CW00616368

Behind a Velvet Light Trap

Behind a Velvet Light Trap

*A filmmaker's journey from
Cinesound to Cannes*

ANTHONY BUCKLEY

hardie grant books

For Mavis, who sadly missed so much of this story.

Published in 2009
Hardie Grant Books
85 High Street
Prahran, Victoria 3181, Australia
www.hardiegrant.com.au
www.hardiegrant.co.uk

Cataloguing-in-Publication data is available from the National Library of Australia.
Behind a Velvet Light Trap
A filmmaker's journey from Cinesound to Cannes
ISBN 978 1 74066 7906

Cover and text design by Nada Backovic
Cover image Hopper, Edward (1882-1967); New York Movie, 1939. New York, Museum of Modern Art (MoMA). Oil on canvas, 32 ¼ x 40 1/8' (81.9 x 101.9 cm). Given anonymously. 396.1941. © 2009. Digital image, The Museum of Modern Art, New York/Scala, Florence
Typesetting by Bookhouse, Sydney
Printed and bound in China by C & C Offset Printing Co. Ltd

10 9 8 7 6 5 4 3 2 1

Contents

PART TWO

PART THREE

Preface

There may be many readers who believe the renaissance of the Australian film industry in the 1970s was its beginning. Certainly Tim Burstall's *Stork* and Bruce Beresford's *The Adventures of Barry McKenzie* spearheaded a new wave but in actual fact Australian cinema was born in 1896 two years after the first Kinetescope parlours opened in Sydney and Melbourne.

However, this is not a history of Australian cinema.

It is a journey of one filmmaker who has had the good fortune to have worked with and for great filmmakers who pioneered the Australian cinema and who had a marked influence on my career. You will meet pioneers of cinema here and abroad – Raymond Longford, Ken G. Hall, Elsa Chauvel, Arthur Higgins, Walter Forde, Louis Edelman, directors Michael Powell, Ted Kotcheff, Rudolf Nureyev, Donald Crombie, Ray Lawrence, Jim Sharman, et al.

For the filmmaker this book will take you into three worlds of cinema. The mystique of film editing, the tasks and torments of the producer and the extraordinary world of the newsreel, the celluloid newspaper of its day.

Acknowledgements

The first of many to be remembered are the librarians at the Mitchell Library reading room of the 1950s who, every Tuesday night and Saturday for a period of two years delved into the bowels of the building to recover volumes of *Everyone's* magazine, *The Picture Show, Stage and Screen, Theatre World* and whatever else they could find related to the history of the Australian film industry – the industry I never knew we had had.

In these more recent times, particular thanks to the following:

Marilyn Dooley of Canberra who read my chapter about Raymond Longford and Lottie Lyell, and who herself wrote *Photo Play Artiste* about the work of these two great pioneers. Lloyd Shiels, veteran Cinesound cameraman, who read my three chapters about the company, verifying that my memory hadn't failed. Gregory Ropert, former assistant editor of mine and filmmaker, for allowing me to read his unpublished thesis about Filmcraft and Colorfilm laboratories. Stanley Moore, editor and mentor, for allowing me to read his memoir. Kevin and Lorna Powell, who read my two chapters about Kevin's father, Michael Powell. Kevin gave me his blessing to publish extracts from his father's letters to me. Donald Crombie for reading my chapters about our work together and reminding me of things I had forgotten. David Williams, retired managing director of Greater Union, who supported Donald Crombie and me so generously with the making of our pictures, for reading my chapters pertaining to that period. In a couple of instances his memory differs from mine. James McCarthy, Christopher McCulloch, Philip Powers and Tim Read for their respective papers about their experiences at Film Australia, which in some cases run counter to mine. Alan Thorne and Angela Raymond for reading and commenting upon my chapter on the making of *Man on the Rim*. The editor of the *Sydney Morning Herald* and their contributors

Paul Byrnes, Richard Glover and Michael Duffy, Scott Murray and Peter Beilby for permission to quote from their valuable record of the film, *Cinema Papers*, David Stratton for quotes from his books *The Last New Wave* and *The Avocado Plantation* and his pieces in *The Australian*, Philip Adams and Bob Ellis, both long-time associates and friends. Lucy Cowdroy, current owner of our family home in Wollstonecraft, for allowing me to revisit and photograph the place of my boyhood. Lane Cove Public Library and Stanton Library, North Sydney, in particular Leonie Masson. Naomi Crago, archivist, City of Sydney Library, for assisting in my search for Heiron & Smith. Last but not least, the State Library of NSW and the Mitchell. Here, by coincidence, my lifelong friend Judy Gimbert works as a volunteer. Judy showed me how to use the index system and microfiches at the library, and proofread the very first draft of this work. My companion, Gary MacDonald, for his patience over the six years it has taken me to write and rewrite by hand, not on the computer, and for his proofreading and his ability to scan material for me on the printer. Raena Lea Shannon, my entertainment lawyer at Frankel's, who read the manuscript and alerted me to what one can and can't say! Justin Fleming, who did the same from another perspective (however, I have graciously declined his recommendation to 'publish and be damned'). Tim Curnow, long-time friend and professional associate from his days at Curtis Brown, who thankfully agreed to be my literary agent and whose notes to each chapter were the first instance of improving my work, only surpassed by my literary editor, Bruce Sims. Bruce has painstakingly and patiently culled, edited and fine-tuned this work to make the flow of the text a much better read than ever before. Thank you. My publisher, Pam Brewster, who has bravely taken on the task of putting all this together. Elaine Menzies knows where all the bodies are buried, and lots, lots more. Private secretary to a couple of my peers as well as to me, Elaine would have to be the world's most discreet secretary, for none of us can ever find out anything about the other! Secretary to me since the early 1970s, her life has many parallels to mine, but our paths weren't to cross until she became secretary to the Australian Film Council. Elaine was also born in Crows Nest, also attended Lady Hay's school and went to the Saturday matinees at the Sesqui. I went to Canada in 1958, she to London and on to Geneva. Her ability to read my handwriting and correct my grammar is legendary. She has typed every draft of this book over the past six years. She still talks to me! From here in Port Douglas I dictate my weekly correspondence to Elaine in Sydney and she emails them back for me to print out and post. The efficiency and craft of stenography is a lost art. Thank you, Elaine.

Photos: Apart from the libraries already mentioned, I am indebted to three people who have allowed me to plunder their precious private collections – Peter James, DOP, and long-time friend, for his on location 'snaps' on *Don Quixote*, *Caddie, The Irishman* and *The Killing of Angel Street;* Peter Hannan, DOP, in London, for on location photos of *Wake in Fright;* and Ian Hanson, film historian, for his pictures of theatres and, in particular, the rare front of house still of *Ali Baba and the Forty Thieves* opening at the State, and Ron Wyndon for his still of me at work in the Cinesound theatrette. Other photos are mainly from my private collection or the press publicity books issued at the time of release of a picture or mini-series.

PART ONE

1

Saturdays At The Sesqui

I was all of seven years of age in 1944. When asked what I wanted for Christmas I evidently had replied, 'a Magic lantern'. It had my mother and father intrigued. Where on earth would I have heard of a Magic lantern? I was accustomed to our Saturday night home movies on Dad's 16mm Bolex projector – evenings held throughout the war by the folks, to raise money for the food parcels that families like ours were sending overseas to our troops. Magic lanterns had never been mentioned.

Dad had placed an advertisement in the paper for a Magic lantern. A gentleman had called from Sans Souci, a Sydney suburb on the southern side of the harbour and a long distance from our home in Crows Nest on the northern side. My Dad later told me it took the best part of a day to go there and return with his find.

It was Christmas Eve and I had been sent to bed early. I could hear great activity out in the dining room. I got out of bed to discover Dad working at the dining room table on a strange looking contraption. I was quickly ordered back to bed. Morning revealed a beautiful, black, shining Magic lantern with a brass barrel lens and an extraordinary collection of glass slides. What Dad had been doing the night before was removing the kerosene wick lamp and replacing it with a forty-watt bulb. Ingenious! My journey into the world of pictures was about to begin.

The Buckleys, however, were no strangers to movies. My father said he could remember the picture show behind the back fence. As a boy he would stand on the upstairs veranda balustrade of our family home and watch the flickering images and the pianist playing under the screen. It was open air in the summer and tented in the winter. It opened as the Rialto in 1910, which was later changed to Albion and then back to Rialto before closing in 1918. It was managed by a pioneer cinematographer, Lacey Percival, before being acquired by Spencers Pictures.

(Top) Queen's Picture Show, Crows Nest, where my father spent most of his Saturday afternoons. Note the retractable roof to the right which, more often than not, used to get stuck on wet days. The art nouveau signage is just visible on the façade.

(Middle) Tented in winter, open-air in summer, the Rialto/Albion played from 1910 to 1918 on Lane Cove Road. The opening of the salubrious Queen's, further down the street, brought an end to the Rialto.

(Bottom) Sesqui Theatre, Crows Nest. I attended the Saturday matinees as my father had done when it was the Queen's.

My father had four brothers and one sister. Three of the brothers had taken to shooting movies as a hobby as soon as movie cameras had become available to the public. Kethel (Keth), my father, had opted for shooting 9.5mm, the unique French gauge with the sprocket hole in the middle of the frame. Brian, a younger brother, had gone with the new 8mm gauge for economy, and the eldest brother, Horrie Pat, my godfather, had decided on 16mm, a somewhat expensive choice for 1928. Horace Patrick Buckley had been a student with the Locke oil expedition in 1922 and graduated with honours from Sydney University with a paper about the expedition's search for oil in Western Australia. In 1929 he was selected by BHP to be sent to Siam (Thailand) to supervise the building of the tin mines for the Siamese government. He took with him his new Bell & Howell 16mm camera. All three brothers were to make movies throughout their lives, but none would ever venture into the professional world of motion pictures.

The Magic lantern was waiting for a home. Patrick Buckley, my grandfather, had built two homes in Crows Nest, 61 Sinclair Street, 'Glen Garrig' in 1909, and 59 Sinclair Street, 'Glendalough' in 1910 or thereabouts: 61 was a spacious, single-storey residence and 59 was an imposing two-storey home with views to the Parramatta River and beyond. (My mother had always insisted mail should be addressed to 59 Sinclair Street, Wollstonecraft. Well, the house faced Wollstonecraft but was firmly sited in Crows Nest!)[1]

I was born on 27 July 1937, not far from No. 59 in a private hospital at the end of Rodborough Street off Falcon Street, Crows Nest, demolished soon after the war.

In the back garden of 59, grandfather had built a walk-in aviary. Dad now set about converting it to the Kings of Crows Nest. Why I chose to call it the *Kings* I will never know. There was a chain of theatres called the Kings, but none in Crows Nest. The Magic lantern now had a home: a screen with hand-operated curtains, a cardboard orchestra of thirty players illuminated by a string of torch-bulb footlights powered by an Eveready cycle battery. Let the show begin!

The Kings at Crows Nest flourished but after a year the same lantern slides were becoming repetitive and my audiences began to wane noticeably. The audience were mainly my parents' friends who were harangued into attending when visiting, and my few friends from school, Lady Hays at North Sydney, which had been built on the site of Crows Nest House.[2] I was a loner from the

---

1   Both homes still stand, 59 Sinclair Street dominating the streetscape with its two storeys, though sadly missing its brass nameplate.

2   Lady Hays is remembered on the bus shelter just up from the school. The original wrought-iron railings of Crows Nest House are behind the shelter.

beginning of my school years. In our outside laundry I found a box of films, which had obviously been put away for a long time. I was curious because the film was not the same as Dad showed us on Saturday nights. I was not allowed to touch his expensive Bolex projector on which he ran the family's home movies backwards and forwards which would keep everyone entertained for hours. Divers at the Manly pool would suddenly come flying out of the water backwards onto their diving boards. His younger brother eating a banana would regurgitate it and place it back in its skin. I thought it was trick photography but it was sleight of hand with the projector. The box of films was Dad's 9.5mm collection which he had started before my parents married. It was thought by now I should be allowed to graduate to my own home movie projector. He had sold his first 9.5mm projector but promised to find me a secondhand machine. This he did at Heiron & Smith in Sydney. They were the leading manufacturers and retailers of billiard and snooker tables and were situated up a very narrow staircase in Castlereagh Street, just down from the Fire Brigade's headquarters. The company also held the Pathéscope franchise in Australia for projectors, cameras and the notable Pathé library of 9.5mm film. How billiards and films came to be connected has never been explained. The Pathé library was at the far end of the billiard showroom. It was always a mystery to me how they got their tables up and down the impossibly narrow staircase. The library was run by a formidable Miss Taylor and her able young assistant, George Browne. Dad had never been content with just hiring the Pathéscope films, but owned his own copies. So a 9.5mm projector, which could project Pathé's tiny little cassette reels[3] and screen 15-minute 300ft reels was installed in the Kings of Crows Nest.

The treasures found in the box in the laundry were treasures indeed and probably had the longest runs in a cinema anywhere in the world! For years, not weeks. Stan Laurel featured in *Stanley is Forgetful*; Mary Pickford and Douglas Fairbanks in *Telephone Marriage*; the adventure film *The Air Pirates*, a William S. Hart western, and, not known to me at the time, a 300 ft reel of a French classic, Abel Gance's *Napoleon* with French notched titles, graced the silver screen at the Kings.

About this time I was allowed to go to the pictures on my own but I was constrained to one particular cinema because I was not permitted to cross tramlines. Crows Nest was a five-way intersection of double tramlines going in four of the five directions. To reach the Crows Nest Hoyts one had to traverse two sets of

---

3   Pathé had invented a unique system whereby their mini reels would only contain one or two frames of the title which was preceded by a notch in the film. When the notch arrived at the projector gate, it would freeze the frame long enough to read the title, and then continue playing the film.

double tramlines. (The Hoyts was also considered to be somewhat of a 'rough house' and not in keeping with Master Buckley's style.) The Sesqui down the road, however, didn't involve crossing any tramlines, so the Sesqui it had to be. This art deco, neon-lit pleasure was built in 1938, the year after I was born. It was named after Australia's sesquicentenary celebrated that year and had been constructed on the site of the Queen's Theatre, retaining its outside walls, and had been my father's boyhood picture show. The Queen's had opened in 1913 at 360 Lane Cove Road, now the Pacific Highway. My father could remember its opening retractable roof. The roof would often get stuck and the rain would pour down into the stalls. The Queen's had quite a reputation. I have spoken to many locals and old timers who remember it vividly. An old acquaintance, Bill Turnbull remembered it as being very salubrious. 'There was a bust of Queen Victoria halfway up the marble staircase, and hitching posts outside for the horses.' Whilst some remembered it as very comfortable and the audiences well behaved, Mrs Whitlam of Crows Nest remembered the 'loud shrieking audiences' at the matinees. 'They used to open the back doors and we would sneak our friends in. It was a big old barn of a place and it didn't have foyers. Nobody with any brains would go to a matinee at the Queen's.' My favourite anecdote comes from Ted Davidson of Killara. He and his mates used to go barefoot to the Queens. He saw Claudette Colbert bathing in asp's milk. 'The remarks were witty, rude and vulgar.' On telling his mother seeing the film was 'cultural', she belted him around the ears. 'You dirty little bugger.'

The Sesqui was altogether a different story. Leslie McCallum, one of the directors of Queen's Theatres Ltd, had transformed his old *Queen's* into one of the finest art deco theatres ever to grace Sydney. McCallum maintained many of the Queen's old traditions, including the novelty band, The Esquire Octette, and the talent quests with prizes of 7/6, 5/- and 2/6. For a comedy routine the Sesqui paid 10/-. This was the early 1940s. I started attending the theatre sometime late in 1943, early 1944. Every Saturday, tenth row from the front on the aisle of the centre block where the stalls rose on an incline towards the stage. I used to marvel at the colour neon changing and how the two sets of curtains rose to the flies and then a silver light curtain parted to reveal the screen. I soon became a member of the Gartrell White Birthday Club conducted by Uncle Reggie Quartley, an old vaudevillian still treading the boards. Gartrell White was the local baker and distributor of Aeroplane Jelly next to Motor Funerals on Pacific Highway. Each Saturday, members of the Birthday Club would be called up by Uncle Reg on their birthday and given an iced Gartrell White cake in a greaseproof paper bag. It was the event of the year we all looked forward to. Nothing like that across the road at Hoyts.

Probably the theatre's most unique feature was the historic panels depicting great moments in Australia's history, which decorated the cinema's walls. The panels had been on Sydney's Queen Victoria Building for the sesqui celebrations and were designed by Edmund Harvey. I used to gaze in wonder at them, probably the only person to do so at the Saturday matinees. My Saturdays at the Sesqui also introduced me to my first Australian film, a re-release of Ken G. Hall's *Orphan of the Wilderness*. Even at this early age I was hooked. I didn't know we made films!

My lobby card collection started with attending the Sesqui give-away matinees. Collecting one-sheet posters was another matter altogether. Around the corner from Bruce Street, near No. 59, on Pacific Highway, was the Sesqui one-sheet billboard, on a fence of a vacant block of ground. The billposter used to come very early on Fridays and Tuesdays because the Sesqui's program was always Fri-Sat-Mon or Tue-Wed-Thur. (The Crows Nest Hoyts was always Sat-Mon-Tue and Wed-Thu-Fri, no class at all!) On very wet mornings it was a steal to peel off the Fri-Sat-Mon or the Tue-Wed-Thur stickers and race back to the Kings and affix them to my next week's attractions! The one-sheeters sometimes were carefully peeled off too and firmly affixed to my picture show's one-sheeter display board. On walking home from school, sure enough the one-sheeter would have been replaced and there would be a fresh Fri-Sat-Mon affixed.

It was called the 'Apex of Entertainment', but for me the Sesqui was a lot more. It was where real cinema came alive at twenty-four frames per second, a speed that was to carry me through over fifty years of working in film. Musk sticks, Fantales, Jaffas, Gartrell White cakes, Reggie Quartley with his bright orange hair and lobby cards – this was Saturdays at the Sesqui.

At Lady Hay's I had become the school projectionist, screening the same education department films through the day to each class every forty-five minutes. Some of the films weren't bad and all seemed to be presented by Stamina Clothes, who used to specialise in school uniforms. It was on one of my first trips into the city that I experienced two incidents that completely puzzled me. I was allowed to take the tram on my own into Wynyard across the bridge and to go to McDowells, men's outfitters opposite David Jones George Street store, to be measured for a new school uniform. The McDowells tailor asked if I dressed on the left or the right. I looked at him blankly. He repeated the question and pointed to my crotch. I still hadn't the faintest what the question meant. Then, on the way back to Wynyard to catch the tram home, I sensed I was being followed by looking in the shop windows opposite. At an intersection a man leant forward and asked me a question. I didn't hear him at first and, obeying my mother's teaching of manners, said 'I beg your pardon?' and he repeated the question. Once again I

(Top) My mother would have hated being referred to as Mrs Kethel Buckley. They had to be married behind the altar at St Mary's, North Sydney, as the Buckleys were Catholic and the Jones Methodist. I became a Presbyterian!

(Right) An extremely rare photograph of the Buckley family together at 59 Sinclair Street. From left to right: Colin (Cole), Noel, Horace (Horrie Pat), Ruth, Brian and Kethel (Keth), my father. He took 16mm footage of the family walking into the garden, which is now archived. The lattice fern house behind became an aviary, which was later converted by my father into the Kings of Crows Nest, where the Magic lantern and later 9.5mm movies flourished.

(Bottom) My father Keth and his brother Brian, with the 16mm camera at the ready, Manly pool, circa 1934.

stared blankly but good sense told me to move on quickly. It was a Saturday, for father was at home. He took over the cooking duties for the weekend. Seated for lunch I began to tell of my two experiences. The first was explained to me by mother and I was greatly enlightened. On describing the second encounter, my father became restless and left the table to go to the backyard. 'And what did this man say dear?' enquired mother. 'Did I take it or did I give it.' She looked at me intensely and said, 'I think you need a haircut!' Father had to stay in the backyard all afternoon as mother spent the time explaining the facts of life to me.

My mother started taking me to matinees in the city. One of Mum's closest friends was Dot Hodges, who ran a millinery shop opposite Strangman's electrical and record shop on Pacific Highway. Dad would come home every Friday with the latest 78 hit record from Strangman's in its brownpaper sleeve boldly marked 2/6. Dot and Mum regularly went to the city on Saturday afternoons to catch the latest show. Coffee at Repins, then it would be a choice between the State, Century, St James, Regent or Prince Edward theatres. If it was the Prince Edward I knew it would be light refreshments at Romanos. My first encounter with a city matinee was at the State Theatre in Market Street and the first film I was to see in this Picture Palace was *Ali Baba and the Forty Thieves*. I can't remember the film but I'll never forget the main titles. I was fascinated as to how barrels of oil being tipped from the top of the screen were washing away the titles for the following title to be seen. No doubt it must look very corny now but in 1944 in a 2,000-seat picture palace I was awestruck. Before the film an organist would rise out of the pit to entertain the audience. The evening performance featured organ and orchestra. I had never seen anything like this before, even though the Kings of Crows Nest had its own cardboard orchestra and organ! At the Prince Edward, however, we always had organ and orchestra at the matinee. The only thing that annoyed me about Mum and Dot's afternoon in town was that we were always late. Saturdays, workers finished at 12.30 or one o'clock. The tram from Crows Nest to Wynyard would always be delayed at the crossing loop in the Wynyard tunnel, waiting for the crowded trams filled with the city workers to exit the platforms. This never worried Dot or Mum but I would become extremely agitated for it meant we would miss the main titles of the film. To this day I cannot tolerate missing the start of a movie. When we were on time I became intrigued with the credit 'film editor' and began to wonder what this person did.

My brother Peter died six days after he was born in December 1944, which triggered my mother's decline in health. She was RH negative blood factor and transfusions were still a year away. The Kings was temporarily closed when my parents were evicted from Number 59 by other members of the Buckley clan but principally Dad's sister Ruth, to whom he wouldn't speak again till some months before he died. Dad had evidently been running two sets of books in his father's wholesale confectionery business, one set for the business, one set for him.

Our life was disrupted for a few years, being moved from one suburb to another until we finally settled at Laycock Street, Neutral Bay where the Kings was reborn. This was post-war Sydney when rental accommodation was extremely hard to find and to acquire a residence or flat, one had to pay 'key money'. This was completely illegal but if you didn't pay, no accommodation. Dad paid £300 to get us into this flat in Neutral Bay.

My first schoolmates were made at Neutral Bay although the three of them went to different schools. I also learnt for real some new facts of life too. My naïvety in matters sexual is typified in the following occurrence. Near where we lived at Neutral Bay was the Bent Street gully with classic views of the Harbour Bridge and the city behind. Two of my newly acquired friends said they had something to show me and we were going to go down to the gully. It was school holidays for I remember all we had on was shirts, shorts and sandshoes. On arriving at a secluded spot in the gully I was told to take my shirt and shorts off, as the other two were quickly doing. One immediately hugged me from behind and the other from the front in vigorous, furtive behaviour as though their lives depended on it. Matters came to an abrupt halt when I asked, in all innocence, 'What are we doing this for?' The two of them took one look at me and fled, leaving me in a state of disarray wondering what I had said. No, I didn't go home and ask mother about it, nor did I have a haircut! But I soon learnt what life was about for that age.

Following in the footsteps of Dad's brothers, I had now been given my own 9.5mm movie camera and had begun to put every penny of pocket money into buying film from Heiron & Smith. Every Saturday, off I would go into town on the tram to put in a two and a half minute roll of film for developing. One had to wait three weeks for the film to be processed and when Pathé introduced Kodachrome, the tiny spool of film had to go back to Paris to be developed. It would take at least twelve weeks before I would see my 'rushes'! Film was so expensive and the rolls so short it was an excellent exercise in discipline as to what to shoot and what not to shoot! No retakes and no tape to wipe. I became fascinated with the process of splicing the film together – editing and making a story out of the material I had shot. As a result the *Sydney Cinema Gazette* was created, to be shown at the Kings on Saturday nights. Miss Taylor introduced me to two English magazines that I would eagerly devour every month, the *Pathéscope Gazette* and the *Amateur Cine World*. Wonderful little journals of the time about how to make films, classics of the cinema and articles by a young man whose career I have followed since this time – Kevin Brownlow. We have never met or communicated but his contribution

(Top) My mother holds my hand and her friend, Dot Hodges, holds the other, in Martin Place. We would more than likely be going to Romano's for a light lunch, then next door to the Prince Edward – Theatre Beautiful for the matinee. If they were running late, lunch would be skipped in favour of afternoon tea at Princes.

(Bottom) My first city matinee was at the State to see *Ali Baba and the Forty Thieves*. I was in awe of the film's main titles being washed off by the barrels of oil and the organist rising out of the stage.

to the preservation of film history and his storytelling abilities about the history of film, I envy and admire. All thanks to 9.5mm. Every Saturday on the Pathéscope projector, and later a Pathé GEM, we saw everything from *The White Hell of Pitz Palu* to *Metropolis* and all the classics in between on 9.5. Miss Taylor's Pathéscope library must have been unique in Australia.

School holidays were spent once a year on my godfather's property at Geurie, western New South Wales. Horace Patrick Buckley was the eldest of the Buckley brothers, to me Uncle Horace, to the rest of the family Horrie Pat. He was the only member of the family, other than my mother, to take an interest in me. He was also the only really 'well off' member of the family. My mother always insisted I be sent first class on the Central West Express, generally hauled by a 38 class steam engine. She felt it wouldn't be right for young Master Buckley to be seen stepping from the second-class carriages of the train. There was only one first-class car on the train and Geurie was a two-carriage length platform. After leaving Wellington I would be all set and ready to get off at Geurie. The conductor used to flag the train till the first class carriage reached the platform. I would be the only one alighting and there would be Uncle Horace, waiting to drive me to his property 'Allandale' on the Little River, a tributary of the Macquarie. When Uncle Horace was seen visiting the village the entire area would be on the telephone to alert each other that his nephew was back. He was a man of few words but I enjoyed his company and he taught me how to cook. He was always intrigued that I brought my 9.5mm camera and just as well I did in 1956, for we were floodbound for a week and it was a spectacular coverage for my *Sydney Cinema Gazette*. Much later he was to pass on his 16mm Bolex to me, and his vast collection of film from Siam in 1929 and his Kodachrome of the 1950s and 1960s.

To earn pocket money I would do odd jobs. One day the local grocer asked me if I could clean up their shop windows. The O'Connors, brother and sister's grocery store, was a somewhat mundane affair with a sawdust-covered floor on the corner of Watson Street and Military Road, Neutral Bay. Being on the corner, the shop had two double windows filled with everything imaginable, which amounted to windows of clutter. I was given 2/6 and allowed to buy five rolls of crepe paper at 6d a roll. I had a flair for doing things with crepe paper for the Kings and by using a strong pair of big scissors one could cut the crepe paper into crinkling ribbons. By mixing and matching the ribbons of colour and hanging them in curtains one could obtain a very effective window display at very little cost. As crepe paper can fade fairly quickly, I had earned myself a job for life – except it didn't pay very well! Favourable comments came from the O'Connors and the customers, more of whom were coming into their shop. The O'Connors were forever grateful. Not so my parents. Surely their only son was not destined to dress Mark Foys and Farmers store windows. A window-dresser in the family? Never! The art of window dressing is akin to the craft of a production designer, a craft I very much admire, but one has to remember Australia in the 1950s was archly conservative and the encouraging of creative expression was unheard of. My mother sought the advice of Mr Kentwell. Gordon and Lila Kentwell ran a lending library and novelty shop at the junction of Wycombe and Military Roads, Neutral Bay. Dad and Mum would borrow five books a week from the library, whilst I used to drool over the Dinky Toys in the shop window. Each Christmas, Mum would order from the Kentwells *The Picture Show Annual* from the UK, year in and year out, which I would quietly devour over the Christmas/New Year holidays. I always looked forward to Tuesdays too, for the local newsagent would have waiting for me *The Picture Show Weekly, Picturegoer Magazine, Film Fun* and the *Mickey Mouse Weekly*.

Gordon Kentwell suggested the only thing for me was to work in the 'fillum' business, seeing my career in film had already started! He knew someone in a film laboratory and as soon as I had completed the Intermediate Certificate at Crows Nest Boys High School I started work for Les Wicks at Automatic Film Laboratories in South Dowling Street, Moore Park, in Sydney. I was all of fifteen and a half years of age – the year 1953.

My mother had insisted on knowing where I was going to work, and with whom. Her indifferent health had reached a stage where she could no longer travel to the city alone, so a family friend, Nellie Periera from Dulwich Hill, was roped in to escort me with mother to meet Mr Wicks. With the manager was a young man from England, Doug Dove, who had come from Technicolor, London, and was being groomed to take over from Mr Wicks when he retired. What both of them thought of this royal escort to approve of my place of employment I will never know.

My first job was in the assembly room, behind the developing and processing machines where the film coming off these machines was prepared, joined from reels onto spools, waxed and dispatched to the film's distributors. Geoff Wettig and Dulcie Shields worked in the assembly room and Alma Murphy in the waxing and dispatch room next door. These three collectively took me under their wing to train and educate me in the ways of splicing and cleaning film. The laboratory supervisor, Phil Markham, was authoritarian and though pleasant early enough in the morning, was a person to avoid in the afternoon, for he was rather fond of the long lunch at the local pub. Working at a bench near me was a silver-haired man of quiet distinction. His name was Bert Cross, father of Clive Cross who, along with his business partner, Arthur Smith, had put the 'sound' into Cinesound. Bert was in charge of the negative processing machines, which, for this laboratory, were relatively new. Max Long was

(Top left) From Lady Hay's to Crows Nest Boys High and my first school uniform. Once again I was appointed the school projectionist.

(Top right) Laycock Street, Neutral Bay. I had just won the job of dressing the O'Connors' grocery shop window. This was to cause concern to my parents, I was later to learn. They clearly did not welcome the thought of a window dresser in the family.

(Right) Late 1953, Prospect Street, Surry Hills. Standing outside Automatic Film Laboratories, where I was to discover we had once had a film industry. The building still stands.

in charge of the positive developing machines which, to say the least, were rather old. I suspect the laboratories had been built in the late twenties or early thirties.

Mr Cross (one never called anyone by their first name until invited to do so) lived at Bronte and I at Neutral Bay. We would walk together at the end of the working day up South Dowling Street to the corner of Flinders Street to catch our respective trams, Bert going east, me going north, except, to save sixpence to put towards another roll of film, I would walk along Flinders, down Oxford and across Hyde Park to Wynyard, a walk of about half an hour. One evening, standing on the corner looking at the Prince Edward Theatre's twenty-four sheeter billboard, Mr Cross turned to me and said, 'Son, get out of the film industry while you can.' I was a little surprised. 'Why, Mr Cross, aren't I doing my job properly?' 'No, on the contrary, everyone is extremely pleased with your work, son.' He paused. 'There's no future in the film industry.' I could sense a tone of bitterness in his voice. Here I was, standing with the man who was the first Pathé-Frères newsreel cameraman in Australia and the unacknowledged cameraman who, with his 100 ft loading (one minute of film) 35 Bell & Howell Eymo, captured Captain de Groote slashing the ribbon at the opening of the Sydney Harbour Bridge in 1932, the only cameraman to capture the event,[4] finishing his career at the end of a processing machine. I said, 'It's too late, I feel there is a future for me, Mr Cross.' 'Too late? You have only just turned sixteen, think about it, travel safely.'

The traffic light changed and I watched him cross the road to catch his tram. Homburg hat, suited, the posture and walk of a man disappointed. I always looked forward to those short evening walks, for each time Bert Cross would tell me a little more of his life and times, and each time would remind me, 'Son, there's no future in it.'

My task in the assembly room was to clean and join the reels into spools, ready for Alma Murphy to wax and pack the print. Placing the velvet around the film soaked in carbon tetrachloride, and winding it through the velvet, watching carefully that the chemical was drying before the film wound tightly onto the reel, was a tiring and time-consuming job, not to mention the smell of the tetrachloride. Extraction fans and Workcover didn't exist, and one was told not to breathe in when applying the chemical to the velvet!

Mr Markham returned from one of his long lunches one day to growl at me that he had a job for me to do. I always had the distinct impression that he really didn't like me, and the feeling was to become mutual. I found it offensive how he used to speak to Dulcie and Geoff. I knew in fact what the job was going to be.

---

4   Both Cinesound and Movietone covered the 'official' opening. Bert Cross happened to be at the event as a 'stringer' with his hand-held Eymo camera and was literally hit by de Groote's horse.

2

The Sentimental Bloke –
Meeting Raymond Longford

Sitting on the floor of the assembly room was a pile of rusting cans, about twelve or fourteen in total. I had previously asked what they were and was told it was some very old film, nothing very interesting. In fact it was a job that had been waiting to be done that no one wanted to do. Dulcie Shields had suggested to Mr Markham that I could be trusted and should be given the job. Little did I know what I was in for. The cans contained a very old film, which had come from the National Library of Australia in Canberra for repairing and re-splicing. It was obviously nitrate film for it stank to high heaven! So I seated myself at the Bell & Howell splicer, not realising I was about to begin a journey into Australian film history that I continue travelling today.

The Bell & Howell splicer is a wonderful machine, operated by foot pedals whilst one's hands do the work of carefully scraping and cementing the pieces of film together. I peddled and spliced, intrigued and fascinated, for ten days. The first thing to do was to carefully load the reel onto the winding plates and then, feeling the edges of the film for broken sprockets, repair and remake all the joins in the print. My first discovery was that although the film was silent, it was not in black and white, each scene was tinted a different tone, hence the number of joins in each print as each tint was separately developed in the laboratory baths, and inserted in its correct sequence in the reel.

Reel one, standard leader of twelve feet from the start mark for the projectionist, main title fades in:

THE SOUTHERN CROSS FEATURE FILM CO LTD
PRESENTS
'THE SENTIMENTAL BLOKE'
C.J. DENNIS
PICTURISED AND DIRECTED BY RAYMOND LONGFORD

Southern Cross? An Australian film? I asked. No one in the assembly room knew the answer and no one had heard of Raymond Longford. I continued my journey of discovery, examining every exquisite frame, carefully re-splicing the old, handmade joins, saving the frames from either side of the join and carefully putting them in envelopes to take home each day. The titles were in prose. My young eyes eagerly read them. Who was C.J. Dennis?

Two weeks later I completed repairing this, to me, extraordinary print, carefully cleaning it, to be sent down to the laboratory at the back of the building, Associated Film Printers, for a 16mm duplicate negative and print to be made.

This was the first major mistake of film restoration and preservation in this country. There is no one to blame. There was not the money to provide for a 35mm negative and print. Eastmancolor processing had not yet arrived in Australia for a tinted print to be made, the National Film and Sound Archive had to wait another thirty years before it would be established. It would have to wait until 2003 for this silent masterpiece of our cinema to be fully restored.

This rediscovery was shown to an eagerly waiting audience at the University of Sydney in 1955 and immediately reawakened an interest in the fact that we had had a film industry, and a search for Raymond Longford began.

In the meantime I was on my way, causing yet more concerns to my parents. For the next two and a half years I spent every Tuesday night and every Saturday in the Mitchell Library ferreting out everything I could find about our Australian film industry and in particular this man, Raymond Longford.

I soon learnt the old saying that behind every good man there is a great woman, and behind Raymond Longford there certainly was – Lottie Lyell, the first star of the Australian screen.

Our old family home at 59 Sinclair Street was only ten minutes walk from Longford's Wollstonecraft home, which I wasn't to learn till much later. We were now living at 77 Alexander Street, Crows Nest and I began writing to him after the press had discovered him working as a nightwatchman on Sydney's wharves, telling him of my discoveries and my research. I forgot to tell him my age. We had no telephone in the early fifties and it would have been extremely impolite to knock on anyone's door unannounced. So I waited and waited.

'There's a letter for you,' said mother. I had only ever been used to letters addressed to Master Buckley on birthdays containing postal notes for 2/6! This was addressed to Mr Tony Buckley and postmarked North Sydney. It was the invitation I had been waiting for. 8 Gillies Street, Wollstonecraft. 'Dear Mr Buckley, I would be pleased to receive you for afternoon tea next Saturday, at 2 o'clock. Yours sincerely, R.H. Longford.'

Raymond Longford stands beside the camera (top photo) whilst Arthur Higgins completes threading the film through the gate in these surviving location snaps taken in 1923. At my last meeting with Longford, he produced these stills and a copy of his talkie script of *Fisher's Ghost* which he had hoped to make in 1934. His silent version, released in 1924 to critical and audience acclaim, he considered his best film. A copy of the film is known to have exchanged hands between two collectors in the late 1970s. The whereabouts of this print is unknown but I hope it has been cared for and that the collector may come forward so this copy can be conserved and restored. These photos are marked on the back as having been printed by C.A. Watson, Parkes, NSW.

Mother insisted I wore an inherited brown, double-breasted suit, which I loathed with a vengeance. (I still hate brown!)

I knew I had knocked on the door rather loudly. I hadn't intended to but I had. I heard the footfalls approaching the door and through the frosted half-pane I saw his looming figure.

The door opened. I'm five feet ten and a half and there, towering above me, was the 'Big Man'. 'Hello, I'm Tony – Mr Longford?' 'My boy,' he quickly turned his head – 'Emilie – it's a young fella – sorry young man, we've been dreading meeting some old codger. Come in.' From the pedals of the Bell & Howell splicing machine to Gillies Street, Wollstonecraft. I had finally made it.

I was shown into a typical Wollstonecraft lounge room. Heavy, stained timber and the sort of velveteen lounge suites that one now probably only finds in the corner of the foyer of the Capitol Theatre! He wore wide braces, a tie but no jacket, and had great presence. Mrs Longford courteously brought in the fine china (obviously already prepared for some 'old codger') and served a generous afternoon tea.

The noted historian on Longford, Mervyn Wasson, had found Mrs Longford very protective of her husband. I had the instant impression that she didn't like me very much, or perhaps she didn't like a young person who would obviously know nothing of her husband's past, intruding on their privacy, opening up a past that perhaps she preferred to forget, stimulating her husband to recall memories in which she had had no part. Worse still, perhaps, arousing the memories of the 'great woman' behind the good man – Lottie Lyell.

Lottie Lyell was born at 7 Terry Street, Balmain, on 23 February 1890. Raymond Longford was born at Hawthorn in Melbourne on 23 September 1878.

By the time Lottie was nineteen she was the leading lady of a travelling theatre group. Her first professional stage appearance was in the role of Maggie Brown in *An Englishman's Home* at the Town Hall, West Maitland, on the 28 May 1909. The role of Mr Brown was played by Raymond Longford. One presumes this was the flowering of the Longford/Lyell partnership that was to quickly make their mark on the establishment of Australian quality cinema.

On this particular Saturday afternoon I knew it was not my place or age to explore the personal side of the Longford/Lyell partnership, except I had already read accounts in the trades that Longford had married his first wife in 1900 when, by his own account, Lottie's parents entrusted the care of their daughter to him. It can be presumed Lyell's and Longford's parents knew each other, for Longford later moved into the Lyell household.

Their stage careers together flourished. From Australia to New Zealand they received rave reviews. Back in Australia in 1910 their lives and careers were to change dramatically, for moving pictures were becoming more and more successful. The man who was to determine their future together was Cozens Spencer.

Charles Cozens Spencer had begun his career by touring with films through Canada, New Zealand and Australia in 1905. He had started his exhibition career at the Lyceum Hall and it was a success from the start. His wife, Eleanor, was billed as 'Señora Spencer, the only lady operator (projectionist) in the world'.

Spencer had been keen to be involved in the making of Australian pictures to play at the Lyceum and around the country. He had made the following observation: 'A film showman in almost every country in the world must have at least a fair proportion of films made in the country in which he is in business. Patrons insist on it. They want to see in the pictures something of their own people and their own country. So showmen have to frame their programmes accordingly. Why should not Australian showmen have Australian films?

'The change, the variety, the freshness that would be got in an Australian picture would ensure its being welcomed by picture lovers all over the earth. For anything with a new atmosphere or note about it – and an Australian picture would have these recommendations – there is always a market in the picture world.'

Spencer had teamed up with actor-director Alfred Rolfe to make a series of dramatic films and newsreels. Rolfe's first film for Spencer was *Captain Midnight* in which, coincidentally, Raymond Longford made his screen debut. But this was not Longford's first involvement with filmmaking. In 1908 he had worked on Cozen Spencer's feature-length documentary, *The Burns Johnson Fight* at the old Rushcutters Bay Stadium. Some footage still survives.

So when Alfred Rolfe left Spencer's Pictures, Longford was put in charge of production and made his directing debut with *The Fatal Wedding* in 1911. Longford and Lyell toured the play in New Zealand, playing the leading roles, and it was a logical transition to move the play to a motion picture. The film was made in an artist's studio at Bondi, the roof being removed and the lighting enhanced by the use of six-foot reflectors made with silver paper stretched over wooden frames. It also brought Lottie and Ray together with a nineteen-year-old cameraman who was to shoot most of their later films – Arthur Higgins.

Spencer opened *The Fatal Wedding* at his Lyceum on April 24, 1911, and it ran for five capacity weeks. Longford estimated that for the outlay of £600 the film had netted some £16,000 in Australasia and England. Ever the showman, Spencer played the film at the Lyceum and major centres with a performance on stage of a children's chorus and a 'tin can band' to synchronise with the sentimental farewell on the screen. Movies were never silent!

Longford and Lyell's second film for Spencer was *The Romantic Story of Margaret Catchpole*. When Lottie mounted Cozens Spencer's own magnificent dapple-grey horse, Arno, and galloped onto the screen as Margaret Catchpole, she effectively became Australia's first film star. The first half of the film survives today.

The profits from *The Fatal Wedding* and Longford and Lyell's next three films encouraged Spencer to build a £10,000 studio complex with its own laboratory at White City, Rushcutters Bay, Sydney. Opened in September 1912 by the Premier, J. McGowan, Spencer screened the event that night at the Lyceum.

Our afternoon tea proceeded comfortably, I had relaxed a little, my cup had at least stopped rattling, and Mr Longford was, I think, both curious and somewhat entertained by someone so young being absorbed with what was unfolding before me.

He asked Emilie to take away the cups and revealed a large cardboard box that had been behind his chair and immediately started to place the most wonderful collection of memorabilia on the table and to open up about his life. It was at this point (out of Emilie's earshot) that he spoke of his great partnership with Lottie Lyell who had been involved in everything from the development of his screenplays to checking and keeping the book of accounts.

At my age I was completely naïve in thinking there was nothing other than a strictly professional relationship at hand but I did notice he spoke somewhat reverently and affectionately about her and said she was totally absorbed in their work together. I later deduced it was obviously a true and loving partnership. He showed me dozens of copies he had kept of programs for their films, some of which he was later to generously give to me to add to my already growing collection.

Longford and Lyell's last production for Spencer's was *Australia Calls* and it took a year to complete. The script was by two *Bulletin* journalists, J. Barr and C.A. Jeffries, who vigorously expressed the *Bulletin*'s weekly campaign of racism and xenophobia against the 'Yellow Peril'.

Australia Calls was also to be Spencer's last film. On January 6, 1913, the infamous 'combine' was born out of Union Theatres and Australasian Films. The first move was to merge Johnson & Gibson and J. & N. Tait to Amalgamated Pictures, the General Film Company of Australasia to merge Wests Pictures, Spencer's Pictures and Amalgamated Pictures. The addition of Greater J.D. Williams Amusement Co. brought the centralising of four partners under Union Theatres and Australasian Films.

When re-splicing the nitrate print of *The Sentimental Bloke* in 1953 at Automatic Film Laboratories there was an additional reel of hand-coloured material of Frank Hurley's *With the Headhunters of Unknown Papua* (US title *The Lost Tribe*). Regretfully the positive perforations had shrunk to the extent they would not fit the holding pins on the Bell & Howell splicer. I managed to repair one splice by hand but it was decided there could be nothing done that would get the print through an optical printer and the reel was returned to the National Library unrepaired.

This rare surviving frame comes from that only splice that could be made. The enlargement above shows the beauty and superb colour registration achieved by the Pathé colour stencilling process, which was carried out in Sydney in Pitt Street near the corner of Bathurst Street, the same building in which Will A. Cathcart and Syd Nicholls began their title card business. Hurley had a considerable amount of his early Papua/New Guinea footage hand-coloured, as well as tinted and toned as most silent films were shown.

Spencer vigorously opposed the merger of his company. The combine were now assured of a supply of imported film, therefore there was no longer a need for Australasian Films and Spencer's Pictures to make films other than the *Australasian Gazette* and *Spencer's Gazette*.

Cozens Spencer, on his departure for Canada, told *Theatre Magazine* in October 1914: 'Picture production has been killed. Today it is dead as the proverbial doornail. Can you believe that this is the only place in the world where pictures are not being made? Such is indeed the case. Australia has become the dumping ground for all the producers in the world, when it could most profitably be taking its place side by side with other picture-producing countries and providing work for thousands of its own people.'

"Dad, w-w-what are these big cracks for ?"

"So as you can get plenty of fresh air and ventilation without going outside."

(Top left) Raymond Longford

(Top right) The spirit of Longford's faithful adaptation of Steele Rudd's novel is typified by his intertitles which were designed and hand-lettered by William A. Cathcart.

(Bottom) Lunch break, *On Our Selection*: Millbank Station, Leeton, NSW. Those named on the back of the photograph are: Arthur Greenaway, Tal Ordell, Arthur Cross, Miss Johnson (Mrs Bob Sheppard) [sic], Olga Nilland, Lottie Beaumont, Beatrice Esmond, Percy Walsh, Jim Coleman and Raymond Longford, left rear.

There is a bizarre ending to this part of the story. After settling on his Canadian ranch he was deeply disturbed by the Wall Street crash of '29. Nerves frayed and his finances gone, Spencer ran amuck, shooting several of his employees before disappearing. Six weeks later his body was dragged from a lake.

I could see the old man was getting tired. It was now four o'clock and I began to make a move to go. 'We haven't finished yet, why don't you come again?' I accepted his invitation immediately and Mrs Longford, escorting me to the door, said I could return in two weeks.

I wrote a letter of thanks, also confirming my next visit, telling my mother I had no intention of wearing that bloody awful brown double-breasted suit!

Two Saturdays on and you could hardly hear my knock on the door. The table had been set and Mrs Longford brought the tea and I could see his box of treasures beside his chair.

He handed me a cream/buff-coloured pamphlet. *The Mutiny of the Bounty*, 1916. In my two and a half years attending the Mitchell Library I had uncovered Errol Flynn's debut for Charles and Elsa Chauvel for their *In the Wake of the Bounty* but this one had escaped me altogether. Shooting had taken place in Rotorua, New Zealand, with some scenes on Norfolk Island and the remainder in Sydney.

Mutiny of the Bounty offers us a rare insight to the practical workings of the Longford-Lyell partnership and in particular Lottie's role in direction. Jack Moller was an extra working for 5/- a day and in a letter of September 21, 1985, to Don Stafford, a resident historian of Rotorua, Mr Moller describes his involvement in the filming: 'I can recall a landing we made on Mokoia Island, two of us rowed the boat and my job was to step ashore and help Lieut Christian who was sitting in the bow ashore. Miss Lottie Lyal [sic] the leading lady was not pleased with our first effort so we had to go out and try again. I stepped ashore, gave Lieut Christian my hand and helped him land. Miss Lyal [sic] said "splendid" this time.'

Mr Longford continued to talk and was becoming more animated, particularly when it came to telling me about the controversies surrounding *The Church and the Woman* and *The Woman Suffers*. *The Church and the Woman* dealt with the controversial subject of mixed marriages between Catholic and Protestant and the responsibility of the priests to honour the confidences of the confessional. The controversy it had created was nothing like that of *The Woman Suffers* in 1918. It opened to capacity business in both Adelaide and Sydney and *Australian Variety*, 30 August 1918, enjoyed its 'rather spicy theme', 'one of the best things done by local producers'. All was going well when the New South Wales Chief Secretary placed a ban on it. Perhaps too spicy?! The advertising was salacious. 'The law of the land punishes the wrongdoer, from petty thief to the murderer; but any man may steal a woman and all she holds dearest, and yet go free!'[1] Longford was convinced the combine had had something to do with it. The Labour paper *The Worker* said, October 31, 1918: 'One cannot help feeling that there is something more in the business than meets the eye ... this much is certain, that while locally produced films are being hampered and stopped, the Yankee Trust is getting a greater hold than ever on the country.'

The *Australian Variety*, November 8, 1918, described it as a 'damn piece of absurdity' – 'a scandalous affair'. The Chief Secretary's Department remained silent. Screenings proceeded in all the other States.

However, Longford had more important things on his mind. Returning from New Zealand in 1915, J.D. Williams exhibitor and showman thrust a copy of *The Sentimental Bloke* into the air. 'Raymond, this is a great book, have you read it?' Assuring him that he hadn't, 'Hell's bells, get busy and read it and tell me what you think of it'.

Longford immediately gave it to Lyell who had nothing but praise for it. Not so the potential backers. All said it wasn't a subject for filming. With the help of Sir David Gordon and Southern Cross Feature Films of Adelaide, Longford managed to obtain the backing to make the picture 'on location' in Sydney and at the White City Wonderland Studios. Longford and Lyell's masterpiece was in the making.

Denied commercial release by Union Theatres, Queensland exhibitor and entrepreneur E.J. Carroll saw it and recognised its potential. He opened *The Sentimental Bloke* at Sydney's Theatre Royal on Saturday, October 18, 1919. It was a huge success and the critics unanimous. 'The eyes of Australia are at last open to what can be done in the way of local film production. The eye-opener has been *The Sentimental Bloke*, which has taken us by storm just as did the book when first published a little while ago,' wrote H.K. Carhall for *The Picture Show*[2] seven days after the release of the film. And was the author as pleased as the audiences? At a special screening in Melbourne C.J. Dennis was seen 'walking rather sheepishly' into the cinema 'not particularly anxious to be recognised'. At the conclusion of the screening Dennis was not only described as being a happy person but 'even astounded'. 'I am amazed at the fidelity with which the written word has been produced as a visual narrative.' 'When I came here, I might as well tell you, I carried grave doubts as to what I should see. At best I expected to see a burlesque – at worst a fiasco. Instead of that I come away

---

1 Page 110, *Photo Play Artiste*, Marilyn Dooley; page 102 *Australian Film 1900-1977*, Andrew Pike and Ross Cooper.
2 *The Picture Show*, page 8, October 25, 1919.

almost believing in miracles. I would have thought it impossible to do what has been done, and the difficulties which I thought would arise have all been admirably swept away.'[3]

For E.J. Carroll it was a box office bonanza, enabling him to finance Longford and Lyell's next four productions. Carroll obtained an extensive release of the film in Britain, and the United States, but the integrity and character of the film was damaged by altering the titles and Dennis verse to suit American tastes. American director Wilfred Lucas shortened 'The Bloke' from 8,000 ft to 6,500 ft for its US release but more was deleted after its first screening at Santa Anna, a small town sixty miles from Los Angeles. Australian producer Beaumont Smith had become involved with its initial release here and assured the *Picture Show Weekly*, '… the usual method is to put members of the firm among the audience to see what impression the picture is making, and to get hints about improvements. When *The Sentimental Bloke* was exhibited we had a full house, and the production was very well received' '… I hope it will be successful everywhere, not only because Mr E.J. Carroll is an old friend of mine, but because a popular Australian film will benefit the industry here as a whole.'

We talked about the film and he became more and more intrigued with the fact I had actually re-spliced the film and that it even existed. I handed him one of my envelopes containing the frames from either side of the joins. He looked into the envelope, touched the bundles of frames for a moment, put them back and handed me the envelope. Perhaps this moment had brought back too many memories.

Longford was already shooting *Ginger Mick*, the sequel, whilst *The Sentimental Bloke* was still in release. Heralded *The Picture Show*:[4] 'Ginger Mick' – Another Australian motion picture triumph. 'Australian enterprise gets a further boost with the advent of *Ginger Mick* as a film celebrity …. Mr Raymond Longford, who was responsible for directing the action of the "Bloke" success, has once more shown his intimate knowledge of Australian life, and in producing *Ginger Mick* has added fresh laurels to his reputation.' Across the board the critics were unanimous that the film was even better than *The Bloke*.

A further sequel followed in 1922, *The Dinkum Bloke*, but this time not based on the C.J. Dennis verse. Released by Paramount Pictures at Hoyts Deluxe on June 2, 1923, it was an instant success and supported by positive critiques. Gaumont paid £2,300 for distribution rights in Britain and it was released in February 1924 as *A Gentleman in Mufti*. Sadly but thankfully only Longford's masterpiece, *The*

3   *The Picture Show*, pp 47/48, May 1920
4   *The Picture Show*, pp 50/51, Feb 1, 1920.

Sentimental Bloke, survives.[5] The team were, however, to repeat their success with Steele Rudd's *On Our Selection* and *Rudd's New Selection*.

Edmund Duggan and Bert Bailey had acquired the stage rights to *On Our Selection* and had reduced the work to melodrama and slapstick. Nonetheless the play was successful for a number of years. But it was not Steele Rudd. Longford returned to the original work. In *The Picture Show*, April 1921, he said: 'I'm making an Australian picture, and I want the people in it to be real Australians. Now your average Australian is about the most casual person under the sun; so if I put the players through their parts over and over again, worrying them, striving to perfect them, they might do good work, but they wouldn't look like Australians. They'd merely be actors, perfectly conscious that they were acting. My way is to let them know the action I want and allow them to go right ahead with it. For a picture like *On Our Selection*, in which it is absolutely necessary that the characters look natural, I think that's the best course.'

But a new difficulty had arisen. Lottie Lyell's health had become troublesome and Longford had to do the picture on his own.

Both films were enormously successful and created a spate of 'bushwhacker' and 'hayseed' imitations. Longford and Lyell continued making pictures but Lottie's health further deteriorated.

On 21 December 1925, at the age of only thirty-five, Lottie died of tuberculosis at her home in Roseville, Sydney. For Longford the grief was enormous; for the Australian film industry it was a tragedy too. In the prime of their lives and at the peak of their careers, the flame was extinguished. Longford would never completely recover, either personally or professionally, though he was to go on working into the 1950s.

Over two full Saturday afternoons I obtained glimpses of his life and times. Exhausted from taking so many cryptically written notes, I'd race up the hill past the Mater Hospital and home to write down in understandable English all that I could remember and decipher.

Here was a true pioneer of our cinema who, with his partner, had battled to achieve their great success, but was he bitter? Was he disappointed? Not so, I believe, for it was on the third and final occasion that I was taken completely by surprise. Mrs Longford, on opening the door, warned me he was not well and not to stay too long. No afternoon tea this day.

I don't know what made me ask the question of an obviously old man, but I said 'What, if you had the chance, would you really like to do now?' He was

---

5 I often wonder if *Ginger Mick* is not lying in the corner of a British film vault and *A Gentleman in Mufti* is not stored somewhere in the vaults of Paramount on Melrose Avenue.

as quick as a flash. He got up out of his chair and left the room, returning only seconds later. Holding a script with a very firm hand, Raymond Longford said 'This is the best film I ever made – ' and, pausing, 'I would love to remake it'.

It was *Fisher's Ghost*.[6] Not one of the classics Longford and Lyell are now known for – but one of our lost films. 'It is the film I would love most to have the opportunity of remaking – I've written a new script – it will be terrific,' his voice boomed.

Fisher's Ghost, set in Campbelltown, NSW in 1826, is about a settler named Farley who is confronted one night by an apparition. The ghost claims to be the spirit of Frederick Fisher who was murdered by a George Worrell.

Longford and Lyell had made the film in Campbelltown for the modest sum of £1,000 in a new production venture supported by Charles Perry in 1924. At the Royal Commission of 1927 into the film industry, Longford accused the head of Union Theatres, Stuart F. Doyle, of having refused to release the film because it was too gruesome. However, despite accepting an unfavourable deal from Hoyts, the box office was to tell an entirely different story. Opening at Hoyts Deluxe, George Street, October 4, 1924, the audiences flocked to the theatre, vindicating Longford's judgement. *Everyone's*, October 8, 1924, strongly recommended the film to the nation's exhibitors: 'There was not a great deal of story to work upon, but the producer has certainly made out a worthwhile one and he has not descended to exaggeration to accomplish this.'

He was about to give me the script to take home to read when Mrs Longford entered the room. 'No, not that one Ray.' She smiled and indicated it was time to go. It was to be the last time – the final visit, for I was about to set out on my journey of discovery overseas.

Mrs Longford worked at the newsagency on Waverton Station. Some weeks later I returned the papers and photographs Mr Longford had lent me to her at the newsstand. She looked at me with great surprise. I was actually returning material she probably thought had gone forever. She smiled and said 'thank you'. I could feel her looking at me somewhat intensely as I began my walk back up Bay Road to Crows Nest. Maybe she had had a change of heart about me, I thought.

---

6   I discovered in 2001 a nitrate copy of *Fisher's Ghost* had exchanged hands between two collectors about twenty years ago. Efforts to find the collector and the film have been unsuccessful.

3

Discovering 'The Hidden Power'

In my first six months of work I was to graduate to the 'dry end' of the positive processing machine – under the watchful eye of Elsie Thomas. The 'dry end' was where the prints came through long drying cabinets onto reels outside the cabinets. One had to watch for the metal staple joins between each reel, snap them off and feed the film onto the next reel. The film didn't travel at a very fast speed like the machines do today. However, sometimes mayhem would occur when a manufacturer's splice in the film stock would part, or a sprocket hole would tear, and there would be an almighty crash as the elevator holding the travelling film would fall to the bottom of the drying cabinet. This would bring the entire machine to a halt and destroy the prints travelling through the developing tanks at the 'wet end' of the processor. The 'wet end' was the charge of Max Long who would immediately stop feeding a new reel into the machine until we could re-thread the film onto the elevators.

Elsie Thomas was the first woman I had met with a biting turn of phrase, a wicked tongue, who couldn't suffer fools gladly and with the drollest sense of humour one could find. We made a good working team and we were never bothered by Mr Markham who was somewhat intimidated by her, a fact which didn't escape her or me! Much later her de facto was to take me under his wing on the filmmaking process. At the 'dry end' we at least could see each other with the soft amber lights over the ends of the machine. It was much darker at the 'wet end' where Max taught me how to join the unprocessed reels from the printing room whilst the machine continued running, without having a nervous breakdown. Underneath the plates holding the undeveloped film, the elevators on which the film ran went down about a floor and a half. By using a clutch one could stop the film travelling in time to join the next reel on to feed into the processor. In this time the elevator travelled up towards you. Only once in my memory did the staple machine jam and panic momentarily took hold of me, when Max thankfully returned early from lunch.

There were two processing machines with two tracks each for the film to be developed and dried. Number one machine was always in use developing the feature film from overseas and the Universal news on Mondays. However, it was altogether a different story on Wednesdays when both machines with all four sides were running non-stop to deliver the *Cinesound Review* weekly newsreel to the theatres across Australia by Thursday morning.

This was to be my next promotion. I was asked if I would like to learn grading and printing. This is a process whereby the grader (nowadays known as a colourist!) looks at the negative of the scene by eye, selects a grade number or 'light', notches the negative five frames from the splice (scene change) so that when the 'notch' hits the gate of the printing machine, the density of the lamp is adjusted by the opening and closing of the printer's gate, to register the 'light' number given by the grader, which is written for the printer operator to adjust when he or she hears the 'notch'. I used to let the film run through my left-hand fingers just above the gate so I could feel the notch and ensure there wasn't a 'missed light'. It was the 1980s before technology took over from the eye of the grader and even then a good grader would often readjust the technical reading of the scene.

It was here I discovered the secret of film editing. I was fortunately assigned assistant to probably one of the most skilled graders of the time, Alan James. As mentioned previously, Wednesday was newsreel day. This entailed starting work at 5am to write the 'light' cards for Alan as he carefully 'eyed' each scene and graded it a number. The numbers on the printer ran from 1 to 22. If the density of the cameraman's negative was 'black' because of the circumstances at the time of filming, then the voltage had to be adjusted and thereby all the light cards rewritten. In the grading process, Alan would describe the scene, which I would write down on the card beside the 'light' number. It soon became very apparent to me that a regular pattern emerged in the structure of each newsreel story. A race meeting is a good example. In describing the scenes, Alan would say:

Long shot (L.S.) racecourse
Wide shot (W.S.) racecourse
Medium high shot (M.H.S.) racecourse
Wide shot (W.S.) bookie's enclosure
Close-up (C.U.) bookie
Close-up (C.U.) punter

(Bottom) Cinesound, March 1956, six months before Bruce Gyngell introduced television to Australians. Ken G Hall directs *The Anthony Squires* film. Across the floor, L to R: Syd Whiteley, editor; unknown; Howard Rubie, Ken G. Hall beside camera blimp; Keith Loone operating; Ray Wiles, camera assist.; Clive Cross, director (son of Bert Cross); Moncia Frogett, continuity; Herbert Hayward, Greater Union Manager, Reg Burbury looks on; Peter Whitchurch, writer/producer with pipe; and Freddie Wyndham on lights. Can't remember why there were so many 'heavies' on the set!

Close-up (C.U.) bookie
Close-up (C.U.) bookie
Close-up (C.U.) punter
High shot (H.S.) fashions
Medium close-up (M.C.U.) woman in hat
Wide shot (W.S.) three women
Close-up (C.U.) woman in hat
Medium close-up (M.C.U.) two women in hats
High shot (H.S.) horses parading
Medium close-up (M.C.U.) horses parading
Close-up (C.U.) horses parading
Wide shot (W.S.) crowd
Close-up (C.U.) starter's gun
Side shot (M.C.U.) horses leaving starting gate

Cinesound, like its competitor Movietone, covered every major race meeting in Australia, of which there are many. I soon learnt to predict the order of shots in a race meeting until one day I said to Alan: 'Wouldn't it be a change if they started with a close-up and pulled back to a wide shot?' Alan stopped, looked at me, looked at the negative he was grading, looked back at me and said 'That would be using your imagination wouldn't it?' Well, if this was film editing, then a Film Editor I was going to be.

It took about two hours to grade the newsreel depending on how long it was. If we opened the can on Wednesday morning and saw it was about 800 feet (nine minutes), we would groan loudly; if it was only 600 feet (six and a half minutes) there would be a cheer. On the law of averages, the newsreel would come in between 630 and 650 feet. I would take the picture negative and soundtrack to the printing room, print the soundtrack first, then the picture, and wait patiently for this first print to come off. Alan would fine-tune a few shots to a different light, or exposure, then the all-day print run would commence. During the morning, as the prints were screened, he would continue to make the occasional adjustment until by the afternoon the prints coming off were perfect. These late prints were destined for the city cinemas and the picture palaces. The earlier, slightly unbalanced prints were dispatched to the country cinemas.

Remember, this is the 1950s. Aeroplanes to the capital cities of Australia took hours to reach their destinations, not one or two as now is the case. The country prints left Sydney on the Wednesday night mail trains, but in both cases, plane or train, the first session at 11am on Thursday in Perth and Sydney, Melbourne and

Brisbane, Adelaide and Hobart, would open with the *Cinesound Review*, right on time. The newsreel being late was unheard of and would have probably brought instant dismissal.

Automatic Film Laboratories held a monthly screening night for the staff and their families. Generally it was a print of one of the many British features the lab used to do and sometimes it would be an imported Technicolor print made available especially for the occasion. I hadn't as yet attended any of these staff screenings as I had to go home to see that my mother was faring okay. Dad worked as the cellarman for Claude Fay at his North Sydney Hotel on the corner of Carlow and Miller Streets and, more often than not, wouldn't arrive home till after ten o'clock. After the death of my six-day-old brother, Peter, in 1944 from the RH negative factor blood complications, my mother had started an early menopause, then called 'the change of life', and a steady decline in her health and general wellbeing. The final straw for her was being evicted from the family home at 59 Sinclair Street a few years later. She was never to forgive Dad's mother, or his sister Ruth, who on the night of our eviction sat in the company's green Ford panel van at the end of our driveway in Bruce Street surveying the scene and making sure we were leaving.

This, coupled with the fact Dad was never home, made her life a miserable one, her nerves becoming worse, which is why she was concerned I would get a good job and be happy. She took a keen interest in everything I was doing and was probably greatly relieved that, although I was an only child, I wasn't a lonely one. I was very much able to make my own world around me. She would devour all my movie magazines, *Picturegoer*, *The Picture Show Weekly*, *Photoplayer*, to read anything she could find about Lana Turner, who was also an RH negative factor blood group person. It was sometimes an effort to persuade her to board the tram at the Oaks Hotel on Tuesday nights and travel only about four miles to the Mosman Kings on my weekly pass from the laboratory. Mrs Gant would be playing the grand piano in the foyer and we were always given the best seats upstairs. Last week's *Cinesound Review* and two features would be the night's entertainment.

The Spit tram to Lane Cove through Crows Nest always waited outside the cinema for the night's program to finish. Sometimes the second feature would be running late because the theatre used to 'switch' at interval the print with the Kings at Chatswood, some ten miles away. If it was very late then the projectionist would drop a reel so we would still get out on time to catch the waiting tram. This weekly journey to the Kings was a complete ordeal for my mother so the thought of getting her across the bridge to Wynyard and another tram up to the laboratory was planning the impossible. The film to be screened for the monthly

(Top) My first job on Tuesday mornings was to cue the music up for each item in the newsreel.

(Right) Chief Cinesound editor, Sydney Whiteley, at his machine whilst I sort the trims.

(Bottom left) Two of Cinesound's many great women technicians: At the Moviola, Queen of Film Editors, Marcia Anderson. Marcia edited the two-minute CinemaScope ads for Peter Stuyvesant cigarettes and the Rothmans Seven Cities series of ads also in CinemaScope.

(Bottom right) Margaret Guihen, the personable, droll and amusing negative cutter at the trusty Bell & Howell pedal splicer.

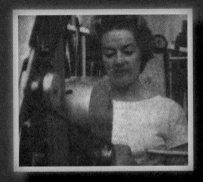

staff night was announced and caused great excitement. It was the first preview in Australia of *Genevieve* with Kenneth More and Kay Kendall. Elsie Thomas said I should bring my parents. I said it was difficult but I would try.

Much to Dad's surprise and mine, Mum said she would like to go. He made special arrangements to leave work early and book a cab. That way he was able to ensure Mum would at least get there. It was not to be.

Having caught the ferry from Circular Quay and the 'jumping jack' tram up to Neutral Bay Junction, I rounded the corner into Laycock Street to see my father standing at the top of the outside staircase to our flat. I thought this very strange. He was waiting for me and had been standing there an hour. As I ascended the stairs Dad said there had been an accident but Mum was okay although badly hurt. I stood at the front door, which opened to the lounge room. The rendered walls were splattered and streaked with blood as was the kitchen and bathroom. Mum had been prescribed the latest tranquilliser of the time, with sometimes bizarre results. It was called Phenobarbital or Phenobarb. I would come home some evenings and think that she had been drinking, except for the fact that she didn't drink. She had decided, as it was a hot summer day and Dad was coming home and doing something for us, to prepare a chicken salad for an easy early tea. The salad bowl was her best Waterford crystal. She opened the refrigerator door, picked up the bowl, turned, had a dizzy spell causing her to stumble and her face to go into the bowl, and both she and the bowl crashed into the interior of the fridge. In the fall she severed an artery. Blood shot everywhere. With no phone at her disposal to call for help, she miraculously managed to stem the flow of blood as she staggered from one room to the other. A neighbour heard her calls for help and phoned Dad at work. He got home just before the doctor arrived. Mum refused to go to hospital in the vain hope she would be well enough to go and see *Genevieve* that evening.

The flat looked as if there had been a massacre. It took the entire weekend to wash the walls down. Mum was lucky to be alive but the look and sense of disappointment on her face was something I can never forget. To this day I cannot cope with the sight of blood, in reality or at the cinema or on television.

I received a very cool reception on Monday at work but all I could say was sorry, my mother wasn't well enough to come. No one would have believed what had happened if I had told them so it was better to keep quiet and get on with my work. Elsie Thomas suspected something serious had happened but I never told her.

Mondays I had to deliver new prints of titles for the theatres, 'Next Friday', 'Soon for this theatre' etc. to the Greater Union headquarters at 49 Market Street.

The Australian Theatre Weekly

Vol. I. No. 4   THURSDAY, 27th MAY, 1915   Issued Weekly

Showing the Latest Star Features
The Supreme Efforts of the World's Greatest Producers

Comics and
Keystone
   Comedies

Interesting
Scenics and
Industrial
Pictures

and the

**Latest
War
Gazettes**

Booking
   Office :
R. TAYLOR
(opp. Theatre)
'Phone
1531
Mosman
Theatre
'Phone
1228
Mosman

Manager:
E. B. BYRNE
Orchestral
Director:
S. R. RAE

Interior of " The Australian." One of the most comfortable and
Best Equipped Picture Theatres

Direction -- A. R. Keeling

The Big Picture House,
Spit Junction, MOSMAN

Printed for the Publisher by Winn & Co., at Ridge Street, North Sydney

The Australian Theatre, Spit Junction, Sydney, May 1915. It was here in the same year Ken G. Hall saw synchronised sound for the first time. The demonstration of sound on disc of Harry Lauder singing was a failure, but it aroused Hall's interest in the possibility of talking pictures. The Australian survived till 1936.

(Top) Des Freeman, Howard Rubie, Ray Wiles, Ian Ryan and me. We Cinesound lads had class. Here, out on the town, December 1956, dining at the Baltimore.

(Bottom) Three Pioneer Mentors to me: third from left, Ken G. Hall, Bert Cross and Sydney Whiteley. Extreme left of photo: Allyn Barnes, Cinesound mixer. Extreme right of photo: Alma Murphy, waxing and dispatch, Automatic Film Laboratories. To her right: Tom Wyldie, manager, Associated Film Printers.

Cinesound 1955. Me at the turntable waiting to cue the music in when the title hit the screen. Marcia Anderson sits behind me, Herbie Hayward from Greater Union to her left, Ken G. Hall, centre back row.

I didn't mind this chore as it was on the way home. On one of these Monday trips I made an appointment to see Mr Hayward. Herbert G. Hayward was on the tenth floor in the hallowed precincts of baronial splendour. To the right as one stepped out of the lift was Norman B. Rydge's suite of offices. Mr Rydge was the head of Greater Union and had taken over from the company's founder, Stuart F. Doyle. To the left of the lift was Herbie Hayward's office. I had written to Cinesound seeking a position as an assistant and had received a letter from none other than Ken G. Hall, assuring me he would do his best to find me a position but it wasn't company policy to take staff from a sister or associated company. Armed with this letter, I presented myself to Mr Hayward seeking a transfer from Automatic Film Laboratories to Cinesound. He was somewhat taken aback by this forthright approach from a seventeen-year-old. He listened attentively and said he would see what he could do.

A few weeks later I was called into the managing director's office at the lab. Les Wicks had retired and the young man from Technicolor, Douglas Dove, had become M.D. 'Aren't you happy here, Tony?' he asked. Assuring him I was, he then revealed that Mr Hayward had made arrangements for me to be transferred to Cinesound at the end of the month. I couldn't believe my ears. I raced home to break the news as quickly as the tram could get me there. 'I'm going to work in a film studio,' I proudly announced. My mother was elated. My father, as usual, said nothing. Elsie Thomas and Alma Murphy were tickled pink with the news and though sorry to see me moving on, were pleased for my sake that I was going to have a future. Alan James was not so pleased as he had to find a new assistant and train him. However, he was very supportive, assuring me it was the right thing for me to do.

Walking up South Dowling Street to the Flinders Street tram stop on my last night, Bert Cross looked at me and said, 'Well, son, at least you're out of the laboratory.' He shook my hand and wished me well and great success. 'But there's still no future in Australian films, my boy!' I watched him board his tram and take off down Anzac Parade to Bronte. It would be twelve years before I would see him again. On Monday I was starting the next leg of my own journey.

4

The Voice Of Australia

In the two and a half years of studying Australian film history every Tuesday night and Saturday at the Mitchell Library I made many discoveries. The library has a complete collection of the *Everyone's* trade magazine going back to the 1920s, and *The Picture Show*, a unique local magazine published for a short time in the late 1900s. My main purpose in attending the library was to find out all I could about Raymond Longford. It was also in *Everyone's* I had learnt about a living filmmaker of the day, Ken G. Hall. I had seen *Orphan of the Wilderness* at one of the Saturday matinees at the Sesqui. I could remember the bold Cinesound Production trademark (logo) at the beginning of the film but not the name of its director, Ken G. Hall. I learnt from *Everyone's* that he was the most prolific of all our film directors with seventeen feature films behind him and the producer of the *Cinesound Review* which I used to print every week. Now I was to start working for him on his weekly newsreel.

Ken G. Hall started work at the age of fifteen too, as a cadet reporter in 1916 for the *Evening News*. He worked as a press man until 1917 when he was offered a job by Gayne (Bob) Dexter, a publicist for Union Theatres and Australasian Films at their headquarters in the Film House in Sydney's Pitt Street, just around the corner from the *Evening News* building. Two years as a cadet reporter had been a great learning curve but publicity was a different ball game altogether. Ken Hall's show business career had commenced. Stuart F. Doyle, the head of Union Theatres, had pretty strong views about publicity in relation to a film's success or non-success. Ken G. Hall: 'The advertising side of this was creative work; you started with a blank sheet of paper and came up with something worthwhile. It had *better* be worthwhile because the publicity man's job was on the line all the time. If the picture flopped he got the blame – always. Stuart F. Doyle had it clearly in his mind. If the picture was a big success, then it was a great picture.

That's what his film buyers and bookers told him because they had bought it anyway. If it failed, the publicist was wrong. You'd taken the wrong angle on it. You couldn't win.'

KG, as he was known, was promoted by Doyle to manage the Lyceum Theatre opposite the Film House, which Cozens Spencer had started all those years ago. It wasn't long before Hall was brought back to the Film House to become the national publicity director for Union Theatres and Australasian Films. In 1925 Doyle sent Hall to Hollywood to 'learn the business of picture making' and to observe the progress Tinseltown was making with sound. KG had seen and heard his first sound demonstration at the Australian Theatre at Spit Junction, Mosman, a suburb of Sydney, in 1915. The demonstration of Harry Lauder singing with the accompanying sound on a disc was a failure. Hall was interested in the progress being made with the development of sound actually recorded on the film. Ken G. Hall's biggest challenge was about to happen.

Back in Australia he was called in by his boss, John C. Jones, who had bought a German film, *Unsere Emden* (*Our Emden*). The *Emden*, a German raider, was sunk by the *HMAS Sydney* in World War I near the Cocos Islands off the northwestern coast of Australia. Jones thought it might be good box office but the film, on viewing, was a disaster. Hall was given the opportunity of remaking all the sequences featuring the *Sydney*. Using his initiative, he approached the navy. Luck was on his side. The *Sydney* would be doing exercises off Jervis Bay, New South Wales, for three weeks. Hall could take his camera and actors and live on board for a week whilst the navy carried out their exercises at sea. Newsreel cameramen Ray Vaughan and Claude Carter, who had established Filmcraft Laboratories, joined Hall on board. KG had written a script recreating the *Sydney* stalking and sinking the *Emden*, retaining the German sequences of the *Emden* and writing new titles, as well as editing the film. He had saved John C. Jones' neck. The film opened at Sydney's magnificent Prince Edward – Theatre Beautiful, on September 21, 1928. Picture palaces of the day normally had a weekly change of program. *The Exploits of the Emden*, the film's new title, ran to packed houses for three weeks.

Around the corner from The Film House, the *Evening News* building had been demolished to make way for Stuart Doyle's greatest dream – an office block for Union Theatres towering over their flagship theatre, the mighty State. Hall was to return to the site of his first job.

When Bert Bailey walked into Ken Hall's new office and announced, 'I believe we are to make a picture together,' it was the first Hall knew about it. Bailey had talked Stuart Doyle into making a 'talkie' of his successful play, *On Our Selection*, which Bailey, along with Edmund Duggan, had adapted from Steele

Rudd's equally successful novel. What both men didn't know was that the film was to be made with an Australian recording system invented and developed by a young Tasmanian. Bert Cross was managing the Australasian Film Laboratory housed in the old Australasian Film Studios at 65 Ebley Street, Bondi Junction. Most of the building had become a rollerskating rink. Bert telephoned KG for an appointment to introduce him to a young radio engineer from Tasmania, Arthur Smith. Bert had given Arthur a corner to work in at the laboratory about a year beforehand because Arthur believed he had the system to get a variable density soundtrack onto film.

'What's it sound like?' asked Hall. Bert told him it wasn't perfect but it was good. Hall listened to the soundtrack but couldn't believe it was possible for a radio engineer to build a sound recorder equal to that of RCA or Western Electric in America. Arthur Smith had! Hall wrote an enthusiastic note to Stuart Doyle but Doyle wasn't impressed. Hall was crestfallen and, according to his own words, thought he had blown his career. Depressed for two weeks, his intercom buzzer rang. Doyle wanted to see him immediately in his office. 'I had another listen to that soundtrack. It's not so bad. It's worth following up.'

To launch *The Jazz Singer* at the Lyceum, as a publicist Hall had used the term Cine-Sound as exclusive to the theatre. Union Theatres had registered the name. Hall took the hyphen out of the name and the great little studio was born – Cinesound.

The filming of *On Our Selection* was not without its technical problems but in the middle of the shoot out at Castlereagh on the Nepean River, some twenty-five miles west from Sydney, Hall was ordered into the city to meet with Doyle that afternoon. 'I want you to start a newsreel,' Doyle thundered. Hall said it was a great idea and he would see to it as soon as filming *On Our Selection* had been completed. 'No,' said Doyle, 'I want it in two weeks.' The Fox-Movietone news was beginning to take business away to the opposition Hoyts. Doyle wanted Hall to act now. KG seconded Bert Cross to find cameramen and equipment. November 1931 the *Cinesound Review* was launched with its proud and unique trademark and motto – 'The Voice of Australia'.

Starting work with a newsreel company on a Monday is not such a good idea. It's the day the footage taken at the weekend is viewed, edited and shot-listed for the writer to prepare the commentary late Monday night in readiness for the newsreel to be recorded first thing Tuesday morning. Remember, this is the very same newsreel that is seen in the cinemas two days later. Cinesound's production base at 65 Ebley Street, Bondi, was shut down in 1948, ending a period of motion picture making on the site commenced in 1915. The Rank Organisation, fifty percent owners of Greater Union at the time, had persuaded Norman B. Rydge, head of G.U., that exhibition was the future, not picture making. Ironically, a few years later Ealing Studios' last film was made in Australia.

Cinesound had moved to an inner Sydney suburb, Rozelle, and into a great barn of a silent picture show, the Amusu. There was certainly nothing amusing about the move and it must have been an extremely sad experience for Ken G. Hall, who had transformed an old skating rink into the country's foremost film studio with an output of box office successes, to move to a dilapidated picture house probably built at the same time as Cinesound's original building.

My first job was to be the projectionist and cutting room assistant. In charge was Sydney Whiteley who, along with Stanley Moore, was to be my mentor in the wondrous craft of film editing. Next door, another mentor, Stuart Ralston, was in charge of the optical department and the Oxberry Rostrum Camera, where the magic of lap dissolves, fades and superimpositions was performed, very tame no doubt by today's standards but to my eyes, wondrous images came from Mr Ralston's printer. The camera department was headed by Ron Horner, who led one of the best newsreel camera teams in Australia, Bede Whiteman, Lloyd Shiels, Les Wasley and, like myself, a very young Howard Rubie and Des Freeman. Two editors who were legends at Cinesound were Marcia Anderson and, upstairs, Wally Batty. Marcia, I thought, had editing's 'glamour' job. She cut the original Cinemascope Peter Stuyvesant theatrical commercials and later the same for Rothmans. I was introduced to Ken G. Hall and his pleasant, raspy voice welcomed me and assured me of a future at Cinesound. I was glad Bert Cross wasn't in earshot. Next door to KG's office was the indomitable secretary, Jean Smith. I recognised her from the photos I had seen in *Everyone's* magazine at the library, as Ken Hall's continuity girl on the Cinesound features. Miss Smith was a force to contend with and I kept a wary distance, though I think she took a shine to me for she always had time to ask how I was doing. Then there was the French editor, Giselle Bougerier, who was a palm reader! At seventeen I hadn't encountered anyone who had this gift. She took my hand one day when she was reading for a group in the cutting room, shrieked, threw my hand down, said something in French and fled from the room. I was quite startled. Marcia Anderson could hardly keep a straight face. She later asked Giselle what my hand had revealed. 'Ah, ooh la la, I have seen double lives but never someone with three lives!' Probably my imagination but I felt for a time some of my fellow staff were somewhat wary of me.

Any time the cutting rooms were quiet, I was encouraged by Bede Whiteman to come round and watch the camera department at work on the studio stage. I was fascinated by the way cameras were moved on dollies and the giant camera crane. At the end of my apprenticeship as the studio projectionist, I was to be given the choice of moving into the editing department or camera. I knew Bede Whiteman was keen for me to move to camera but I also knew where I really wanted to go.

Projecting the newsreel rushes every Monday morning, then projecting the edited stories on Tuesday morning for recording, had me enthralled. The transformation from sometimes 2,000 or 3,000 feet of coverage of a story on Monday morning to a one-and-a-half minute story by Monday night was, to me, a miracle of editing. More so because we were not allowed the luxury of a positive print cutting copy, the negative itself was edited. Movietone over at Camperdown had a budget for what is called the 'work print' whereby the editor can chop and change the shots at will. Not so at Cinesound. A 'work print' they could not afford. Greater Union's priority was a low-cost newsreel at no matter what the cost! If one makes a mistake editing negative, that's it! If I scratched the negative by incorrectly threading the projector, then the story was useless. So extreme care had to be taken. The C&W projector sprockets had been modified because the negative sprocket hole is marginally smaller than the positive print to allow proper registration and steadiness in the camera. The Moviolas on which the film was edited had specially made gates with green velvet runners to allow the negative to pass through the editing machine without being scratched. Mind you, black and white negative film is a pretty tough commodity, not like colour film negative, which will reflect a breath or a fingerprint. This procedure was not greeted with approval by either the cameraman or the editors, but this was the Cinesound practice and we had to adhere to it.

Ken Hall's 'presence' was not unlike Raymond Longford's. A tall man, perhaps not quite as big as Longford, but you certainly knew when he walked into a room. He had a sprightly walk and his raspy voice added to his charm and character. He also always wore a light blue-grey casual jacket zipped up the front, quite trendy for the 1950s. It was his memory for particular shots that fascinated me. From the thousands of feet of film projected on Monday morning, if Syd Whiteley hadn't used a shot KG had remembered, he would ask Syd why he hadn't used it. So as soon as I had completed projection of the edited story I would be assigned the task of foraging in the trim bins holding all the unused film, to find the shot KG wanted included in the story. The recording of the newsreel was a wonderment. KG would direct John Sherwood or Charles Lawrence on how to read the story, I would spin in the opening disc, Hall would use a cue light for the commentator and raise or lower his left arm for when sound mixer Allyn Barnes had to raise or lower the music.

Because the stories didn't have to go through the process of 'negative cutting' i.e. matching the negative to the positive 'work print' images, Cinesound very often had a time advantage over our opposition Movietone in getting our prints to the theatre screens. Mondays and Tuesdays the main theatre had to be kept clear for the *Cinesound Review*, Wednesdays to Fridays the theatre was occupied with a variety of documentaries, commercials for the cinema and travelogues for the various states' tourist commissions. I often had to screen shorts for recording of narration and mixing for outside independent producers. One such was John Heyer's *The Back of Beyond*. Heyer was editing and post-producing the documentary at Merv Murphy's Supreme Sound Studios in Sydney's Paddington, when a massive power failure occurred. Heyer rang Hall to see if Cinesound could assist. This documentary was something entirely different from anything I had seen before. Made for the Shell Film Unit, it tells of the legendary Tom Kruse and his mail truck traversing the arid desert route of Australia between Birdsville and Maree, delivering the Royal Mail to the people of the outback. It won the major prize at the Venice Film Festival and launched Heyer's career to become one of the world's great documentarists.

Ken G. Hall had won an award of a different kind in 1942. It was the Oscar, the Academy Award for his production of *Kokoda Front Line*, the world's first and only newsreel to be so acclaimed and honoured. During World War II the footage taken by the newsreel cameramen was controlled by the government's Department of Information and allocated after censoring to Cinesound and Movietone for their newsreels. The cameraman Damien Parer happened to be in town on leave and Hall seized the opportunity of getting Parer before a camera to introduce and close the newsreel. Hall wrote Parer's script and got Parer to heighten Australians' awareness of the war on their doorstep. The result was a triumph. Terry Banks' judicious editing, Peter Bathurst's passionate delivery of Hall's patriotic commentary and the somewhat ironic use of Wagner as the newsreel's score, can still bring a choke to the back of the throat at retrospective screenings.

Ken G. Hall in my time at Cinesound gave the weekly *Review* a quality quite different from that of Movietone. The opposition news was highly professional and very slickly produced, whereas the *Review* was known for editorialising particular subjects, and at this Hall was in his element. Issues of the day were debated by the newsreel and government policies were often questioned. I could never establish whether this got KG into trouble with his masters at 49 Market Street or not.

Colour had arrived in Australia in about 1955. At Avondale Studios in Sydney, Charles Chauvel was completing the first feature film to be shot in colour, *Jedda*, and at Cinesound Ken Hall was producing and directing *South Pacific Playground*, a featurette (as shorts were called) on Sydney's famous northern beaches. Both films were using the Gevacolor process from Belgium, which had to go to Denham Laboratories in England for developing and printing. Just like my 9.5mm Kodachrome, we used to wait weeks for the rushes to be returned. Colour wasn't new to Cinesound for Ken Hall had pioneered experimental colour *Cinesound Reviews* in the 1940s with a spectacular newsreel *Call of the Surf.* It was filmed in Solarchrome, a bi-pak colour process similar to Cinecolor, used by Monogram and Republic pictures, developed by George Malcolm and Arthur Higgins at Supreme's laboratories in Paddington. Arthur had filmed *The Sentimental Bloke* in 1919 for Raymond Longford.

Bede Whiteman poked his head into the cutting room one morning to ask Syd Whiteley if I could be available the next day to help on the sound stage as the camera department was short of staff and the studios had been hired by an independent cameraman. It was Arthur Higgins. It was a revelation to watch a silent days pioneer still at work in 1956. His method of lighting infuriated Bede Whiteman. Arthur would walk around the set, look at the lights with his beady eyes, adjust the lens aperture accordingly and film. He had never used an exposure meter in his life! His images were always perfect. Bede could never fathom it. I don't think I can recall ever seeing a cinematographer do likewise. Arthur was intrigued that I could be so interested in the history of Australian cinema for a person of my age. He was even more intrigued that I had met Raymond Longford. I had the opportunity between set-ups of hearing Arthur's reflections on the great man.

It was about a month later that I was called out to the reception desk. It was Arthur. 'Here, son, I've done this for you. I think it might help you. I hope you find it interesting.' And off he went. Written carefully on several pages of lined foolscap paper with an ink fountain pen Arthur had made a complete list of every silent feature film he and his brothers Tasman and Ernest had shot, along with the details of cast and director and producer. I was to pore over this document and treasure it for years. It was to be the basis of my unpublished manuscript 'Our First Sixty Years' and a documentary I was eventually to make about our cinema.

The time had come to make the decision. For me it wasn't hard. I was summoned to Ken Hall's office. 'Well, son, how are you finding it?' I was in extreme awe and as nervous as hell. 'Well Mr Hall, I would appreciate the opportunity of moving into the editing department.' 'Excellent – it's where the film is made. Tony, I have had particularly good reports. We are starting a new projectionist in two weeks, then you can move. It's a great craft my boy – you have a great future.' Once again I was thankful Bert Cross wasn't in earshot. I went around to the camera department. I could see the look of disappointment on Bede Whiteman's face as I explained to him my choice for a career. He was completely understanding and wished me well – 'Make sure you always cut my material well!' I think I would have made a good cameraman but it was the magic and mystery of putting all those shots together to tell a story. *The Hidden Power* of editing as Kevin Brownlow so rightly called it. Maybe I would now get the chance to start a story with a close-up and not a long shot!

Syd Whiteley was in charge of the editing department at the *Cinesound Review*, though Stan Moore was the principal editor and it was to Stan I was seconded. Stan gave me excellent training and many opportunities. My job on the *Cinesound Review* was to select the music tracks for each item, synchronise them, and also play in the opening music to each story from a disc. The newsreel was recorded 'live'. If the commentator 'fluffed', the optical film would be rewound in the dark room and the other side used. One had to be careful when the processed track was returned from the laboratory to ensure the right track was synchronised to the picture negative. Most of the library film was on optical film, which was easy to synchronise, splice, whatever, for one can 'see' the track without having to hear it. I became so familiar with the library of stock music I could pick the right mood for each story and lay up the music without ever playing it. The music tracks were kept in one of two film vaults at the end of the editing department corridor. Another vault was behind the projection box.

I soon discovered an Aladdin's cave of film treasure. The Cinesound picture library containing all the off-cuts of all the newsreels of the past twenty-five years, nitrate-tinted footage dating back to the *Australasian Gazette* of the 1900s, the complete nitrate film record of Australian aviation history from Spencer's newsreels and the *Gazette*. Complete 1000 ft reels of lavender background projection plates used in all the Cinesound features of the 1930s and '40s. Some of these plates showed wonderful street scenes of Sydney travelling in front of its famous trams. Nitrate prints of *Cinesound Reviews*' colour editions, including *Call of the Surf* and the negatives of every newsreel produced since 1931. The back vault was the Aladdin's cave. It contained all the negatives of Ken Hall's feature films plus the first print made of *On Our Selection* in 1931, nitrate prints of *For the Term of his Natural Life* (1927) and two reels of *The Adorable Outcast* (1928), prints and negatives of the wartime propaganda documentaries including *100,000 Cobbers* and an intriguing collection simply marked *KYA*. Investigation revealed it was *Know Your Ally* and it was produced and directed in Australia by none other than Frank Capra, with contributions from other directors including Hall. I asked Syd Whiteley who looked after the films in the vaults. 'No one son, they're just a lot of old films the boss made years ago.' I sought permission in my spare time to rewind and clean the negatives. 'That's fine, son, if you want to,' said Syd, 'but son, don't waste too much time on them; they're of no value now.' Every spare hour or at lunchtime I would retrieve one double can at a time (a double can, like a cake tin, held two reels of negative, one picture, one soundtrack) and rewind them carefully, checking for lifting splices or broken sprockets and repairing them where I could.

———————

Marcia Anderson was intrigued with what I was doing but couldn't fathom why I was doing it. 'Who will ever want to see them again?' she asked, making it very clear she thought they weren't worth seeing in the first place.

Clive Cross, the son of Bert Cross and the Cross of Smith & Cross, the inventors and manufacturers of Cinesound's sound system, was now a producer/director of documentaries at the studio. Clive had his own dour personality, which was at odds with the culture of Cinesound. Nonetheless it was not the newsreel but Clive who gave me my first big opportunity. The editors found it difficult working for him and I was told that I would be cutting my first film. It would be for 'Mr Cross'. I could see, even at my young age, what the problem was. The year was 1956. Cinesound editors all worked at a frantic and sometimes frenetic pace. Clive Cross's style was a slow, methodical and considered approach to editing; evaluation of every shot and every cut was his way of making a film. The short was for one of the studio's clients, the Tea Council of Australia, and hosted by a famous radio personality, John Dease. Titled *The Magic Leaf*, it was a fifteen-minute film on how to make a cup of tea! It was probably the subject matter that set the other editors scurrying away, but for me it was my all-important break. It was also a frustrating time for Clive Cross. I was only available to edit his film Wednesday, Thursday and Friday as I had to be on the newsreel Mondays and Tuesdays. I seem to remember it took about a month to cut and then I was shown the credit card listings. Clive asked what credit I would like. I said it didn't matter, but on informing my mother, she was adamant it should be Anthony and not Tony. I dutifully reported back to Mr Cross as I, like everyone else, called him, and he said 'That's good. I like that because your first and second names have seven letters.' 'What's important about that?' I asked. 'It looks better, son, and it's a lucky number.' Having been born on the 27th of the seventh month 1937, maybe he was right. From that day on the credit was nearly always to be Anthony Buckley.

The credits were painted on glass by Will Cathcart whom I was still to meet, but I spoke to him on the phone every Monday night to dictate the titles for the week's newsreel. I kept the glass title for many years. My first credit. Film Editor.

The newsreel was the flagship of Cinesound in the eyes of Ken Hall, but it was the documentaries, short travelogues and the cinema advertisements that were the bread and butter of the company. Even in 1955 the newsreel was heavily subsidised by Greater Union, even though a 'film rental' was charged by the distributor, British Empire Films (BEF). BEF's film handling distribution centre was next door to the studio, and was run by an earnest enthusiast, Cec Kelly. It was from Cec that Syd Whiteley built up the newsreel music library. Syd would just lift the main and end titles from any English film he liked and integrate it into the library! I don't know how many *Cinesound Reviews* finished with the music from *Temptation Harbour* but there were quite a few as it was Syd's favourite.

Cec and BEF used to provide the occasional print of the latest British feature for Friday night staff and family screenings. Reg Burbury, the company secretary, encouraged me to check the print in our vault of *On Our Selection* (1931), Ken Hall's first talkie, to have an anniversary screening on one of these nights. The print was only just still screenable. On examination I could tell the nitrate print had shrunk and it would be a task to get it through the projector. The projectors being as old themselves, I felt I had a chance. The night Reg had organised was a full house and I was a bundle of nerves. The print was in ten single reels, which meant there had to be a 'change over' from one projector to the other every ten minutes, rather than the usual twenty. Being a nitrate print, one had to be 'on hand' at all times. By the time I had threaded the next reel up, being particularly careful to ensure the print was sitting on the sprockets and the carbon arc rods were re-trimmed, it was time to change over to the next reel. It was close to ninety minutes of hell! At times the print was so noisy going through the projector it could be heard in the theatre. Reg sneaked round the back way to enquire how I was going. 'I don't know Mr Burbury but we're up to reel eight, so keep your fingers crossed.' 'Son, everything's crossed – good luck!' The film got to the end, barely in one piece, and the evening was a triumph. After twenty-five years the picture was still very funny. I stepped down from the projection box into the theatre and received a round of applause for my efforts. Applause for a projectionist ... now that's really something.

The Cinesound team of cameramen were a marvellous band of men whose hearts and souls were the lifeblood of the newsreel, the *Cinesound Review – The Voice of Australia*. However, we were all in for a shock or two, which were to shake this venerable organisation to its foundations.

Shock number one. A staff meeting was called by Ken Hall at three one afternoon in the theatrette. No one was given a clue as to why we had been called together. The theatrette was packed. I, being a junior, sat right at the back. Through the door to the left of the screen strode KG. Over six feet in height, and still the proud head of the company whose glory days were long since gone, he stood before his brigade and announced he was leaving the company he and Stuart Doyle had founded. The silence was deafening. Some gasped, others were too stunned to react. It was my first experience of seeing grown men cry. Syd Whiteley rushed from the theatre, tears streaming down his face. Stuart Ralston[1] put his arm around my shoulder and said, 'It's the end of an era, son!' and he asked me to rush over to the corner store to get him a packet of Bex powders, to which he was regretfully addicted. Was Bert Cross going to be right after all?

Hall announced he was leaving to go to head up Frank Packer's new television station, Channel Nine, the first station to go to air in 1956 in Australia. Packer had chosen the right man. 'Ken, I've got this television station! It's a fucking licence to print money, Ken, you've got to come over and run the bloody thing.' So said Packer. But what of Cinesound? – Hall, incidentally, never swore.

Shock number two. Hall announced he had negotiated with Packer a contract for Cinesound to fully provide the newsfilm coverage for Channel Nine's nightly news bulletin for ten years! Cinesound was to be fully re-equipped with the latest 16mm cameras from overseas and editing gear from Eastons Australia. In one fell swoop Ken G. Hall had extended the life of the *Cinesound Review* to be the 'voice of Australia' for another decade. It was a coup that saved the life of the company.

It was mayhem! An entire new form of news presentation had to be learnt from scratch, as well as maintaining the weekly service to the cinemas. Writers' offices had to be built and cameramen trained only to shoot 1 x 100 ft roll of film for each story. (Try that discipline today and perhaps the standard would go back up.) A cameraman was expected to virtually edit the story in the camera to facilitate the short amount of time allocated each afternoon to editing the story. One thing for sure was that the Cinesound team were well trained in editing the original film! Single system Auricon cameras and Bell & Howell 'Eymo' cameras had to be imported. Single system cameras recorded the sound direct onto the film. Separate sound recording in sync with the camera at this time for news was still a long way off. Editing single system sound was a nightmare, far worse than 35mm. For 16mm the sound was twenty-six frames in advance of the picture and one didn't have the latitude one had with separate sound and picture editing. I think it was

---

1   Stuart Ralston took a great interest in mentoring me at Cinesound, just as his partner, Elsie Thomas, had done just a few years before at the laboratory.

the first time I heard expletives on a regular basis in the cutting room. Writers were trained to write so many words a second and each filmed story had to be accurately timed as there was never time for a rehearsal.

Channel Nine's studios are at Willoughby on Sydney's lower North Shore and Cinesound's studio was at Rozelle, an inner suburb on Sydney's south shore! This was a thirty-minute journey each night across the old narrow Gladesville Bridge in Jack Allen's Morris Minor, across the Lane Cove River onto the single lane bridge at Figtree, then up to Willoughby, sometimes arriving at telecine with only ten minutes to spare. For the first few months I would travel with the film in Jack's Morris in case there were any last minute changes whilst we were travelling and a story had to be removed from the reel. Later, as things settled down, the writer would just pick up the reel and hurtle off. Of course there were the scary moments if the tram had broken down on the old Gladesville Bridge or if there was a breakdown anywhere for that matter. One must remember there were no fax machines in the 1950s, so the script could not be sent ahead, no videotape, no satellite, no computers, and the mobile phone was still some twenty-five years away. Surprisingly we never missed a bulletin, though one night I remember threading the telecine machine as the news was going to air.

Channel Nine pioneered the screening of the races from Randwick on Saturdays after the news. The Australian Jockey Club had installed processing machines on the course to assist the stewards and the newsroom had access to the footage at the end of the afternoon. I know nothing about horse races except where the furlong posts are. When the footage arrived it was a relatively easy task to 'assemble' the races (it was hardly an editing job) and put them in race order on a reel for transmission. This, thankfully, was done at the channel, and after transmission I would tidy up and file the reel away for the librarian to pick up on Monday. It was all a very straightforward routine and provided one with some extra pocket money each weekend.

Monday at Cinesound. Syd Whiteley was in early as usual, it being newsreel day. I walked in and was greeted with, 'Shit, son, all hell broke loose on Saturday night.' I looked at him, somewhat perplexed. 'They couldn't find the reel of the races, but the engineer finally did.' I had filed them in the usual place but no one but the librarian would have known where. Ken G. Hall was relaxing at his Bellevue Hill home about 9pm when the phone rang. It was the boss, Frank Packer, holding a dinner party not far from KG's home. One of Frank's horses had done well at Randwick that afternoon and he wanted his guests to see the race, could KG kindly arrange it about 9.45? He explained the Saturday night movie was underway. This did not deter Frank Packer. 'Put the bloody race on in the next commercial break,' said Frank. Hall then rang Syd and asked where would I have put the races! An on-duty engineer finally found the reel, the movie was interrupted and the race was re-run for the proprietor and his dinner guests!

The story has become somewhat exaggerated over the years to nearly becoming apocryphal. In Gerald Stone's excellent and very entertaining insight into the Nine Network and the Packer influence, *Compulsory Viewing*, he relates a different version as told to him by Bruce Gyngell who had taken over the news at the station long after I left Cinesound and the Channel Nine news. Packer may well have pulled the same stunt on Bruce but it seems highly unlikely and too coincidental. Anyway, the above story is the true and original one so I hope this sets the record straight.

1956 was only four years after the Korean War and the western allies were still on alert. The world was in the grip of the Cold War and national service had been introduced in Australia to provide a back-up of trained personnel in case of a further break-out of hostilities on the North/South Korean borders. National service was by a ballot draw and though one couldn't win the lottery, I won selection for 'nasho'. Full training was three months in camp followed by two years of occasional weekend and week-night training with the CMF, the Citizens Military Forces. Employers were obliged to hold open your job, so Gunner Buckley 2/757043 commenced training at Holsworthy Military Barracks south of Sydney in 1956. I stayed in contact with my peers and mentors at Cinesound, who wrote to me whilst I was 'interned', and much to my surprise Ken G. Hall wrote on two occasions.

Whilst we were supposed to take national service seriously, I found it somewhat of an administrative farce. I was given permission to take my Pathé 9.5mm movie camera with me and covered the events, exercises, etc. for my *Sydney Cinema Gazette*. I thought this quite a triumph. I was obtaining footage not available to Cinesound or Movietone. For a loner, the thought of national service was daunting but in fact it was to be one of the best learning curves of my formative years. I was billeted in a hut with eleven others, six beds on either side (or was it eight?) and the sergeant's cubby-hole at the far end. All twelve came from all walks of life and though at times I sensed a reserve about me, we seemed to all get on well with each other. We collectively thought it was a bit of a chore and we soon learned never to admit to being an expert at anything, for the answer would involve doing totally the opposite thing. The captain would ask if any one of us was expert with boats. Hands would shoot up and they would be on kitchen duty next week. Nighttime exercises were a joke and I devised a way of skirting around them in our heavy greatcoats and arriving at the designated spot on time and looking impeccable!

No one queried why we weren't covered in mud. We were allowed one weekend home in three and I have to admit I used to dread the 8.30 red rattler from North Sydney Station all the way to Holsworthy on a cold winter night. I was absolutely hopeless at firing guns so I became a teller and plotter in the Royal Australian Artillery. I liked that we wore berets and not the slouch hat.

I had, over my period at Cinesound, become good friends with cameramen Des Freeman and Howard Rubie. Howard was into boats and all things that sailed, and Des was involved with acting classes and making short films, which were far and away more contemporary and imaginative than anything else being made locally at the time. I wanted to travel and the three of us planned to go overseas together.

The year 1957. Stan Moore had moved on from Cinesound to become a feature film editor for Lee Robinson and Chips Rafferty, two mavericks of Australian cinema. Lee and Chips had set up an independent company to make Australian feature films and co-productions, something that had not been attempted before. Their Southern International Studios were based at 65 Ebley Street, Bondi Junction, in the old Cinesound Studios. Their first venture had been a modest black and white feature, *The Phantom Stockman* (1953), then *King of the Coral Sea* (1954) followed by their first co-production with the French, *Walk Into Paradise* (1956) filmed in Eastmancolor in Papua New Guinea. (For its American release it was retitled *Walk Into Hell*, as this was considered a more commercial title.)

Stan Moore was finishing *Dust in the Sun* at Southern International and telephoned me to enquire if I would like to join him at the studio as his assistant editor. Stan was about to start work on Lee's second co-production with the French, *The Stowaway* (*Le Passager Clandestin*) (1958) with Martine Carol, Roger Livesey, Serge Reggiani, an ambitious venture being shot in English and French on the island of Tahiti. Andy Helgeson had been brought in from Queensland to replace Ken G. Hall and the new management style had brought about change to such an extent, several Cinesounders left the company or retired. To me the opportunity to work with a top professional editor was one I could not afford to refuse, in particular a man whom I knew and respected. I went to see Mr Helgeson. He was not perturbed and wished me well. Leaving Cinesound was a somewhat emotional event and I was very moved that at the age of twenty I was thought of so highly. Little did I know I was to return in a quite different capacity five years later.

5

'There's No Future In It, Son!'

For Australian filmmakers to be making feature films at all in 1958 was a miracle in itself. To be attempting co-productions with foreign countries was thought to be sheer madness! After Ken G. Hall's *Smithy* (1946) and Charles Chauvel's *Sons of Matthew* (1948) the Cinesound Studio at Bondi was closed and feature film production shut down. Cinesound had moved to the Amusu at Rozelle to keep the newsreels going as it fulfilled the Australian quota for the theatres. A few maverick independents – the McCreadie brothers, Cecil Holmes – tried but in the end failed to make a go of it. Pagewood Studios lingered on until the closure of Ealing Studios in London. There was no government support whatsoever and Robert Menzies, the Prime Minister, made it known we had no actors or filmmakers in Australia for a government to support. Put in this context, Lee Robinson's venture was a bold and extremely brave vision for an industry that no longer existed and was not to receive any recognition or government support for another fifteen years.

The Stowaway was the second film made by Southern International under the French co-production agreement with Discfilm, and French producer Paul-Edmond Decharme. Robert Dorfmann of Silverfilm later became part of the team. Dorfmann was a very successful producer in France with such credits as *Jeux interdits* (1951) and *Gervaise* (1955). The script was based on the novel by Georges Simenon and adapted by Lee Robinson and his associate, Joy Cavill. Joy was part of Southern International from the beginning. A very competent continuity girl, she became associate producer with the group and later became a successful producer in her own right. Filmed at a cost of £250,000 in Tahiti and on board the ship *Calédonien* which regularly visited Sydney, Lee directed the English version and his French associate, Ralph Habib, directed the French version. The film was not received well by the critics but for me it was a wonderful experience. Graduating from the genre of newsreels and shorts to the world of feature films is every moviemaker's dream. In 1958 it was thought only achievable if one went

Stanley Moore sitting at the Westrex Editer editing *The Stowaway*, while I file the off cuts.

overseas and then there were slim chances of achieving that goal. Here I was being given the opportunity of assisting an already established feature film editor, Stan Moore, on what in effect was a 'continental' film being made in Australia.

Stan was editing the film on a new Westrex editing machine from the US, similar in method to the famous but noisy Moviola, but a completely different mechanism. Where the Moviola operates in a similar manner to a projector with a shutter movement, the Westrex used a prism system and subsequently was a very quiet machine in operation – the forerunner to the German Steenbeck. Although seldom used, it also had a projection system built in to screen onto the wall at the back of the machine. Cutting room procedure was quite different from that of the later flatbed machine and absurdly different from editing on computer systems. My task was to break each slate (scene) down by its number and wrap the sound and picture together. The slate breakdown system for editing by Moviola, or in this case the Westrex, is a far more efficient system than that of the flatbed. The soundtrack and cutting copy print of each scene is edge numbered in sync for each slate so that even a few frames cut by the editor can be safely filed away in case those frames are required again to lengthen a scene or rearrange the dramatic context of the editing of a particular sequence. Clive Cross had given me the opportunity of my first screen credit but Stan Moore gave me the chance of cutting my first scene for a feature film. It was the Tamurea dance sequence Stan gave me to edit. It is a vigorous and lively traditional Tahitian dance, filmed in the notorious Quinn's Bar, and gave me plenty of opportunities to experiment. I could move the shots around in various ways for there was extensive camera coverage. Of course my cut was far too long but Stan patiently suggested where it could be shortened and with the final trimming the dance was included in the film.

Whilst the editing and post-production sound on *The Stowaway* was proceeding, Lee Robinson was back in Tahiti filming, once again in French and English, *The Restless and the Damned*, but this time as producer with Robert Dorfmann. The director was Yves Allégret. The French version was completed as *L'Ambitieuse* and released but the English version was never released theatrically. It finished up on American television as *The Climbers* and elsewhere as *The Dispossessed*! It was very apparent to me that this time Bert Cross may be right. I could see no future at Southern International. Despite Lee's ambitions and the great team around him, the company was severely under-capitalised and had to close its doors. If you thought making an independent Australian film in 1958 was a miracle, having an Australian film obtain distribution and theatrical exhibition was next to impossible. Despite these obstacles put up against Australian films obtaining release, and in the 1950s those obstacles were substantial, Lee managed to get the studio's films released through Universal. Generally in second-run houses in the wrong end of town, including neglected picture palaces seating two and a half thousand people. Nonetheless, Lee would stand at the door counting the numbers going into the cinema to make sure the distributors were accounting correctly.

My plans to go overseas with Howard and Des had faltered so I decided to go on my own. My peers urged me to stay. Two American films were coming to be made and more were to follow. Stanley Kramer had announced the filming of *On the Beach* in Melbourne and Warners had announced Fred Zinnemann was coming to make *The Sundowners*. I couldn't see how these two productions could help me further my career as they were to be with foreign stars and foreign crews with little opportunities for the locals, though Des did get a job on *The Sundowners*.

So in October 1958 I sailed out of Sydney Harbour on the Orient Line's *Orcades* for Canada and the future. From number 13 Pyrmont I waved to my parents and friends, not realising it would be the last time I would see my mother.

6

Seven Miles From Sydney And 10,000 Miles From Care

The *SS Orcades* pulled away from number 13, Pyrmont on a crisp, sunny afternoon, October 7, 1958 at 4pm precisely. Maintaining a Buckley tradition, my 16mm MCM camera whirred away the first roll of film on what was to become a journey of four years. It was a big decision for me. I was disappointed when Des and Howard couldn't make the trip but Des hoped he could follow the next year. Mother's health was not improving but she insisted I go as the opportunity may not present itself again. For me, my worry was the gap it would leave in her life.

In the months leading to my departure I tried to gain as much knowledge as possible about the Canadian film industry and what opportunities could be sought. My film history work had attracted the attention of the New Melbourne Film Group and Garth Buckner, their co-editor of *Film Journal*. He had suggested I write to their Canadian correspondent, Guy L. Coté. Mr Coté replied on 22 June, 1958, with a summary of the effects of the Canadian recession but also a paragraph of encouragement:

'One thing about Canada and the Canadian film industry is that it is not yet mummified by strong unions. It is therefore possible for a young man with talent, drive and imagination to make his way to the top in a relatively short time.' I knew I had the drive and the imagination but did I have the talent? Mr Coté then went on to recommend I approach four particular companies for employment, which I planned to do on arrival. Friendly and positive advice like Guy Coté's is incredibly valuable to a youngster starting out. I took a leaf out of his book and have tried to offer the same to others throughout my career.

As the *Orcades* steamed past Fort Denison, the bastion built in Sydney Harbour in 1857 to protect Sydney from the Russian invasion, I felt a tap on my shoulder. 'Isn't your name Tony Buckley?' the voice enquired. 'You buy your records from our store in Neutral Bay.' I recognised the man but had never known his name. 'Hi, I'm Laurie Catley.' Laurie was on his way to North America to show the Americans how to suspend passionfruit seeds in cordial. Laurie and I became good friends on the voyage.

My cabin, berth 585, was on the water line of the ship, the porthole sometimes resembling a Bendix washing machine. Bright sun streaming in one minute, then dark blue-green water would plunge the cabin into complete darkness. I had a lower berth and thankfully there were only two of us sharing the three-berth cabin, Jim, that's all I ever knew him as, occupying the berth opposite.

Auckland, Suva and Honolulu were the main ports of call before our arrival in Vancouver. A seventeen-day voyage. For me, only twenty-one years of age, it *was* a voyage of discovery. Meeting people from all walks of life, seeing places for the first time that one had studied in geography class, experiencing the Pacific and its islands, an interest which has continued to this day. One must remember this was what was called a 'line voyage', not a cruise. Despite this, the captain would take us off course to show us Pacific islands not on the regular steamer route. My camera began to whir away. I had brought with me five 100 ft rolls of 16mm Kodachrome, one for each port of call and two for Canada, which was all I could afford at the time. These five rolls of film began the recording and preserving of a journey which was to continue halfway across the world to 1962.

Shipboard life was a completely new experience. Laurie Catley was the driest humorist on board, who met his match with Professor Jim Peters, a Presbyterian minister with an outrageously wicked sense of humour, on his way to lecture at Harvard.

The late afternoon of 23 October, 1958, the *SS Orcades* entered the Drake passage, which leads into Vancouver. Journey's end. Adventure begins? Laurie Catley and I moved into our respective rooms at the YMCA and on Saturday set forth to explore the city. On the Sunday, Jim Peters, with whom we had become good friends, was giving a sermon so Laurie and I went along. This was a little unusual for me, for I am not religious. My father and his family were Catholic and my mother Methodist, and as a result had to be married behind and not in front of the altar at St Mary's, North Sydney in 1935. My first day going to the Marist Brothers at North Sydney was also my last. I took an immediate dislike to the priests and brothers, to such an extent I refused to go back. I was then enrolled at Lady Hay's and for my religious teaching sent to the Presbyterian Sunday school at the end of Sinclair Street and Shirley Road. Our family wasn't dysfunctional, we were just of three different religions. One could also say typically Buckley!

Monday the search for work began. With the list Guy Coté had given me I set forth to see CBUT television, Artray film studios, Telefilm labs and Mr Parry at Parry Film Studios in North Vancouver across the Lions Gate Bridge. Parry was interested in employing me the next year but would it actually happen and what would I do in the meantime? It was farewell to Laurie who was leaving for Banff on *The Canadian*, the pride of Canadian Pacific's train service. The weather had become wet and drizzly, typical for Vancouver at this time of year. I assessed the situation of waiting for a job and my bank balance, and made the big decision to go east. Monday, November 3, I boarded *The Canadian* for the three-and-a-half day journey to Toronto and the future.

My fourth precious roll of Kodachrome began to whir through the camera on this most spectacular rail journey in the world. First morning, up at dawn to grab a seat in the Dome car and sit firmly there till dinnertime in case I lost my seat. I sat in awe of the majesty of the Rockies till late afternoon when *The Canadian* pulled into Banff and I stepped out to get a shot of the train and experience the cold of a Canadian winter for the first time. The journey across Canada through the Rockies and across the prairies is a book in itself, but this memorable trip by train is now no longer possible.

Regretfully Toronto was not to my liking. I found it cold in every sense: the people, the place and the attitude. It certainly came as a shock after the warmth and friendliness of Vancouver. It has changed a lot now and of course it hosts one of the world's best film festivals. I applied to several companies and found a job with a small outfit, Ministar Films, about three quarters of an hour out of town via the subway and the streetcar (tram).

On the day before I was to start work with them, I happened on the sales office for Crawley Films and promptly walked in to enquire about employment on their new series I had heard about. The sales manager asked me to waste no time in writing to the production manager in Ottawa and to stress my experience with 35mm film, which momentarily I thought a little odd. In the meantime he was going to ring Ottawa to advise them to keep a lookout for my application. If I were successful it would mean fifty weeks continuous work. I put pen to paper immediately and the next day started with Ministar Films. This experience put the nail in Toronto's coffin as far as I was concerned. Run by an extremely conservative management, the outfit was very small and way behind the times. I was surprised. The purpose of coming overseas was to learn and gather experience that I could take back to Australia with me. It was not to be. By the third day I was teaching them. The money was not good and in fact there was very little for me to do. My heart sank.

(Top) A line voyage to England or across the
Pacific in the 1950s had to be booked at least
twelve months in advance to secure a berth.
Our first port of call was Auckland. Then it was
across the Pacific via Suva and Honolulu to
Vancouver.

(Bottom) In Vancouver I caught The Canadian
to Toronto. This super streamliner was a far cry
from travelling on the Central West express to
Guerie, NSW.

CANADIAN NATIONAL RAILWAYS

DELIVERY
CHECK

PASSENGER'S
RECEIPT

Excess
Check No.

Amount
Collected $

From OTTAWA, ONT.,

To PENN. STATION
NEW YORK

Route

SUSPENSION BRIDGE

Transfer Co.

Account
To be
Delivered
To

S.S. QUEEN ELIZABETH

State delivery point, i.e., Residence, (Street and Number),
or name of Hotel, Railway Station, Steamship,
or Steamship Wharf, and date of sailing.

READ CONDITIONS ON BACK

Form
B 7

40-46-01

CANADA

BY

Canadian
Pacific

I got back to the YMCA about six on the Friday night to find a letter for me post-marked Ottawa. I didn't wait to get to my room to open it. It was an invitation to attend Crawley Films in Ottawa for an interview. It was now or never. I wrote a nice letter to Ministar and thanked them for giving me a week's employment. If I didn't get the job in Ottawa I had just enough money for the bus fare back to Toronto and two weeks rent at the Y. I had to take the risk. I found the Greyhound Bus Terminal and bought a one-way ticket. Always the optimist. At 11am Sunday I left Toronto for Ottawa and was at the YMCA by seven o'clock.

Next morning I awoke to an amazing sight. Snow had fallen overnight as far as the eye could see. I went downstairs and out into the street and despite the cold just stood there in awe. I had breakfast, obtained a map and discovered Fairmont Avenue was about a half an hour's walk from the city. Unprepared for the sudden snowfall, I set forth and arrived at Crawley Films about nine o'clock. I asked the receptionist if I could make an appointment with Mr Glynn, their production manager, if possible that day. I was asked to wait whilst she enquired. In less than a minute Mr Glynn appeared, ushered me into his office and introduced me to Fergus McDonell, who must have given him the nod somehow, for the next thing I knew I was asked to sign an employment contract and by ten-thirty I was sitting in Fergus's cutting room officially at work. I had been questioned closely about handling 35mm film and the reason for this was that, apart from the English crew brought over to do the series, Crawley's staff only had experience in 16mm. To which I said it didn't matter, film was film no matter what the gauge. I detected a hint of the inferiority complex bestowed upon Australians at the time by Prime Minister Menzies, and was a little horrified the same was being applied to our Canadian cousins.

It was Monday, 24 November 1958. I had been in Canada exactly a month and was at work. In 1958 Crawley Films, founded by Budge Crawley, was Canada's largest film studio with 150 people on staff, a handsome three-storey building which dominated Fairmont Avenue, housed the administrative staff and the sound and editing departments, with three of the most modern recording theatres I had seen. A canteen, which Cinesound never had, served everything from sandwiches to three course meals and was very much appreciated on a day of blizzards!

The editing team was headed by Fergus McDonell who I was soon to learn was one of Britain's finest and well-renowned editors. Included in his enormous list of credits was Anthony Asquith's *The Way to the Stars* and Carol Reed's *Odd Man Out*. The other senior editor was Paul Harris, a Canadian with a somewhat droll sense of humour. Paul had his own assistant and I was to assist Fergus. In the assembly room across the corridor sat Charlie, a wonderful Canadian of mature years who was the chief splicer! The fact that I didn't have to do the splicing somewhat amazed me so I was always nice to Charlie for fear of ever being given the job! A young Barrie Howells was my companion assistant. Further along the corridor was the documentary division on which Crawley Films had built their fine reputation. Here was Wendy McDonell, wife of Fergus, with her laconic assistant Robert (Bob) Beattie, with whom I was to become good friends. I was the odd one out. No one in the building had ever encountered a forthright Australian before. I could not help myself at times in taking the piss out of Tony Hanes, much to the delight of the Canadians, for I had not come across such a 'British' person before. Charlie on the splicer would be aching with laughter at some of the asides I would hurl at Tony. The McDonell clan were soon to 'adopt' me for the duration I was to be in Canada.

The Royal Canadian Mounted Police (RCMP) are probably one of the most famous and accomplished of all police forces in the world with a proud tradition, and of course their familiar bright red uniformed 'Mounties'. The RCMP series had been talked of for a very long time and I believe Budge Crawley had worked for years to bring it to fruition and had actually backed it with his own money, a risk most producers will not take. It was to be thirty-nine half-hour episodes, all shot on 35mm. Although I had only seen a glimpse of American colour television beamed across the border, I could not for the life of me fathom why the series was not being shot in colour. Even as early as 1958 it was clear colour television was the future. There was an incredible amount of preparation for the series. Crawleys had to bring in every piece of equipment from the UK. The cameras rolled on December 1 at Alymer, a small town on the Quebec side of the river at Ottawa and at Chelsea, a little further north in the hills of the Gatineau where a small studio had also been built. The Gatineau is an area renowned for its breathtaking fall (autumn) colours. It was extremely well organised and a difficult shooting schedule for it had to be tailored to the seasons, a not insignificant task for the writers. Fergus was to eventually direct two of the episodes and this was to be my first experience of watching filming on location.

My first day ended and Paul Harris invited me and another member of the staff for dinner and a look at the classifieds to find me accommodation. There and then we found a place not too far from the studios in Caroline Avenue. It was a German family who had a very nice room and full board, lodging and laundry for $18.00 a week. The boys were very impressed. I could move in on Saturday when their tenant was moving out to get married. I returned to the Y somewhat dazed. Twenty-four hours in the capital, I'd found a job and lodgings and had started work. I hadn't even had time to write home that I was no longer in Toronto.

Saturday I moved from the Y and set up home with Frans and Maria Glaubitz and their three children (two of whom were teenagers) at 43 Caroline Avenue, home for the next year. It was to be the happiest year of my life.

Ottawa, November 1958: Here was a city of contradictions. The nation's capital in Ontario sitting astride the Ottawa River with her sister city Hull in the province of Quebec. Beautiful parliamentary buildings, a busy retail commercial centre, lovely landscapes but archaic laws that were a leftover from prohibition days. I thought it bad enough when the wine disappeared from the table on *The Canadian* when we crossed from one province (wet) into another (dry), but to have to have a licence to buy a bottle of wine I could not believe. I warned Dad that if he felt like a drink, he should not come to Ontario.

My domestic routine soon became very settled. The Glaubitz family ate together in their kitchen and I was seated at a low table in their living room, on my own, in front of their 24" TV set. Their German food and hospitality was superb and on Wednesday I would be invited to watch the evening's television with them. I became addicted to Milton Berle.

Sundays invariably fell into a routine of going to the McDonell's for lunch, which generally extended into the early evening. Some Sundays Bob Beattie would join us. The McD's lived in the very pleasant suburb of Rockcliffe which involved travelling in two streetcars from where I lived.

Also working at Crawley Films was a young Polish lad, Christopher Malkaveic, who was also a good friend of Bob Beattie. Bob invited both of us down to his family home at Welland on the Welland Canal near Niagara Falls. In the family's magnificent De Soto, sporting the biggest fins I had seen on a car, Mrs Beattie took us to Thorold about twelve miles from Welland, to see the operation of the double locks of the canal, the only double locks of their kind in the world. In the afternoon we had a sneak look at the mighty Niagara Falls, where the whole of the next day was planned. A storm had just passed and a huge rainbow had formed over the Horseshoe Falls. The next day we spent at the Falls exploring every aspect, including their somewhat hilarious museum containing the barrels of those who had gone over the Falls in them! Another roll of Kodachrome through the camera and bugger the expense! On awakening the next morning I was somewhat startled to look down over the end of the bed through the window to see a large ship's funnel going past the back of the garden.

At Crawleys we were extremely busy and the operation of the RCMP series was a well-oiled machine, with each episode being delivered on time. I had been given extra duties of splitting the dialogue tracks with their overlays for the dubbing editors.

Easter was looming and the temptation was too strong. New York beckoned.

The train from Ottawa arrived at Montreal at 7.30pm and the train for New York wasn't due to depart until 10.30. I went for a walk to see the sights of Montreal but the cold soon had me retracing my steps to Union Station. I was booked in the third division of the train, which was twenty-three carriages long. There were people standing and sitting everywhere until we reached the American border where they attached two more coaches to the already overlong train. I had a window seat that was placed above a heater and I boiled all night.

My first glimpse of New York was at 6.30am as we travelled along the Hudson River. I could see the outline of the great skyscrapers in the distance. Soon the train went underground to Grand Central Station, a huge terminal, with trains arriving and departing on two levels. Watching my pennies, or I should say nickels and dimes, I had booked into the Y, which was opposite Penn Station, some distance from Grand Central. I took my first New York cab to the Y and was promptly reminded by the driver that one tipped in America! I have been paranoid about tipping in the United States ever since.

Despite the rain and the cold and hardly any sleep, I stepped into the streets of New York to see the sights and the shows. Twelve noon, first stop Radio City Music Hall. The theatre itself is overwhelming with its superb art deco design and seating six thousand people. I sat in front of the first balcony to watch the Easter Pageant, followed by the legendary and longest chorus line in the world, The Rockettes. I could hardly contain myself. Then one of the two mighty Wurlitzers was played for ten minutes whilst the stagehands re-anchored the screen. The lights dimmed and the curtains and tabs opened to reveal the biggest wide screen I had ever seen. The Metro-Goldwyn-Mayer lion appeared, which the audience applauded, and *Green Mansions* with Audrey Hepburn and Anthony Perkins unspooled. In a letter home I commented, 'The show starts all over again and I might add you can stay there as long as you like and the admission is only 90 cents. How they do it I don't really know. The stage show would have cost a mint of money to produce.'

I emerged from Radio City Music Hall at 4.30, had a quick bite to eat and walked the short distance through the freezing rain across Rockefeller Center to the NBC TV studios. Perry Como was rehearsing his show in the studio to go to air that night live. Como was a class act with loads of style but on this occasion I was far more interested in the fact the program was being transmitted in colour. I was less than twelve feet from a 28" RCA monitor watching the superimposition of a rabbit with Como and the colour fringing was barely noticeable. The tour of

CANADA'S MOST MODERN FILM STUDIO

19 fairmont avenue ottawa

Crawley Films Limited

1 DUNDAS SQUARE, TORONTO   1467 MANSFIELD STREET, MONTREAL

(Top left and bottom right) The *R C M P* series was an initiative of Budge Crawley, who recognised the importance for Canada to have its own film industry making films and series telling Canadian stories. The parallels with our Australian film industry at the time didn't escape me.

(Bottom left) The doyen of British film editors, Fergus McDonell, here directing an episode of *R C M P*. Note the crew jacket he is wearing. Much of the series was shot in bitterly cold weather.

Series Shot by Crawley Films in the Gatineau Hills

806-C2

The production of the television series "R.C.M.P.", we think, is the first step towards establishing entertainment film-making in Canada on a firm and continuing basis. The decision to pioneer television film production in this country was made on the premise that we can make a place for ourselves in the world television market by choosing subjects which can be made in Canada more efficiently than anywhere else in the world.

We think that the "R.C.M.P." series will be profitable to all concerned because we can produce the factual story of the Royal Canadian Mounted Police more effectively than can the Americans in Hollywood or the British in London, and we can sell it in the world TV market in competition with their production.

Canada has a large and growing group of competent actors and actresses; there is no shortage of acting talent. Writers in this country show every promise of rapid development, and we are extremely pleased with the work of the outstanding Canadian authors who provided most of the scripts for "R.C.M.P."

If there is any shortage, it is in the field of directing. While there are some excellent Canadian directors for live television, there is a definite lack of Canadian directors for entertainment films for television. It will take some time before we can develop in this country directors who can compete successfully with their American counterparts in the television film production field.

I should like to add this final word: "R.C.M.P.", while respecting the traditions and customs of the Force, is full of real entertainment and excitement. We are confident that viewers will enjoy these exciting stories of the Shamattawa detachment, "R.C.M.P.".

— F. R. (Budge) Crawley, President, Crawley Films.
  Executive Producer, "R.C.M.P."

The main street of Aylmer, Quebec, doubles as the main street of Shamattawa in several episodes of "R.C.M.P." Here, a camera crew gets some winter footage.

26-C

Summer and winter the cameras rolled, recording on film an episode of "R.C.M.P." every five working days. Camera operator Norman Allin directs operations from his camera platform.

79-C

Bundled up against the 20-below-zero cold, a camera crew moves in for a close shot during the filming of the television series "R.C.M.P." Assistant director Peter Carter looks on (left).

22-C

..with star performance and direction!

NBC ended at seven and then I rushed off to the Mark Hellinger Theatre where I had managed to obtain a seat to see *My Fair Lady* with Pamela Charles and Edward Mulhare. I had chosen a musical for my first show on Broadway deliberately. From the inception of long-playing microgroove recordings, LPs, I had been collecting Broadway shows, something one would rarely see in Australia.

Up at 5.30 next morning and to Times Square for breakfast, then to the top of the RCA Building, seventy floors in thirty seconds, losing one's stomach in the lift on the descent. Not a good idea after breakfast. Then the long walk to the Empire State Building, still the grand dame of skyscrapers. Had lunch at the top, then down to Pier 43 to catch the 3.30 steamer around Manhattan Island, a three-hour trip for the princely sum of $2! Back to Times Square and dinner and a quick change of clothes, to whiz up to the Booth Theatre to see Anne Bancroft and Dana Andrews in *Two for the Seesaw*. I thought coming out of the Mark Hellinger the night before to find New York blanketed in snow was really something but it was nothing compared with the sight before me on turning the corner from the Booth Theatre. I was swept up in the crowd outside Lowes State Theatre where the world premiere of *Some Like It Hot* had been taking place. To this twenty-year-old aspiring filmmaker, it was like walking into God's heaven. Spectacle, klieg lights, it felt as though there were a million people in Times Square. Then the crowd screamed, I was pushed forward and there she was, Marilyn Monroe herself posing for the photographers and then into her car. It was only a glimpse I have to stress but she was only twenty feet away and that 'glimpse' has stayed with me ever since. Despite the million people, I turned around and there was Jenifor Jordon who had just left Crawley Films to go to Vancouver with a friend. It was off to supper at the Hotel Victoria to share the day's excitement with each other, and home to bed at 2am! It was fortunate the YMCA were liberal with their hours.

New York had totally won me. How soon could I get back?

The RCMP series ground on and Bob Beattie was to leave assisting Wendy to go and try his hand at the Playhouse in Pasadena, California. Meanwhile Barrie Howells and I planned a big train trip in the summer break coming up. The *Twilight Limited* to Chicago and the *Atchison Topeka and Sante Fe* from Chicago to Los Angeles and HOLLYWOOD! Barrie and I left Ottawa on Friday evening, July 17, 1959, changing at Toronto the next morning for Detroit where we caught the New York Central's *Twilight Limited* to Chicago. We only had one night in this great city. We just walked and walked to see as much as we could. State Street had to be the brightest street lighting we had ever seen. Next morning to

Dearborn Station to catch a Standard *Sante Fe* train to Union Station, L.A. This time I had brought ten rolls of Kodachrome with me.

Train travel then, as now, is still the most rewarding way of seeing a country. Buses are all very well travelling down the main streets, but trains travel through the backyards of a country, the heartland of a place, and America is no exception. In the next two weeks Barrie and I were to see all the things everyone sees and does on visiting Los Angeles and San Francisco. Of course for us the studios and environs of Hollywood and Beverly Hills were of the most interest and we must have walked for miles. One morning, however, the notorious LA smog beat us and we had to return to the YMCA. Our eyes were red raw and aching terribly. More importantly for me, Fergus McDonell had arranged for us to meet his relative, Walter Forde, and had arranged for a private visit to the Disney Studio with Alan Jaggs, a long-time friend of his. Being interested in drawing since an early age, animation completely fascinated me (it still does) and this was something I was really looking forward to.

We were invited out to South LA Pier Drive to meet Walter Forde and his wife and set forth in what we both thought were LA's excellent buses. The locals were not so complimentary. To meet with Walter Forde was, for me, the next most important person to Raymond Longford for Forde, like Longford, was a true cinema pioneer. Walter Forde was born in Bradford in 1898 and after a successful career in music halls, became Britain's most successful comedian in early slapstick shorts. In 1919 he made a series of shorts known as the Zodiac Comedies and in 1921 made the two-reelers *Walter's Winning Ways* and *Walter Finds a Father*, both box office champs. In 1923 Forde went to Hollywood to make what were known as two-reelers for Universal Pictures. He returned to Britain in 1927 to make his first feature film for Walton Studios, *Wait and See*, immediately followed by *What Next?*, two comedies written and directed by Forde and starring Forde with Pauline Johnson. His last silent film, *Would You Believe It*, came just too late. Talkies had stolen a march on the golden age of comedy.

The Fordes were charming and gracious. Mr Forde took us on a drive of luxurious homes of Beverly Hills and the heights of the Hollywood Hills, giving Barrie and me a first-hand commentary.[1] Next day we were to meet Alan Jaggs at the Walt Disney Studios.

Why my interest in animation? I had been attracted to drawing from the beginning. I loved the comics and in particular Jim Banks' quintessential Australian

---

1   Unlike Raymond Longford, Forde moved into talkies with ease directing for Michael Balcon one of Britain's biggest hits of the thirties, *Chu Chin Chow*, described by Leslie Halliwell as 'a curiosity'. Available on DVD.

character, Ginger Meggs. Ginger started out as a strip Banks called 'Us Fellers' in the mid-thirties in the broadsheet *Sunday Sun and Guardian*. The full colour supplement was *Sunbeam's*. HITCH YOUR WAGON TO A SUNBEAM heralded the masthead. I have three framed broadsheets from March and May, 1936, Ginger Meggs occupying the whole front page, on the back of which is another famous Australian strip, *Bib and Bub* (*Snugglepot and Cuddlepie*) by May Gibbs. The quality of colour printing on newsprint in the thirties is remarkable. I collected Ginger Meggs annuals and have an ageing plaster cast of Ginger. I became a Sunbeamer of Cousin Marie, and later a Chuckler as a member of the Charlie Chuckles Club in the *Sunday Telegraph*.

This paper was running a colouring competition to celebrate Ginger Meggs' transfer to the *Telegraph* from the *Sun*. It was Ginger and his gang riding his billycart down a hill. It was a cinch for me to colour the cartoon but I added one thing extra. The numberplate on Ginger's cart was blank. New South Wales had just introduced a new car numberplate registration. From the old black and white plates of two letters and three numbers, the State was going to three letters and three numbers, black letters on a bright yellow background. I gave Ginger a numberplate AAA001 and won the prize; a valuable Malvern Star bicycle which I could never learn to ride and which totally intimidated me. I fell off so many times I became an embarrassment to my friends and eventually sold it to buy my new Pathé Gem projector for the Kings at Laycock Street, Neutral Bay.

About the same time, early 1950s, I had won a half scholarship with a correspondence course with the Art Training Institute of Melbourne, 'Australia's Foremost School of Commercial Art'. I have no idea whether this was a commercial con or a bona fide course, but everything I submitted won top marks. I reached the Intermediate Certificate in high school and won top honours in technical drawing. I fiddled with watercolours for a while but film was my obsession and animation was film.

Alan Jaggs met us at the Walt Disney studio gate and I was immediately transported into a world I would never have believed possible for a young bloke from Sydney to achieve. Alan had a guide take us on a complete Cook's tour of the entire studio and backlot where Barrie and I saw the sets of the *Zorro, El Faca Bacca* and *Texas John Slaughter* series, and *Zorro* in the making. The guide left us at this point and Alan took us to the Editing Block. Two buildings with no fewer than 200 Moviolas (editing machines) including the seven-head Moviola on which *Snow White* had been edited. They were in a state of tidying up, having just completed *Sleeping Beauty*. The studio was accustomed to producing three to four hours of theatrical material a year but when television arrived, the studio's output went to 106 hours a year! We saw the unique multi-plane cameras, the animation rooms, the girls inking and painting, where they transfer the paper drawings to celluloid cells. In early character development stage was *101 Dalmations* with an incredible amount of work being done. The studio had just completed filming *Third Man on the Mountain* and had just begun *Swiss Family Robinson*. It was an extremely rewarding experience to see a Disney feature in the making and to have the rare opportunity of talking with the animators. At this time Disney himself supervised every aspect of production.

The journey back to Chicago (via the Grand Canyon) on the *A, T & Santa Fe Chief* was a lot swisher than the journey out, with a Dome car to relax in. I don't think we could have fitted another thing into our two-week schedule. We now had two days travelling in which time to reflect and try and absorb all we had seen. There were two rolls of Kodachrome left for the last great spectacle Barrie and I were to experience. To see the Grand Canyon at dawn was worth an early morning change of trains. Even the best travel writer in the world would be hard put to describe the sight that greets you as you approach the Canyon rim, the colours and moods of the Canyon throughout the day, and I was hoping the Kodachrome unspooling in the camera would catch some of its magic appeal.

We returned to Crawleys to discover the RCMP series was getting behind schedule. The sound department wasn't coping. I was put onto sound editing which pleased me greatly but the hours were becoming longer and now the weekends were being worked. It didn't take long before someone complained to the union shop steward who was obliged to refer it to management, who then placed a complete ban on overtime for ten days. The irony was that the cause of the overtime was Paul Harris, who was the union secretary, and the head of sound, who was the union president! The union executive was pretty shocked at this turn of events. There was a shortage of available sound editors and three of us who were assistants were subsequently elevated to the post of sound editor, giving me my first Canadian credit on the episode *Back to School*. Then, as suddenly as Barrie Howells and I had been promoted, we were promptly demoted, for the company couldn't afford to pay the extra salaries. I decided it was time to move on and made a booking to sail from New York on January 21, 1960, on the *RMS Queen Elizabeth* for Southampton. Knowing of the Atlantic Ocean's tantrums in the winter, I thought the bigger the ship the better, and the fare strangely wasn't any dearer than the other lines.

The RCMP series was reaching a conclusion so my timing was right. The series was a landmark for Crawleys and Canadian television. Humour percolated through the entire series, which lifted RCMP from the usual cops-and-robbers

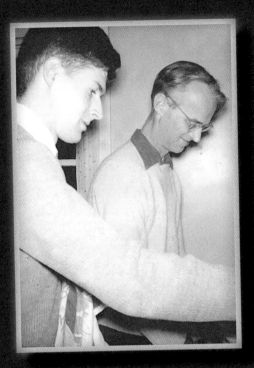

(Top left) In the kitchen with Fergus McDonell.

(Top right) Walter Forde, pioneer British director, related to the McDonells on Wendy's mother's side of the family, made me and Barrie Howells, my travelling companion, very much at home the day we visited. In many ways he reminded me of Raymond Longford. Both men started their successful careers in the silent film era, but where Forde furthered his career in British talkies, Longford didn't master the new medium.

(Bottom) My first Halloween, Canada, 1958, with the McDonell clan at their home in Rockcliffe, Ottawa. Many happy Sundays were spent here, winter and summer.

genre. I had no sooner made my announcement I was leaving when I received an enquiry from the National Film Board of Canada as to my availability. It was very encouraging and enhanced my confidence, but did I want to live in Montreal? Beautiful city, and the NFB had an international reputation which would have been a slap in the eye for Stanley Hawes at the Commonwealth Film Unit who would only accept applicants if they had achieved the Leaving Certificate in education. No, it was to be London or nothing.

From home, not very encouraging news. Southern International had collapsed. With three films completed and still awaiting release, Lee Robinson was forced to close the doors. Stan Moore was returning to Cinesound and Syd Whiteley had announced his retirement. I figured Bert Cross would have been pleased with the decisions I had made so far.

Fergus McDonell had arranged for me to meet people in London and some introductions to an independent commercial channel, Associated Rediffusion. Crawleys invited me to stay and join their documentaries department, but with a taste of drama firmly under my belt I confirmed I was moving on. The decision to leave wasn't easy. I had made a lot of friends, more than I had expected. A letter from home to say Grandma had died and Dad had bought a secondhand Ford Prefect to 'get Mum out of the house'.

The farewell dinners began.

On Saturday night Bob and I went to the very beautiful Toronto Odeon to see *On the Beach*. I thought the film excellent and was relieved to discover so many fine Australian actors in the supporting roles. John Meillon, Lou Vernon, John Tate, Grant Taylor, Ken Wayne, et al., and it was good to hear the Aussie accent coming through on the soundtrack which was greatly enhanced by a rich, dramatised orchestral score of *Waltzing Matilda*. I commented on Ross Woods' superb black and white photography. I felt very homesick.

Farewell to Beattie, a good friend. The train quickly pulled out of the station and gathered momentum for its journey to the Big Apple. Leaving Canada was sad in one sense but not in another. Despite all the friends I had made, I still found the country 'strange' and a 'little foreign'.

The heavy seas the *Queen Elizabeth* had encountered had forced our sailing to be delayed by twelve hours, which I put to good use. A revisit to Radio City Music Hall where I was once again overwhelmed with the show and those glorious Rockettes. In the evening a special treat at the Plymouth Theatre – second row centre to see Claudette Colbert and Charles Boyer in *Marriage Go-Round*. A very funny show in which we find Boyer lamenting the fact that they have twin beds, to which Colbert's pithy reply, 'Well, the short walk could always be rewarding,' brought the place down. The following afternoon brought an even bigger treat. Front stalls, aisle seat for *Gypsy* with Ethel Merman making the entrance down my stalls aisle from the back of the theatre. Splendid.

I went down to the docks with my ever-faithful MCM camera to film the mighty liner's arrival. She was certainly the worse for wear, with huge rust marks over her enormous bow. It was cold and windy and all I wanted to do was get on board and be on our way. I had to wait until 8pm before I could board and it was 11pm when we finally sailed, passing Staten Island and the Statue of Liberty at midnight. One journey was over, another about to begin.

7

Letters Home: 189 Cromwell Road – 'Hurry, My Milliner Is Waiting!'

Friday, 22 January 1960. The *Queen Elizabeth* could, at best, be described as a floating mausoleum! With very few passengers for this winter crossing, one could walk the lengthy companionways for hours without seeing a soul. A few of us attended the cinema to see *Pillow Talk* and *Our Man in Havana* but the orchestra played to an empty dance floor as passengers retired to the warmth of their cabins after dinner. I found a way up into first class, which, at ten o'clock in the evening, was even more depressing. Vast lounges, with their high, heavy British art deco ceilings, devoid of people and the band waiting anxiously for the clock to strike eleven so they could stop playing and repair to the tourist class bar which was still open. For the Cunard Line the writing surely must have been on the wall, even in 1960, that the halcyon days of Atlantic crossings were over. For me, though, I could wander wherever I chose without interference or stewards and pursers waving a finger at me saying not to go here or there. Whilst waiting to board in New York, I heard an Australian accent, 'That case has come a long way,' and looking at the Orient Line label he introduced himself. This Aussie was from Melbourne and had just arrived from spending five years in the Yukon. How do I remember these incidents? Well, in many cases I don't, much to my embarrassment. Of other incidents I have a clear memory. It is from letters home to my mother, which she kept, every one, that I am able to piece together my encounters of three and a half years overseas. I knew she had kept them but it wasn't until 2003 that I had the courage to revisit this time, about which I wrote home in meticulous detail.

Luggage and passengers loaded at Southampton, the boat train sped its way to Waterloo where, on arrival, my eyes popped and my jaw dropped at the sights I saw en route in my cab to the Overseas Visitors Club in Earl's Court, to be met by my old chum Barry Prentice. The first day in London and the search for a job begins.

Monday, 15 February: 'I had two promising interviews last week and it will be February 22 before I hear from the BBC, so one has to be patient. My most important interview however is to come this Friday afternoon at four with Mr John Gutheridge at Pinewood Studios… I also have a tentative appointment with Mr John Heyer at Shell.' I think on reflection I must have been the only Australian reject from the BBC at the time. I went for three interviews, two of these at their recently acquired Ealing Studios, but with no luck. Fergus McDonell wrote from Canada telling me the BBC had written to him about employing me. He was somewhat dismayed to learn later that I hadn't got the job. John Gutheridge was editing *The League of Gentlemen* at the time and spent a good two hours with me showing me around the editing department at Pinewood which was very generous, but regretfully came to nothing. John Heyer, whose landmark film *The Back of Beyond* I had screened at Cinesound only a few years before, didn't have any positions either. In between the search for employment I became your typical 'innocent abroad', gawking at everything. A letter home: 'Oh yes, before I forget, saw 'is 'ighness the Duke (of Edinburgh) last Thursday night arriving for the premiere at the Odeon Theatre of *Sink the Bismark*. All very posh and gay.' Gay? Did we really use the word in this context in the sixties?

Barry Prentice and his crowd were good fun and company and we had many active evenings at the pictures, the OVC watching television, and numerous slide evenings. Oh those bloody slide nights! Will one ever be able to forget them? It was getting back to the OVC one evening at 6.30 from my interview at Pinewood that I received a message to ring a Mr Willows urgently at Associated Rediffusion.

Out of sheer desperation I had gone into their headquarters on the corner of the Kingsway and The Aldwych near Australia House on the Strand to enquire if they had any vacancies. Somewhat audacious in the sixties in London for it was customary to write or telephone. Much to my surprise I was advised that they did have a program vacancy and I was interviewed on the spot and given a conducted tour of their enormous enterprise. No promises were made so I thought that was the end of that. At 6.30 would Mr Willows still be there? He was. Could I come out to Morden on Sunday to meet with him to discuss employment with Rediffusion and have afternoon tea with him and his wife? Mrs Willows had prepared a huge, typically English afternoon tea whilst Mr Willows briefed me on being the second editor in the films department on a new series, *Farson's Guide to the British*, a quarter hour program to be telecast every Thursday night and hosted by Dan Farson. The first editor was Mike Batchelor and their supervising editor was Charlie Squires, whom I was to describe in a letter home as 'the funniest man – England's Syd Whiteley!' I stayed in touch with Syd at Cinesound and Stan Moore at Southern International throughout my sojourn in the UK.

Could I start tomorrow morning? The hours were long – 8.30 to 6.30 – a forty-four hour week except Wednesdays and Fridays when we finished at six. The union at the time were fighting for a forty-two hour week. Salary wasn't mentioned and I wasn't about to ask. On my first visit to the pay office I opened the envelope and went back to the cashier and asked if they may have made a mistake. 'No, your salary as a film editor is £28.10.0 per week.' Despite the fact this was the union minimum, which accounted for Rediffusion's difficulty in obtaining editors from the studios, this was far and away above what my colleagues were being paid in their respective jobs, which was between £9 and £11 per week. So I had to keep very quiet about how much I was earning.

At the same time as starting work I had moved to 189 Cromwell Road, South Kensington SW5.

February 20, 1960: 'I have joined Barry Prentice's friends in a very big and spacious flat just round the corner from the OVC. They're a grand crowd; Trevor an Australian Pom, Andrew a Kiwi, Dave a Kiwi, Warwick a Kiwi, Ray an Aussie and myself. Dave is leaving on Thursday for the Continent. There's tons of room, with our own bathroom, laundry, two big bedrooms (one in fact was quite small), a huge living room and a good kitchen. It's only 30/- each for the rent and we put in 30/- each for the food etc. It's very good and I'm very happy about it. Trevor is more or less in charge and like the others is very reliable. They are excellent cooks and the meal is already cooked when I get home.'

Trevor specialised in ginger cake and hot custard, which was to become the signature dish at 189. Moving in with this buoyant group and starting work was the beginning of two of the happiest years of my life. With so many coming and going to the 'Continent', everyone practised their 'bonjours', 'bonsoirs', 'mercis' and 'gracias' from their phrase books. One of the boys discovered the curious 'Hurry, my milliner is waiting.' I have often wondered if anyone ever found use for the phrase and if ever, where and why!!

24 April 1960: 'Des has arrived and is very well and of course is busy trying to find a job. Howard never made it overseas, deciding to concentrate on his career at Cinesound. Des opted to go to New York at first to further his studies in theatre.'

He was a welcome arrival in London and we repaired to the local in Earl's Court where he introduced me to vodka and lime, which is my preferred drink to this day (sometimes a double, and I'm anybody's!). At home and in Canada I

(Top) Looking for work in London was dispiriting. I must be the only Australian reject from the BBC! I don't know who took this picture, but obviously I had been to the newsreel theatrette behind, where – if nothing else – it was warm.

(Bottom) London, Earl's Court, 1960. Halcyon days at 189 Cromwell Road and my introduction to vodka and lime, which is still my favourite aperitif.

rarely drank alcohol at all but in London we used to enjoy a weekly visit to the pub. None of us could overindulge because we couldn't afford it. Dave and Warwick had left 189 and Roy had moved in. Our flat was wedged between two floors of the four-storey terrace. The flat below was occupied by a group of terrific, but very much to themselves New Zealand girls, and the flat above by three English girls, Anthea, Rosemary and Judy, and Olive, an Aussie and a yodeller! Overall we socialised more with the girls upstairs.

5 May 1960: 'You were asking who does the laundry? I do!! Heavy laundry like sheets, pyjamas, etc go to the OVC where they do the lot for 2/- and the shirts we all do ourselves *and* iron them if you please! Wonders will never cease I know! I suppose Dad is roaring his head off! We saw *Summer of the Seventeenth Doll* last Sunday night at the Odeon and it wasn't too bad really. It didn't have anything like the drama of the play or for that matter the Cinesound newsreel sequence.'

That was a typical week for us at 189. There were extended weekend trips to the Lakes District, Devon and Cornwall, and over to Bath. One Easter we all traipsed off to Edinburgh, driving there and back and thinking nothing of it. Back at work on Tuesday morning the staff at Television House thought we were all mad driving such a distance in one weekend. Little did they realise that distance is nothing to an Aussie or a Kiwi. Our journey coincided with the Edinburgh Festival.

September 4, 1960: 'Arrived back last night from a very successful journey despite the horrible weather … the festival of course was the highlight and the shows we saw were excellent. Joan Sutherland was magnificent in *I Puritani* and the revue *Beyond the Fringe* was so witty and clever they should bring it to London.'

Our travel experiences were recorded by the ever-faithful ageing movie camera but I had changed to using Agfacolor, not only because it was much cheaper than a roll of Kodachrome but I liked the 'look' the colour stock gave to the English countryside. I had indulged in the purchase of a silent 16mm Siemens projector, which was to entertain us with the movies of our trips through the winters of our content.

Life, however, was anything but normal at Television House. When television came to Australia in 1956, Cinesound and Channel Nine had embraced 16mm cinematography and editing very quickly. The newsreel crews were already conversant with 35mm single system sound and the changeover to 16mm single system Auricon cameras was relatively smooth. (Single system is the optical sound recorded directly onto the same roll of film as are the images.) So it came as quite a shock to arrive at Television House to find Associated Rediffusion shooting exclusively on 35mm picture and separate magnetic sound. The expense must have been enormous. The irony was, I had been employed by Crawley Films in Canada because I had had 35mm experience, whereas the Canadians had been using 16mm exclusively, and I was employed by Rediffusion because I had had 16mm experience and was the only person on staff who had. 16mm was still eighteen months away at Television House and even then when I was asked to edit a major documentary on Lyndon Johnson and the American elections, the editors didn't want to know about it, nor for that matter did Telecine! The picture was 16mm but the sound was still 35mm, and limited the length of the picture reel to 400 feet (eleven minutes) that to me seemed to defeat the object of the economic savings of using the 16mm gauge. Trying to maintain synchronisation between 16mm to 35mm on the editing synchroniser is an editor's worst nightmare come true!

Television House was an eight-storey building employing 800 people at the Kingsway and their studio at Wembley. Rediffusion was the biggest of the commercial television operators broadcasting Monday to Friday only, when Associated Television (ATV), later London Weekend Television, would take over to broadcast Saturday and Sunday only, one of the many idiosyncratic peculiarities of the ITV network. The company had been established by a group of ex-naval people headed by Captain T.C. Brownrigg. Our 'superior officer' as she used to be referred to, was Deborah Chesshire. There were so many naval people on staff I used to refer to the left side and the right side of the lift well as the port and starboard sides of the building!

The editing department was on the sixth floor but I had been allocated a cutting room on the eighth floor on the port side near Freddie Slade's dubbing suite and the sound department. Next door was another tiny room which housed the Rediffusion library, administered by a pleasant young man, John Rowe, and his assistant Eve. I was allocated my first assistant editor, Rosemary MacLaughlin, whose job was to synchronise the rushes and do the editorial filing. One could hardly swing a cat in the room with the Acmiola (the British version of the American Moviola and most definitely not my favourite machine) taking up the best part of the room.

Farson's Guide to the British was not unlike producing the weekly *Cinesound Review*. It was a fifteen-minute program going to air every Thursday night. We were generally only about a week and a half ahead of transmission date. Editing would take place Thursday, Friday, Monday. Dan Farson and his producer would look at the cut Monday, last-minute adjustments made, sound laid up, work print (cutting copy) sent off to Humphries Laboratories for negative cutting Tuesday, graded print delivered Thursday morning. In the meantime the work print would come back from neg cutting and Freddie Slade would mix and record Dan's voice over to picture either late Wednesday or Thursday morning. I would synchronise the final mix to the newly delivered print from Humphries and it would be dispatched early afternoon to Telecine at Wembley Studios for transmission that evening. Thursday afternoon Rosemary would have the rushes ready for the next program and the whole process would start all over again.

After six months I began to wonder what my next task would be as the series was reaching its conclusion. I had also become a tad paranoid for, stuck away on the eighth floor away from the main editing department on the sixth, I was beginning to wonder if my work was satisfactory. No one had ever commented about my editing of the series and I would only see the supervising editor when he was on his way to the dubbing suite and would wave to me from the corridor on the other side of the light well. So I went to see Charlie Squires. 'Was everything okay Mr Squires?' 'Son, you are up there because Mike and I don't have to worry about you, you're doing fine and we want you to do some drama editing soon. Carry on!'

The drama was *Echo Four-Two*, a spin-off from the highly successful series *No Hiding Place*, but television drama in the 1960s was a drama in itself! The filmed sequences could be anything from three shots of a car going past to a five-minute dialogue sequence, which were used to integrate into the telecast of the play or drama series whilst sets were changed and actors moved to their next scene, for the show went to air live! The editing and preparation of the filmed drama inserts was relatively straightforward. Care had to be taken to ensure each sequence was in its correct running order and the start marks on both picture and sound clearly identified with white grease pencil to assist Telecine to correctly cue the next drama insert. Prepared on 2000 feet spools, a reasonably heavy weight, Rosemary and I would take the train to Wembley whilst Rediffusion's courier would deliver the film. On one occasion the courier wasn't available and we had to cart the film to Wembley on the train! Taxis were unheard of at Television House headquarters!

The editor and his assistant had to be present at the rehearsals and broadcast in case the director made last-minute changes, or a splice might lift on the film as Telecine would forward and reverse the filmed sequences throughout the rehearsals. I found drama going to air live a most nerve-wracking experience. A kinescope (referred to as a kine) would be made as the program went to air. These were the real pioneering days of television broadcasting. Fergus McDonell had been my great editing mentor in Canada and Michael Batchelor was to guide me in my drama editing at Rediffusion. He was the first editor to alert me to cutting on the syllable in dialogue editing to make the overlays seamless and therefore the transitions from one shot to the other less noticeable or jarring.

I was given a wide diversity of programs to edit at Television House. Some great documentaries – *People and Pantos*, an intriguing insight into the history of pantomime, something that is intrinsically British to this day, *The Dubliners*, a thirty-minute special about the great writers of Ireland. My favourite series was *Questions in the House*, a fortnightly program which went to air at 10.30 every second Friday. Sometimes the show would go to air live with just short film clips to introduce each item but on other occasions I would have a complete thirty-minute all-film documentary to make. These 'specials' would come about after a question was asked in the House of Commons about a controversial issue which the House would be debating and being commented upon by a very questioning British press. Some of the issues of the day would make for some very strong material going to air. One of the most controversial issues of this time was conditions in prisons. A question had been asked in the House of an extremely challenging and provocative nature, necessitating the abandonment of our already prepared program, to work fifty-two hours in four days to edit, dub and print a two-reel, twenty-minute piece, all on 35mm, to go to air on Friday night. Exhausted and stretched to the limit, the effort was well worthwhile. The show received excellent reviews in the *Sunday Times* and *The Observer* and even favourable comments about the editing. I always thought *Questions in the House* one of Rediffusion's better programs.

The journalists downstairs in the *Questions in the House* production unit were headed by David Frost and New Zealander Alan Martin. As with the drama programs, I would go to Wembley with the film in case there were any last-minute changes before we went to air. Alan Afrait had replaced Rosemary as my assistant editor. He was a very pleasant and talented young man who quickly went on to be one of Britain's finest editors. It was announced that Dan Farson was going Down Under with Rollo Gamble to do *Farson's Guide to Australia*, but I was to temporarily bow out as a group of us at 189 were about to set off to 'do' the Continent!

8

Five For Europe: A Telegram From Home

$\mathbf{B}$arry Prentice had booked to go home; his firm wanted him back and therefore he wasn't able to come on the planned trip of Europe. Des was away in Scotland filming the RAC rally around Britain from where he sent us all a postcard assuring us the Loch Ness monster wore a kilt ... a wet one! Roy was generally busy preparing Agony downstairs in Cromwell Road for the big trip. Agony was an ancient blue Bedford panel van which we had acquired for the enormous sum of £60! The old girl had just returned from a journey all around Europe and here we were, preparing her for another! The social whirl between the three flats of 189 continued. *Settled out of Court* with Nigel Patrick, 2/- in the Gods, *Chin Chin*, a tragi-comedy (?) with Anthony Quayle, 3/- in the gallery; the prices in the Gods were creeping up. I had just taken to wearing glasses for the first time. I had thought the plays we were going to see were naturally 'soft' or 'out of focus' because we were in the cheap seats in the gallery. I mentioned this one day to Eve in the library next door to my cutting room and she suggested perhaps it would be a good idea to have my eyes tested. She said the same thing had happened to her until one day she was in the Kingsway and hailed a pantechnicon thinking it was a double-decker bus! My 'new eyes' revealed what I had been missing all this time from my seat in the Gods.

Meanwhile, upstairs my portrait was being painted! Anthea had taken to dabbling in oils and had been trying her hand at portrait painting. I think practically everyone in the building had had their portrait done and now it was to be my turn, except Anthea had decided my canvas had to be bigger than the others she had painted. There was great anticipation among the girls in the flat with whom Andrea shared as I went upstairs for my sittings. Then the evening came when her work was revealed to me. I was so startled at what I saw, I couldn't say anything. I think I muttered something polite, or at least I hoped I had, and immediately repaired downstairs to where the boys were eagerly waiting to know what it was like.

Before I could say anything there was a pounding at the door and Judy from upstairs burst in to abuse the daylights out of me for being so cruel and ungrateful and disappeared as quickly as she had appeared. We all looked at each other with incredulity. It seems that on my departure Anthea had burst into a flood of tears and rushed to lock herself in her bedroom. It is reproduced here as a courtesy and an apology to dear Anthea, along with another effort or two done over the years. Unlike the writer, they haven't faded for they have never been exposed!

Roy worked hard on the preparation of Agony for our big trip. Ted Peach from Western Australia joined our intrepid team, answering an advertisement we had placed in the local paper. The fifth member of the team, Don, a Kiwi, had done likewise. We had decided on a basic anti-clockwise tour of Europe. There was nothing particularly original about the route we were taking because thousands before us had probably done much the same journey. Would Agony make it was the question uppermost in our minds. Roy worked for the Automobile Association in Leicester Square and the AA had supplied us with a complete route map of our proposed itinerary. It totalled 8,836 miles! My 16mm MCM camera was on the verge of giving up the ghost, so I went back to the people from whom I had purchased my Siemens projector and they found me a reconditioned 16mm Eumig in excellent condition with three very good lenses. Des had scored a windfall for me in obtaining ten rolls of 16mm Kodachrome for the trip from his company at the wholesale price, saving me £1.4.0 a roll. We were to leave for Paris May 29, 1961.

Letter home, May 28, 1961: 'Here it is 1.30am Sunday morning, bathed, packed and nearly ready for our departure at 4.30 tomorrow morning. Rediffusion were rather upset (much to my surprise) to see me go although they are hoping I can rejoin them in September. It's nice to know there may be a job for me when I get back … I haven't managed to get anything packed off for your birthdays, so I trust you can change this note at the bank, and both of you have a drink and perhaps you could get tickets for a show, perhaps *My Fair Lady*. Anyway Dad, have a happy birthday next week and same to you Mum for the 15th. All my love and till next time from somewhere in Europe. Tat, ta!'

There was to be no next time.

Dawn, May 29, we intrepid five set forth for Dover to meet the ferry to Calais. A few hours after we had left, a telegram was slipped under the door at 189. One of the residents leaving for work noticed it and placed it on the hall table. Coming home from work that evening, Olive, from the top flat, noticed the telegram was addressed to me. Thinking it was only a bon voyage greeting she took it upstairs and left it for a while, when something told her it may be something important and she decided to open it. Olive wasn't prepared for the shock it contained.

We had arrived safely in Paris Monday evening and set up our tent, which attached to the side of the van, in one of the public camping sites on the edge of the city. Four slept in the tent and I slept in the back of the van. We prepared our first meal and planned our first day in Paris.

Olive knew a friend of Des's, Françoise, who lived in Paris, and somehow managed to contact her. Tuesday morning and I thought something strange was going on when I saw Françoise arrive at the camp and talk to Des and Roy. Thinking no more about it, we decided to go off and see the sights but Des decided to stay behind to 'fix his camera'. We arranged to meet at the Eiffel Tower and I had just finished taking a shot from the base of the tower when Des arrived and the others sauntered off. Des suggested we sit down on a bench near the Tower and here had the unenviable task of breaking the news. Mother had died at St Ives Hospital, North Sydney, at about 6am on Sunday, May 28. It seems that Mum and Dad had been planning on Friday night what they were going to do in rearranging the garden over the weekend when, at 4.30 Saturday morning, she collapsed from a burst ulcer and had bled badly. Within the hour she was admitted to hospital and by late Saturday night her condition was described by the doctor to my father as 'excellent'. They would keep her in hospital for two to three weeks till her condition had built up. Dad went home to get a good night's sleep. At 5.30 Sunday morning the phone rang and by the time Dad reached the hospital Mavis Buckley née Ellis-Jones had passed away. A tiny clot of blood which reached the brain caused a cerebral collapse.

It was a sunny, bright, spring morning in Paris. Looking at the Eiffel Tower, my head was reeling trying to take in the brief message of the telegram. It was the first day of our adventure and my whole world had suddenly collapsed around me. What to do? Obviously make contact with home, but how? In 1961 a long-distance telephone call was an exercise in itself to organise. There was no such thing as direct dialling. My parents had only just moved and hadn't had the phone connected but I did know father's work number, although under the circumstances he wouldn't be at work. Des found a post office and suggested sending a telegram.

It was looking out the window of the post office at the Parisians going about their everyday business that I realised the world had not stopped. I was transfixed at the scene before me to the point I couldn't think of what to say in the telegram. I finally drafted some words together to the effect that I would try and make contact by phone when we reached Madrid. It was only after sending the telegram that I realised I had made one of the biggest decisions of my young life. I was going to continue the journey. I was not going home. There was no point, for that part of my life was over. My decision to go on must have seemed at the time to the boys somewhat callous; I don't know, I never asked, though I'm sure there must have been a sense of relief that I had decided to continue our journey together.

We set off on June 1 to Spain via Bordeaux, Biarritz, over the Pyrenees to San Sebastian and then the road to Madrid via Vitoria and Burgos. I began to study the phrase book so I could construct a sentence to make myself understood when I arrived at the Madrid post office to call home. I sat in the square opposite the post office practising for about an hour and finally braved it up to a window at the counter and in halting Spanish spelt out the words requesting a call to Australia. The elegant woman behind the window looked at me and asked, 'Are you from Australia?' in perfect English. She tried in vain for hours to get through but to no avail. Mail was being sent to Lisbon so it was decided to move on. We arrived in Lisbon on June 9 and crossed the harbour to the campsite at Tarfaria on the Atlantic coast. There was a pile of mail from home, from friends, relatives, Mum's sister Gwen, all waiting at American Express. I opened them all and then folded them up and put them away. It was only in 2003 that I have unsealed the cache and read them. Strange to read them, from such a distance.

We spent three days in Lisbon, moved back into Spain travelling no doubt by now the well-worn tourist route through Italica, Seville, Cadiz, Gibraltar, across the Sierra Nevadas, Granada and the bullfights!

Granada, 18 June 1961: 'In the evening we went to the Plaza de Toros for the bullfight. The atmosphere was tremendous, then at 7pm a fanfare of trumpets and in paraded the horses, toreadors, matadors etc. I looked at the first bullfight through the viewfinder of the camera, however, when looking at it with the naked eye it was a little sickening. After the first three (fights) my stomach returned and I'm afraid to admit it, but I enjoyed the proceedings, except the actual kill.'

On arrival in Venice we realised we had underestimated the impact Venice would have on us, and that night we decided to vote to stay an extra day to enjoy the city's unique sights. It was at this point our Kiwi colleague convinced the rest of us he was odd! On hearing we wanted to stay the extra day, Don exclaimed, 'What

The Intrepid Five for Europe, despite the news from home, was a journey of a lifetime. Falling down culverts in the middle of the night, broken axles, bullfights, didn't deter any of us.

on earth for, once you've seen one city you've seen them all!' VENICE?? We were all somewhat flabbergasted and have been dining out on the story ever since.

Our journey was to be a total of ninety days with all the usual highlights creating splendid memories. Throughout, we would pick up our mail from the American Express offices. Letters of sympathy were still coming from home, but I would put them aside, quickly read those from father, which weren't too encouraging, but it wasn't till we reached Brussels that the impact of mother's death hit home and hit home badly, all caused by going to the pictures! As my birthday had been only four days previous, I suppose that didn't help either.

30 July 1961, Brussels: 'I came back to the camp to put the washing away in case it rained, then went into town to the pictures which after ten weeks was quite a break. It was *Rebecca*, quite old, but I always remember Mum saying how good it was and how she had enjoyed it so many years ago. So I went to see it. It was extremely good, only wish I could make pictures like that, alas. I thought of Mum quite a lot through the film. It took me back so many years to when on Monday or Tuesday nights we would go down to the Kings at Mosman and later to the Kings at Chatswood and enjoy so many films. They were the only outings she ever used to get. I remember particularly *Wuthering Heights*, that was like

Rebecca today. But I don't suppose there's any use in lying here remembering, for all that's finished now, forever and forever … After ten weeks I look back on this trip and think how fortunate one is to have been given the opportunity to see and experience all the wonderful things that made up Europe. It has been an extremely lonely journey, no companionship really, but still I don't possess the qualities that make people wish to know you closely. I sometimes regret not having gone home immediately and the number of nights I've stayed awake here trying to sort things out … All I hope and pray is that I've done the right thing and that everything works out for the best.'

In hindsight I find it a very strange entry to have made. Talk about feeling sorry for oneself. I realised halfway through the trip that if I had not continued I would never have coped if I had returned home. Strange too, for we all still see each other at our regular 'Old Farts' luncheons, to which their spouses are not invited! (The ladies have retaliated by having their own.)

On returning to 189 Cromwell Road it didn't take long for life to normalise and our daily routines to resume. Associated Rediffusion reappointed me as one of their team of senior film editors. Life at the coalface had become a little more civilised with the union having won shorter working hours for all the employees. Letters from home soon indicated I would have to return to Australia so plans were made to obtain a berth on the first available ship in 1962. Shipping was still at the forefront of travel and one had to book months in advance. The Super Constellations flights to Australia were only affordable to the well heeled or company executives.

From the time of arrival to my departure from London was two years nearly to the day. London had awakened me to so many things. The riches of theatre, how to read a newspaper, and becoming aware that journalists were given by-lines and one soon became familiar with a particular journalist's style and views. The *cinema*. What an awakening. It was my greatest learning curve in two years. I had collected the *Picture Show Annuals* since boyhood, read *Picturegoer* and *The Picture Show* weeklies, which would arrive three months after publication in Australia, but I was totally unaware of *Sight & Sound*, *Films and Filming* and what we called 'continental' cinema. Every Monday night was spent at the National Film Theatre on the South Bank (I am still a member) where the program opened my eyes and mind to another world of celluloid riches. I would walk sometimes in a daze across the windswept Hungerford Bridge to the tube at Piccadilly to go home to Cromwell Road, where I'm sure I bored everyone witless about what I had seen that evening. It wasn't only 'foreign' cinema that intrigued me, but also the accessibility to the history of American cinema at the NFT. One Monday night double bill I vividly remember was Lloyd Bacon and Busby Berkeley's *42ⁿᵈ Street*, and Ernst Lubitsch's *Trouble in Paradise* with its risqué main title superimposed over a double bed. Remember this was twenty years before the advent of VCRs and movies on videotapes. Some silent classics were available on 8mm and 9.5mm if you could afford a projector. 16mm was virtually the preserve of the film societies.

Going to the National Film Theatre where pristine 35mm prints (sometimes nitrate) were screened was an eye-opener. Another Aladdin's cave of cinema treasures. I would devour the sometimes vitriolic critiques of *Films and Filming*, the more considered judgements of *Sight & Sound*, and the insights to film through the eyes of Dilys Powell, Alexander Walker, Penelope Gilliant, Roger Manvell, Paul Rotha, Peter Bucker and Australia's own Gordon Gow to mention only a few. The films which I can remember vividly were Visconti's *Rocco and his Brothers* and Nino Rota's haunting score, Satjit Ray's *The World of Apu*, Antonioni's *L'Avventura*, Bergman's *Wild Strawberries*, Fellini's *La Dolce Vita*, and a strange film, *La Notte Brava* which Raymond Durgnat in *Film and Filming* was to describe as 'a brantub of semi-crude, semi-poetical erotica' which must say something about me, and last but not least Michael Powell's *Peeping Tom* which I was to see again some years later with the master himself.

February 3 1962. On board the *RHMS Bretagne*, Southampton: 'Left Southampton on the voyage that I must admit I hadn't been looking forward to. Des, Roy, Derek, Ted, Robin, Judy, Olive and Elizabeth all came down to see me off.'

9

Another Cinesound Exclusive!

My return to Australia was not a happy one. Dad was waiting on the wharf and we travelled to Lane Cove to the weatherboard house he and my mother had moved to before she died in 1960. It was an extremely unsettling experience. I was fortunate in obtaining a job straight away at a new film company, Ajax Films, started up by Brian Chirlian primarily to make TV commercials for the British Tobacco Company in an old Bond Store in Argyle Street in Sydney's Rocks district. I didn't stay long. I was not happy either here or at home. I just could not settle. Someone at Cinesound had heard of my return and telephoned to see if I would come back to the company. I immediately said yes and, returning to my old employer, I was faced with the biggest challenge of my life.

I had left Cinesound as an assistant editor earning £14.10.0 per week in 1958 and returned as supervising editor in 1962 earning £40 per week. Not a lot had changed. Some new faces. Michael Ramsden was director/producer of the Cinesound Channel 9 news crew and I the producer of the *Cinesound Review*. Some of the newsreel team would often be seconded to do news stories for the television bulletin. It was an extremely efficient and professional operation, producing the best evening TV news bulletin in Australian commercial television. Not so for the *Cinesound Review*. No fault of the editors and news team. There was no producer. Ken G. Hall had had a total hands-on approach to the *Review*. He would often editorialise the feature item of the newsreel, whereas Movietone would deliver the news straight without opining. Andy Helgeson was not a producer. He wasn't even a filmmaker, hence the newsreel had been left to founder. The 1960s saw the demise of the newsreel the world over: the *Universal* and *Metro News* along with the *Paramount News*, 'The Eyes and Ears of the World' were three of the first to go. The *Gaumont British News*, 'bringing the world to Australia', was the first to go in Britain. *Movietone* and *Pathé News* were hanging on, as were *Movietone* and *Cinesound* in Australia, though 'the voice of Australia' was no longer the voice that audiences once heard.

The newsreel theatrettes where people could while away an hour or so seeing the Australian and world news, travelogues and cartoons, were rapidly being converted to 'continental' cinemas. I presented a paper to Helgeson and GU outlining a case for abandoning the weekly *Cinesound Review* and issuing twelve colour *Reviews* a year along the lines of *Look at Life*. The idea was mulled over for about six months but 'no' came the reply. 'See what you can do with the *Review* to liven it up a bit.' So I took the bold step of planning as many full reel 'specials' as possible on specific subjects, rather than the usual diet of five or six stories in each reel, which audiences saw every night on television. The legal arrangements Cinesound had with Channel Nine entitled the Nine news access to any item in the *Cinesound Review* for Nine to use in their *Weekend Magazine*. This practice used to upset the exhibitors no end. What was the point of showing a newsreel when everyone had probably seen most of it the week before at home? I slowly introduced the idea of newsreel specials by using a by-line or sometimes a full screen title, *Cinesound Special* or *Cinesound Exclusive*. Andy Helgeson wasn't at all interested, so I just went ahead and waited to see who would scream first.

Chief cameraman John Gilles supported me and somehow or other we managed to get Ross King onto a plane to Honolulu to cover the World Surf Life Saving Championships in Hawaii. The surf wasn't too hot but the newsreel certainly was! I had bought the rights to a pop song from an emerging and highly successful local group called The Atlantics. They had a new 'surfing' instrumental number 'Bombora' which, by the weekend the newsreel hit the theatres, was number one on the charts. The timing could not have been better. The Atlantics and Cinesound had a hit on their hands. I had literally drowned the newsreel commentary by Ken Sparkes with the strident and effective instrumental. Despite the success, the next Monday I was carpeted by Andy Helgeson for spending £5 for the music for the newsreel. One wasn't supposed to spend money on the newsreel, just cheap library music. 'Hey, that's not a bad reel,' said Michael Ramsden, 'we'll have it for the *Sunday Magazine*.' 'No way,' I retorted, 'Michael, sorry, it's a Cinesound exclusive.' He initially thought I was joking but I remained firm, Nine couldn't have it. He went to see Andy Helgeson who told him it would be okay. It was time for me to put on the first 'wobbly' of my career and I stormed downstairs to see Helgeson. I had been told to liven up the *Review* and I had. Nothing more was said and Nine didn't get the Surfing Special. I think Ramsden respected me for standing up for the rights of the newsreel and we got on, I felt, even more so than previously because I had taken my stand.

If Andy and GU thought it a bit rich spending £5 for the music for a newsreel, it wasn't to be long before they would have a pink fit for I was about to spend £35 for six songs for a *Cinesound Review*. I had begun collecting the 45s of a new group called The Beatles. It was announced they were going to come to Australia. It was obvious to me that here was a golden opportunity to put life into our ageing newsreel. I wrote to the entrepreneur Ken Brodziak in Melbourne seeking permission for Cinesound to film the Beatles in concert at the Sydney Stadium (the House of Stoush as it was once called). It was weeks before a reply came. In the meantime I planned two newsreels on the Beatles' visit to Australia, keeping as much of our plans away from the Nine news team as possible. We alerted all our 'stringers' in New Zealand and Australia, wherever the Beatles were to tour. Stringers are local cameramen who shoot the occasional story for the newsreel but are not in the full employment of the company. Brodziak finally replied. We could film the Beatles but not record them. Okay, no problem. I had already sought permission to use thirty seconds of each of six songs from EMI. 'Oh! It's only the newsreel,' they said, 'that'll cost you £35.' 'Done!'

Our team of cameramen were all fully briefed to only film the Beatles with their mouths behind the microphones so we could not see what they were actually singing. It was just as well! Soundman Bill Dukes' wonderful recording of that night at the Stadium is a collector's item. All one can hear is the crowd and, faintly in the distance, the Beatles! It was easy to mix the 45s of the group singing into the sound of the crowd at the Stadium and mix out again. Our scheme worked. To open the newsreel special I had selected a piece from a Visnews item of the group singing overseas, but the footage was mute. Careful study of the clip revealed they were singing 'I saw her standing there'. I bought a new copy of the 45, transferred it to magnetic sound and put it on the Moviola. It synchronised perfectly. The second song I had chosen to overlay on our coverage of the impact of the Beatles tour was 'Misery'. Not much notice had been taken of this song but it had become a particular favourite of mine. Radio jocks had ignored it. In the first weekend's release of the newsreel, suddenly 'Misery' hit No. 2 on 2UW's weekly hit parade. The old newsreel had never had this much power!

For the first newsreel of the Beatles in Australia I had put 'Cinesound Special' at the top of the title because it was pretty obvious that Movietone would have similar coverage. For *Beatles at the Stadium* I went all out. After four quick shots of each of the Beatles synchronised with 'Oh yeah – oh yeah' four times, the biggest 'Cinesound Exclusive' title Will Cathcart had ever devised filled the screen. By

CINESOUND EXCLUSIVE!
ENTIRE NEWSREEL
The BEATLES AT THE STADIUM!

The poster artists hand-painted the outdoor display advertising for the newsreel theatres every Wednesday night ready for the Thursday morning programme changeover. In 1964 this day-glow poster was one of many to cover the entire facade of these theatres for 2 weeks!

1964, attendances had waned at the surviving newsreel theatres; people no longer went to the movies to see the news. For two momentous weeks *The Beatles at the Stadium!* changed all that. The news theatrettes had queues extending along the footpaths and at most cinemas that regularly played the *Review* it was being rescreened either after the interval or at the end of the program as an encore. In GU theatres it played for two weeks instead of the usual one, then came the greatest coup of all! Movietone played Hoyts theatres exclusively and Cinesound GU exclusively. The Beatles reel was so popular in the second week, Hoyts booked the reel. It was to be the first and only time the *Cinesound Review* was to play on our competitor's screens.

Helgeson called me into his office. 'Oops, it will be that £35 I had expended on the music,' I said to the staff as I went downstairs. No. The Beatles management and lawyers had been in touch with Greater Union. What rights did we have and how did we acquire them? I had all my paperwork, permissions and licences at the ready to show them. Out to the studio came a contingent of lawyers and the Beatles manager. My paperwork was studied and then the reel was screened to them. The company secretary from Greater Union, Eric Saunders, was present, along with an apprehensive Andy Helgeson. The lights went up at the end. The contingent had a quiet mull to themselves, when a spokesman leant forward to Eric and Andy. 'Well done, that's terrific, everything seems to be perfectly in order. Could we by any chance have six 16mm copies, four for the "boys" and two for the company's library?' There was relief all round. What had happened became clear in a conversation later. Ken Brodziak had in fact no rights whatever to license us to film the Beatles at the Stadium. However, the reel had such an impact on their manager, no action was taken against Cinesound or Brodziak.

These were the dying days of the newsreel. The Beatles had saved the *Cinesound Review* for perhaps another year but the Beatles had not been our biggest story of the year 1964, for either Cinesound or Movietone. It was the night of February 10 when all hell broke loose. Movietone's feature story always headed their newsreel, whilst Cinesound's feature story always closed the reel. We had put the reel to bed this particular Monday night and our feature was an item on General Douglas MacArthur culled principally from our library. It was a straightforward newsreel with three short light items to begin with. Will Cathcart had his titles to do; John Moyes had his shot list to which to write the commentary. It was 7pm and time to go home to Clifton Gardens.

It was coming up to ten o'clock when the phone rang. It was John Gilles: 'I'm on my way to Jervis Bay. The *Melbourne* has cut a destroyer in half – we had better hold the reel, I'll ring in later.' I quickly agreed and said I would alert the boss and the laboratories. I rang the lab manager at home to get the lab ready to take negative from 5am. Left a message at 2SM for Phil Haldeman, our commentator, also their breakfast announcer, and alerted John Moyes, our commentary writer, at home. Rang Bill Dukes, our senior soundman. Everyone was on standby. The ABC had radio bulletins continuously. It was a horror story. At 8.56pm the aircraft carrier *HMAS Melbourne* sliced the destroyer *Voyager* in half causing a huge loss of life. I arrived at the studio at 5am to discover the launching of the *Voyager* in our library. By this time John Gilles had phoned in that he and his Cinesound cameramen, and those of the Nine news, were on their way to the Balmoral Naval Depot where the survivors were being brought. By mid-morning it was known there were eighty-two dead. I decided to drop the three items at the front of the reel and move the MacArthur story to the front – and ditch it altogether if necessary. Our first negative arrived by late Tuesday morning and I began the editing of the newsreel. By early Tuesday night we had the *Cinesound Review* recorded and off the sound went to the laboratory. Back before midnight for syncing and return to the laboratory for the regular Wednesday morning grading, on schedule. One feels guilty admitting that, for a newsman, it had been an exhilarating twenty-four hours of bringing the news to the cinemas, when for the navy, the relatives and the nation it was one of the blackest nights in our history. The thought of it now still sends shivers down my spine.

Our one-reel 'specials' were produced as often as we could find a subject to suit the entire length of the newsreel. I dispatched Kevin Thurger to Northern Australia to do a full reel on crocodiles, which for its day worked particularly well, but I got into trouble (again) when management wanted to know why a cameraman had been sent away for over a week!

It was clear the end was approaching, but instead of ending the life of 'The Voice of Australia' on a high note the powers-that-be decided to merge the two newsreels to create the *Australian Movie Magazine*. The result was dire! Cinesound and Movietone were great newsreels, two of the finest in the world that maintained their standards through thick and thin, matched and sometimes eclipsed their international counterparts. The *Australian Movie Magazine* was a pale shadow of these two great reels and finally limped to a miserable fade out.

Before I close this chapter there are three more stories to tell.

I made mention of the Aladdin's cave behind the projection box at Cinesound prior to my departure overseas in 1958. On my return in 1962 to take over as supervising film editor and producer of the *Cinesound Review*, it was evident that the vault had not been opened in my absence. This cave of nitrate treasures was in danger of chemical deterioration and subsequent oblivion. Those I respected at the studio couldn't understand my concern. Here were all of Ken G. Hall's eighteen features, including a couple of tinted silents from the days of Australasian Films, Frank Capra's *Know Your Ally* and hundreds of reels more. I took it upon myself to get in touch with the National Library of Australia's newly appointed film officer, a young Ray Edmondson. I told him of my dilemma and that I needed an accomplice to assist in moving the collection from Cinesound to Canberra. I was not telling the management, for if alerted I would have been ordered to take the lot to the tip. This more or less happened twice previously. In 1926 Norman Dawn wanted the convict hulk *Success* to burn and sink for his epic *For the Term of His Natural Life*, so it was loaded with all the nitrate prints that could be found in the vaults of 65 Ebley Street, which included all of Spencers Pictures output from 1910 and the production of Australasian Films which now occupied the site. Bert Cross told me this story in one of our perambulations after work up South Dowling Street to the tram. Even now it makes my stomach churn to repeat it here. Then when Cinesound was moved in 1948 to Rozelle, only a fraction of the company's collection could be housed at their new premises, the remainder being sent to the tip! Two-thirds of Australia's silent and sound film history gone forever. It couldn't happen a third time.

Ray and I set forth to save the collection. The manager, Andy Helgeson, enjoyed a long lunch and generally didn't return before three in the afternoon. I arranged with Ray for the library to send a large delivery truck to arrive no later than 2pm. The entire morning was spent moving nearly a thousand cans from the vault behind the projection box, around the back of the sound stage and stacked near the delivery dock door but hidden from view behind the large cloth 'cyc' (cyclorama) which most stages have. The truck was an hour late and arrived at 3pm. I cannot remember who kept a lookout for Andy but what had virtually taken all morning to remove from the vault took only half an hour to load into the truck. It left for Canberra at 3.30!

I went home that evening and it suddenly struck me what I had done. An entire studio's output from 1931 to 1946 was on an anonymous grey truck travelling to the nation's capital and no one had been told or given the opportunity of giving approval. I later wrote to Herbie Hayward at Greater Union and told him of the heist. Some weeks later I received a letter thanking me for my efforts and it had been a wise decision. I never told Andy Helgeson, there was no point. The truck arrived safely at its destination and the National Library had the beginnings of a collection which was to grow to such an extent over the next twenty years that a National Film and Sound Archive would be created. My accomplice in crime was to be its prime mover.

Helgeson had a penchant for pornographic film, something I hadn't encountered at my young age. They were crudely made 16mm films produced after hours over at the old Spencers Studios at White City overlooking the tennis courts. Allyn Barnes, the studio's principal sound recordist, used to acquire these films from his associates and tease me I was too young to project them and that he was to be projectionist on such occasions, until he got into an awful mess one evening with film all over the floor and not on the projector. I had to get the show running again. I looked through the porthole of the projection room in startled amazement at what I saw. The films were so badly made I couldn't for the life of me see how anyone could be aroused by such amateurish performances ... for the want of a better word! The films weren't kept on the studio premises but in the vault at the local police station!! It used to amuse we juniors and the staff when we would spot the Sergeant of Police from Balmain wandering up the road with the 400 ft cans of film under his arm. This meant Andy was having a 'clients' screening'.

One of these clients' screenings, however, went very badly wrong! Cinesound had just secured a new client, to make their theatrical and television commercials. It was one of the country's most respected cordial manufacturers and Andy had always thought it would be a good idea to 'entertain' them in appreciation of being awarded their contract. There was a small problem, of which Andy was unaware. The family owners were deeply religious. I was standing in the foyer when a group of agitated executives stormed through, followed by a somewhat flustered Andy who was at the same time brazenly laughing. He wasn't laughing when asked by head office why we had lost such a valuable client.

After the Petrov affair, which Bede Whiteman had covered splendidly for the *Review*, the government had given extra powers to the Australian Security and Intelligence Organisation (ASIO) to the extent they had developed their own film unit. In the mid-sixties there was to be another scandal, referred to as the Skipov affair. Prime Minister Menzies was hellbent on telling the Australian public about ASIO and the excellence of their work. Menzies instructed that a television documentary be made featuring some of the intelligence footage taken by the ASIO unit of the surveillance of Skipov. What ASIO intelligence officers thought of this idea has never been revealed. Menzies received assurances from Frank Packer that Channel Nine would telecast the documentary, this at a time when commercial television stations were reluctant to program documentaries. Having received clearance from ASIO, an officer from the organisation arrived at Cinesound with the footage. For reasons never explained to me, sound recordist Allyn Barnes was the contact person between me as the editor and ASIO. The officer would sit in the cutting room all day watching my every move. At the end of the day I would have to remove all the trims (left over pieces of film) from the editing trim bins, roll them up and hand them to the ASIO officer, who dutifully took them away, returning the film to me next morning. No film was to stay on the premises overnight.

The footage was nothing less than amazing. ASIO had lenses and recording equipment the professional industry was not to see for years. Long lens shots taken on extremely fast film, also not available to the industry, from buildings on the opposite side of the street looking into darkened restaurants with only a candle on the table, yet the image perfectly clear, a little grainy perhaps, and crystal clear radio sound from the microphone hidden in the candle. Another scene was taken of a person being watched by ASIO making a telephone call, from a camera several hundred yards up the other end of the street.

The routine of wrapping up every piece of left over film and sound, as well as the edited reel, would take place every evening and taken away to be returned and hung back up again the following morning in the bins. Allyn Barnes and I didn't think the film was very good but the content had us fascinated. I actually expressed the opinion to the ASIO officer supervising me that I didn't think it a good idea to show this footage to the public as it seemed to me to reveal the workings of a department which would weaken, not strengthen, our security. There must have been others in high places who thought the same for the film never saw the light of day. One day this ASIO officer arrived to make sure there was not one frame of film lying in the bottom of the editing bins or in any corner of the room. He was never seen again. I must confess I would be intrigued to see the archival collection of ASIO, which I believe is now in the National Archives.

I was offered a job by the new television network, Channel Ten, to start up their editing department and John Gilles to set up their news and current affairs camera teams. So John and I left Cinesound, with I must confess great sadness, and fortunately didn't become involved in the merger with Movietone. I think that would have broken my heart. For with the closure of the *Cinesound Review*, I knew the end of Cinesound was not too far away. After Ken Hall's departure in 1956 the great team of news people kept the heart of the place alive with the production of the nightly Channel Nine news footage and the *Review* until the mid-sixties. But with no direction and an uninterested head office, the place began to falter and more and more of the staff left for greater opportunities elsewhere in television. The Channel Nine news, I believe, still reflects their Cinesound foundations.

10

Forgotten Cinema And The Australian Renaissance

The move to Channel Ten had initially been a wise one and head of news and current affairs, Lionel (Bill) Hudson, had given John Gilles, head of camera, and me, relatively free rein in setting up the film side of the news division. A small 16mm processing machine was installed next to the news cutting room but we soon had to expand into the main film programming assembly area because management wanted a nightly current affairs program. It was to be called *Telescope* and it didn't take long for the show to establish its own style and sometimes create controversy with management, for more often than not the show expressed opinions. A terrific team was put together with John as chief cameraman and me as editor, Tony Ward as presenter and writer, with Tanya Halesworth and a bright new anchor man and commentator, Bill Peach. Stewart Young from Cinesound had come over to look after sound and John Wallace, Cinesound's editor for the Nine news, moved over to take over Ten's news bulletin, whilst I concentrated on our new show. Wayne Le Clos, an up and coming editor, came aboard before he set off overseas. It didn't take long for Bill Peach to become a household name and a television 'star', though he will probably hate me for saying it. Ten, however, had gone way over budget on its launch opening night show *TV Spells Magic*, shot on 16mm black and white by John McLean and edited by me for expatriate director Robert Flemyng. My flirtation with Australian television was to be short-lived.

As a result of cutbacks on budgets and staff, less than six months after establishing *Telescope*, which had a growing audience, I could see the writing on the wall and decided it was time for me to move on. The announcement of my departure from Ten wasn't greeted with much joy. Bill, Tony and John Gilles in particular pleaded with me to stay with the team. An opportunity had opened for me back at Ajax Films, whose editing department was headed by my old mentor, Stanley Moore. I was restless and it meant I was going back to film.

My farewell was held at a wonderful old and historic watering hole, the Clifton Gardens Hotel, whose doors were about to close as it was to be demolished as a result of residents' protests about noise. Well, I'm sure we helped it along for I don't remember how I got home and I only lived a short distance away on the corner of Morella and Iluka Roads. For all I know it may have been the demolishers that morning who asked us all to leave. The team unfortunately was destined to break up and *Telescope* to close. It had given the ABC ideas for a nightly current affairs show of their own, *This Day Tonight*, and it wasn't long before Bill Peach was seen right across Australia. It is somewhat satisfying to look back and realise that the *Telescope* team were the pioneers of this type of nightly current affairs program, long before *TDT*, and has become the norm for every channel. It has never been previously acknowledged by television historians.

Stewart Young and I had become very good friends at Cinesound and, naïvely or otherwise, set out to make television documentaries of our own, on our own. Our first was *Here Remains a Memory*, a twenty-five minute black and white film about the history of The Rocks, an historic precinct in Sydney, then under threat of massive redevelopment. A noted Australian architect, Harry Seidler, was building a tower of apartments on Blues Point on the north side of the harbour, and the plan was to develop Blues Point with several other tower blocks. There was a public outcry. Diagonally opposite, on the southern shore under the shadow of Sydney's famous Harbour Bridge, the government revealed a similar proposition for the development of the historic Rocks. The outcry became a tumult of protest. With my godfather's Bolex 16mm camera, Stewart and I spent nearly every weekend over a twelve-month period, or when we could afford the stock, filming every nook and cranny of the district. At night at Cinesound, in his own time, Freddie Wainwright filmed our stills on the great Oxberry camera.

Our timing could not have been better. The Rocks development had become a major controversy and the new Channel Ten was looking for Australian programs. I think we sold it for about $250 but it served our purpose of making a film hopefully to be seen. The critical response was surprisingly positive as were the viewer ratings. However, I must confess I saw the film about five years ago and asked the Archive not to let anyone see it, or I should say *hear* it. The narration was dreadful purple prose, which I didn't realise at the time and no one told me.

The next two documentaries we made together were somewhat better. *They Shot Through Like a Bondi*, a twenty-five minute history of Sydney's trams, which was the biggest tramway system in the world, was well received, as was our third documentary *When the River was the Only Road*, a history of Australia's wonderful paddle steamer era. Phil Haldeman, one of radio station 2SM's 'Good Guys' and the highest rating breakfast announcer in Australia, did the narration. I thought our documentaries would never sell to the ABC, which was virtually a closed shop, and I wanted to crack the commercial networks, hence the use of Phil for our commentaries, but sell they did. I think all three documentaries covered their basic costs, excluding our salaries which were non-existent of course. One must be reminded in this story that there was no government funding for independent filmmakers in the 1960s. What you made was made on the smell of an oily rag and your hard-earned wages. The government's only funding was the Department of Interior's Commonwealth Film Unit which basically made propaganda shorts for supply to Australian embassies, *Australian Diary* for the cinemas and occasionally a quality 35mm documentary for theatrical release. The CFU didn't come into its own till the end of the sixties and the early seventies, as Film Australia.

In a letter home to my father in 1961 I had mentioned that nothing had come of my book though I had received letters from the British Film Institute in London and Angus & Robertson in Sydney expressing cautious interest. I had also noted that on re-reading it, 'some of it badly needs re-shaping'. This was an understatement. I had called it *Our First Sixty Years* and it was the result of my two years research in the 1950s at the Mitchell Library after my restoration of the nitrate print of *The Sentimental Bloke*. In fact the text was an endless list of credits and titles l culled from the trade paper *Everyone's* from 1929 and *The Picture Show*, an Australian publication of the late 1900s and early 1920s. There were no reference works available until Andrew Pike's and Ross Cooper's pioneering work *Australian Film* arrived in 1977. Why not use the 'book' as the basis for a film on the history of the Australian film industry? Everyone thought I was mad. 'Who would want to see it?' I was repeatedly asked. I was haunted after the 'heist' of the Cinesound collection to Canberra by Marcia Anderson's comment as to why on earth I wanted to save those dreadful films!

So with a borrowed Bell & Howell projector, Stewart Young and I sat through every Australian film of which there was a print, virtually every weekend in the upstairs lounge of my home in Clifton Gardens for nearly two years. It was arduous, never mind the labour of love! When we found a sequence or a scene worth duplicating we would switch the projector into reverse to the beginning of the sequence, stop the projector, put a paper carefully around the print, switch the machine back on and go to the finish of the scene, stop the projector, put another paper around the print, then gently rewind the print and repeat the procedure with every title. We must have done this at least a hundred times. The papered

Poster for *Forgotten Cinema* in 1966.

print would then be returned to Canberra to the National Library where they would make a dupe negative of the papered section, wherever possible from their fine grain master, sometimes from the print itself, and then a work print from the dupe neg for our editing process. We would try and get through three or four features each weekend. Some were so bad we would look at each other and query if we really wanted to see more, and quickly dispatch it to the ever-growing pile on the floor. Editing the material was equally tortuous. Our first satisfactory cut was over two hours! Pioneers Ken G. Hall, Bert Cross and Elsa Chauvel were extremely cooperative and gave us splendid interviews but I knew we couldn't sell a two-hour documentary to television, so ruthless we had to be. I finally got it down to precisely sixty minutes and I was not going to take another foot out.

If we were going to sell to commercial television then I would have to have a recognisable commercial narrator. Phil Haldeman was called again and he was amazed at what we had achieved. The whole work had taken two years. I submitted it to the 14th Sydney Film Festival in 1967 and David Stratton programmed it for three screenings at the then Sydney University venue. The Festival this particular year was held at both the University and the Cremorne Orpheum. I had made up a collage poster from the stills I had collected originally for the book and Grahame Jennings, production manager at Cinesound, arranged the printing of the poster which, with the help of some of the gang from 189 who had come home, plastered the builder's hoarding opposite the Cremorne Orpheum and around the University. The first screening was a little frightening for it got a standing ovation which was repeated at the later screenings. Could it be sold, however? The film had opened the eyes of the Festival audience to something that had never been discussed before, that Australia had had a cinema of its own, established in 1896, and movies had been shown here since 1894.

The papers soon picked up on it and a groundswell of support had started, led by Senator Doug McClelland. *The Film Weekly*, the industry's trade paper, observed, 'Anthony Buckley's *Forgotten Cinema* was scheduled to be screened in the Federal Senate this week following a request for a print of the feature by Senator Doug McClelland. Screening was to be held during the dinner adjournment. It will be interesting to learn Senator McClelland's comments and those of his colleagues. But it will be even more interesting if the screening helps raise some interest in Australian production among the members of our government. If all the politicos were as interested in local filming as Senator McClelland then maybe the struggling film makers of Australia would really get somewhere.'

At Question Time in the Senate on September 21, 1967, Senator Douglas McClelland took the initiative. From *Hansard*:

AUSTRALIAN FILM INDUSTRY

Senator McCLELLAND – Is the Minister representing the Postmaster-General aware that last night there was shown in Parliament House an excellent documentary film produced by one Anthony Buckley entitled 'Forgotten Cinema', which sets out the history of the Australian film industry? ... Is the Minister prepared to ask his colleagues to join him to view the second screening which will take place this evening, and if they do not come away holding their heads in shame for their failure to do anything to encourage and foster this type of important Australian industry, will they at least give some consideration ---

The PRESIDENT – Order! The honourable senator will ask his question, not make a statement.

I could only afford two 16mm prints and even the laboratory sold them to me for cost price which was their generous contribution to our effort, and Greater Union had foregone any royalties. One print was for the festival circuit and the other to send around to the TV stations in the hope I would find a buyer. I knew it would be pointless sending it to the ABC for they wouldn't accept a narration read by a 'popular' breakfast announcer. Bruce Gyngell had devised 'the Seven revolution' so I sent the print to Seven. The phone rang. Gyngell wanted to see me. 'You've created a bit of a stir Tony, with this – congratulations.' Goodness, I thought. 'How much did it cost you?' Gyngell asked. I stupidly wasn't thinking fast enough and told him the truth. '$3,500 Mr Gyngell – ' 'Call me Bruce, I'll pay $3,600.' Cripes, a profit! I had to confess to Stewart and everyone else, I was amazed. We were going on commercial television. Even more amazing was the announcement that *Forgotten Cinema* would screen on a Wednesday night at 9.30, immediately following Channel Seven's most successful weekly hit, *The Mavis Bramston Show*, Australia's most-watched program. I heard much later that the chief programmer for Seven, Glen Kinging, a very nice man, thought Gyngell stark raving mad. One, he had bought a documentary, two, it was an Australian documentary, and three, he wanted it programmed following *The Mavis Bramston Show*!

Well, history was made. The audience stayed and it was a ratings and critical success. It was also to win for ATN7 a 'Penguin' for best documentary in the Television Society of Australia annual television awards. We were bowled over. Our festival print travelled the country so I ordered a new print which then went to a couple of overseas festivals, winning a meritorious citation at the San Francisco International Film Festival. Australian television viewers, festival audiences and the politicians had been reminded an Australian film industry had existed, and it was time for one to exist again. Remembering Bert Cross's remark 'There's no future in the film industry, son,' I felt vindicated by my belief in our industry and I was still only thirty years of age!

11

Michael Powell and S.Y.M.

Brian Chirlian's Ajax Films had outgrown their premises in the Argyle Bond Store at The Rocks and they had leased the old Warringah Hall next to the primary school at Neutral Bay on Sydney's lower North Shore. The hall itself was converted to a not-so-sound-proofed studio and the surrounding rooms were adapted to make-up and wardrobe rooms, offices and cutting rooms et al. It would be an understatement to say conditions were cramped.

Then, on 27 September 1965, Chirlian announced to the staff that Ajax were going to make a feature film and the company would be acquiring a second studio at Bondi Junction in Sydney's eastern suburbs. The film was *They're a Weird Mob*, with Walter Chiari and Claire Dunne, and was to be directed by Michael Powell, the maverick of British cinema. It was to be edited by Gerald Turney-Smith, an English film editor who had immigrated to Australia.

The second studio was none other than the old Cinesound Studio at 65 Ebley Street. This building had had more reincarnations than Nellie Melba had had farewell performances. Built in the 1900s as a rollerskating rink and studio for Australasian Films, it became a talkie studio for Cinesound from the early 1930s till 1948 when Cinesound moved to the Amusu Theatre at Rozelle. Then for a short time it became the bottling plant for a new American soft drink, Canada Dry, a brand Australians didn't take to. After Canada Dry failed it became a studio once more for Lee Robinson and Chips Rafferty's Southern International Films, followed by Visatone Productions and then Ajax Films till the 1970s. The building still stands in 2009 and is home to a Manchester showroom. The side and back of the building have not been altered and are still recognisable as in Cinesound's day. It should be heritage listed. A group of film historians wants to revert the building to a cinema and film museum.

Editing *Age of Consent* in the air-conditioned, bamboo-lined shed with the best view in the world. The trusty Westrex Editer in the corner. For film editors, please note the 17.5mm magnetic track running in sync with the picture work print (cutting copy) through the synchroniser. Customs duties at the time were such that it was more economical to import 17.5mm stock than 35mm. It was a nightmare to handle and to gear the reels to take up in ratio with each other. Michael Powell never came into the cutting room, preferring to dictate his suggested edits in the theatre looking at the cut footage on the big screen. Very unusual.

At the behest of film editor Stan Moore, I rejoined Ajax Films at the end of 1965 at their Neutral Bay studio whilst the features department was set up at their Bondi premises. The schedule was frantic. Television commercials and sports documentaries were the main staple of the company. Sport was anathema to me but I always won the golf tournaments and the Rugby League to edit, two sports I still fail to comprehend. The TV commercials were the bane of my life! One director of TV commercials the editors at Ajax sought to avoid was Jack Lee, a noted British director of such features as *A Town Like Alice* and *Robbery Under Arms*. Strangely I got on well with Jack but I had no patience for the pedantic style of cutting that typified television commercials, or agency producers' behaviour.

'I say, old boy, we need to add four more frames to the corn flakes hitting the plate,' Jack's pukka voice would intone, or 'No, old boy, we need to take three frames off the cigarette in her mouth.' This would go on ad infinitum!

Jack Lee was always full of enthusiasm and jolly, and if the clients were ever getting on his nerves then Jack never showed it. Sitting at the Moviola, I often pondered what Jack really thought about his new-found career in television advertising after such a long and distinguished role in British cinema. It was on the advice of Paul Rotha that Jack took a film course at London's Regent Street Polytechnic and in 1938 joined John Grierson's GPO Film Unit as an associate producer. In 1947, he directed his first feature film, *The Woman in the Hall* with Jean Simmons, and this was followed by *Once a Jolly Swagman* with Dirk Bogarde. It was *Robbery Under Arms* that brought Jack to Australia where he met Isabel Kidman, the cattle heiress who was to become his second wife in 1963. It was to be a coincidence that the last feature to be directed by Jack Lee, *Circle of Deception* (1961) was also to be the last film I saw at the Odeon, Kensington, before leaving London for home in 1962. Jack died in 2002 at the age of eighty-nine.

They're a Weird Mob was a box office sensation after its premiere at Sydney's palatial State Theatre. Though there can be no doubt that Tim Burstall and Bruce Beresford were the beginning of the new wave of Australian cinema in the seventies, it was Powell's film which aroused an awareness that the time had come for the re-establishment of an Australian film industry, making Australian stories for our own audiences.

With *Weird Mob*'s success, Michael Powell announced plans for a second film and the fledgling NLT Productions, set up by Jack Neary and TV personality Bobby Limb, was to bring Walter Chiari back to Australia for their first feature film, *Squeeze a Flower* (originally titled *Squeeze a Flower, Squeeze a Grape*).

The phone rang in the cutting room. Mr Chirlian would like to see me. 'Sit down, Tone.' There were no formalities with Brian, straightforward and to the point. 'Mr Powell would like to see you about editing his new film.' Though I had edited many drama inserts at Associated Rediffusion, I had not edited a feature film. 'What can you show him?' Brian asked. I naïvely answered *Forgotten Cinema* which was all I could think of at the time. 'Good idea, Mickey is only available Saturday morning, set up a screening in the small theatre at Bondi will you, for ten o'clock – thanks Tone.'

'Thanks Tone' indeed! Cripes, what on earth was I doing showing a documentary on the history of Australian movies to an icon of English cinema, the founder, with Emeric Pressburger, of 'The Archers' film company which was to leave an indelible mark on world cinema?

10am Saturday was confirmed.

My early introduction to the films of Michael Powell had been at the Arcadia Theatre, Chatswood, one wet afternoon during school holidays, when I had actually gone to hear the organist. The vast stalls of this art deco gem were empty except for me and two hatted ladies. Onto the screen came the familiar Archer's trademark (as logos were once called) and then appeared the main titles for *Stairway to Heaven*. The year was probably 1947,[1] I was all of ten years of age and I could not make head or tail of this Technicolor and dye-monochrome picture. So I thought it wise not to mention my schoolboy experience.

I arrived early at Ajax that Saturday morning, checked the theatrette was clean, threaded the film on the Bell & Howell projector, checked focus and waited nervously for the maestro to arrive. I couldn't work out why I was being considered for the job. I knew Gerald Turney-Smith wasn't available. However I later learnt that Powell had heard and read of *Forgotten Cinema* and had actually asked to see it.

On his arrival he could see how nervous I was and he immediately set out to make me comfortable by sitting down to chat. I indicated the film was ready to roll and that I would leave him in peace to watch it. He was having none of that and invited me to sit with him during the screening.

It was the worst hour of my life!

When the lights came up Powell leant over, gently touched me on the knee and said, 'You are a sensitive young man,' and left the theatre. I felt that I (and the film) had really blown it.

Sunday night at home at Clifton Gardens. The phone rang. It was Powell. 'I would like you to cut my film.' I was shaking so much I was sure he could hear

---

1 The film was released in 1946 as *A Matter of Life and Death* in the UK but films almost always did not reach Australia until a year later, and sometimes longer

(Top left) Michael Powell does his
last-minute checks whilst camera
operator John McLean keeps his
eye on the weather.

(Top right) Hannes Staudinger,
DOP, listens to Michael Powell
re his requirements for the next
scene. Camera operator John
McLean hovers nearby.

(Above) Harold Hopkins and I
became good friends during
and after the shoot of *Age
of Consent*. As with the late
John Hargreaves, I have always
thought the industry has
underrated and neglected this
fine actor.

(Left) Helen Mirren listens
to Rose Lindsay and Michael
Powell discussing the film's
making. Rose approved of
Peter Yeldham's adaptation of
Norman's novel.

me rattling. I graciously accepted and told him I wouldn't let him down. 'I'm sure you won't,' he said.

So was to begin a long and warm relationship – the mentor and the mentee! – and a whole new world of filmmaking which was to launch my career in feature film production. I was also to be referred to as SYM (sensitive young man) for quite a few years to come.

Age of Consent is a popular novel by the late Norman Lindsay, noted Australian artist and writer of the 1920s and 1930s, and famous for his portraits and drawings of voluptuous women, more often than not noted for scandalising society matrons and the church, not to mention the censor! James Mason was cast as the artist Bradley Morahan and also as Powell's co-producer, a relationship about which I had grave doubts. The nubile model in the story, Cora, was to be played by newcomer Helen Mirren who had just come from the Royal Shakespeare Company. The screenplay was adapted by Peter Yeldham. Little did I know that I would still be having the pleasure of working with Peter to this present day. Powell was sixty-three and with him came his twenty-three year old son, Kevin, to experience and learn the crafts of production management and producing from his father and production manager John Pellatt. He was also to be unit manager. It was to be a lasting friendship.

Powell had selected Dunk Island[2] on the Great Barrier Reef as the main locale for the film. Thursday, March 7, 1968 saw the departure from Sydney of cast and crew of approximately sixty people for the island, including me and my assistant editor, Peter Buchanan. Powell had decided to have the picture cut on location wherever possible. He felt it was rather difficult for the director to communicate with his editor when they were 1800 miles apart. For me to be on location for a major film was quite an experience, as it was for all the crew. Whilst the resort's hotel facilities were okay, the accommodation was nothing less than primitive. Non-air-conditioned cupboards is the best way to describe the rooms, which had to accommodate two crew members to each cupboard. I shared with the hairdresser, Robert Hynard. Hair and make-up, along with wardrobe, are the first to be required each morning, so when Rob got up for crew call at five I would get up too and set forth to the cutting room. The Moviola (actually a Westrex Editer that was much preferred by this editor and was in many ways the forerunner to the Steenbek), trim bins, spare cans and bobbins, all the cutting room paraphernalia, had all been transhipped from Sydney. Our chief of sound, Paul Ennis, and his

---

2   Dunk Island Resort is today one of the premier five-star resorts on Queensland's Barrier Reef. A far cry from the days when *Age of Consent* was filmed

assistant, Daryl Price, had the onerous task of bringing a complete projection and sound system to the island for the screening of daily rushes.

These were screened to the crew and the residents of the island (a rare privilege) each evening after dinner at nine o'clock in the huge tent erected as a combination cinema and production office. The crew fearing the worst, and the residents anticipating the best, the show would soon be underway. If the evening's proceedings resembled Ashton's Circus, it was purely coincidental.

The first few days were spent setting up the cutting room in an old tin shed with probably one of the best views in the world. Assistant editor Peter Buchanan was quite handy in the carpentry department and finally we were set up with a reasonably sophisticated facility, except there was no air-conditioning.

Then tragedy struck. Principal photography was to commence on the Monday after our Thursday arrival. Saturday afternoon I was watching the filming by Hannes Staudinger and John McLean, with hand-held Arriflex's, of the island's bat colony, when a courier appeared holding a telegram for Powell. The main generator being transported from Sydney had been placed on a barge in Townsville for the final leg to Dunk Island, but the barge carrying the genny had capsized halfway. I remember vividly the look on Powell's face. His first comment was 'Is everyone okay? Is there anybody hurt?' He was assured no one was injured. A massive reschedule took place on the Sunday and filming commenced on Monday without the generator. It was another week before a replacement reached us.

I spent the first ten days on the set watching Powell work, a rare chance to observe a master at his craft. This enabled me to take in his shooting style and anticipate what he was going to expect in a first cut of the picture once rushes had begun to arrive on the island. The weather was hot and humid and at long last our first batch of rushes arrived from Colorfilm in Sydney. Despite having the windows and doors open, the film began sticking to itself. Worse, the mirrors on the Westrex Editer began to deteriorate, but the final straw came when I, and the film I was cutting, were pulled into the machine. The moisture adhering to the celluloid was unbelievable. An air-conditioner was requested and much to our surprise an air-conditioner arrived. Peter and I were soon working in the comparative lap of luxury, much to the envy of our fellow crew members. In the meantime, shipments of dry ice were being brought from the mainland to keep the raw film stock and the camera equipment as free as possible from humidity.

In the first assembly cut of the various scenes I noticed one between James Mason and Jack MacGowran where there was a 'two shot' of them both and a close-up of Mason but not of MacGowran. At rushes that evening your SYM was taking notes from Mr Powell (as I always called him) when I took the liberty of mentioning my observation of the lack of a close-up. He looked at me with a steely eye, smiled and curtly said, 'You won't need it.' The words of a very confident director. He was right.

A considerable amount of *Age of Consent* is set in artist Bradley Morahan's (Mason) shack that had been specially designed and built on the island by art director Dennis Gentle. However, our first day's filming was held up when it was discovered the Mitchell camera wouldn't fit through the door of the shack. Ooops! Then the weather decided to have tantrums, rain and wind set in for nearly two weeks. But nothing was going to stop Michael Powell. Rain or sun, we continued to film. Powell never missed a trick. One morning James Mason, on one of his days off, wandered down to the cutting room with the view. Peter and I were standing outside having morning tea. James wanted to know how I was and what I thought of the footage. The conversation led to the sound level of his dialogue, with which sound recordists Paul Ennis and Lloyd Colman were continuously wrestling. 'Oh,' said Mason, 'I much prefer to control my performance in the post-sync (ADR). I never give my full performance vocally when filming.' He was totally accustomed to revoicing all his performances, even when studio sync sound quality was perfect.

Like a tailor measuring and cutting his cloth, the physical cutting of celluloid makes one 'feel' a craftsman. The film running through one's fingers, threading the machine, rewinding, holding the bobbin on your left thumb and balancing the speed of the rewind so as not to burn your fingers, is an enormously satisfying experience, the same a tailor I'm sure gets from sewing and stitching the cloth – at the end of the day a suit – and, for the editor, a reel of film. Not so any more. Editing the celluloid film was the basis of the craft for over eighty years till the invention of the Lightworks and Avid computer editing machines. There are now several brands and methods of electronic editing. The modern electronic way gives the editor more choices, but I'm not convinced it makes the editing any better.

The procedure in 1968 was quite different. Australia uses the British/European method of slate order when filming, i.e. 1 to 600 or whatever. If a slate is missing in rushes, the assistant editor picks it up straight away, long before the rushes screening, whereas the American system of using the scene numbers is prone to error and mislaid scenes. Peter Buchanan would break down the slates individually and the continuity sheets would state which slate was which scene. (A film is not shot in scene order.) Uncut sequences awaiting missing scenes would be joined together to make up the reel of film. It was then I would run the reel on the Westrex to trim and tidy up the rhythm of the reel, just like the tailor at the sewing machine.

Easter weekend saw the entire unit move to Cairns, the tourist capital of Far North Queensland. Not so in 1968. A quiet country town with a few motels and the Great Northern Hotel and Hides as the premier places to stay. The cutting room was set up in the Tradewinds Motel. Peter and I actually had a motel room! And the rushes were screened at the Tropical Theatre. This was paradise! Ten days' filming in and around Cairns and Green Island and the next move was to Brisbane, where fate was to change James Mason's life. In a tiny role near the beginning of the film set in Brisbane, Bradley Morahan encounters Meg, played by an up-and-coming actress of the time, Clarissa Kaye. They *were* to fall in love. Returning to Sydney to complete filming, Mason would spend his first few days in the dubbing theatre at Ajax 'looping' all of his lines in the film. Mason, with his distinctive British voice, wanted to do Bradley Morahan with an Australian accent, to which, surprisingly, Powell agreed. It is totally unconvincing and is one of the serious flaws in the film. On wrap, I would be waiting in my Morris 1100, James would quietly slip away, and I would drive him to Marrickville, an inner Sydney suburb, to Clarissa and her mother's home, a modest, semi-detached cottage. This way, James had total privacy, not having to ask the switchboard operator to call cabs to Marrickville. It would not have been long before the gossip columnists would have been on his tail. Long after *Age of Consent* was completed they were to marry.

Four days after the last clapper had fallen, the rough cut of *Age* was ready to screen. Whilst editing had been proceeding on Dunk Island, sound editor Tim Wellburn and his assistant, Gary Kildea, were preparing the post sync loops to be done on our return. As sequences were cut they were sent to Sydney for copies to be made, which enabled Mason, Mirren and MacGowran to revoice their lines before their return to England. The rough cut hadn't been seen by Powell, he having left me alone till this time. The day for the big screening was also the day of the cast and crew wrap party. If Powell was nervous at seeing the work he had entrusted to this unknown cutter, he didn't show it. By noon all was over and there was a look of relief on everyone's face, not to mention mine. On the following Monday, some ten weeks after shooting had commenced, the real work of fine cutting began. Michael Powell was to be this editor's dream. He viewed his film only in the theatre and never in the cutting room, stated what he liked, what we should drop, alter and rearrange, and at no time ever hovered over my shoulder whilst I was editing. I think he only ever entered the cutting room once and that was to say 'Good morning' and 'Oh, by the way, I think it's time you stopped calling me Mr Powell. Michael will do nicely.'

(Top) James Mason 'doodled' every day on the pages of his script. In his caricature of me he added a clipping from the column of a newspaper which says 'A CUT ABOVE THE REST'. Nice.

Mason was intrigued with Australian 'strine' and would phonetically write it down on his script and practise on his days off. His distinctive British voice, however, made his attempts at 'strine' unconvincing and irritating. It is the one major flaw of the film.

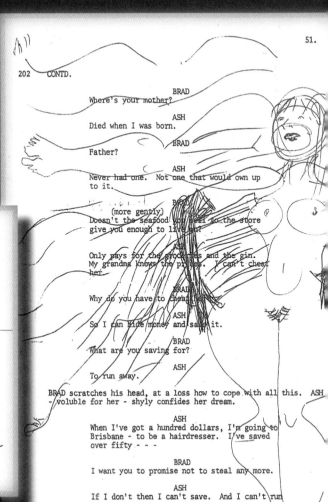

THIS THAVIN SCUTTA STUP UTPYED TID DULLUH SNIDVANCE FRA STOULEN CHOOK.

S POL AHD YI MN URRLE

hooja Hefta chayta?

haday n sgeving for.

wanchata promiss nit ta stailinimove

51.

202   CONTD.

                                    BRAD
Where's your mother?

                                    ASH
Died when I was born.

                                    BRAD
Father?

                                    ASH
Never had one. Not one that would own up
to it.

                                    BRAD
            (more gently)
Doesn't the seafood you sell to the store
give you enough to live on?

Only pays for the groceries and the gin.
My grandma knows the prices. I can't cheat
her.

                                    BRAD
Why do you have to cheat?

                                    ASH
So I can hide money and save it.

                                    BRAD
What are you saving for?

                                    ASH
To run away.

BRAD scratches his head, at a loss how to cope with all this. ASH
- voluble for her - shyly confides her dream.

                                    ASH
When I've got a hundred dollars, I'm going to
Brisbane - to be a hairdresser. I've saved
over fifty - - -

                                    BRAD
I want you to promise not to steal any more.

                                    ASH
If I don't then I can't save. And I can't run
away.

12

Home To Avening

With the completion of filming, Michael's partner, the actress Pamela Brown, arrived and they set up residence in Beach Road, Double Bay, one of Sydney's fashionable harbourside suburbs. This was the beginning of getting to know the real Michael Powell, or at least I thought it was. Michael would ring the studio and insist I join he and Pamela for lunch at Beach Road. I would arrive with script and notepad and they would remain unopened. Michael would be preparing lunch and Pamela and I would retire to the veranda to talk. Michael purely wanted to enjoy a social occasion and there were to be many at Beach Road. Sometimes we would be joined by David Crocker, Michael's first assistant, and Peggy Carter, our make-up artist, and Kevin Powell, Michael's son.

Michael could talk on almost every subject known, and was intrigued to know what I thought of the current political scene in Australia, especially the movements that were starting in Melbourne and Sydney to establish an Australian film industry supported by government. I would remind him politely it was time for me to return to work and this 'beast' he had created. The afternoons would always finish with a laugh, something I was not used to seeing on Dunk Island. Miss Brown had the master well and truly in control, but never let him know it.

Michael had commissioned noted Australian composer Peter Sculthorpe to compose the score for the picture and no better choice could Michael have made, though as we will see later, this was not to be the case from Columbia's viewpoint. Sculthorpe was already established as one of Australia's finest classical composers with, among others, his glorious 'Sun Music' suites. He had already scored one feature film, a children's story – *They Found a Cave* – in 1962. Sculthorpe had been brought up to Dunk Island to watch the filming and to soak in the 'atmosphere'. The music was recorded to picture at Ron Purvis's Natec Studios in the old 2UE

Radio building in Bligh Street, Sydney. Ron's studio was quite small for a largish orchestra but he had devised a new projection system that enabled conductor and orchestra to sit in front of the screen whilst we all sat behind the screen watching the picture in reverse. It was the first time I had seen music recorded to picture.

The nudity in *Age of Consent* was superbly handled by Powell and was to cause a lot of comment, mostly favourable, but the Americans couldn't cope with the frankness of the nudity. In the medium close-ups of Cora (Helen Mirren) posing for artist Bradley Morahan (James Mason), the water falling and rising over her pubic region was allowed to take its natural course on the screen. There was nothing obscene about it. Extremely lyrical. But no, for the US version I had to replace all the shots of Helen with extreme long distance shots, so much so it could have been anyone playing the role. Kathy Trout had been employed as Helen's understudy and double for Ron Taylor to do all the underwater shots. Helen was determined to do her own and do them she did. They are some of the special moments of *Age of Consent*.

Sun Herald, critic not credited: 'James Mason turns in a masterly performance as Bradley Monahan [sic] a vagabond-hearted painter who escapes from the emptiness of fashionable success to the idyllic freedom of an island off the Barrier Reef … Peter Yeldham's screenplay and Michael Powell's direction combine the lazy indifference and timeless atmosphere of the South Seas with a lively vein of comedy to make this film distinctive entertainment.'

Unusual for a writer to win praise from a film reviewer in the 1960s.

My godfather, Horrie Pat, had sold 'Allandale' at Geurie and moved to Port Macquarie on the New South Wales coast north of Sydney, where I continued to visit him. He rang in great excitement, which was untypical of him, to tell me *Age of Consent* was coming to the local cinema. I said I would come up and join him for the opening, my intention being to bring him tickets for himself and his friends. On arrival at the large cinema I introduced myself to the manager, told him I was the editor of the film. 'Oh! Congratulations, but Mr Buckley has already bought every seat in the lounge of the dress circle for tonight, Saturday and Monday.' It was true, the lounge was packed with all his business colleagues, friends and associates. The Port Macquarie cinema was normally on a weekly change of program but Horace Patrick Buckley is credited for the film running three weeks, he was so proud to see my name up on the screen.

Uncle Horace was to bestow upon me his 16mm Bolex camera, so that the journey of the Buckleys on film would continue. Regretfully he was not here to see my other achievements and is buried in Port Macquarie Cemetery. The Bolex, though, continued the tradition.

Columbia's executives in LA nearly went spare at the nude scenes with Helen Mirren. Like the one here, it had to be replaced with a long-distance shot of the scene, making it indistinguishable as to who was playing Cora.

On the film's release in London later in the year, the critics were a typical case of point and counterpoint but it took the doyenne of film critics, Dilys Powell, to put the film truly in perspective.

The *Sunday Times*, 16 November 1969, Dilys wrote: 'A curious thing about the cinema just now. So many nudes, so little of the sensuality which used, occasionally, to inform the well-dressed screen; the nuder the pruder. But then it can take more than a beautiful body to look sensual. It can take an actress. It has Helen Mirren. The screenplay is based by Peter Yeldham on a Norman Lindsay novel. An Australian painter (James Mason) withdraws to the Great Barrier Reef, but presently encounters a wayward thief of a girl who keeps her harridan grandmother in gin by skin diving and crayfish catching. There, then, is the model he needs to revitalise his work … some embarrassing over acting in secondary roles is atoned for by James Mason's decently controlled performance; and Michael Powell shares with us his pleasure in the Australian landscape. But Helen Mirren is the heart of the film. Splendid in nudity, unconscious of its own grace, her very flesh seems to act.'

Regretfully neither the overseas critics nor the audiences were ever to hear Peter Sculthorpe's splendid score, except in Australia. Columbia thought the score too 'sophisticated' for the general audience they saw for the film and chose Stanley Myers to re-score the picture. For the Australian season this was eventually to be a calamity. *Age* ran at the Rapallo from July 1969 to the end of February 1970, a record season of seven months, only to move to 'Nine suburban theatres – exclusive'. These were the halcyon days when you dressed to go to the pictures in town and waited months for a film to reach your local cinema. (Now you would be out on 150 prints and off in three weeks!)

The only problem for *Age* was what was happening to the prints as a result of the long seasons in the capital cities. Projectionists were taking frames of the close-ups of Helen Mirren in the water from the prints, under the pretence of the print having broken and needing re-splicing. This went on to such an extent there was very little of Helen left standing there nude, and Columbia had to order additional reels from the London laboratory to replace the damaged reels that had been printed in Australia. One problem. The score on the imported reels was that of Stanley Myers and the score on the Australian prints was Peter Sculthorpe's. On reel changeovers in the cinema, it became extremely irritating going from one score to another then back again. It must have been heartbreaking for Powell. Worse for him was Columbia's reaction to Paul Delprat's wonderful paintings for the titles. Paul had designed them also as a homage to Norman Lindsay. His first painting is one of Helen Mirren naked, raising her left arm up holding the torch, being the Columbia lady. Columbia was outraged. Thankfully the paintings and Peter Sculthorpe's score were recently restored by Columbia's archivist Grover Crisp in Hollywood, but I digress. Back to Mr Powell:

Nov 21   4 Albermarle St W1

Dear Tony,

I waited to write until the film opened and I could send you a report. The Trade & Press were well attended in spite of a heavy week for the critics with the London Film Festival opening. We got a good press from the trade and from the better papers like *Times* & *Telegraph* … It seems (from returns) to be doing very well in Australia but you are the only person to give me some idea of audience reaction, except Maureen who wrote that people loved the film. I hope it's true. Many people here do and many more will if we work hard. Helen has had a remarkable press and she is safely launched with her work in the theatre to back it up. In eighteen months she ought to be one of the most sought-after of young actresses: and she will be one of the best. She is playing good parts and has at last slimmed down, losing about a stone and looking splendidly strong and lovely. Pamela has cut you out, especially for you, these reviews from the Sunday papers. (I am sending Kevin a set to pass on. It looks as if this is one Australian film that the whole world will like. That is until 'Return of the Boomerang' eclipses it.[1] Stanley Myers' music is sensitive and clever but no better than Peter's. But the dubbing by Hugh Strain (at Warwick Films) was definitely superior to our version … I don't think you need fear about the future of Australian films. You are started now. Canada has made ten films this year & will make ten next year. And they – and I hope Australia – have no intention of copying Hollywood: only of telling their own stories in their own way. I have led the BFA and the Canadians into a Co-production Treaty, the Unions have been persuaded, on both sides, & I expect to see the treaty signed soon. Australia will surely follow. Pity you haven't got a Trudeau at Canberra ---

You will certainly see me next year if you don't come here first! My Love – Michael.'

The above letter is both poignant and historic. It was the beginning of nearly twenty years of regular correspondence between the two of us and the occasional

---

1   *Return of the Boomerang* was the working title of *Adam's Woman*, directed by Phillip Leacock (see Chapter 14)

surprise phone calls enquiring after the welfare of his son Kevin, whom he dearly loved and worried about and to whom I was to become mentor, confidant, advisor, lifelong friend and Michael's spy! Historic and poignant because Michael in his letters revealed himself in a way his autobiography and other biographies don't and can't, and shared his visions and dreams for his future and mine in film, for he always included me. Dreams and visions, sadly, which were never to be realised. I was sceptical on many occasions but went along supporting him with letters of enthusiasm wherever I could. One must remember Michael's career slowed dramatically after The Archers were dissolved and his long partnership with Emeric Pressburger had come to an end.

They're a Weird Mob brought a boost, albeit temporary, to his morale and career. *Age of Consent* revealed a master returning and he knew his next film had to be the winner he was in need of. He pressed on with his ambitious plans for his film of William Shakespeare's *The Tempest*. He was planning it initially to be filmed the same way he made *Black Narcissus*, in the studios with glass plate photography, until he was persuaded to go to Cairo.

A long silence followed. No communication till Kevin Powell rang one night to tell me *The Tempest* had collapsed. His father was stoic. I wrote to him with my commiserations. He was unstoppable.

Jan 24

Dearest Tony,

I met Garlinsky in a pub and he talked of you with great affection. We are planning a film in India 'Taj Mahal',[2] which is nearly halfway to NSW isn't it? It would star Noureyev [sic] as the Prince Shah Jahan. I have sent a synopsis to Kevin. Please cast your eye over it. This is a subject we planned with Korda. His death eclipsed it. Now it is being revived. There seems to be interest & finance. So let's hope it brings better fortune than 'Tempest' …

… Of course the world is mad. But we aren't. NO artist is. Poets are called mad because they are sane …

She [Pamela] sends you her love. So do I. Michael.'

In the next ten years after *Age* I visited London on several occasions, generally associated with a picture I was editing in Australia with post-production in

---

2 *Taj Mahal* was the love story of Shan Jahan and Mumtaz Mahal. Nureyev was to play the Emperor Shan Jahan, Lord of the World. Omar Sharif was to play Rajput Warrior Noble, Chandra Gurta Mauriya and Michael wanted an Indian or Persian as the Princess Mumtaz Mahal, Ornament of the Palace.

England. It was on one of these trips that I was invited home to Avening. I was working for Rudolf Nureyev (Chapter 16) on *Don Quixote* and I had just vacated Rudi's house where the picture was edited, moving the film to Pinewood Studios in preparation for dubbing, when the telephone rang. It was Michael. Why not get away for the weekend, he suggested. It was to be a welcome escape.

I stood at the Pinewood roundabout that Friday afternoon when at great speed a Land Rover hurtled around the corner and screeched to a halt. It was the maestro. 'We're off to Avening and Pamela will look after you.'

It was at Avening in Gloucestershire that I was to get to know the real Michael Powell. A man at peace with the world, surrounded by his marvellous collection of books and his screenplays waiting to be produced, and Pamela Brown, his companion, partner, lover, of many years. Michael was never an easy person to get to know, or to manage at times, but here at Avening, in an environment in which he felt secure, he became a different person. I know it's a cliché to say behind every good man there is a great woman. Well, here at Avening it was proven true, and the woman was Pamela Brown. Before dinner, Pamela and I were told to put our walking boots on for we were about to go for the first of our three walks that weekend. It was a weekend full of talking, listening to his ideas, visions and plans, not to mention enjoying his culinary surprises. Pamela was clearly his backstop and didn't discourage him from talking about his next production-to-be. I didn't raise the subject of *The Tempest* for fear of opening old wounds and in any case I knew Michael didn't live in or dwell on the past. But he was keen to talk about *Taj Mahal* and how to work with Nureyev. There was much to talk about, and Pamela and Michael roared their heads off at some of the anecdotes I had to relate.

The next time we would see each other would be on the set of *Caddie* (Chapter 18), a sad period for Michael as Pamela by this time had contracted cancer and he was called back to London. I was to learn of her death not long after.

Oct 5   Lee Cottages, Avening

Dear Tony – Thank you for your sympathy and for going with me to Beach Road that night. Pamela died peacefully and almost unknowingly just after midnight of Thursday of that week. She had a long and gallant struggle against arthritis and diabetes, complicated by cancer at last, but she was lovely and funny to the very end and we were so close during the past year that we were like one person. She taught me what love really is. All the time she was in hospital & after hospital I wrote every morning – she made me write 1000 words a day – then I would fill a basket of soups and pâtés and ice creams and coffee (hospital food is as bad in England as genius can make it), pile Johnnie[3] into the Rover, drive over to Gloucester and spend the rest of the day in and out of her room, always reading her what I had written. She never criticised, just asked questions, sometimes praised, sometimes said, 'Go and write what happens next'. But she was the most wonderful audience and I always knew when I had gone wrong. Although she was racked with pain in all her joints, covered in bed-sores from losing so much weight, she kept control of everything and everybody. She came home because she wanted to be there and we got a personal nurse to live in and look after her, a dear little Welsh girl whom Pamela took to at once. We agreed together to accept the Sydney invitation because of seeing Kevin, and the doctor approved it, but apparently as soon as I had left she started to go. We knew, I suppose, that all the year she had been slowly fading away but week after week went by with no special crisis and even the doctors were talking of another minor op. in November and planning how long she would need the nurse. Within a week of coming home – and how glad she was to be home – she was dead. She's buried in Avening churchyard not 300 yards from her cottage, which she loved. She always said it was the only real home she ever had. By flying back on Sunday I was able to arrange everything with her mother and sister (that's all she had and she kept them at arm's length) and the funeral was on Wednesday. Johnnie came to it and was very good. It's a beautiful place. I was very sorry not to see more of you and your production. I shall get the book from the library. I wish you and Australia the very best of luck with it, because it's important. There was a good feel about your unit at work. You can't mistake it when it's there … Dear Tony, I'll send you something to remember Pamela by, as soon as I can think and sleep again. My love, Micky.'

It was to be the first time he had signed himself 'Micky', which is how he was known to all his peers and his family. Three weeks later another letter arrived.

Oct 24   Lee Cottages, Avening

Dear Tony – Kevin tells me your first cut is about three hours. Perfect! So far I can't bear to touch or change anything. Luckily I'm having to be busy … (*At this point he went on to describe his plans for another three films, one to star Dustin*

---

3   Johnnie, sometimes called Johnson, was Michael's dog.

Hoffman & Claudia Cardinale which would have been very intriguing, then back to Pamela) The autumn was always Pamela's favourite time of the year and this year the leaves are wonderful. I have just put a huge bunch of every colour on her grave. It's a comfort that she is buried here and I don't find it morbid to go down with Johnnie & have little talks. Particularly as Johnson always interrupts them. Yesterday he sat on the piece of heather I had planted and flattened it. But every so often it comes over you and then there's nothing to do, but think of her lovely, funny, kind way of living with a very difficult man.

My love and the best of luck with the fine cut - Micky

And finally –

Feb 2   Lee Cottages, Avening

Dear Tony – Thank you for your lovely letter and news of your lovely lady 107 minutes old. Ladies can kill but it's more permanent when they have charm & a sense of humour, vide Greta Garbo. She lasts! And so I hope with Caddie…

On my occasional visits to London after *Caddie*, Michael would always take me to his favourite club, the Saville, for dinner and/or drinks. One evening he rang the hotel to tell me we were going to the theatre to see *The Day After The Fair* which I knew was starring Deborah Kerr, playing in a theatre on Shaftesbury Avenue. Michael had had a long association with Kerr since he and Emeric cast her in *The Life and Death of Colonel Blimp* in 1943.[4] Her triumph was in my favourite of all Michael's films, *Black Narcissus*. He had obtained the best house seats in the centre front row of the mezzanine. I was captivated and once again awestruck at the privilege of seeing such a fine actress performing, I felt, just for us. Michael had leant forward resting his chin on his hands and stayed in this position through the entire performance. We repaired for our pre-ordered gin and tonic at interval. He looked at me and said, 'Isn't she splendid?' I discreetly asked if we would be going backstage at the end of the performance. 'No, Tony, the past is the past.' I studied his face during the second half of the play and I could sense all his memories rushing back.

Michael was to go to America and work in residence with Francis Ford Coppola and Martin Scorsese, about which much has been written elsewhere. These working relationships brought new life and vigour to Michael and he was

---

4   Powell had cast Kerr three years beforehand as a cigarette girl in *Contraband* but her only scene was deleted in editing.

Pamela Brown and Michael Powell at home at Avening, Gloucestershire. I took this photo on Michael's camera and he later sent the snap to his son Kevin.

to meet Thelma Schoonmaker, Martin Scorsese's film editor. They fell in love and married to begin a full life together. Thelma came along at exactly the right time. America was discovering Michael Powell's films for the first time and their revival was taking him across the States, lecturing and presenting some of his greats – *A Matter of Life and Death* – *Colonel Blimp* – *The Red Shoes* – *Peeping Tom*. Michael once said to me that *Peeping Tom* was his favourite film. He screened it to a somewhat stunned crew at the mix of *Age of Consent*. He sat on the console of the mixing desk and I watched his expressions throughout the screening. Michael was having a wonderfully wicked time.

When David Puttnam arrived at Columbia, Michael rang me one night to tell me the good news that David was going to reinstate Peter Sculthorpe's original score for *Age of Consent*, but where was the music? I had kept the original quarter-inch tapes of the score that Ron Purvis had given me for safekeeping. I despatched them immediately to Thelma but before she could start work on reassembling the score, Puttnam was sacked from Columbia.[5] Throughout 1989 I knew Michael's health was not the best. Nonetheless in typical fashion he soldiered on and was finally honoured at London's National Film Theatre with a retrospective – a

---

5   At the beginning of 2004 an archivist at Columbia found the original answer print of *Age of Consent* that had been despatched from Australia with the Sculthorpe score. Restoration has now taken place.

salute from a country that never really recognised him. His health began to fail before Christmas and he wanted to go home – home to Avening. Martin Scorsese suggested to Warners that it might be nice if they could provide their company jet to send Michael home. They did so generously and graciously, and two weeks later Michael Powell flew home to Avening.

I'm not convinced Michael will ever rest in peace – he has too much still to think about – too many films still to be made – and I'm sure he is up there to remind we filmmakers to be true to ourselves and our own cultures. Michael Powell wasn't just a great British filmmaker, he WAS British film and Avening will become the shrine to British cinema and perhaps its greatest son.

13

'The Locomotive That Drives Everything Else'[1]

'Through the exciting seventies and at the end of them, I hope there will be established here a film industry, not yet as great as those in other countries, but so great that its ultimate greatness cannot be denied and cannot be prevented. And if this does come about, then this will be one of the most delightful things for me personally because I will feel that I have had some part in it and I will feel it is a thing worth having done.'

Prime Minister John Gorton

Robert Gordon Menzies, former Prime Minister before John Gorton,[2] would turn in his grave to hear Gorton's words now. Menzies could never see the need for an Australian film industry, for we didn't, in his opinion, have the actors or the talent, and why was there the need when we had the best of British and American pictures to see and experience the performances of the visiting Royal Shakespeare Company or Britain's National Theatre. (This was the arch-monarchist who wanted our decimal currency called the Royals!) Worse, Menzies' Postmaster General opined before the House in 1964: ' I do not think we have many good script writers in Australia ... we have not many good actors in Australia ... we haven't producers and we haven't directors of high quality at present.'

Prime Minister Gorton's statement, made at the annual presentation of the Australian Film Institute Awards in Canberra on December 2, 1969, came like a breath of fresh air after the stultifying years of the Menzies regime. It was to blow a gale when Whitlam became Prime Minister in 1972. Gorton's announcement

---

1   Chapter heading, a quotation from producer, director and reviewer of the time, and long-time friend, Michael Thornhill.
2   Harold Holt succeeded Menzies and later drowned attempting to swim in wild seas. Gorton then became Prime Minister.

was an historic occasion for us all, for it was the first time an Australian prime minister acknowledged the existence of an Australian film industry. The Prime Minister promised the establishment of a National Film & Television Development Corporation, the setting up of an Experimental Film Fund and the appointment of an interim Council to plan the establishment of a National Film & Television School.

All of this had not happened overnight. It was the result of several years of activism by filmmakers and writers that began in Melbourne and Sydney in the 1960s. The agitation gathered momentum when debate on the Vincent Report into the industry was abandoned. The Vincent Committee had been established to inquire into the Australian film and television industry but was seen by many as a 'token gesture' to quieten the dissidents. Not so the relatively conservative Film Editors Guild of Australia (FEGA), of which I was a member, who published a report, 'The Conspiracy of Silence', claiming the press as a whole had ignored reporting the committee's findings because of its corporate links with the television network proprietors. FEGA's paper created quite a stir within parliament and was strongly supported by the Australian Writers Guild and Actors and Announcers Equity, as it was then called. These stirrings finally led to the establishment of the Australian Film Council[3] in 1968 by Roland Beckett and myself, to bring together an extraordinary group of eclectic and disparate unions, guilds and associations who worked harmoniously together for nearly ten years fighting for the same cause. Regretfully this has never been repeated. Roland and I were both members of the PDGA, the Producers & Directors Guild of Australia, and we both felt the only way to succeed in influencing government was to speak as one voice.

The activists who dominated the scene were many but primarily it was filmmaker Cecil Holmes and writers Sylvia Lawson and Colin Bennett, the film reviewer of *The Age*, and film reviewer/filmmaker Michael Thornhill of *The Australian* who argued vigorously through their writings in various papers and periodicals for the local film industry. The ranks swelled in Melbourne, led by Tim Burstall and John B. Murray, and in Sydney by Tom Jeffrey and Roland Beckett.

In Melbourne, advertising guru and, later, sometimes film producer Phillip Adams, teamed up with popular quiz show contestant and historian Barry Jones

---

3   Members of the Australian Film Council: Actors & Announcers Equity Association of Australia, A.B.C. Senior Officers Association, A.B.C. Staff Association, Australian Cinematographers Society, Australian Film Institute, Australian Film Producers Association, Australian Motion Picture Studios Association, Australian Society of Authors, Australian Theatrical & Amusement Employees Association, Australian Writers Guild, Film Editors Guild of Australia, Feature Film Producers Association, Institute of Motion Picture Technology, Musicians Union of Australia, National Film Theatre of Australia, National Institute of Dramatic Art, Producers and Directors Guild of N.S.W., Sydney Film Festival.

to use their political clout in the issue. Though Jones was a staunch but sometimes dissident member of the Victorian State Labor Party, he was also a close friend of John Gorton. Both icons brought considerable influence to bear on the Prime Minister. Though Harold Holt had established the Australian Council for the Arts, Gorton was to go a lot further with the establishment of the Australian Film Development Corporation and the Experimental Film Fund to be administered, through the Council, by the Australian Film Institute. The Interim Committee to investigate the formation of a National Film & Television School was announced. Peter Coleman, NSW Liberal politician, was appointed chair.

The Australian Film Council became active on the issue of having an apprenticeship scheme incorporated in the establishment of the Film School's charter, but this was not in favour with the committee or John Martin-Jones, who had been appointed to oversee the establishment of the School. As a practising producer; to me this is still a grave oversight in 2009.

The Australian Film Development Corporation, under the chairmanship of merchant banker John Darling, opened for business in March 1971 with Tom Stacey appointed as managing director. In the same month, a vote of no confidence in the Prime Minister John Gorton resulted in a tied vote and, holding the casting vote, he voted himself out of office, leaving the country with Billy McMahon as a regretfully inadequate Prime Minister. Gorton's resignation caused considerable disquiet within the industry for it was feared his initiatives would be shelved. There was a threat that plans for the Film School would be abandoned and Phillip Adams resigned from the Interim Council. From the parliamentary backbench, Gorton spoke out. He urged the Parliament to accept the recommendations of the School's Interim Council 'instead of rushing around in circles seeking some way to evade them'. He was spot on.

The Tariff Board Inquiry commenced in September 1972 and concluded just days after the election of the Whitlam Labor Government in December 1972.

The winds of change were to become a cyclone.

Whitlam's government established the Department of Media to encompass the AFDC, the ABC and the Commonwealth Film Unit, with Senator Doug McClelland as Minister. It was McClelland who urged parliamentarians to see *Forgotten Cinema* and 'hang their heads in shame for what had not been done for Australian cinema', before being brought to order by the Speaker.

The Tariff Board report was tabled in Parliament on June 30, 1973. However, a visit to Australia by the President of the Motion Picture Association of America, Jack Valenti (no friend to any nation's film industry) in February had brought the industry onto the streets in protest and was to eventually bring the Minister unstuck. Tom Jeffrey had quickly formed FIAC, the Film Industry Action Committee, to organise the protest. McClelland was taken aback at the ferocity of the demonstration, led by director Peter Weir, actors Kate Fitzpatrick, Graeme Bond and over 200 others. Even Ken Hall was spotted lost in the crowd at one stage. Police had to be called to control the crowd overflowing onto the roadway outside the Chevron Hotel in Kings Cross.

McClelland hosted a luncheon next day for Valenti and though the Minister said all the right things about 'concerns about foreign ownership' it was clear some months later, as the Tariff Board's recommendations for the establishment of a solidly based film industry were slowly being whittled away, that Valenti's visit had been sinisterly effective. The only survivor of the recommendations was the scrapping of the Australian Film Development Corporation, which had become extremely controversial, to be replaced with the Australian Film Commission, but it wasn't till April 1975 that the AFC became a reality.

The industry by now distrusted McClelland because of his cosy relationship with Valenti which was made worse when *The Australian* newspaper published on their front page a letter McClelland had written to Valenti inviting him to nominate names for the board of the new Commission. All hell broke loose. My phone rang. 'Could I talk to Tony Buckley please, I have the Minister here?' 'Which Minister?' I enquired, wondering what on earth a church was ringing me for. 'No, no,' said the caller, 'Doug McClelland wishes to speak to you.' 'Fine.' McClelland came on the line and asked me would I go on the board of the Australian Film Commission. I said I was flattered and asked how long I had to reach a decision. 'Oh, Tony, I need to know now as I'm about to go into the Cabinet room.' Obviously he detected I was somewhat startled so I immediately said 'yes'. Sure enough, only four hours later the press release was issued in time for the late afternoon and early evening newspapers.

It seems Whitlam was furious with the publication of the letter to Valenti and all names submitted to recommend to Cabinet had been scrapped by the Prime Minister.

With my career as a film editor and my appointment to the AFC Board, I had to stand down as vice-president and secretary of the Australian Film Council. The Council was heavily time-consuming but completely rewarding and worthwhile, a great initiative that perhaps should be revitalised and reactivated today.

14

Mercer Clips And Hollywood

I was fortunate in my early career to have such great mentors – Ken Hall at Cinesound, Fergus McDonell in Canada and Michael Powell. My next mentor was to be one of a different kind, a genuine Hollywood producer. Louis F. Edelman had arrived to produce a film entitled *Return of the Boomerang* (until about two months before its release when the title was changed to *Adam's Woman*). The first thing I learnt was that this was a producer's film and not a director's picture, a fact that intrigued me throughout the production. The director was purely a gun for hire and left the picture upon completion of filming.

Edelman was of the old school. Already in his late sixties, he was elegant in his attire, gracious in demeanour and manners, quietly spoken and extremely knowledgeable. The true professional. We were to get on well. He was curious about my interest in the history of cinema but for me he was history of cinema himself, well, at least Hollywood history. I had been a collector of Busby Berkeley soundtracks since I had started work and to discover I was going to be working for the man who had produced Berkeley, Dick Powell and Ruby Keeler was unbelievable. Louis F. Edelman, sometimes credited Lou Edelman and sometimes not credited at all, was born in New York on 18 May 1900. It was Irving Thalberg who gave Edelman his first job in production at Metro. Later he moved to Warners as a script editor and script doctor. His first credit was for *Shipmates* in 1931 and later in 1934 he shared the writer's credit for *Flirtation Walk* with Delmar Davies. Directed by Frank Borzage with Dick Powell, Ruby Keeler and Pat O'Brien, it was nominated for an Oscar for Best Picture. (Capra's *It Happened One Night* with Gable and Colbert took the Oscar.) Between 1935 and 1939 he produced and acted as an associate producer on sixteen films, mainly solid studio potboilers with strong casts. On most of these he went uncredited.

However, Edelman's greatest film was unquestionably *White Heat* (1949) directed by Raoul Walsh, starring James Cagney, Edmond O'Brien and Virginia Mayo. Through the early 1950s he worked with some great directors – Michael Curtiz, Andre de Toth, Roy del Ruth – and some great actors, among them James Cagney, Gary Cooper, Doris Day, Gordon Macrae, Broderick Crawford and Claire Trevor. The films themselves were respectable but unmemorable.

When Edelman moved on to television he quickly established himself in the new medium with the highly successful series *The Life and Legend of Wyatt Earp*. He had just acquired ownership of *Wyatt Earp* after the rights period of sixteen years had lapsed and reverted to him. Louis encouraged me to think about becoming a producer. 'But Tony, remember to have the rights in your work revert to you and own it, it's the only way to survive.' Subsequently Louis Edelman lived off the income from licensing repeats of *Wyatt Earp* to syndicated television for many years, enabling him to fund and develop projects of his own.

Looking at his impressive body of work, I could not help but be totally perplexed as to why he had chosen *Adam's Woman* for what was going to be his last major work for Warners. The script by Richard Fielder, based on a story by Lowell Barrington, was not very exciting, and the choice of Phillip Leacock as director was even more perplexing. Whether he felt the same about the script as I did, I'll never know, but the direction was lacklustre despite the scale of the production. Filmed in Panavision, it was only the third film to be shot in the anamorphic[1] process in Australia. The first had been *Long John Silver*[2] in Cinemascope in 1954, only one year after Cinemascope had been launched by 20th Century Fox into Hoyts cinemas, and *Smiley* in 1958.

Edelman had secured a 'negative pick up' for the film from Warner Bros. This means that the film is made for $2.5 million, for which Warners pay $3 million on delivery of the finished film, giving the producer a profit of $500,000. Louis Edelman kept a very tight rein on the budget. Set in Australia in the 1840s it was a mish-mash of colonial history and based on some local historic figures. Beau Bridges, youngest of the Bridges family of actors, quite unconvincingly played an American convict, Adam Beecher, wrongfully transported to the colony, Jane

---

1   Anamorphic, which applies to both Panavision ® and Cinemascope ® is the camera lens process where the image is squeezed onto the 35mm frame and unsqueezed in projection to give an image wider than the standard widescreen format.

2   The negative for *Long John Silver* was processed overseas and a black and white dupe neg was sent back to Australia to Automatic Film Laboratories where I would print the rushes for the editor's cut. It was also being filmed as a 26-part television series. As a feature it failed in the U.S. and to try and recover some of their investment, the producers edited episodes of the TV series into two 'B' features *Under the Black Flag* and *South Sea Pirates*. I think they would be rather fun to see now.

Merrow played a fiery Irish woman, Bess – Adam's woman. The casting of the principal supporting roles was strong but couldn't save the film. From the UK and Ireland came John Mills, James Booth and Andrew Keir. Local actors, headed by Peter O'Shaughnessy, Clarissa Kaye, Doreen Warburton, Peter Collingwood, Harry Lawrence, Harold Hopkins, Katy Wild and Mark McManus; all acquitted themselves with fine performances.

The town built for the film near the banks of the Shoalhaven River at Nowra, southern New South Wales, was a splendid piece of production design by local art designer Dennis Gentle (*Age of Consent*). It was the first time I had seen the practice of 'special effects' which I used to think was done on an optical printer. Special effects expert Milton Rice was brought from the States with a hundred or so pipes with which he lined the banks of the set, connected the gas, and on cue from the director, the flames would exit the doors and windows, and on 'cut' the flames would be 'switched off'. Except on one of the many repeated takes, on 'cut' the town continued to burn and off-screen standby hoses had to suddenly be brought into play. It was on these all-too-rare occasions that the rushes of the 'out' takes were more entertaining than the 'okay' takes.

The cut was finally locked off and despatched to Hollywood where Lou presented the picture to the executives at Warners. It was too long, they said. Recut. Usually at this point another editor would be brought in but Lou insisted that I be brought over to do the recut under his supervision. I had found the whole editing experience rather weird. Phillip Leacock returned to America immediately the shoot had been completed, when the producer took over. I later received a note from him wishing me the best with the picture and never heard from him again. I doubt if he ever saw the finished film.

My travels around the world had been by liner, cargo ships and trains, but I had never been on an aeroplane. The day of my departure was the day Neil Armstrong landed on the moon, which was being televised live as I waited for the taxi to take me to the airport. In 1969 Sydney's Kingsford Smith International Airport was primitive by anybody's standards. From terminal buildings built of weatherboard, one walked out onto the tarmac to join the waiting plane. Mine was a Boeing 707 sporting its Pan American livery. I was directed to the forward staircase, for I was being flown first class. It was a style of travelling to which I quickly adapted, but not to be repeated for many years! The plane flew via Pago Pago and Honolulu to Los Angeles. I think it took all of twenty-four hours.

Though I thought the cutting rooms at Warners would be super swish and equipped with everything, I still took the precaution of packing my own utensils – grease pencils, scissors, all the paraphernalia of the cutting room, including a couple of boxes of mercer clips. When editing, one (used to) run the strip of picture through a synchroniser which sat in front of you on the cutting room bench with the separate soundtrack running beside it. As the film is not yet spliced, it was clipped together in frame by four-pronged fibre clips, the prongs of which fit the sprocket holes in the film snugly, enabling the film to continue its way through the synchroniser. I was told the clip was designed by a Mr Mercer, but I didn't realise it was an Australian invention.

In Canada and the UK they used ordinary paper clips, having to remove them at every scene change or cut to feed the film through the synchroniser, then re-clip it on the other side of the machine. The mercer clip eliminated all of this bother. I could never understand why it was never used overseas.

For a filmmaker, no matter what one's age, looking across at the vast sound stages at Warner Bros' studios at Burbank, California, for the first time must be something like an archaeologist discovering a lost city in the jungle. It still impresses me when I visit.

Not so the cutting rooms, however. Austerity was the key. A bare room, with a bench, a synchroniser, a chair, a Moviola and a bowl of paper clips! The American editors in the same block in which I was housed were fascinated by my mercer clips. They would come into my room and politely stand and watch, as I would wind the film through the synchroniser without a hitch. They really could not understand why they were not using this remarkable invention. It wasn't long before the marvellous Italian hand tape splicers were to be introduced and quickly adopted by every editor in the world, relegating cement splicing to history. Not so for the neg cutters, for them the editor's tape splicing was the bane of their lives. The editors would forget to skip two frames at the head and tail of each shot, which is what the neg cutter needs when cement splicing the negative, which in effect becomes a weld. This practice continues today although some films are now graded onto tape or hard drive and retransferred to celluloid for projection screening.

The recut and deletions only took two days so associate producer Art Brodie took me under his wing for that week to show me the inner workings of Hollywood and the Playboy Club! At Lou and Rita Edelman's house in Beverly Hills I gazed in awe at the contents of his study. There on crowded shelves were all the scripts of the films he had produced, superbly leather-bound with gold embossed lettering. The room was a complete treasure trove of Hollywood history.

Adam's Woman was given a world premiere at the Center Cinema in Canberra on March 19, 1970, followed by a respectable season at Sydney's palatial State

(Top) Louis Edelman's production of *Adam's Woman* was grand in scale but soft on plot line. Adam (Beau Bridges) has been transported to Australia by mistake and placed in a chain gang of convicts.

(Bottom left) Adam's Woman was played by Jane Merrow.

(Bottom right) The Governor was played by John Mills, here with Beau Bridges.

Theatre. The film had only a modest release overseas, most people seeing it much later on aeroplanes with the new-fangled device called 'inflight movies'.

Lou never revealed whether he was disappointed in *Adam's Woman* or not, but he was sure about one thing, he wanted to make Australian movies. I introduced him to Alan Seymour's play, *The One Day of the Year*, for which I had taken an option to make a feature film, and film reviewer/film editor Michael Thornhill had written the screenplay. Lou was quite taken with it and made some suggestions for strengthening the script even more, which I think Michael took on board. However, Lou could not get away from the idea one had to have at least one American lead. There were months of Sunday morning phone calls from him in LA (Saturday afternoon their time) to me in my home at Clifton Gardens, about getting the film off the ground.

I had moved to Clifton Gardens, a suburb overlooking the harbour adjacent to Sydney's Taronga Park Zoo, after my father had decided to move to the NSW Central Coast, to live with his de facto, to whom I could never relate at all. Reflecting on the ten years I spent in my two-storey 'maisonette', part of a large Federation style house, this was a very happy period in my life, personally and professionally. Dinner parties were a regular occurrence and one didn't have to look for an excuse to host them.

I had protested to Lou from the outset that any American actor in *The One Day of the Year* would be seen as ridiculous and laughed off the screen. He finally came to terms with this decision but then it all became too hard for him to comprehend an Australian film with only an Australian cast. It was clear to me that the film was just not going to happen. This was before script development funding and government supported production funding became a reality in the re-establishment of an Australian cinema. Michael Thornhill had done a superb and powerful adaptation of Alan's play, which Michael was to direct, but he had to wait till 1974 before he was to direct his first feature film, *Between Wars* with Corin Redgrave. It is still a much underrated Australian film, though a critically well-received film at the time here and in London.

The Sunday morning phone calls between Lou Edelman and me became fewer and eventually I didn't hear again, till I received a message from Rita that he had died on January 6 of a heart ailment. It was 1976, a defining year for my career. Rita died on November 3, 2000, aged ninety.

Reg Goldsworthy was a radio announcer and producer who decided to move into movies in late 1967. With American partners Commonwealth United Corporation, he formed Goldsworthy Productions to make three low budget 'quickies' for $300,000 each, with Eddie Davis, a former second unit director, who by the time he arrived in Australia had become an aged American television director. The films were *It Takes All Kinds, Color Me Dead* and *That Lady from Peking*. Only *Color Me Dead*, an inferior remake of *DOA*, the thriller directed by Rudolf Maté in 1950, obtained a release in the States. Primarily made for the new American colour TV services, the three films were subsequently released in Australia to derogatory and derisive reviews and remarkably short runs. I had won the task of editing *That Lady from Peking* (originally *The Girl from Peking*) as soon as I had returned from *Adam's Woman* at Warners.

Eddie Davis was a pleasant enough man but had a complete distrust of film editors, obviously through some very bad experiences. When I arrived at the Film Academy studios in Mitchell Street, North Sydney, I found 65,000 feet of rushes (very economical shooting), which had been put in scene order and not slate order, ready to screen. Eddie would not allow assembly of his film whilst he was shooting, such was his distrust of editors. Over the week I viewed all the rushes with Eddie and dutifully took notes. The coverage was so basic there was nothing in the footage to challenge an editor. I took my leave and told him I would have the first reels within a few days.

'That lady' was Nancy Kwan, who had risen to temporary stardom in *The World of Susie Wong* in 1960 for Ray Stark and Paramount. It had obviously been a long time between drinks for Miss Kwan to arrive in Australia in 1969 to play the role of Sue Tan Chan, who in fact was not the principal character despite her star billing, shared by Carl Betz and Bobby Rydell. It didn't take long to have two complete reels ready to show Mr Davis. He seemed to be dumbfounded at first, saying nothing. Then he turned to me and said, 'Well, son, you are sure some smart editor – just continue and finish the picture,' which over the next four weeks I did.

Davis was very appreciative of my work and said he hoped I would do all his pictures in the future. The thought horrified me, a budding career dashed by B pictures. Fortunately there were to be no more Davis quickies and Reg Goldsworthy soon folded the company. *That Lady from Peking* was lucky to get a release as a support but not until 1975 at the Village Twin in Brisbane! It would be a curiosity to see today for it had the most eclectic local supporting cast which included Don Reid, Owen Weingott, Sandy Gore, Graham Rouse, Kevin Goldsby, Penny Sugg, Robert Bruning, Ruth Cracknell, Jack Thompson and Tom Oliver. Now here's a thought: *Adam's Woman* and *That Lady From Peking* as a double bill in revival. They could become late night cult classics.

The Ajax Film Centre at Bondi had a very busy schedule. Whilst I had been editing *Age of Consent* and *Adam's Woman*, Stan Moore, my mentor at Cinesound and Southern International, had moved from Ajax's Neutral Bay studio to take over as Film Centre's manager. The studio serviced the Goldsworthy pictures, *Age* and *Adam's Woman* with crew, facilities and equipment. Stan also was editing *Squeeze a Flower* and in the cutting room next to mine Englishman Charles Rees was cutting Tony Richardson's *Ned Kelly*.

Despite all this industrious activity, we were making only hybrid, pseudo-Australian films, none of them true to themselves. Even in Michael Powell's brave attempts – *They're a Weird Mob* and *Age of Consent* – the Australian characters portrayed were still caricatures. All this was about to change with the arrival in Australia of a Canadian director to make what is arguably still the best film yet made in our country.

15

Le Reveil Dans La Terreur
– Wake In Fright

A more unlikely pair to be associated with what has become an Australian classic you could not imagine. Jack Neary, a savvy, suave, shrewd and perfectly down to earth theatrical entrepreneur and manager. A gentleman of show business. Bobby Limb, a vaudevillian entertainer, a true showman, who with his show business wife, Dawn Lake, was to create for Ken Hall one of Channel Nine's longest running and most successful live entertainment shows, *The Sound of Music*.[1] Jack and Bobby had formed a television production company, NLT (Neary Limb Tinker) to supply television programs to the networks. They became involved with an Australian business tycoon, Sir Reginald Ansett, who had taken over ANA (Australian National Airlines) to become Ansett-ANA. The trio subsequently engaged Motion Picture Investments, a company headed by Sir Reg, to invest heavily with Group W, a division of Westinghouse Broadcasting, to make ten feature films, the first of which was *Squeeze a Flower*, directed by Marc Daniells.

I have not been able to establish how Kenneth Cook's 1961 novel *Wake in Fright* was chosen for their second film, except the book had been optioned for a film more than once. In 1963, Joseph Losey optioned the book for a film to be made starring Dirk Bogarde. Nothing became of this proposal and Morris West optioned the rights for a film to be produced by himself. Once again, nothing happened with this venture and Morris West, who had acquired his option cheaply, then onsold the option and rights (while still under option) to NLT for a much larger sum, with West making a handsome profit on the exercising of the option. Ken Cook always felt very bitter about this, and felt he had been ripped off. NLT had acquired the rights in association with TV producer Bill Harmon, and Howard Barnes and Maurice

---

1   This was before the Robert Wise 20th Century Fox movie with Julie Andrews.

Singer representing Group W's interests. British producer George Willoughby was brought in to physically produce, and Ted Kotcheff chosen to direct the picture.

Evan Jones, a Jamaican who emigrated to London, was chosen by Ted to adapt Cook's novel. Evan had written Ted's very interesting film, *Two Gentlemen Sharing*. In fact, the structure of the two films is very similar. The West Indian dance sequence in *Two Gentlemen Sharing* is the two-up game in *Wake in Fright* and the party in *TGS* is the kangaroo hunt in *WIF*. In an earlier version of the script, the kangaroo hunt (about which there was and still is much controversy) had become a pig hunt. It was only after Ted Kotcheff had been on his first survey for locations in and around Broken Hill, in western New South Wales, that the kangaroo hunt was reinstated. Producer George Willoughby was horrified by the decision. Ted was fascinated with what he saw in his survey of Broken Hill. A tough and very closed union-controlled town. Every night of the week, men go out to shoot the kangaroos, generally after much drinking. Ted was adamant this had to be in the film if the film was to be a true depiction of life in the 'Outback', the sort of life not featured in John Heyer's *The Back of Beyond*! Cinematographer John McLean was engaged to film actual hunts over a series of nights with his Arriflex camera. John was to be engaged as camera operator for the film. The survey was before Christmas and this, too, fascinated Ted. Santa Claus, silver tinsel hanging from the shops and public buildings, when it was 100° in the shade. The height of the Australian summer. Another facet of the country's culture caught Ted's eye. The nine o'clock ritual at the RSL (Returned Servicemen's League). Each evening at nine the lights are dimmed and everyone, no matter whether they are dining or playing the poker machines (slot machines), stands to attention whilst the Last Post is played to remember those fallen in the wars. Then, after a minute's silence, the lights are brightened again and the evening routine continues. All of these observations were conveyed back to Evan Jones in London. (Evan wasn't to visit Australia till the 1980s.) How Evan so brilliantly captured and adapted Ted's observations without visiting the country he was writing about has always intrigued me.

Wake in Fright attracted the attention of the press, as had Nicholas Roeg's *Walkabout* only a few months before. It was also something of an experience for Broken Hill. *Mad Max* was still some ten years away. The production company was fully aware the town was totally union-controlled. All members of the crew were made temporary members of the local union by the company and on the quarterly Button Day, when all the workers of the town proudly wore their union button, the crew did likewise.[2]

2   Jane Perlez: 'Button Day in Broken Hill is a serious matter. A pastry cook in one of the 36 hotels (for a 30,000 population) refused to start work until another cook put her button on. Having it in her handbag

Initially I thought Gary Bond was a strange choice to play the Australian teacher. John Hargreaves, a rising young Australian star, had always been considered for the role and would have been splendid, but the producers wanted someone they thought was a rising English star. I asked George Willoughby, our producer, one day, why Bond had been chosen. 'Oh, don't you realise Tony, Gary is the new Peter O'Toole.' What a peculiar way of casting, I thought! Nonetheless, Gary Bond works in the role but was destined to become a star of the West End and virtually disappear from the silver screen. So much for being the next O'Toole. The last time I saw him was backstage after a performance of *Joseph and the Amazing Technicolor Dream Coat*. Gary had built up a huge fan club by his performances in the West End theatre. Sadly he was to die from an AIDS-related infection at the peak of his theatrical career.

I became very good friends with Bill Harmon, one of the producers of the picture for NLT, an American who had come to Australia in the 1960s and for whom I was later to edit some of his ambitiously produced movies for television. In this field Bill was very much a pioneer of what was to become the 'telemovie' concept. Much later he was to become very well known with the (then) salacious and titillating series, *No 96*. Bill spent a lot of time on location in Broken Hill and was very enthusiastic about the film's international chances. 'This is going to be the biggest picture ever made in Australia,' he told Jane Perlez of *The Australian*. 'This picture is more in the modern genre and I just hope it will make people aware of the kangaroos and stop all the brutality.'

Brutality is an understatement. The footage shot by John McLean on that survey was brutal and uncompromisingly disturbing in the extreme. I was ever thankful it was only a black and white 'work print' (cutting copy) to work from, though the negative of course was shot on Eastmancolor stock. I don't think I could have looked at the work print if it had been printed in colour. The survey was very helpful to Ted Kotcheff in finalising the shooting script and story boarding the kangaroo hunt, for I was to use a lot of the actual survey footage of the hunt in the editing of the 'staged' hunt, which was filmed by the location main unit much later. Though Powell and Edelman had insisted on colour cutting copy, George Willoughby came from what I call the 'mean' school of producers and wanted to save as many pennies as he could, hence we only ever saw black and white rushes and had black and white footage to edit. I thought this made it extremely difficult for the director of photography (DOP) to assess his work, as well as for the art

wasn't good enough.' To further public relations with the Barrier Industrial Council, Kotcheff had its president play the trumpet in the classic RSL scene in the film.

director[3] to assess his craft. It was Brian West, the British cinematographer who, on landing in Australia, looked up at the blue sky, back down to the ground, and declared Australia was 'one stop over-exposed'.

───────

Ted Kotcheff[4]: 'Last night, jotting a few notes, my wife peered into the room. Saw a perplexed face or what she imagined to be. Said, 'Why don't you just stand up and say to those editors: "to edit a film, choose the best bits and put them together", and sit down and screen your film.' '

If only it was this easy!

Kotcheff[5]: 'In a Bach fugue – each chord is superb – but each chord contains harmonic tensions which demanding musical resolution, lead to a new chord and when all the chords are put together there is created a running counterpoint. **So it is the editor's and director's job to go through the material, find the beat chords and find the right order to release their contrapuntal energy:-** or as my wife said, 'A cut should be unforeseen & unexpected yet inevitable. Nothing I dislike more than the predictable – you know 2 people in L.S.[6] walk toward camera.'

I have received continuing praise over the years from film critics and peers for my editing of *Wake in Fright*. Yet it was a total and exhilarating, collaborative experience between Ted and myself. Though there were occasions where I would have gladly throttled him (and no doubt likewise) both of us were guided by Evan Jones' script. Flashbacks seen in the picture as extremely short cuts were there on the page, carefully scripted.

Towards the end of the film, there is a homoerotic scene between the alcoholic Doc Tydon (Donald Pleasence) and John Grant (Gary Bond) where Tydon advances towards Grant attempting to pour beer down his throat, intercut with a swinging bulb in a light shade coming backwards and forwards towards camera, until it freeze frames at the point of Tydon's or Grant's ejaculation (or both) and cuts to black. Every cut of the swinging light is superbly scripted by Evan Jones.

The two most challenging scenes in *Wake in Fright* are the two-up game in the first act and the kangaroo hunt in the second act which takes up the best part of a complete reel. Both took weeks to achieve the final cut of each sequence, the two-up

---

3   The title 'production designer' was not used then. It's still not used by the Academy of Motion Picture Sciences at their Academy Awards, favouring 'art direction'.

4   Ted Kotcheff quoting Sylvia Kay from his lecture on editing to the Film Editors Guild of Australia (FEGA) delivered whilst we were editing the film.

5   From Ted Kotcheff's notes to his FEGA talk.

6   L.S. script abbreviation for a long distance shot.

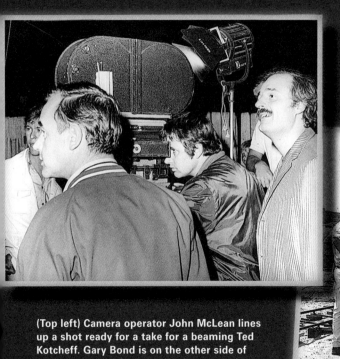

(Top left) Camera operator John McLean lines up a shot ready for a take for a beaming Ted Kotcheff. Gary Bond is on the other side of the camera, as DOP Brian West contemplates his exposure. On arriving in Australia it was West who looked at the sky and proclaimed Australia was 'one stop overexposed'!

(Top right) On location outside Broken Hill. Director Ted Kotcheff looks at the battered car being readied for the kangaroo hunt while camera and grips crews prepare the lights and dolly tracks.

(Right and bottom) On location in Broken Hill.

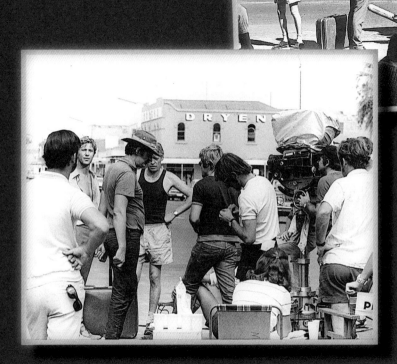

game being the most difficult of all, because of its fixed location in the gambling hall at the back of the café, whereas the kangaroo hunt proceeds forward at a frantic pace from day into night. How do you make a game of men betting on the toss of a coin in the air interesting and exciting when it is played five times in the scene?

Kotcheff achieved this by a clever amalgam of camera angles and unique crowd shots. Unique because the scenes were filled with genuine players and extras picked off the streets. Kotcheff prowled the pubs of Bondi Junction in Sydney, just up from the studio, just prior to the scheduled filming of the game, soliciting the men at the bars and persuading them to come to the filming of a few games of two-up.[7] Mistaken at times for a poof on the prowl for some excitement, Ted didn't have much luck at first (I was surprised in this area he wasn't thumped!) but his gentle persuasion soon resulted in the most marvellous and motley collection of faces one can imagine.

Filming took place at the old Ross Wood[8] Studios in Paddington whilst the Bondi Studios of Ajax were being prepared to shoot the interiors of Doc Tydon's hut in Broken Hill. *Wake* is called a 'split shoot'. Only the exteriors were shot in the environs of the Hill and the interiors filmed in Sydney. Another of producer George Willoughby's economic measures.

Australia was still adjusting to having changed from imperial pounds, shillings and pence to the new decimal currency of the dollar. Bank notes were all new and though permission had been given to film with fake money, which was supposed to be collected at the end of each day's filming, some of the players didn't hand their money in and it later turned up in the bookies' enclosure on the following Saturday at Randwick Racecourse. The facsimile money was so good it wasn't detected immediately and all hell broke loose later with the authorities.

I wasn't allowed to go on location at the Hill with the main unit for the duration of the shoot so I had to prepare the kangaroo hunt on my own for the first screening of the film on Ted and the unit's return from location. Our only communication was via the director's notes, when he had time to do them, or the extremely rare telephone call which had to be hooked through an operator. It is an editor's worst time on a picture, the first screening of the assembly cut. Here one sees warts and all and it is at this point the editor's real relationship with the director begins.

---

7   Two-up is an illegal gambling game on which bets are placed on the toss of a coin (a penny), 'heads' go to the better, 'tails' to the house. Thomo's was Sydney's most notorious house from where many of the extras and the callers were selected to play the scenes in the film. The law tolerates two-up in certain outback towns, Broken Hill being one.
8   Ross Wood was one of Australia's leading cinematographers.

Kotcheff[9] (It's a)

- 'highly personal relationship
- intimate one
- spend many weeks together working irregular hours in confined surroundings
- obviously the editor must be one for whom you have a basic liking and whose intelligence you respect
- someone whose taste and judgement you can trust because sometimes the film is entrusted to him [sic] to be finished
- one usually knows the editor one is going to make it with when timing the length of the first cut
- if your rhythm sense differs, you're in trouble
- editors range in type from a near director to a pair of scissors
- everyone has a contribution to make and should be encouraged to make it: then filmmaking becomes an enjoyable process why I think the producer should be allowed to make a suggestion (much laughter from the assembled editors)
- he should be the director's alter ego and they should be as one as to what the film is striving to do and trying **together to discover the most exciting way of doing it**
- I like an editor who has a positive attitude to the material, a clear opinion about it and a frankness about expressing it. I want another mind working: telling me what is bad, a performance a shot: what is clichéd,[10] what is unnecessary, heavy-handed, clear or unclear. The editor is one of the few people on a film who is intimately involved but still objective.
- When I shoot a sequence, I have for the most part a fairly good idea of how I would edit it.
- Always interested to discover what the editor will see in the material: most times he sees things which I have never dreamt of: what new order.
- **A composer is not necessarily the best conductor of his own music, so sometimes an editor knows a better way to achieve what (a) director is striving to say.**
- I like an editor who takes a strong stand … the editor's entry into a picture comes at a psychological moment. The director is fatigued: at the end of shooting: you see the rough assembly: (I like it long and loose) and immediately you know if the editor has worked the material and done the basic spade work. It gives you a psychological boost.

9   From Ted's talk with FEGA members, 1970.
10 Evan Jones – 'The first thing to do with the obligatory scene is cut it.'

I wasn't sure if I fitted any of the above criteria but I must have done something right with that first assembly for Ted turned to me and said, 'I'm really looking forward to getting started on Monday.' What I wasn't prepared for were some of Ted's foibles. The cutting of both the two-up game and the kangaroo hunt were exhausting, but rewarding. It was the editing of Doc Tydon's scenes that turned Ted on. There is a scene in the hut where Tydon is playing an aria from *La Traviata* from an old 78rpm 12" record on a wind-up gramophone. The next thing I knew was hi fi speakers appeared in the cutting room, a bench was cleared for Ted to lie down on, whereby he then proceeded to play opera loudly whilst I attempted to edit the picture. I thought this contrivance was initially to annoy me to get my fire and energy up or whatever going. But I was wrong. The playing of opera was to get Ted inspired as to how to cut the scene. It was to be ongoing until one day I exploded and said I had had enough and the bloody thing was to be turned off and stay off.

Of course this outburst only encouraged Ted all the more till he put his head around the door and said he was taking me and Wellburn to lunch. I protested vehemently that I was too far behind to go to any lunch. This made Ted more determined than ever. Tim Wellburn[11] had been our sound editor on *Age of Consent*, and was in charge of our post sync (ADR) on *Wake* of the actors returning to England whilst we were still editing. He then created the amazing soundtrack for the kangaroo hunt, which the UK sound editors found they could not recreate with the car effects they had. I digress. Ted Kotcheff's protestations became louder than mine so I was finally dragged off to lunch. He took Tim and me to a fashionable restaurant, The Hungry Horse in Paddington, where I was to enjoy escargots for the first time. I think it was about 5.30 pm when the maitre d' asked if we were staying for dinner.

I was poured back to the studio.

Ted's strategy had been right. He could sense the tension that can build up when editing, particularly when working on long and difficult sequences. As writers get what is called 'writer's block', an editor can also get 'editor's block'. One can sit in front of the editing machine for hours at a time fiddling with the scene and not achieving anything.

The Morris 1100 got me home to Clifton Gardens on the other side of the harbour, how, I won't think about even now! But next morning I left for the studio

11 Tim Wellburn's sound editing precision would have driven a saint to despair. On *Age of Consent* sync sound was unusable on much of the track because of the wind. If you ever have the opportunity of seeing the film study the waves closely. Tim hand-synched each lap and crash of the waves onto the shore with finite accuracy.

A player about to toss the coin. Note the extras, many of whom were regulars at Thomo's two-up game, an illegal activity often raided by the police.

before five and had an entire reel ready for Ted to see by 9am. I have always been and still am a morning person.

You could always expect the unexpected with Ted. Editing the swinging light shade homoerotic sequence between Pleasence and Bond, the subject of perversion came up. I looked at Ted over the Westrex Editer: 'Well, go on then, tell me what perversion is.'

'Well Tony,' he stated, with his infectious giggle gathering momentum, 'Imagine two people in a vat of honey having sex wearing only their Wellington boots.' It was something even my vivid imagination had not contemplated. Looking sternly at him, 'Well go on then – '

Ted, with relish, then explained that if one of the couple was not enjoying the experience of having sex in the vat of honey, then it was perversion. I was beginning to think having the hi fi on whilst cutting was somewhat akin to being perverse. After this interesting aside I continued working on the film whilst we had another burst of opera from the wretched hi fi.

One day he asked if I would mind having his attachment on the picture, who had been on location in Broken Hill, come and observe the editing process for a week. I didn't mind. A handsome young man wearing cap, scarf, sweater, jeans and gym boots, the young people's outrig of the time, entered the cutting room and introduced himself. 'Hi! I'm Peter Weir.'

It was to be another three years before I was to find myself editing for this promising young filmmaker at Film Australia.

It became very apparent to me early in the editing process that Ted Kotcheff had very little support, if any, from his producers. George Willoughby was completely intimidated by him and really didn't understand what Ted was trying to achieve with his picture, and the other producers, including Bill Harmon, seemed to have moved on, for neither of us ever saw them in the cutting room. I told Ted of Louis Edelman's suggestion that I should consider becoming a producer. Ted endorsed the idea for he felt I understood where writers and directors were coming from.

Wake in Fright was finally locked off. Tim Wellburn and his team completed the dialogue and sound effects editing and the tracks were packed off to London for the final mix to be completed and for composer John Scott to add his haunting, evocative score.

Once again we were prepared for the colour grader, this time at Technicolor, not to get the first print right. As usual they tried to make the red earth green and the clear blue sky bleached to the usual European grey. DOP Brian West soon put them on the right track but in fairness they only had a black and white work print to work from. Not a wise producer decision when the picture is in colour.

What we were not prepared for was the vigorous and sometimes vicious critique the film was to receive. Though the producers were confident the National Film Board of Australia, at the time the official advisory board to the government through the Minister for the Interior, would recommend *Wake in Fright* to be the official entry for the Cannes Film Festival, the chairman, Ian Hamilton, advised Jack Neary and Bobby Limb that it had been refused endorsement by the Board. Despite this refusal of recognition of an Australian film, the selection panel for the Festival International du Film, the governing body of the Cannes Film Festival, selected the film as the official Australian entry in competition for the 1971 Cannes Film Festival.

On its release in October in London, the British film critics had a field day. Some of their responses:

The Guardian, Derek Malcolm: '…The story is a little long-winded and melo-dramatic but what makes the film absolutely is its cruelly accurate observation of a certain type of Australian life, an observation heightened by some very good playing indeed in the minor parts. The brutal environment of the outback is reflected in each of them with a sense of inevitability it is hard to get out of the mind.'

The most scathing of all reviews was to come from Dilys Powell. In a long piece under the heading 'Flowers of Violence' for the *Sunday Times*, Ms Powell was disturbed to find a shift to brutality in the cinema in reviewing *The Crimson Gang* and *Outback*.[12] Of the latter she had this to say – 'Now and then I am asked whether the cinema is changing for the better or for the worse. Better, I always say; not perhaps the routine pieces, but the serious, the searching films improve; they explore, they extend the range. I am bound to add, though, that lately I have noticed a change of another sort. I think the cinema in general is becoming more repulsive … perhaps it will be argued that the intention of *Outback* is to excite disgust with crudeness, to invite us, severing ourselves from those sweaty drunks, to recognise a generally tough goodwill which teaches the visitor to know his own weaknesses. Maybe. Myself I find that the film excites disgust, period; that the young schoolmaster ends up not a wiser but a more degraded man; and that the spectator is degraded with him. Meanwhile in the cinema we increasingly degrade ourselves. Not of course that I would deny anyone such pleasures, not that I would censor anyone's kangaroo-hunt. But if that is what you want, testicles to you.'

Meanwhile at home there was a more positive analytical response. Colin Bennett, one of our most respected film critics of the time, observed in Melbourne's *Age* – 'One way and another, Australians stand condemned. They suffer at the hands of two directors from overseas, descending on us armed with local tales of the outback.

These men, with their disparate styles – violent realism, poetic lyricism – have the guts to dare what we have never dared bring to a screen unaided. One, Canadian-born Ted Kotcheff, takes a Kenneth Cook story and tears to shreds the Weird Mob ethos and the romantic myth of mateship. The other, British cameraman Nicholas Roeg, uses a children's tale by James Vance Marshall to retell the myth of the Noble Savage and his doom.

Is it an Australian trait, a blind spot in our character, to refuse more than most peoples to see ourselves as others see us, let alone film what we see? Insecurity-complexed, we will knock everything about Australia but ourselves, and we will shun those who paint our faults larger than life, in either a city or outback context – unless it be blatantly satirical.

Wake in Fright tends to disintegrate in spots, like its hero. Purposely, it has no finesse, few nuances or subtleties. Kotcheff's only imposed bits of 'art' are a seduction, unsuccessful in both senses, and some swinging light globes. Yet, served especially well by editor Tony Buckley, he manages an intense feeling of

---

12 *Outback* was the international English title for *Wake in Fright*

claustrophobia in his semi-documentary, demi-semi-caricatured portrait of the sweaty boozers of a desolate clime.

It is high time someone made a *Wake in Fright*, a healthy exaggeration of our unhealthiest side.'

I leave the last word to veteran filmmaker turned reviewer, Phylis McDonagh, one of the three McDonagh sisters who pioneered feature filmmaking in the 1920s, and their *The Far Paradise* thankfully survives. Phylis, now deceased, wrote her column, 'Curtain Up', for the weekly *North Shore Times* – 'The other night I saw a double crime perpetrated on the screen. The first was the murder by subject-content of what, from the point of view of direction, photography and acting is the best film ever to come out of this country. The second was murder on a more literal scale. The unbelievable screen record of a bash-up by a wild carload of drunken outback rioters let loose on a joy-hunt among a pack of bush kangaroos – including the joeys.

The sequence I refer to explodes in scenes of horror and sickening brutality as the 'roos are mowed down in a welter of jerking, writhing limbs before the hail of bullets.

The senseless carnage goes on as daylight fades and torchlights are directed by night on the defenceless animals.

These are scenes so beyond the human pale that they degrade the watcher…

This is a clinical sequence – in the same sense as a filmed surgical technique is reserved in a documentary vault for specialised viewing.

What makes the whole chilling murder trail inexcusable is that it is presented at a leading city theatre in the form of entertainment.

When first shown in Canberra, *Wake in Fright* was refused official sponsorship for entry in this year's Cannes Festival. It did show there, however, and was hailed as a masterpiece.

Perhaps the values of animal life differ on the Continent, or the technical brilliance of the film may have outweighed the humane protective values…

There is a casting triumph in the person of Donald Pleasence, who brings to life the role of a debauched and alcoholic medico living on the fringe of civilisation.

The late Chips Rafferty leaves as a living memorial his characterisation of an outback police officer.

I close this review with a hope – and a prayer. May the Canadian director, Ted Kotcheff, decide to linger in this country and give us a sample of his superb film-sense in the production of further Australian pictures.

He is what our still struggling film industry has long awaited and needs. – P.McD.'

It is Miss McDonagh's second last comment in her review that caught my eye. Having lived in Canada I can see why and how Ted Kotcheff caught the Australianness of our culture so successfully. Life in Canada – the Yukon, the prairies and in the vast northern wilderness – is no different from the Australian outback. Only there it is bloody cold for most of the year and, here, bloody hot. Canadians and Australians have a lot in common. We have survived imperial empire colonialism and have our own stories to tell. Both countries are continually fighting the onslaught of Americanisation of our respective cultures. Canadian and Australian filmmakers I believe have missed a golden opportunity to do co-productions and share our stories. An exchange program of Canadian directors occasionally working here, and Australian directors working there, would strengthen both Canadian and Australian cinema culture and identity.

The French certainly recognised something 'different' in Ted's insight into Australian mateship and their life in the outback. As *Le Reveil dans la Terreur* (Waking in Terror) the film enjoyed a ten-month season as a 'version originale' at a cinema on the Boulevard Saint Michel in Paris.

In Australia the film soon disappeared from the few city cinemas it was playing and it didn't reach the suburbs. It was not until its one and only television release some years later on Network Ten that general audiences had a chance of seeing this powerful film, and then only after eleven o'clock in the evening. Surprisingly this screening was strongly supported and endorsed by Bill Collins, presenter of the network's *Golden Years of Hollywood*. Bill I admire very much indeed, for his love of and dedication to the movies he has presented to Australian television audiences for over thirty years, on all the channels except SBS. In fact he is known as 'Mr Movies of Australia'. I had noticed his *Golden Years of Hollywood* movie one particular Saturday night was Alfred Hitchcock's 1949 production *Under Capricorn*, set in Sydney in 1830. I had also noted that Bill's scheduled following film was *Wake in Fright*. I was somewhat astounded, for I felt this was not a Bill Collins film and certainly not what his regular following would be expecting.

Bill wasn't very far into his introduction when I realised I was wrong in thinking it wasn't his type of film. Here is an abbreviated quote of what he had to say:

'*Wake in Fright* is any Australian man's story or any Australian woman's story. Think about it. Put yourself in his place and this film makes a lot of dramatic sense. It's about aspects of Australian life which are revolting, which you may not accept yourself, but in certain situations you accept them, go along with them, or you go under. It is frightening, this is a horror story as far as I am concerned and I say no more about the events, just think of this man facing so many dangerous corners. It is tragic.'

More recently, in the volume *100 Greatest Films of the Australian Cinema*, in his appraisal of *Wake in Fright*, Bill had not changed his mind. 'As far as I am concerned *Wake in Fright* is one of the finest and truest films ever made in Australia.'

THE SEARCH FOR *Wake in Fright*

July 1996. Bobby Limb, business partner of Jack Neary (co-founders of NLT – Neary Limb Tinker), telephoned inviting me to lunch to discuss the whereabouts of the negative and soundtrack of the picture. Bobby tells me the rights have reverted to him and Jack and they would like to see the public have access to the film once more. I confidently tell Bobby that it would be in London at one of the laboratories, probably Technicolor or Kays, where I knew a lot of Australian films had been sent for their overseas sales requirements to be serviced. Murray Forrest, CEO of Atlab, gives me the names and addresses of all of London's labs and their managers and I dutifully write to them, carefully pointing out the cans may also be labelled 'Outback'. A complete dead end is reached. It is not to be found.

However, the manager of Kays Laboratories alerts me to the fact they are holding the negatives of nineteen Australian films for which they cannot find owners! I suggest he advise the National Film and Sound Archive in Canberra.

Correspondence with the head of United Artists, based at Pinewood, confirms that MGM/UA lost all rights to the film in 1991. Through 1996 and 1997 I search France, Germany and Spain where a Spanish dubbed print is found but no supporting materials. Then in January 1998 the Dublin Film Festival director telephones to say they have located a print with UIP in London. This turns out to be the only known Technicolor print of the film in existence. My long-time associate Peter Rose is then based in London with UIP and confirms they have no rights to the film and he arranges for the print to come to the Archive in Canberra in June 1999.

But where is the negative? UA come to my assistance again, advising they had returned the negative to the film's producer, George Willoughby, in 1986, who in turn lodged the materials with Lancair, a bonded warehouse at Heathrow. A search of the London telephone directory doesn't reveal the company's whereabouts. My secretary Elaine Menzies conducts a companies search for Lancair between January and March 2000. I finally make contact with a Tony Liffen who explains that Lancair had gone into liquidation and that the negative had been sent to vaults in Pittsburgh in November 1998 for Eyemark Entertainment. He has no record though on whose instruction it had been sent.

Through July 2000 to January 2001 I correspond with Florien Dorffman seeking access to the film because of its importance to Australia's film culture. Ms Dorffman's interest in the film soon wanes and Eyemark becomes King World Productions, a subsidiary of CBS Television. Now finding the task somewhat daunting, I ask the National Film and Sound Archive to take over negotiations in July 2001. This proves to be a mistake and seeing no progress being made, I ask Ausfilm in Los Angeles in 2002 to pursue the case, which Megan Worthy takes on with professional zeal and makes a breakthrough. She makes contact with Harvey Rappaport at CBS who must have wondered what he had struck with an enquiry coming from down under about an obscure Australian film which was obviously of no interest to CBS, or anyone else as it turned out. Mr Rappaport locates some 16mm prints, which are sent to the Archive in July 2004. I email him thanking him for his trouble and imploring him to make one final search for the negative. Probably out of despair to get rid of this ratbag continually emailing, Mr Rappaport personally goes to Pittsburgh and discovers a container marked 'For Destruction'. He has the container opened and discovers can after can of 'Outback' – 'Wake in Fright'. Not only the negative and soundtrack, but tri-separations and 35mm magnetic mixing tracks et al. He advises Megan Worthy at Ausfilm in LA and he authorises for the materials to be immediately packed and repatriated to Australia, where they are delivered to the National Film and Sound Archive in September 2004. I was never game enough to ask Mr Rappaport what date had been on the manifesto at the vaults for the film's destruction.

A nightmare of legalities had to be endured to satisfy the Australian Film Commission and the Archive before restoration could begin. To this end my entertainment lawyer, Raena Lea-Shannon at Frankel Lawyers, offered her services pro bono and has worked tirelessly to clarify ownership of the film and to protect the interests of Bobby Limb and Jack Neary's heirs, both having died before the film could be brought home.

Curator and preservator Anthos Simon commenced the restoration of *Wake in Fright* at Atlab in Sydney, March 2007. From making my first enquiry with Atlab's CEO, Murray Forrest, re the London labs, to Anthos commencing work on the film, had taken eleven years.

The *Wake in Fright Inc Trust* was formed to 'own' the film and, in association with the National Film and Sound Archive, appointed Madman Entertainment of Melbourne to be the Australasian distributor.

16

Ballet In The Bedroom

First day's rushes reveal what a picture really is going to be, an 'A' feature or a 'B' feature. You can read the script till the cows come home but it won't really tell you how the director will translate it to the screen. *Age of Consent* definitely 'A'. First day's filming on Dunk Island revealed the film had a 'look' and some style. *Adam's Woman* strangely nearly fell into a chasm between 'A' and 'B' but the anamorphic Panavision photography saved the day by giving the picture a 'big look'. *That Lady From Peking* was definitely a double 'B', no two ways about it. *Wake in Fright* deserves a double 'A'. Not so the next two films I was to edit.

The production of motion pictures regretfully encourages ambition above ability. I don't think anyone sets out to make a bad film but the so-called glitz and glamour of our trade encourages the ambitions of writers and directors whose abilities to deliver are just not there. A television director does not necessarily make a film director and vice versa. I should add at this point one may see glamour and glitz at a premiere of a movie but there the myth ends. Making films from their inception to delivery is a damned hard slog for all concerned.

Regretfully Warwick Freeman's one and only attempt at feature film direction wasn't helped by Kit Denton's and Rae Knight's verbose adaptation of *Demonstrator*. Freeman was influenced at the time by an MGM film, *The Strawberry Statement* which was MGM's vain attempt to enter the 1970s contemporary cinema away from their usual stock and trade. Halliwell summed it up: 'One of a short lived group of student anti-discipline films of the early seventies, and about the most boring.' – *Demonstrator* was also attempting to deal with contemporary issues, the student anti-Vietnam war demonstrations. Not even Bob Young's music could save the film. On opening night, 31 March 1971, at the less than salubrious Town[1]

---

1 Formerly the Esquire, Cameo.

cinema in Sydney, I discovered Warwick Freeman in the projection room wanting to take yet another scene out of the film. I felt very sorry for him. It was by now 114 minutes and should have been no longer than ninety!

Sunstruck was designed to be a starring vehicle for Harry Secombe, the popular Welsh singer, better known as one of the three Goons from *The Goon Show* with Peter Sellers and Spike Milligan. (*The Goon Show* was about the only thing my father and I had in common. We would roar our heads off every week whilst my mother fled to the back of the house!) The first day's rushes were to reveal a soft 'B'. In a strange sort of way it was the comedy version of *Wake in Fright* if there ever could be such a thing.

The project began as *The Education of Stanley Evans*, later *The Immigrant*, hence Immigrant Productions, and finally *Sunstruck* was chosen in post-production. Stanley Evans (Harry Secombe) is assigned to the one-teacher school of the town. Stanley transforms his unruly rabble into a successful choir who perform at the Sydney Eisteddfod and win a 'special effort' certificate, much to the town's delight. The love interest is nicely played by Maggie Fitzgibbon, and there are lively performances by John Meillon, Bobby Limb and Dawn Lake. However, it was lacklustre and basically dull.

Do well it did not. After a world premiere in Parkes in central New South Wales on 18 November 1972, the film had a short season at Sydney's Rapallo Theatre where *Age of Consent* had played for over seven months.

Lacklustre or not, the film gave me a marvellous opportunity to experience the music scoring and the final sound mix in London. The musos were only available at night to record at an old hall in Queensway off Bayswater Road, and the sessions went late into the night. On one occasion, Harry offered me a lift home in his Rolls Royce. In London I used to stay with Peter Hannan, a top cinematographer from Cinesound, and his wife Annou, at their very comfortable flat above a rustic shop in Holland Park just down from the police station. Approaching the Hannan's flat, Harry swings the Rolls Royce over the kerb and parks on the footpath, asking me to remain seated whilst he swung by the rear of the vehicle to open the door for me as a good chauffeur would. A constable walking down from the station must have thought I was someone important and said 'Good evening, sir,' to which Harry put on his best Neddy Seagoon accent and said, 'No, constable, he's only a bloody Australian.' He roared with laughter and drove his Roller into the night, leaving a somewhat bewildered policeman as I scurried up the stairs.

I don't remember who phoned. It may have been production manager, Hal McElroy, or it may have been the producer, John Hargreaves (pronounced Hargreeves). It doesn't matter now, the call was to enquire would I be prepared to assemble, but not edit, a ballet film being shot in Melbourne with the Australian Ballet. Four weeks work only but pay was reasonable. I said 'yes', not realising this venture was going to be one of the 'events' of my life. The ballet was *Don Quixote* with Rudolf Nureyev and New Zealand prima ballerina Lucette Aldous, and was to be directed by Nureyev and Robert Helpmann. The music by Ludwig Minkus, based on a ballet by Marcus Petipa, and superbly orchestrated and conducted by John Lanchbery, had had successful seasons in Sydney and Melbourne since 1970. The Australian Ballet had formed a partnership with International Arts (an independent company, headed by Peter Bowen and headquartered in Sydney's Double Bay) and the Australian International Finance Corporation. I'm not sure to this day where the actual investment funds came from, but I believe a good proportion was from the States and the remainder from Australian investors and the Australian Ballet Foundation. The original budget had been $500,000 plus but this was soon to blow out to just under $700,000.

The stages were the recently vacated hangars of Melbourne's Essendon aerodrome, totally unsuited for filming, a more miserable place one could not possibly find in which to stage a ballet with the world's leading star of the dance. Bleak and cold, despite being late November,[2] the draughts blew with a vengeance around the place. Art department, set construction, make-up and wardrobe and my cutting room were all housed in makeshift divided sections of the hangars, with the main hangar being the number one shooting stage. Because everything had to be built and supplied from scratch, gantries, grids, lights etc., the entire Australian film industry was brought to a halt so the gear needed to make the picture could be brought in from the studios in Sydney, Melbourne and other places. The head gaffer, the venerable Tony Tegg, nearly went spare trying to obtain enough light for Geoffrey Unsworth to light the enormous stage. Every klieg, brute arc, redheads, lights of every make and size in the country, were on this Melbourne stage.

Geoffrey Unsworth knew I had edited *Age of Consent* for Michael Powell, for whom he had been camera operator on *The Life and Death of Colonel Blimp* and *A Matter of Life and Death* (*Stairway to Heaven*). He was renowned as Britain's supreme artist of colour cinematography, with *The Laughing Lady, Jassy, 2001 – A Space Odyssey, Murder on the Orient Express, Superman – The Movie* and, my

---

2   November, the start of the Australian summer.

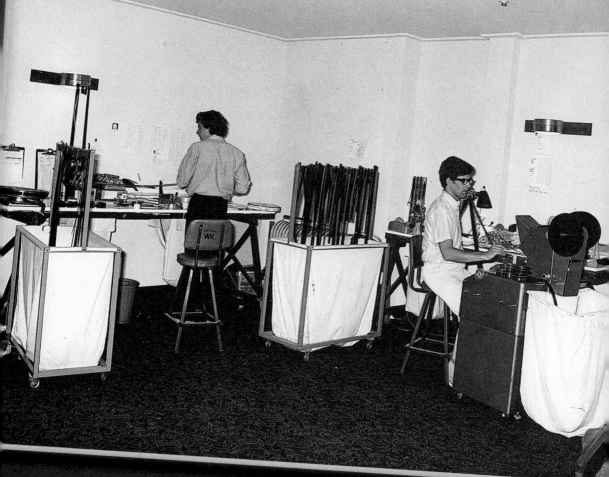

Editing Warwick Freeman's *Demonstrator* on the trusty Westrex Editer whilst assistant Warwick Hercus syncs rushes, sometimes having difficulty controlling his mirth!

favourite, *Cabaret*. He was working with Roman Polanski preparing *Tess* in Brittany when he died of a heart attack. His superb sensitivity of lighting for colour film had begun at Technicolor in 1937.

My cutting room was set up with a Moviola adjacent to the main hangar. The idea was to enable Nureyev to see his footage during the day between set-ups. He was rarely to take advantage of the facility.

Robert Helpmann arrived and presented me with his shooting script. Continuity Lyn McEncroe and I peered at this somewhat thin foolscap document, which bore no resemblance whatsoever to a film script, as we knew them. What sort of a picture was this going to be, we wondered. The 'script' was never referred to again. John Hargreaves arrived from England to be the producer. Hargreaves was a fragile, pleasant man who we were soon to learn was feeling the dreadful strain of being out of his depth. Hargreaves knew the studio system like the back of his hand where he felt secure in the knowledge that everything is at a producer's fingertips, in a well-run studio such as Pinewood. Though being filmed in an aeroplane hangar could be thought of as a studio base, it was still a 'location' picture, which brings with it all the problems associated with filming on location, a far cry from the well-equipped stages and back lots of Britain and Hollywood.

Hargreaves was very quickly intimidated by Nureyev (as was nearly everyone else) and remained in his office most of the time. Hal McElroy did a stoic job running the show but it wasn't long before one could sense the budget running away and this was something Hal had no control over, only the producer does – whereas in fact we didn't have a producer in the real sense of the role.

I was to assemble the film, and Wallace Potts, Nureyev's partner, one of the assistant directors, was to edit the film in London. Potts had made a film of Nureyev's production of *Raymonda* and Nureyev felt that Potts was the only person who should edit his film. Now assembly editing, a practice of the time, unique to British editing, is a practice whereby the assembly editor prepares all the okay takes, shot out of sequence, into sequence order, removing only the tops and tails of each take. I have never utilised this practice as I deem it to be a total waste of time, as do most American and Australian editors. I suspect the British unions may have had something to do with the continuance of the practice.

When first day's rushes came in, I would 'cut' the film together so it would run as a dance sequence. Nureyev could later pick his takes on the Moviola. My assistant, Geoff Portman, would synchronise the rushes and after screening would break them down to edit. There were many temper tantrums on this set. Whilst I was cutting, Geoff would go around to the filming stage and quickly scuttle back to report on whom Nureyev was abusing today! The film crew didn't suffer too much but the corps de ballet had a terrible time. In fact Nureyev took quite a shine to one of our camera operators, Bill Grimmond, a very straight Australian. This greatly amused many on the floor, who still dine out on this story.

Nureyev would look at the film, swear a lot about the dancing, and not say a word to me or anyone else. Helpmann had very quickly taken a back seat and retreated. As I began the edit, I noticed that when Nureyev landed en pointe in close-up (CU), he would remain stationary and be in the same position in the next shot. I asked Geoffrey Unsworth to come round and look. He immediately saw the problem I was seeing. Could he persuade Nureyev, when landing en pointe, to continue to move out of frame and move into frame, so that when cut together there would be a fluid motion in the dance, thereby making the editing seamless and less noticeable? Geoffrey brought Nureyev round to the cutting room to explain to him what we were both recommending. Nureyev studied the cuts backwards and forwards but could not grasp what we wanted him to achieve. Needless to say, the editing at times is quite noticeable because I had to wait for his feet to 'settle' before cutting to the next shot. In the minaches it wasn't a problem. In fact, Nureyev learnt quickly that he could make up his whole routine by cutting not from the two-camera coverage, but from the many takes of a minache to achieve the absolutely perfect performance. Cunning of him. Editing – the hidden power, as Kevin Brownlow so rightly observed.

Tension on the set at times was extreme. Although there was always two-camera coverage, Nureyev would insist on endless takes. All his material had to be shot first. He had only a four-week period available for his sequences to be completed. As his schedule became tighter, the shooting day would go well into the night.

Although Nureyev is credited director, the unsung heroes of the filming were Unsworth's camera operator, Peter MacDonald, and ballet master and co-first assistant director with Potts, Bryan Ashbridge. Watching Ashbridge on the set, one immediately sensed control of both the filming and the dancers. He would work quietly and efficiently, directing the dancers to their positions, whilst Nureyev sat on the camera crane having the recommended shots explained to him by Peter MacDonald. Ashbridge was in complete control of the floor. It was just as well.

We had been filming for two weeks and I thought it was time Nureyev should sit down and look at his cut footage. Lyn McEncroe, one of Australia's leading continuity girls (now called script supervisors – if you please!) was at breaking point. Lyn never swore but she would storm into my cutting room and say, 'How can I do continuity where there isn't bloody any!'

The eventful day arrived, Nureyev nodded his head at me, and we rolled the film. It looked pretty good but not a word was said. The reels finished, Nureyev looked at me, smiled and walked out of the room. Well, at least there was no swearing.

The production took a dreadful toll on John Hargreaves. Art director Bill Hutchinson was going way over budget, purchasing thousands of dollars worth of Persian carpets, cutting them up to form 'original' patterns for the carpets that were to be used in the film. Fine for theatre perhaps, but an incredible waste for film, when cheaper fabrics would have done the same job. However, the horse had bolted. John Hargreaves came and sat with me in the sun one afternoon between the hangars. Tears were softly running down his cheeks. 'I've lost control of the film, Tony.' I felt dreadfully sorry for him. He didn't have the security of the studio at Pinewood to support him, where his work normally excelled. I wondered what would be in store for him on the picture when he returned to England.

The schedule was now completely squeezed, to the point the 'Enchanted Garden' sequence was shot on Nureyev's final morning. I watched with incredulity. Saturday morning, early start, the corps de ballet going through their paces, two cameras rolling, while at the edge of the set the limousine waited to take Nureyev to the plane for Paris. Only in a couple of instances were there second takes. More about this extraordinary sequence later. Nureyev left the set, no goodbyes, and went straight to his plane.

I continued to cut the film into shape, particularly the last day's footage. Geoff Portman and I looked at it, packed it up and despatched it to Pinewood, expecting never to see it again. Not till it was released anyway.

Filming had been completed in time for everyone to be home for Christmas, most of the crew being from Sydney. It was two days before Christmas Day. The phone rang. 'Tony, can you be on the plane Boxing Day for London? I have just secured you the last seat. Nureyev is insisting you finish the editing of the film.' Hargreaves, sounding a little more relaxed now he was on his home turf, but nonetheless somewhat apprehensive in case I was going to say no. There was nothing stopping me, the seventies were beginning to look pretty lean employment-wise, so I said 'yes'.

Boxing Day I boarded the plane. First class. I was incredibly impressed, this time it was a 747! Was I dressed appropriately? I wondered. Outside the plane it was a typically hot, sunny Australian Christmas. Some twenty-nine hours later I was being greeted at Heathrow by a well rugged-up John Hargreaves with limo driver, to be driven down to Iver Heath, through endless snow flurries, and to awaken next morning in the guesthouse near Hargreaves' home to a blanket of snow covering the English countryside. Echoes of Ottawa all those years before.

I was invited that day to meet Hargreaves' wife and family and enjoy their Christmas hospitality. John reminisced about some of the great British pictures he had been associated with. It was time to go back to the guesthouse, and it was then John Hargreaves dropped his bombshell. 'I'll pick you up in the morning at nine and we will drive you to East Sheen. Rudi doesn't want to edit the film at Pinewood. He has made room for you at home. You will be very comfortable, and the room is excellent. Rudi will be back from Paris after New Year's Day.'

What had I let myself in for? I rang Hal McElroy in Sydney from the guesthouse that evening, which wasn't easy in the days prior to ISD. I told him the news. He laughed, 'Hey, mate, you'll be right,' and then offered some ribald remarks on how to look after myself. 'Very funny,' I retorted. He laughed even more. No one could imagine, not even Hal, the adventure I was about to begin – moments of pressure to get the film to Nureyev's precise satisfaction and other moments which can only be described as downright hilarious!

Fife Road, East Sheen, faces or backs on to, depending on your view, Richmond Park. It's a glorious location. Nureyev's house, according to Hargreaves, had belonged to Sir John Guillerman. A handsome but not overstated pile, its gravel driveway was only a short distance from the road to the front door, with a modest turning circle, which was not good for limousines. Standing at the front door of the large entrance hall, a handsome staircase went up to the left to Nureyev's and Pott's quarters.

The geography of Nureyev's bedroom has to be carefully understood to fully appreciate the circumstances associated with the editing of the film. It was actually three rooms without doors, but a wide-open rectangular archway opening between the two main rooms, and a smaller doorway to the third room. The podium level was a spacious but austere room in which was a magnificent four-poster Jacobean bed. Two steps down from the podium level was an area similar in size, off which was the bathroom. The room, I assume, would have normally been a sitting room but it was unfurnished and became the cutting room in which I was to work for six weeks. Two more steps down was Nureyev's dressing room, which was also the entry point for the three rooms. All faced Richmond Park. So, on entering, one turned right into the middle room, behind which was the sight of the imposing bed two steps up.

On arrival I was introduced to Clare, seventy-five, Rudolf's housekeeper/cook and keeper of the house. A marvellous woman who spoke no English, or very

King of Gaffers, Tony Tegg, confers with DOP Geoffrey Unsworth re the light sources and exposures. Tegg had to comb every studio in Australia to obtain every available light to illuminate the vast stage which was an aircraft hangar. Every Kleig, Brute Arc, Redheads, you name it, it still wasn't enough to give Unsworth the exposure he needed for the Gypsy Encampment scene, set by moonlight. Regretfully the restoration of the film a few years ago has made the subtle, moonlit sequence into something akin to Bondi Beach on a bright summer's day. It was the biggest lighting job ever undertaken for a film in Australia.

little, and I spoke no French. We got on like a house on fire. She escorted me to Rudolf's suite of rooms where the middle room was stacked with cans containing a total of 100,000 feet of film, three trim bins (trolley with canvas bags which hold the 'trims' of film one is cutting) and a pretty good editing bench at the window facing the park, and thankfully an American Moviola. (The English had developed their own version with a spy glass called an Acmiola, which was a pain to use.) So all I had to do was start to sort out all the film and prepare to start work.

I asked Clare if I could go to my quarters to unpack. She pointed to Rudolph's Jacobean bed and vanished. I quickly followed her down the stairs to clarify I wasn't Rudolf's new partner, or whatever she was thinking. 'Non, non, non!' she exclaimed. Of course I was sleeping in that bed! Knowing Rudolf and Wallace were not due to arrive from Paris for about a week I thought, 'Well, what the hell.' I had to sleep somewhere.

So my first night at Fife Road was spent in the bed of the great dancer, pondering on the four posts of the bed and wondering what sights they had seen and what stories they could tell. Next morning, thankfully Wallace rang from Paris. I told him of my predicament. He immediately laughed his head off, thought it was extremely funny and said he had to tell Rudolf straight away. After a pause he asked me to put Clare on. I shouted down the stairs, could she pick up the phone. I heard much French spoken and put my receiver down. The phone rang again. It was Hal in Sydney: 'How's it going mate – comfortable, everything okay?' he enquired. I told him of my previous night's predicament. He laughed like a drain! He and Wallace would have got on well together. Within minutes Clare rushed into the room, gesticulating, gesturing, 'Oh la la, monsieur!' Nonetheless she was very amused and hurriedly escorted me to my quarters through Rudolf's bedroom. Facing my bedroom door was the narrow staircase, which meant I had access without having to disturb anyone or go through Nureyev's quarters. I discreetly locked the connecting door and finally made myself at home.

Nureyev was performing at the Paris Opera with Fonteyn, and Wallace was coming home early to assist me prepare the film for Rudolf's return. I began to wonder if my editing the film was going to cause concern for Wallace. It regretfully did, for he was to leave Rudolf two weeks after my arrival, unannounced, which caused some drama. I had presumed there was a big difference between his production of *Raymonda* and our production of *Don Quixote*, which Rudolf had obviously recognised, hence my summons.

On Nureyev's return he locked into a strict schedule. After breakfast I was permitted to enter his quarters at 8.45 sharp and start work, whether he was up or not. Most occasions, if not all, he had showered but wouldn't dress till after his masseur had been. He would leave for Covent Garden rehearsal rooms on the West Cromwell Road at 9.30 and sometimes Clare and I wouldn't see him till late that night after a performance.

Clare was on duty all the time and I would wait up till he returned in case he wanted to see the reel I had cut that day. Most nights he would look at the film. Some days, when he was free from rehearsals, he would pore over every take of the dancers to ensure I was getting the best of the dance and not worrying too much about disjointed cuts unless they were obvious to both of us.

The routine of the house was interesting. I would eat all my meals in the kitchen with Clare, but on Sundays Rudolf insisted we both had breakfast with him in the Summer Room facing the park. Sometimes nothing much was said, other times he would ask my opinion of something he had read in the Sunday papers. They were very pleasant occasions and he seemed to enjoy the company of having breakfast quietly together.

His rehearsal and performance schedule was gruelling and sometimes the masseur would have to come twice a day, for though Rudolf was only in his mid-thirties he was already becoming muscle-bound.

The cut was proceeding well and I had reached 'The Enchanted Garden' sequence, our last day's filming at Essendon. I alerted Rudolf to advise when he might have a day off to assist me, for I knew he was concerned about the standard of the dancing. It would be unfair to criticise the ballerinas for inferior performance, as the circumstances it was filmed under were extreme. However, Rudolf had a field day. He examined every 'take' in detail, sometimes roaring with laughter and others screaming abuse at the dancing. We ripped endless footage out of the scene, marrying together what remaining shots we had, to try and make what was left of the scene have some cohesion.

A year later Mike Harris in *Variety* and our local *The Australian* was somewhat critical of my editing for the landing en pointe. He wondered why 'The Enchanted Garden' scene was so well cut, whereas the rhythms and fluidity of the editing were missing in the rest of the picture.

'With the exception of the Enchanted Garden sequence – all girls plus Sir Robert – the lack of unison by the dancers is often most conspicuous.

And the directors, or Unsworth or his operator, should have noticed the intrusive movements by extras at the edge of frame. During a particularly beautiful dance sequence, the eye is drawn away from the principals to some bird fanning herself.

Ultimately, much of any blame to be levelled must be directed at the editor, Anthony Buckley. What chance he had, or how much actual control over the selection of shots he had is known only to the director(s); but for whatever reasons, there is little smoothness in the progress of the film in cinematic terms.

All the same, *Don Quixote* has movements of magical beauty. The Enchanted Garden sequence mentioned before, for example, is pure classical ballet, and exquisitely filmed. And so, also, is our first meeting with the main character.'

Little did he know!

Whether I am a master of editing or not, I don't know. One thing I do know is that I became the master of the faux pas at Nureyev's home.

Breakfast as usual with Clare. 8.44 I ascend the stairs as usual to commence work at 8.45. On entering the room I encounter the startled look of a man in bed (not Rudolf) to whom I bid 'good morning'. He grabs the sheet, covering himself as he flees the room. I look to my left and see Rudolf looking at me from his dressing room two steps down from the 'cutting room'. It was the wickedest grin one could encounter, to which I responded with 'hmmph' and a huff, and proceeded to the Moviola. From the corner of my eye I could see he was beaming!

It gets worse. Nureyev, one could tell, appreciated the long hours being put into the editing of the picture. He invited me to join him for dinner with his guests on the forthcoming Saturday night, to which he was also inviting Geoffrey Unsworth. Dame Margot would also be attending after their performance at Covent Garden. Clare had the regular caterers, for Rudolf was pernickety about how his food was cooked and served, particularly his steak – bleu – that is, seared on the outside quickly, rare on the inside. Though the house was centrally heated, big houses always seem to feel chilly and I always wore a neat V-necked cashmere sweater. I thought on this occasion I would wear a tie. I continued to work at the Moviola when I heard Rudolf ascending the stairs. He took one look at me and said, 'I see – dressed.'

I could hear the limos arriving on the gravel and went downstairs to assist Clare with the guests' coats. Dame Margot arrived escorted by a strikingly tall, handsome blond man. Clare took Dame Margot's coat and I took the man's extremely heavy black overcoat and cloaked it in the vestibule.

The dinner for twenty was one of those occasions where one has the good fortune to reflect 'memories are made of this'. How privileged I was to be there and included. I felt a tad embarrassed, however, for I was seated at the end of the table facing Rudolf at the head of the table several metres away. Dame Margot was nearby and Geoffrey Unsworth in the middle. She wanted to talk about Australia and many of the other guests, I could tell, were wondering 'who's the bloke at the end of the table?'

Talking of Australia, Dame Margot surprised me when she declared, 'My most happy memory of my entire career was in Australia.' I was expecting it to be a performance at one of our capital theatre cities. No. 'It was in Darwin,' she continued, 'an open air performance on a warm balmy night in front of several thousand people – you could hear a pin drop and then tumultuous applause.' I was beginning to feel homesick.

The dinner was winding up. I excused myself from the table to assist Clare with the guests' coats. Cars were arriving, people were leaving, when Dame Margot and her escort appeared. Clare had Dame Margot's coat at the ready and I knew where I had put the gentleman's heavy coat. I stood there holding it open for him to put on, when he turned and gave me a look of total disdain. I quickly retreated with the coat. I looked across the vestibule and there was Rudolf with that wicked, bemused look again. The Dame was going home alone and the 'escort' was staying the night.

Thankfully the next morning was Sunday and I didn't have to appear upstairs in the 'cutting room' with the Jacobean bed. But it was breakfast as usual in the Summer Room, despite the late hour of the night before. I carried some of the dishes in, following Clare. There at the table, with the same look of disdain, was the guest from the night before. I quickly indicated quietly to Rudolf I would eat in the kitchen. He rose from his seat, said nothing, but indicated for me to sit down. Breakfast proceeded as normal for a Sunday.

The best weekend of all was when Rudolf asked would I stay in for the weekend to dine with his girlfriend from Paris. She had come over to London with a girlfriend on a shopping spree. They were hilarious. I asked Rudolf her name. 'In French you would not understand – "Douci Pouci" – in English it translates to "Sweet Pussy"' – and looked at me with a straight face.

The relationship between Robert Helpmann and Rudolf was cordial but cool. Bobbie only ever came to one screening of the assembled footage at the house. He sat on a stool near the editing machine whilst Rudolf sat on another stool in the far corner of the room. Every time I glanced over at him he would throw his eyes skywards at the commentary coming from Helpmann.

The film was very close to its final fine-tuning. Helpmann announced that Peter Bahen, the administrator of the Australian Ballet, was arriving from Melbourne. It was thought best to present the film to him on the big screen at Pinewood's main mixing theatre. Bahen arrived at the appointed time after the long flight from Australia. I like watching the body language of someone who hasn't seen the film one is working on, to observe where they become restless when a scene isn't working, or to watch their reaction where a scene is working but more work should be done with it.

The screen at Pinewood is HUGE. I seated myself in the row behind Bahen about two seats to his right. Helpmann and Nureyev were seated separately several rows behind. Ten minutes into the screening Bahen promptly went to sleep and remained so till about fifteen minutes from the end, when he suddenly stirred himself, sat up and watched the finale. The lights were still coming up when he hauled himself out of the seat, turned round to everyone and declared, 'It's a bloody disaster!' – and stormed out of the theatre. Hargreaves was quite shaken, as was Helpmann. Nureyev looked determined.

Next morning I was still in my room when I heard a car arrive on the gravel drive. Before long I could hear much shouting. Curious, I cautiously opened my door, which faced the staircase leading to the front door. There was Rudolf, shouting at the top of his voice, holding Peter Bahen by the scruff of his overcoat and hurling him out the door, followed by Bobbie rushing past Rudolf before he was to suffer the same fate. This was an amazing sight, one I have never forgotten. Bahen was a solid, big man but Rudolf certainly had the strength to lift and propel him out onto the gravel driveway. I was so mesmerised I wasn't thinking quickly enough to get back into the room. As he slammed the door, Rudolf looked up, saw me, smiled that wicked smile and enquired if I was ready to start work.

It was really only a polish now, but the distributors were flying in from New York and screenings were soon to be set up in the West End. Rudolf had a penchant for 'doing the beat', though how he found time, on his schedule, I really didn't know. Looking at the film continuously on the small screen of the Moviola doesn't allow one to get a 'feel' of what a motion picture is really doing until it is seen on the big screen. Every two or three weeks we would book a 'double head' screening of the picture and soundtracks into a Wardour Street screening room to see how our work was proceeding. The cans of film would be put into the boot of either Rudolf's car or the limousine provided by Pinewood. John Hargreaves would join us for the journey into town. Wardour Street is off Shaftesbury Avenue, the street of theatres, just up from Piccadilly. On the approach to Piccadilly Circus Rudolf would ask to be let off, 'I am wanting some fresh air,' and requesting that he be allowed to walk the rest of the way whilst I and the projectionist were readying the reels. If Rudolf arrived some twenty minutes later looking grumpy, I knew it would not be a good reaction to the cut. If he came in beaming with that wicked look on his face, generally to me in an aside, I knew it would be a good screening. Rudolf would have scored a half-hour beforehand in the Piccadilly tube toilets, which was one of London's most notorious 'beats' at the time. John Hargreaves could never fathom why he wanted to walk such a short distance from Piccadilly to the screening room.

The pace was now a little more relaxed and Sunday nights Rudolf would spend with the Goslings at their apartment in South Kensington. On one occasion I was invited too, and was to see them again after Rudolf had left on tour. Watching him relax with his adopted 'godparents' was akin to watching Michael Powell with Pamela Brown at Avening five years before. Nigel and Maude Gosling were the ballet critics for *The Observer*, both writing under the nom de plume Alexander Bland. Her maiden name was Lloyd, and as Maude Lloyd she was described as 'one of the most beautiful and important dancers in the British ballet', later dancing with Peggy van Praagh, who was to become the artistic director of the Australian Ballet.

Rudolf Nureyev defected from the Kirov Ballet during their Paris season in 1961. Dame Margot Fonteyn called the Goslings to ask if they could take Rudolf under their wing. Fonteyn was deciding on an offer to dance with him. The Goslings happily became his surrogate parents, though Maude made it clear, 'I never tried to be his mother,' that would have been an insult to his own mother, whom he adored. Rudolf was not to see his own mother and family for another twenty-six years.[3]

Clare worked around the clock at Fife Road, a fact not lost on Rudolf. I can remember one evening, when he was quite relaxed, having just finished looking at the reel I had cut that day, when he offered me a glass of his favourite wine, Pouilly-Fuissé. We repaired to the kitchen where Clare was about to go to her room and she started to get the wine for us. No, Rudolf insisted she retire and *he* would serve the wine. He asked would I mind taking Clare to Covent Garden for the last performance of *La Bayadère* which he was dancing with Dame Margot. Would I mind? The big night came and there was a limousine to take us from Fife Road to Covent Garden. They were the very best house seats, as you can imagine. It was well into the performance when I first recognised the music and then the dance. The pas de deux Fonteyn and Nureyev were dancing was the same pas de deux Lucette Aldous and Nureyev danced in *Don Quixote*. The sneaky bastard![4] Just as the curtain was coming down on the finale, Clare grabbed my hand, pushing her way past those seated in our row to a hidden staircase which led us eventually onto the stage wing on the left-hand side. It was a breathtaking moment watching

---

3   Maude Lloyd died at the age of 96 in December 2004. She never got over Rudolf's death in 1993. 'I always said he would be there to hold my hand when I went, and was quite sure that he would'.

4   In fact it was John Lanchbery who took the pas de deux from Minkus's *La Bayadère* to strengthen the climax of his *Don Quixote*, which Lanchbery thought was a major weakness of the work.

Forever watchful on the set, Nureyev was fascinated by the editing process. Grateful for the two-camera coverage, he soon learnt that by combining alternative or 'out' takes from all the other footage, he could manipulate the editing of several takes together to produce, in his eyes, the perfect Minache. This technique became essential in the editing of the Enchanted Garden sequence.

the heavy curtain rise and fall, revealing the splendour of the crowded auditorium as Dame Margot and Rudolf took curtain call after curtain call. When the final drop has occurred, bewigged and liveried footmen then hold the curtain apart as each star takes their individual bows. It was at this point, as Rudolf was taking a bow, that Dame Margot noticed me, rushed over with her bouquet and said, 'Here Tony, please hold these for me.' I could feel why, it weighed half a ton. To see an opera house from this angle is a wondrous sight and with Rudolf and Dame Margot holding court, something unique.

Clare and I found our way back into the street and were prepared to look for the District Line to take us home to Richmond, when a chauffeur came forward to enquire if we were Mr Nureyev's guests. So home Clare and I went in fine style to enjoy a pot of tea in the kitchen together. The servants back in their quarters on a high after a night with the stars.

It was some years later, when walking down the Croisette at the Cannes Film Festival, that I heard a voice call 'Tony!' I looked around to see Wallace Potts striding towards me. 'Rudi's here, he just spotted you. He would like to say hello.' I looked beyond Wallace's shoulder to see Rudolf's beaming smile, warmly rugged up against the chill wind blowing off the Mediterranean. We spoke for a while. He had plans for another film and hoped I would do it. It was the last time I was to see him. It was to have been *The Sleeping Beauty*.

17

Insular Fairyland
– Anyone For Croquet?

The 1970s have sometimes been described by contemporary writers about film as 'the renaissance of the Australian cinema' – but at the time the facts were anything but that. Whilst the political wheels had been set in force by Jones, Adams, Burstall, Becket and Jeffrey et al., plus the Australian Film Council, and the seventies did see the establishment of the Film & Television Board of the Australian Council for the Arts, the Experimental Film Fund and the Australian Film Development Corporation, the practical side of the industry was in rapid decline, sparking high unemployment rates and the beginning of the decline of 'studio' employment as we knew it in favour of a new phenomenon; the 'freelance contractor'. Whereas a large percentage of our film crews had been employed on overseas films being made in Australia, there were few if any locally made films in regular production till the middle to late seventies. Studios survived on the production of television commercials, sponsored documentaries, whatever they could find. The corporate video was still fifteen years away.

Facing unemployment, and after much soul-searching and procrastination, sitting in a park in Chatswood one day I decided to accept an offer as film editor at Film Australia, employed specifically to cut a half-hour drama, *The Choice*. Although I was extremely depressed at the thought of working at Lindfield, *The Choice* was to be the turning point of my career. Now there are two very different points of view about Film Australia in the industry and I have to admit that my view places me in the minority.

The Commonwealth's involvement in making documentaries goes back to 1911 when James Pinkerton Campbell, forty-three, was appointed official government cinematographer to the Department of External Affairs. His employment was terminated after eighteen months' stormy relationship with his employer and

Queenslander Bert Ive was appointed official Commonwealth cinematographer, a post which he enjoyed till 1939. It wasn't until the legendary documentarist John Grierson visited Australia in 1940 that any serious thought was put into creating a permanent base for the making of government propaganda films. The Department of Information Film Unit had started at Burwood after the war and moved to specially built premises at Lindfield, a leafy, northern Sydney suburb, in 1961. Stanley Hawes had been brought from Canada in 1946 to head up the Commonwealth Film Unit (CFU) as producer-in-chief, and though he was not known for any filmmaking 'style', to his credit he was politically skilled to take on the mandarins of the public service in Canberra. Hawes is renowned for saving the Film Unit from abandonment and extinction in the 1950s by tackling the government at the highest level and convincing them of the need for a national filmmaking organisation, loosely based on the prestigious National Film Board of Canada. There is little to show, however, that John Grierson was Hawes' mentor as he claimed. Hawes held some extremely strange beliefs – that music and sound effects should never be mixed together and that wide-angle lenses be locked away to prevent their use by the Unit's cameramen. He also didn't believe that specialist film editors be employed, insisting that directors had to edit and track lay their own films. It was not till the advent of dramatised documentaries that editors were officially recognised and employed.

My depression was caused partly by the fact that I was a reject of the CFU by Stanley Hawes in the 1950s when I was seeking to start my career in film. It was impossible to obtain a job at the CFU unless you had reached and passed the School Leaving Certificate but in those days, if you didn't intend to go to university, when you reached Intermediate Certificate standard at fifteen years of age you started work or sought an apprenticeship in one of the trades.

The CFU was basically established by the returning war correspondents and war cinematographers who had been in the service of the Department of Information and thence the Department of the Interior (DOI). However they weren't filmmakers or producers, even though they were employed as such. The films from the CFU in this period were monumentally dull, especially Jack Allen's *Australian Diary*. I was at the cinema one night when the title *Australian Diary* hit the screen and the entire audience groaned! Stanley Hawes did lift their game (as did Gil Brealey much later) but the Unit didn't produce anything at the time equal to John Heyer's *The Back of Beyond* for the Shell Film Unit.

Arriving at the CFU I was introduced to the public service for the first time, and croquet. There, on the lawn opposite, a croquet court was laid out where the game was played in the lunch hour with sometimes gentlemanly vigour! Now here was a real learning curve! I discovered the world of form-filling-in, for one did not start or complete a procedure unless it was 'signed off' by a public servant employed for this purpose. I was to find I was continually in trouble for not having obtained the 'right permission' to do whatever it was I was doing. The evolution of the freelance contractor drove the regular staff dotty! I was ever thankful to one of those rare beings in the public service (and they do have them), Stuart Jay, who was extremely sympathetic and appeared never to be fazed by the malpractices (of the public service regulations) the contractors continually perpetrated.

What I couldn't accept was the nine-to-five routine of the place, no matter the reputation of quality and art it may have had in filmmaking. Starting time was 9am and clock-off time, including the telephone switchboard, was promptly executed at 5.06pm – not one minute less nor one minute more. I couldn't fathom how a film editor could actually leave film on the Moviola or in the synchroniser, switch it off and go home at precisely 5.06 without having finished the sequence being cut. It was bizarre. Of course there were those who were the exception to the rule. Chief editor Tom Foley was one. An eccentric maverick filmmaker Graham Chase was another, along with David Haythornthwaite, with whom I was destined to make the Unit's most famous and popular film. They would ignore all the rules and work on regardless, and on many occasions sleep overnight in their cutting rooms. The rituals entrenched in the place could never be coped with by freelancers like me. Rushes were screened every morning, mute, straight from the camera, without selected takes having been chosen, nor synced up, even if there was dialogue to camera. These rushes sessions would go on interminably. I baulked and refused to attend rushes until they were synced up and were only the print takes. Rule 74ZB broken under Public Service regulation 67K etc. etc. etc.

The sheltered workshop atmosphere of the place was enhanced by the silence of the corridors at morning and afternoon teatime. Some would spend an hour at tea break and heaven forbid if you were looking for anyone immediately after lunch. Fridays were best avoided by staying well and truly in your room. I am convinced the 'long lunch' was conceived at Film Australia. Led by one dour wag of the sound department, the senior staff would repair to Roseville any time after twelve o'clock and not be seen again until well after four o'clock in the afternoon – then would drive home promptly at 5.06. Some would no doubt say halcyon days. I think not.

I did respect the fact the place had a reputation which the 'commercial' studios did not have. At Cinesound one had to face the banality of Bill Carty's two-reelers to edit for the Queensland Tourist Office, with bland commentaries and equally banal music scores made up of Chappel and KPM library music. Yes, there were the rarities of something special like Cec Rubie's[1] *The Play's The Thing* for his NSW Education Department, but in the main nothing of the standard the CFU and Film Australia were attempting to achieve. The frustration was how they went about it.

My first 'stint' there was editing, and later I was invited as a contract producer. That first 'stint' was *The Choice*, an innovative half-hour drama about drugs in schools. The director, Donald Crombie, had graduated from the National Institute of Dramatic Art (NIDA), worked for the CFU in the 1960s and, like most of us, went to London. He worked for the BBC from 1969 to 1971. Looking at Donald's rushes was a revelation. Here was a first-class cast giving totally convincing performances and I was impressed by how many extras filled the screen. I mentioned this fact to Donald, poring over the Moviola. He looked at me and burst out laughing. He was only allowed twenty extras in the playground of the school, but his placement of his extras gave the impression there were a hundred or more. That is direction!

I had optioned the book *Caddie* in 1970 and although I had chosen a screenwriter I hadn't selected a director. Fate had just lent a hand. I invited Donald to read the book with a view to directing his first feature. He was to accept. *The Choice* had really started something.

Incredible Floridas was a different challenge altogether. A study of the Australian composer Richard Meale and his homage to the 19th century French poet Arthur Rimbaud, Peter Weir gave me some challenges in film editing with one of the most stylish and haunting short films of that decade. Peter and I had met briefly on *Wake in Fright*. Peter was already established as a director with his independently produced film *Homesdale*, and Film Australia's feature *Three To Go* where Peter had directed the episode *Michael* for visionary producer Gil Brealey. Brealey was later to leave Film Australia to set up the South Australian Film Corporation for premier Don Dunstan. Two visionaries working together.

In 1973 the name Commonwealth Film Unit was abolished in favour of the more embracing name, Film Australia.

Tom Daly had been brought out from Canada to advise Film Australia on the *Challenge for Change* program he had pioneered for the National Film Board of Canada. Though there was enthusiasm for the idea, only one of the proposed series ever got off the ground. Peter Weir was given the task of directing *Whatever Happened to Green Valley?*, an hour-long program about life and social issues facing the residents in a new Housing Commission estate on the far-flung edges of Sydney's western suburbs. The idea was to film these issues affecting the

---

1   Cinesound cinematographer Howard Rubie's father.

estate, then screen the result to the citizens at their community hall, filming their reactions and incorporating these into the finished documentary. It became a huge undertaking. The Canadians had had great success with the format in tackling social issues facing the underprivileged and working class, and the problems facing them and the indigenous people of that country. *Whatever Happened to Green Valley?* was a tentative start to an Australian *Challenge for Change* program but sadly was never continued.

Caddie was still two years away when Crombie and I teamed up again, this time as director and producer. *The Fifth Façade* was to be the 'official' government film to celebrate the opening of the Opera House by the Queen on 28 September 1973. I made it clear from the outset that the film couldn't spend six months in the cutting room after the opening ceremony, but had to reach the screen the very next week. I can remember the glazed looks on everyone's face. Who is this upstart contractor from the freelance world? It was all or nothing. Would the cinemas take it at twenty-nine minutes (a three-reeler)? Yes they would, if it was in the same week of the opening of the Opera House. *The Fifth Façade* didn't conform to Film Australia's house style such as an *Outlook*, which was a maximum of fifteen minutes (two reels) or *Australian Diary* (ten minutes). Denys Brown, producer-in-chief who succeeded Stanley Hawes, expressed concern but when assured the film had a distributor for its theatrical release he relented. With only six months to go we started pre-production immediately with production manager Damien Parer at the helm to organise schedule, shooting dates of rehearsals, the Opera House itself, music clearances and a host of other things that went into a strict timetable that had to deliver in more ways than one.

Donald Crombie felt it was essential to have Joern Utzon's commentary about his masterful work. This was not going to be an easy task. Utzon had been sacked by the NSW government for overruns and had returned to Denmark. Sam Wannamaker was to direct the first opera to be performed, *War and Peace*, Jim Sharman *The Threepenny Opera,* and Birgit Nilsson was to sing in the Concert Hall. Our plan was to film all final rehearsals, editing and recording up to the Saturday opening day where we had rostered every cameraman on Film Australia's staff to film the momentous event in 35mm widescreen Eastmancolor.

During the planning stages Utzon responded to one of my letters. He would do the narration provided we recorded it in Denmark. This had come about thanks to Bill Wheatland, Utzon's former assistant architect, who had made representations to his old boss on our behalf. There was great excitement at the news of this break-through, not only in our team but right through the corridors of Film Australia. But getting Donald to Denmark was far more complicated than buying an overseas airline ticket. One had to make application to the Overseas Visits Committee, a rigid Commonwealth bureaucracy, whose sole purpose seemed to be to frustrate and prevent public servants from travelling overseas, particularly filmmakers who were regarded as 'junior officers'. My saviour at Film Australia, Stuart Jay, once again came to the fore. He knew how to play the system and Donald's authority came through on the morning of his departure to Copenhagen. Bill Wheatland travelled with Donald to Helebeck for the recording of Utzon's commentary, and his presence proved to be invaluable. Donald remembers vividly one extremely poignant moment about the visit: Wheatland and Utzon were reminiscing about their times in Sydney. 'Utzon went very quiet for a few moments, then said softly in his Danish accent, "Ah, Bill, we should have finished it." It was one of the most moving moments I have witnessed.'

There were two rival films being made at the time but we didn't let on to the media that we had Utzon.

Sam Wannamaker came to the studio to record his narration, the two commentaries were married together and the mix was completed for the first two reels.

The opening of the Opera House by the Queen went without a hitch and Colorfilm Laboratories worked the weekend to process and print the negative. By Monday night editing (by Richard Hindley) had been completed and the three-reeler opened in each capital city the following Thursday, in Sydney at the Embassy, echoes of Cinesound days by now a distant memory.

Boxing Day 1974: I was enjoying a late Christmas repast at the Beecroft home of fellow Film Australia producer Tim Read and his wife Adrienne, when the news came through that Darwin had been flattened by Cyclone Tracey. I can't remember all the circumstances of how Film Australia had a 35mm crew either in Darwin or nearly there at the time, but we hit the phones to suggest we put out a one-reeler 'newsreel' to the cinemas immediately. Colour TV was less than six months old and although its take-up was growing, it hadn't yet become a threat to cinema-going, nor was it in the majority of homes.

The footage brought from Darwin showing the destruction and havoc was top-rating documentary material. By using, with permission, actual 'grabs' from radio broadcasts, I was able to put the 'newsreel' together without the use of a narrator, which gave an immediacy to the reel not normally associated with a newsreel. Within four days *Cyclone Tracey* was playing in major cinemas right across Australia. Within days Bob Kingsbury was in Darwin with a 16mm crew making the memorable television special of the disaster, *When Will The Birds Return?*

With the newsreel of the cyclone it was thought we had possibly created Australia's last major 'newsreel'. Little did we know that just over a year later, a train travelling from the Blue Mountains to Sydney would derail and crash into the stanchions of a major bridge at Granville, bringing down the bridge, crushing a section of the train and killing eighty people. It was late morning when I heard the news on the car radio driving to Lindfield. As with *Tracey*, Film Australia mobilised itself and, using the same format, issued a 'newsreel' simply titled *Granville*, which hit cinema screens four days later. This was the last major newsreel. A sombre note on which to end an era. The event is commemorated every year at the bridge where eighty roses are thrown onto the railway tracks, and has become known as the Day of the Roses.

Speaking of trains, hereby hangs another tale, and one of a more cheering kind. For reasons I cannot possibly remember I asked in the tearoom one day (a ten minute break – oh, very well then, twelve minutes!) whatever had happened to what I described as 'that green engine that used to haul the Newcastle express'. Talk about waking up the sheltered workshop! I hadn't realised I was surrounded by train devotees. Head of music – dour, urbane James McCarthy – peered at me and said 'You would be referring, young man, to 3801 I presume?' I liked the 'young man' but 3801? What on earth was that? I was soon to learn, wasn't I. McCarthy and film editor Ian Walker descended on my office and a film was born. McCarthy and director Chris McGill had already submitted a proposal to the film committee for a short subject about the 38 class locomotives, but it had fallen on deaf ears. I studied their submission but felt Chris was not right for the project. I had seen David Haythornthwaite's recent work at FA and felt he was right for the task. Naturally McGill was not happy with my decision but this is what producing is all about. A slot was found in the *Outlook* strand, which were occasional two-reelers on various subjects of the 'national program', produced for the cinemas. Director David Haythornthwaite set about writing a scenario based on an idea of the train travelling through time across the countryside with dramatised 'memories' and without narration. The idea appealed to me. House cinematographer Dean Semler came on board, along with fellow cameraman Ross King to head up second unit, Wayne Le Clos as editor and James McCarthy suggested George Dreyfus to compose the score. One could not have wished for a stronger or better team. And so *A Steam Train Passes* was scheduled for a six-week winter shoot.

Now, having an idea for a film is one thing – making it happen is another, more so when it involves a train. Fortunately 3801 had recently undergone a refit and the railway enthusiasts endorsed and fully supported making the film and providing volunteers, which would help their case eventually for the engine's full restoration. Not so the New South Wales Government Railways. They just didn't want to know about it. So it was off to see the Minister for Transport who thought it was a splendid idea and issued the appropriate public service authorisation for the film to be made, provided it did not disrupt the passenger and freight services on the line we would be provided with to shoot our film. Fortunately for us, the location chosen was centred on Blayney, NSW, a bleak and extremely cold place in the middle of winter – but ideal conditions to film steam.

You may well ask who in the end is in charge of the railways. The system was broken up into divisions, with the superintendent of that particular division having the final word, not head office, on what you can do and when you can do it. The superintendent at Blayney was delighted with the thought of us filming in his jurisdiction and felt it was an additional challenge to facilitate our shoot, scheduling our filming stops within the regular timetable. The main difficulty was finding sufficient time between regular trains to film not one but two, three and more 'takes' of 3801 steaming past hauling the vintage carriages, then being allowed the time to back up the track to do the run again. Trains may move at speed, but shunting in reverse is a different matter altogether. Filming took place day and night over the next six weeks. Radio stations were receiving phone calls from intrigued listeners saying they had seen 'this ghost train' travelling past at night. What was it? Where was it going?

Actors are well trained to hit their 'marks' that are discreetly placed on the floor, and to deliver their lines, in theatre and film. The camera-dolly pushers likewise have their 'marks' to follow, which are placed on the set. Try getting a steam train to stop on its 'mark'! David Haythornthwaite created an evocative flashback, set in World War II in a pub with young soldiers on leave waiting to catch their train back to their barracks. The soldiers are enjoying their last beer, looking out the window of the pub across to the railway station, when 3801 moves into view. After several takes of the train, requiring it to back up some way along the track, 3801 finally came into view and stopped right on the 'mark', letting off a marvellous burst of steam.

The opening sequence of A Steam Train Passes is still, for me, one of the great moments of picture and sound working together in film anywhere. To 'coal' a steam engine for that day's run commences about four in the morning, a ritual beautifully captured by Dean Semler's camera and Howard Spry's recording. We follow the preparation of the engine to the point where 'steam's up' and 3801 begins to move out of the shed on to the turntable, which moves the engine around to its designated track to begin its journey. As the engine begins to move off the turntable, amid the cacophony of steam and engine, George Dreyfus's haunting score begins. It sends a tingle up my spine when I hear it to this very day. The marriage of George's score and the authentic sound of the train is one of the triumphs of the film.

In the early stages of editing by Wayne Le Clos, it was clear to David and me we needed no commentary, but we did need to find a way to explain to the audience what 3801 was, and why there was a film about it. The newsreel libraries had nothing, yet it was known that Cinesound had covered the launch of 3801 in the forties. By now of course the news had spread among the train buffs about the film. One had recalled seeing a *Cinesound Review* years before, but it no longer existed according to their records. Enter Roger Mackenzie.[2] The phone rang. 'I think I may have something you're looking for' said the voice. Roger came up to Film Australia. Always dressed meticulously in suit and tie, no matter what the weather, under his arm he had a reel of nitrate[3] film. Nitrate film is to be respected at all times and, having spent my formative years at Cinesound whose entire vaults contained nitrate film, I was accustomed to handling it and recognised the familiar 'smell' when Roger lifted the lid off the can. There, in pristine condition, was the *Cinesound Review* with its main item heralding 'Monarch of the Rails', photography J.S. Fletcher, film editor Terry Banks.[4]

Hearing Peter Bathurst's familiar voice delivering the stirring, patriotic and somewhat nationalistic narration, I knew immediately it bore all the trademarks of a Ken G. Hall production. It was decided to place the newsreel item at the beginning of *A Steam Train Passes* before the main title, as though the newsreel was being seen at the movies, and then dissolve to our journey beginning.

Film Australia's rigid discipline of 'house style' not only dictated the length of the film but everything else, right up to its delivery. Before a film could be 'locked off' it had to receive the approval of the producer-in-chief prior to the mix of the sound being transferred to optical soundtrack to enable prints to be made. I arranged a 'double-header' screening – picture and sound not married together – for Denys Brown to see at 4pm Friday afternoon. Denys I had every respect for; a pleasant, conservative man, he was not a filmmaker but a capable administrative leader. As I recall, only the producer was allowed to sit with the producer-in-chief at this 'approval' screening.

The lights came up, there was a significant pause, then Denys looked at me and said, 'But it's not finished, Tony, why haven't you played me the commentary?' I

---

2   Roger Mackenzie, a film editor and collector. When researching *Palace of Dreams*, a film to celebrate the 75th anniversary of the Greater Union Organisation, historian and researcher Graham Shirley alerted me to the fact that Roger had footage of the State Theatre Orchestra filmed by Frank Hurley in 1934 for a 'B' support, *Cinesound Varieties*. Ken Hall hated this film so much he later had the negative destroyed. Collectors are very private people and incredibly secretive about their collections. Once afraid of being sued, the studios and the industry are now thankful to embrace them, for very often these are the only people who will have the missing footage to enable the restoration of a film. Vale Roger.
3   Nitrate film is highly combustible if not stored in the right conditions and was used till the 1950s.
4   Terry Banks edited Cinesound Review *Kokoda Front Line,* which won an Oscar for Ken G. Hall.

explained there wasn't any and, politely, that we didn't need any, and that it was a journey through time to observe, remember and enjoy. I could see he was quite troubled by this development and he indicated he would talk to me on Monday. I spent the weekend working on a strategy to handle this situation to ensure we didn't have narration forced upon us. Well, I need not have bothered. Very first thing on Monday, before all the various production meetings got underway, my phone rang. 'Mr Brown would like to see you right away.' I walked into his spacious office. 'I've been thinking about your film – I think it's a good idea – let's hope it works, ah, go ahead and finish it – thank you.' I thanked him and quickly left in case he changed his mind. Haythornthwaite, Le Clos, our whole team, were anxiously waiting in the corridor. We all had an early celebratory morning tea.

A Steam Train Passes opened at the Ascot Theatre[5], Sydney, as the support to *Barry Mackenzie Holds His Own*. The Ascot had one of the biggest screens in Sydney and was the city's first stadium cinema. *Bazza* was to hold his own at the Ascot for many weeks, but the talking point became the short.

Word of mouth began to spread. The phone rang. I recognised the voice immediately. It was Harry Griffiths, 'young Harry' from Roy Rene's (Mo) *Macackie Mansions* radio days. Harry started waxing lyrical about a film he had just seen that afternoon. He thought it the most satisfying, evocative film he had enjoyed in years. It was our short, *A Steam Train Passes*, not the feature.[6]

So what of Film Australia? In 2007 the government announced the creation of a new super film authority merging the operations of the Australian Film Commission, the Film Finance Corporation and Film Australia to commence operations July 2008. Britain got rid of its National Film Unit, the COI, in the early sixties. The National Film Board of Canada reinvented itself with the establishment of digital cinemas across the Dominion, to bring documentaries to its people. So what did Film Australia mean to anyone? What is the 'National Program'? Is anyone aware of it? Why does the government want to keep it? The need for shorts in cinemas, which Film Australia handsomely served, ceased at least twenty years ago. What was Film Australia achieving that wasn't already being done by the ABC and SBS and, more importantly, our independent documentary

---

5   The Ascot Theatre, Sydney, was built (and so named to screen the Australian premiere season of *My Fair Lady*) by the Virgona family, independent exhibitors who owned the North Sydney Orpheum (a barn of a place) and the Cremorne Orpheum (an art deco treasure). Warners had had a dispute with Hoyts Theatres and guaranteed the film to the Virgonas who in turn guaranteed their theatre. Hoyts were obviously horrified at this likelihood and after more than a year of negotiation, Warners returned to the fold and *My Fair Lady* opened at Hoyts Century Theatre where it was to play for two years. The Virgonas meanwhile had to be content to open the Ascot with Cliff Richard in *Summer Holiday*.

6   *A Steam Train Passes* is still Film Australia's most popular film.

I was to return to Film Australia in the 1990's at the invitation of Executive Producer, Chris Oliver, to produce the four part series *The Celluloid Heroes* to celebrate Australia's centenary of cinema. Writer and director, Robert Francis, created three of the four episodes, and Donald Crombie created the remaining episode. It was a mammoth three-year task. Nigel Westlake wrote the score for the Melbourne Symphony Orchestra and Bryan Brown was the narrator. From the USA we brought Cinesound's star of the thirties, Shirley Ann Richards, to appear along with many other Australian pioneers of film. This photograph is Australian film history. L to R front row: Philys Cross, Stars of the series Michael Pate, Shirley Ann Richards and Bill Kerr. L to R back row: Me, Alex Ezard (Cinesound's and Shirley Ann Richard's make-up artist and later a producer at Film Australia), Chris Oliver, Clive Cross (the man who with Arthur Smith put the 'sound' in Cinesound), Writer and director Robert Francis.

filmmakers? If Film Australia had been developing small digital cinemas across Australia, reaching out into our regional areas where, believe it or not, they are starved for information and entertainment that documentaries can and are providing, I would have been a strong supporter.

However, I found the organisation caught in a time warp of timidity, such as that which enveloped it when they hadn't the drive, nous, not to mention vision, to take on the *Challenge for Change* program so successfully embraced by the National Film Board of Canada. What is there that is so sacrosanct about this National Program that couldn't be serviced by the independent documentary filmmakers of Australia, from an office in Sydney or Melbourne or, for that matter, Gulargambone? Hopefully the new entity, Screen Australia, can get a handle on this 'National Program', even if the government can't. There I rest my case.

18

... 'You Wanna Make A Film About A Woman???!!'

So exclaimed Michael Tarrant, the then head of Columbia Pictures in Australia, with whom I had made an appointment to invite Columbia to invest in *Caddie* and to distribute worldwide. I had figured that, as Columbia had financed Clarence Badger's *Rangle River* in 1936, Ken Hall's *Smithy* in 1946, and a distribution guarantee for Michael Powell's *Age of Consent* in 1967, it might be time for them to put their toe in the water again.[1] Not so! Columbia liked the story, even thought it was commercial. Tarrant, after initial reservations, became surprisingly positive in that he thought it was the best thing he had read locally with an international ingredient. I asked what that was and he replied, 'It is about a woman, and there are some valuable markets for that subject.' However, was it for Columbia? The word naïve began to enter this up-and-coming producer's vocabulary.

However, nothing compares with my bizarre encounter with one of the heads of the Rural Bank of NSW, which had moved from Martin Place, Sydney's centre of banking, to the corner of Oxford Street and Wentworth Avenue, now called Whitlam Square. I was ushered into a vast office, in the corner of which was one very large but bare desk, except for one black telephone, a blotter on green baize, a glass top and a small desk calendar. Behind the desk sat a stern-faced gentleman. He too said, 'So you wanna make this film about a woman?' After speaking for about a minute on the reasons why I thought the Rural Bank should invest in our motion picture, he looked at me, looked at his desk calendar, looked back, paused and said, 'Sorry – I was just making sure it wasn't April Fool's Day'. Naïve now became my byword for what was to come.

---

1   It should be pointed out that the only reason for overseas films being made in Australia up until the early 1970s was to extricate monies earned by American pictures locked up by our stringent tax laws of the time.

I am continually asked what a producer does. Well, in the following chapters you are about to find out.

Editing the kangaroo hunt reel in *Wake in Fright* was exhilarating but damned exhausting. It was a Saturday and it had been a long week. I decided to wrap about five and by the time my Morris 1100 got me across the bridge to Mosman en route home it was just coming up to 6pm. The newsagent was closing up so I quickly bought the Saturday papers when a book on his shelves caught my eye. A black and white cover of Sun Books, 'the autobiography of a Sydney barmaid' in small print, then just the one word in bold – *Caddie*. I purchased it and continued home to Clifton Gardens where I prepared my tea and set off upstairs for an early night. Early night indeed. I opened the cover of the paperback. The title page says: *Caddie, A Sydney barmaid, an autobiography written by herself.* The frontispiece informed me the book had been first published in 1953 by Constable, the year I started work, but it hadn't reached paperback till Sun Books published it in 1966. The cover said 80c, 8/- – it was the year Australia changed from imperial to decimal currency.

Dymphna Cusack, in her introduction describing the 'bright May Day in 1953' when Caddie was launched onto the English market with 'rave' reviews, says: 'It was the triumph of Caddie's life. For the distinguished writer and critic, Michael Sadler, and for me, the book's success continued the belief we had had in it from the beginning.'

Strangely, the book had not been noticed by filmmakers. In 1953 there was no Australian feature film industry per se. In fact, I hadn't realised there had ever been one till I respliced *The Sentimental Bloke* in that very same year *Caddie* was published.

It was now 4am and I hadn't been able to put the book down. I turned out my light, only to notice the first light of dawn breaking. The year, 1970.

What to do? This book was screaming out to be made into a major film. A couple of phone calls on the Monday morning put me in the direction of the author's agent in London, Stephen Durbridge, who was later to point me in the direction of Curtis Brown in Sydney. I could have an option for £100 for twelve months, renewable for a maximum of three further years. What was an option? Durbridge courteously explained in a long-distance phone call from London what rights an option gave me. Though I was being paid a then handsome $190 per week to edit *Wake in Fright*, £100 was quite an amount per annum to find to give me the rights to develop the book into a feature film, particularly in light of the fact that I had no idea what I was doing. So I raided the savings bank and arranged my first international bank transfer. I'm sure Stephen Durbridge was

(Top) DOP Peter James and director Donald Crombie
line up a shot with Takis and Helen in Sydney's Botanic
Gardens.

(Right) Where a producer should be on a set – out of
the way. Production manager Ross Matthews and me
waiting for the 1st assistant director, Hal McElroy, to call
a wrap!

(Bottom left) Jack Thompson and Donald Crombie
discuss the filming with Caddie's daughter Catherine,
visiting the set for the first time. Slightly overwhelmed
by the experience at first, Catherine confided how
pleased she and the family were with Joan Long's
adaptation of her mother's book.

(Bottom right) Our star, Helen Morse, as Caddie.

wondering who on earth was this ratbag from Down Under, and what was he going to do with this book.

I thought it would be appropriate to commission a woman to adapt the book to a screenplay. I had met Joan Long when she was researching and writing *The Pictures That Moved* for Alan Anderson at Film Australia when I had stolen a march on them with *Forgotten Cinema*. Neither film conflicted and we got on well together. I had also been impressed with her script for Christopher McCulloch's *Paddington Lace*, a widescreen theatrical short, also for Film Australia. I rang her at Lindfield to tell her what I had done. Would she adapt the book for me if I could raise the money? 'Tony – that's very nice of you but I have never written a feature film,' she said. I quickly pointed out that I hadn't produced one. 'Let me have a think about it,' Joan courteously replied. Before I had time to put my copy in the post to her in the hope it would convince her, she rang. 'I popped into Lawsons and found a secondhand copy – you're right, it has to be made – I'll have a go but I am very apprehensive attempting something this ambitious.'

So our journey began.

I had invited Donald Crombie to be our director not long after finishing editing *The Choice* and shortly after delivery of Joan's first draft screenplay. Although Donald had repeated what Joan had said about a first feature, I knew he could achieve what we were both looking for. The first draft naturally was over-length and overwritten. This I have discovered is always the way with a first draft adaptation of a book. The adaptor keeps faith with the author's work, and it is not until the second and third drafts that the screenwriter's skill is seen at its best, when they are putting themselves into the adaptation. For example, in the book *Caddie*, her Greek lover returns to Australia and is killed in a car crash three days before they are to be married. It was just too much to expect an audience to accept and it didn't seem believable, so out it came. Even then it was a long haul for Joan to bring the script down to what we all thought was the appropriate length. Donald's director's eye on the script at this point was of great help to Joan.

When I had sent the script to Michael Tarrant at Columbia I had also sent it to David Williams, the managing director of Greater Union. David was aware of my involvement with the industry as the producer of Greater Union's *Cinesound Review* and my production of *Forgotten Cinema*. I didn't reach the tenth floor of 49 Market Street. David phoned, thought it was the most depressing script he had ever read. 'It will never work, Tony.' Not cheering news to break to Donald and Joan.

Michael Tarrant declined Columbia's involvement, suggested I make contact with Graham Burke, the managing director of Roadshow. So I commenced a two-pronged attack on the marketplace. The Australian Film Development Corporation (AFDC) had been formed by the Federal Government to bankroll Australian films, headed by Tom Stacey and investment manager Nadine Hollow. Tom wasn't too enthusiastic overall about the project, probably having much the same reaction as had David Williams, but not saying so in as many words. Nadine Hollow, however, was wholly supportive. We had arrived at a budget of $375,000 for a period film set in the 1920s and '30s, on a six-day, six-week shooting schedule. Little did we know!

The AFDC was demanding we raise $125,000 from a distributor based on Greater Union having put up this amount for *Picnic at Hanging Rock*, but relented after pressure having been brought to bear because we had allowed $40,000 of our budget to be allocated to distribution and publicity, which Roadshow was to take over later, freeing up our budget for the production of the feature. Graham Burke had a very favourable reaction to the script, quite the opposite to that of David Williams, which becomes very relevant later in this chapter.

Roadshow would come on board and Graham suggested Joan and I meet with him in the Garden Court at Sydney's Wentworth Hotel to discuss strategy on handling the AFDC's sub-committee who were sending mixed messages out re the AFDC's reaction to our application for funding. We had learned that Tom Stacey was now flatly opposed to the project receiving investment funding.

Joan had had the brainwave of suggesting I apply to the International Women's Year committee for investment. Although we had a male director, the book had been written by a woman about herself, and the script was adapted by a woman too. Much to our surprise and incredulity, not to mention pleasure, International Women's Year offered an investment of $50,000. Roadshow confirmed their $25,000 and both these initiatives took the AFDC completely by surprise.

I had approached Len Mauger at the Nine Television Network but Len wasn't too keen on the idea of investing in Australian films. However, he agreed to read it and to get back to me.

Michael Thornhill, who had produced and directed *Between Wars* with Corin Redgrave two years previously, had become a strong supporter. He and I go back many years as friends, both as editors as it turns out, and through his publication *Sydney Cinema Journal*. He had tricked me and the entire industry when I declared one day how impressed I was with the editing of a new editor in town by the name of Anthony Edgecliff (his company name is Edgecliff Films to this day). He roared with maniacal laughter. He claimed he could never get a job under his real name for he was considered too much of a radical, so he invented Anthony Edgecliff. I told Michael of Len Mauger's procrastination. I was at the Crombies' house in

Kissing Point Road, Turramurra, when the phone rang. It was Thornhill in full flight – 'Ah! Jesus Christ Buckley – ring bloody Mauger and offer him $30,000 investment and $30,000 licence fee – now – ring him now,' and hung up. With the fear of God I phoned Len immediately. 'Okay,' said Len, '$30,000 investment, $30,000 licence fee – but – it's in perpetuity – no negotiation.' 'Agreed,' I said. Producers will do or say anything for money. I was learning fast.

I notified the AFDC and Roadshow. Tom Stacey phoned. 'Well, you've got your money.' The gruff tone of his voice indicated he didn't concur with the AFDC board's decision to invest. However, he later said to me how pleased he was that everything had worked out.

From Roadshow's Sydney office, Gregory Coote and Robin Ball came on board (Robin Ball was to become Robin Campbell-Jones and, much later, Mrs Robin Burke). In the meantime, parallel to all this activity, the search for Caddie had commenced months beforehand.

It was a morning in February 1975. Donald Crombie and I were to meet our first contender for the role of Caddie at my flat in Lane Cove. It was long before intensive casting was to commence but this actress was en route to Melbourne to play a lead role in Pat Lovell's production, *Picnic at Hanging Rock*, and today was her last opportunity to meet with us. Her name – Helen Morse. Our meeting? Interview? What should one call it? Here we were, Donald and me, two new kids on the block meeting with an actress who had already become renowned for her role as Marion in the splendid ABC television drama of the same name, and in Sandy Harbutt's contemporary bikie drama *Stone*. Her director on *Picnic* had already made an impressive debut with *The Cars That Ate Paris* – Peter Weir. We talked and had tea. All very pleasant, and then it was time for Helen to leave. We wished her well with *Picnic*. Would she mind doing a screen-test for the investors when she returned? 'Of course not,' she replied, and departed.

Donald and I looked at each other and we said – more or less in sync – 'but that's her – she's Caddie!' We both realised this couldn't possibly be, we had purely been mesmerised by the moment and we now had to set about to find our Caddie. Over forty actresses were auditioned but the presence of Helen continued to haunt us both.

May 29 and 30, screen-tests were booked.

The search for Caddie's Greek lover, Peter, was made somewhat easier by the casting of Takis Emmanuel by Tom Cowan the previous year for his film *Promised Woman*, in which Takis played Manolis, a Greek immigrant. Takis was the right age and had the right 'presence' to be Caddie's lover. Jack Thompson was cast in the role of Ted, who gives Caddie her nickname based on his Cadillac car because, like his car, she had 'class'.

The cast Donald put together for *Caddie* now looks like a who's who of Australian actors and actresses: Jacki Weaver, Melissa Jaffer, Jane Harders, Kirrily Nolan, Lynette Curran, June Salter, Robyn Nevin, Pat Everson. On the male side much the same in luminaries, particularly the casting of the two Rabbitos – Sonny and Bill – Drew Forsythe and Ron Blanchard. They were backed up by John Ewart, John Gaden, Willie Fennell, Les Foxcroft, Phillip Hinton, Bryan Niland and Lucky Grills.

Putting our crew together was bringing the usual reaction – 'Oh! I haven't done a feature before.' Fortunately our director of photography, Peter James, had shot one small children's feature for Chris McCulloch in 1972, *Avengers of the Reef*. As with our actors, the crew credit list on *Caddie* is now a venerable who's who of the Australian cinema.

Shooting was to start on Monday, August 18 1975, for a six-day, six-week filming schedule. Takis Emmanuel arrived August 10 on SQ752 at 6.45am to commence rehearsals and wardrobe fittings.

Unit manager Errol Sullivan queried me about the schedule. He felt that we were going to be stretched to achieve it and that perhaps we should be looking at cutting the script. After the first week's filming Donald declared we couldn't possibly shoot the picture in the time allocated. How right Errol was!

I felt for writer Joan Long who worked with Donald every Sunday for the next three weeks of the shoot trying to eliminate scenes. At first Joan declared that it was like taking one's arm off, but by the end of filming she felt we had taken not only both arms off but her legs as well! In six weeks we filmed in some forty locations, including three days of the main bar interiors in the old Cinesound Studios at 541 Darling Street, Rozelle. Other pub scenes included the Mercantile in The Rocks, Sydney, Sir William Wallace, The Bald Face and the Kent Hotel, all three in Balmain, the latter later becoming 'Caddie's Restaurant'.

The six-day shooting schedule was a killer. Saturdays one normally tries to wrap late afternoon, for one can sense the energy level drop after lunch on this last day of our working week. Not so, from an entry in my desk diary of Saturday, August 23, the end of our first week's filming. Donald Crombie has written: '2 a.m. Your crew is sitting here drinking your beer and your red wine in your office in your time. Mr Williamson (focus puller) requests a cutter over the lights as it offends his eyes. Mr Seale (John Seale, camera operator) regards the watermelon as obese. Camera Dept requests Tic Tacs to be organised in office.'

(Top left) The closure of Cameron Street, Edgecliff, was a boon to our ability to film as well as a long-term benefit for the residents. However, filming was momentarily suspended to welcome Michael Powell and his son, Kevin. Michael took a keen interest in our filming techniques with very few lights and small crew. Here talking with Donald Crombie and me, he was interested to learn of Donald's background in documentaries. It was my documentary, *Forgotten Cinema*, with Stewart Young, that won me the position of film editor on Michael's *Age of Consent*.

(Top right) Also visiting that day was author Dymphna Cusack who 'discovered' Caddie, and screenwriter Joan Long, here pictured with Helen Morse and me.

(Right) The *Caddie* crew shot (1975) is literally a who's who of Australian film and television today. Cinesounder Syd Mayo is centre foreground. Caddie's daughter Catherine and Helen Morse at left rear.

I doubt if our steely-eyed, intrepid production accountant, Treisha Ghent, would have permitted such extravagance!

Unit manager Errol Sullivan had his hands full the following Saturday of our shoot in the inner Sydney suburb of Glebe. Next to our location, the owner had decided it was the right day to do his home renovations. The fellow was totally uncooperative until Errol arrived on his doorstep with a slab of beer. Quietness reigned, and further slabs of beer continued to arrive. Errol sat with the renovator and filming was achieved, but poor Errol was legless on wrap!

Saturday, 6 September: End of third week of filming and an historic moment in Australian film history. Fellow producer and director Tom Jeffrey brought pioneer producer/director Ken G. Hall out to visit us on set in what was once his bustling Cinesound Studio. How would he feel? What memories would watching our filming bring back to him? Was it a wise idea, I couldn't help thinking. KG had been my mentor from the time I had started at Cinesound in 1955 and had continued to be an advisor thereafter. He had taken a keen interest in the development of *Caddie*, stressing all the time to me that I had to be 'commercial'. His favourite time for talking was Sunday morning about 9.45. He would ring and his gravel voice would ask 'How's it going, son?' Echoes of Bert Cross. On arriving at the studios he couldn't get over how art director Owen Williams had recreated a 1920s pub interior on the old sound stage. DOP Peter James was taking a last meter reading when first assistant director Hal McElroy called 'Quiet!' for a take. Peter said he was ready. Hal: 'Okay everybody', when KG leaned over and asked Peter, 'When do you put the lights on?' 'They are on Mr Hall,' Peter explained. KG couldn't wait till the following Sunday to make his regular call. He rang on the Tuesday knowing we would have seen Saturday's footage Monday night. 'How was the exposure on the pub scenes?' he enquired. 'Terrific,' I assured him. Coming from an age where film was only 10 ASA and every brute arc and klieg light would be burning with glaring intensity down on the set, and on the poor actors, Ken Hall couldn't get over the fact that the colour film and the lenses were now so much faster, which enabled such low-key lighting. I knew he would never be convinced until he saw our fine cut early in 1976.

There were many hilarious incidents on this wonderful bar set. Donald's favourite is about our elderly extras who were 'actuals' from a nearby old people's home. 'They were supplied with real stout and beer and couldn't work out why the barmaids (Helen Morse and Jacki Weaver) sometimes served them and sometimes not. Art department Graham "Grace" Walker crawled around their legs with film cans containing burning incense. "What are you doing, son?" asked one oldtimer. "Making smoke," replied "Grace". "What for?" asked the ancient.

"The film," said "Grace". "What bloody film?"was the next question. Probably this same gentleman was the one who pushed the bar door marked "gentlemen" open, only to find sound recordist Des Bone crouched over his Nagra recording machine, then struggled in the darkness (of the set) and found a length of picket fence that he anointed, to the ire of the nurse.'

We later had a second VIP pioneer film visit on location in Cameron Street, Edgecliff. Cameron Street had been chosen for its old terrace houses which typified Sydney of the 1900s, and in particular a stand-alone cottage where the closing scenes of *Caddie* were to be filmed. The residents had been campaigning to have the street permanently closed, for it was used as a rat run by motorists in the morning rush hour, to take a short cut to New South Head Road and the city. Though the Council disapproved, the police gave us permission to close the road completely to facilitate filming for two days. The residents were delighted. So were we.[2] Our second visitor was Michael Powell, accompanied by his son, Kevin. Powell, like Ken Hall, was intrigued with how small our location crew was, and how Peter James was basically using only reflectors. (There is an exquisite scene of Helen Morse in a phone box where she strikes a match to read the telephone directory. There was no lighting other than that of the match.) Filming was halted to allow various crew members, who had been on *Age of Consent*, to say hello to 'the master'.

Film editor Tim Wellburn was progressively editing as we shot and had an assembly or first cut ready a week after completion of filming. It never ceases to amaze me, the impact a first cut of a picture has on one. The script has been scrutinised by writer, director, producer et al. Rushes are viewed, everything is okay and then WHAM, the first cut is screened and there is your picture, warts and all. The scenes that you thought were working are suddenly not working at all. This only applies to maybe three or four scenes, but with *Caddie* we had made a thumping oversight. There was a long 'dolly' shot of Caddie and Peter (Takis Emmanuel) walking along Balmoral Beach at night, talking about their respective pasts. These sorts of scenes, involving camera dollies and the laying of tracks for the camera to run along, take hours to set up, rehearse and film. On the page there is absolutely nothing wrong with the scene. Likewise at rushes. However, in the cut of the film it was absolutely boring. It completely stopped the energy and progression of the story. It was information we, and the audience, didn't need to know. One complete night's filming on the cutting room floor!

2   As a result of the closure for filming, the authorities later closed Cameron Street permanently, making it into a cul de sac.

What is not on the cutting-room floor is the extraordinarily long tracking shot at the beginning of the film. The opening scenes are set in a heritage-listed precinct of one of Sydney's great Federation suburbs, The Appian Way, Burwood. It was planned to do a tracking shot looking through the windows of the house at Caddie preparing to leave home, the camera moving from left to right, then back right to left, following Caddie moving from one room to another. The problem was, being the last shot of the day the light was beginning to fade. The shot was rehearsed and Peter James went for a take. The shot was declared to be far too long and a retake was needed. The light had gone. On seeing this scene, all three minutes of it, at rushes the next evening, it was quite obvious there was more brick wall than glimpses through the windows from the veranda. We had only a day in The Appian Way and a re-shoot was out of the question. Hence all the end titles became the main titles! This achieved two things. It settled the audience down and gave time for Patrick Flynn, our composer, to firmly establish the musical themes for the picture. I think Peter James still winces when he sees this scene, as does Donald.

Friday, January 23, 1976, 3pm. Our day of reckoning! We had commenced mixing the sound and music on January 7. Patrick Flynn's music fitted like a glove. Before we had commenced pre-production I had given him tapes of my records of Isham Jones and his Orchestra from the 1930s, and a recording (a favourite) of the torch singer Ruth Etting singing 'Mean to Me' which I thought typified Caddie's life. Patrick knew we couldn't afford to buy the rights to 'Mean to Me' but very craftily (and legally) managed to incorporate a couple of bars of the melody into the main theme. The day had come to play back the final mix of the film to our investors before the film went to the laboratory to become the print we see and hear at the cinema.

In attendance were Graham Burke, CEO of Village Roadshow, the champion of the film with Robin Ball; Greg Coote and Len Mauger, who had come in at the death knell; John McQuaid and Peter Martin, two full-time commissioners from the newly formed Australian Film Commission, with staffers John Daniell and Carly Deans; Ken Hall, Joan, Donald and me.

To Joan's, Donald's and my relief, the screening went off without a hitch until someone mentioned the length of the main titles. Donald Crombie refers to this as the Smith's Crisps syndrome. His drollness is to be enjoyed: 'I was mortified by their length and died a thousand deaths (and still do) every time the film was screened. I said in defence that I had an aversion to people eating during films, so I told them I had designed the credits of *Caddie* to cover the time it takes to eat a packet of Smith's Crisps and crunch up the empty packet and throw it under the seat and that this should occur just as the director's credit faded from the screen. I don't know if anyone believed me but there was no more discussion on the length of the titles.'

An enthusiastic Graham Burke declared it was definitely a film for Greater Union. I was mortified. Their CEO was David Williams who had hated the script and thought it would never work. I drew Graham aside to break the news. He was now even more determined. 'We'll get Greg (Coote) to speak to him.' Greg was in charge of the Sydney and NSW operations of Roadshow. He said Graham was right and it was an ideal film for David to open Greater Union's new flagship, The Pitt Centre, in the heart of Sydney. I thought this move would be doomed from the outset. Greg Coote, however, persuaded David Williams to come and see the film before we locked it off at the laboratory. Greg suggested strongly that Donald and I sit through the screening with David.

There are few end credits on the picture, as explained earlier, so the lights quickly came up in the United Sound dubbing suite. David was sitting in the back row to my far left and I was on the aisle. I think Donald was sitting behind me on the other side of the sound mixing desk with Peter Fenton and Ron Purvis, our mixers. David looked right at me and said, 'Well, I was wrong, wasn't I?'

I didn't – couldn't – say a word.

There are not many CEOs who will ever admit a mistake or admit they might be wrong to anyone in earshot. He was genuinely enthusiastic about what he had just seen and declared *Caddie* had to be one of the three opening films of his new triplex on Pitt Street. It was to be the beginning of support for our next four pictures from David Williams and Greater Union.

Roadshow were delighted and Robin Ball put together the best possible publicity campaign to launch what was still a somewhat rare breed, an Australian film. The catchphrase for the film proved elusive until Greg Coote came up with 'Life's tough enough for a woman alone, but with two kids and the Depression … it's a bugger!! … But not for *Caddie*.' The one-sheeters and daybills were printed and hit the streets till the censor came down on us like a ton of bricks and banned the use of the word 'bugger'. The decision was absurd and ridiculous. So the new posters had this peculiar blank space where the word 'bugger' had been.

Thursday night, April 8, 1976, *Caddie* opened Pitt Centre 3. Little were we to know that it would play here in this 480 seater, four sessions a day, for the next fifty-four weeks, a record still not broken for a multi-screen complex or an Australian film. Mind you, the opening night was not without its drama. In the middle of those wretched main titles the film snapped in the gate of the new

(Top left) Standing beside one of our two humble one sheeters outside the Cinema Rex, wondering if anyone was going to come. They did, including Jeannine Seawell who advised me to put on the poster that the film was French subtitled, which was unusual for the time in the Marché du Film. I still have one of the posters with its message scrawled across the top.

(Top right) Cannes, 1976. The Carlton Hotel. It was to be another ten years before we could afford to stay at this venerable pile.

(Left) The patio bar at the Carlton. I am sitting with Jill Robb, fellow commissioner of the AFC, whilst Jeannine Seawell talks with Peter Rose.

projector. I remained remarkably calm. Fortunately the film was not on a platter and the projectionist had it back on the screen within minutes.

The Australian press is an unpredictable beast when it comes to the local film industry. They either ignore you or take you to their heart. Be assured you can't and don't buy them. During the shooting the year before, the weekly and daily coverage by the papers – *The Sun, The Daily Mirror* (long both defunct) and *The Daily Telegraph*, not forgetting *The Australian Women's Weekly* with their colour cover of Helen Morse – was extremely positive. Of all the coverage my favourite headline comes from Leigh Bottrel's piece in *The Daily Telegraph*, October 3, 1975, Super Sheila Takes on the Ockers. Fortunately for us the film didn't let them down and the reviewers and their reviews reflected this, though Romola Costantino in *The Sun Herald* may have gone a little overboard: 'Caddie is a fascinating, outstanding film. It is in the best sense a woman's picture … Joan Long's screenplay avoids melodrama and comedy, making every point concisely, the accent is on visual messages … One feels that the story isn't sufficiently contained in its present length – that one has missed some of it, especially at the end. But it's still a masterpiece.'

The film struck a chord with our more conservative press and my favourite curmudgeon of the written word, Paddy McGuinness, had this to say in *The National Times*, 19-24 April 1976, referring to Helen Morse and her co-stars who had created portraits of 'authentic Australian women, with absolutely correct accent and intonation which had contributed immeasurably to the very firm feeling of local habitation'.

Donald Crombie remembers: 'The last scene in *Caddie* was improvised … it was vaguely worded as to what should happen. We shot this scene on the last day in the studio, I remember sweating blood over lunch, then sitting on the bed with Helen talking about what we should do. I think Helen and I basically talked it through, then Helen and the kids went for it.'

These in hindsight were the halcyon days of the revival of Australian cinema. Our stories were being told, but more importantly our voices were being heard for the very first time. No phoney pseudo-English accents that Cecil Kellaway and Jocelyn Howarth had to give in their day for Ken G. Hall, no pseudo-American voices attempting to be Australian, just our own voices at long last, on our own screens. This surely has to be one of the most significant achievements of our cinema of the seventies.

We were persuaded, with the success of our domestic openings, to take the film to Cannes, for the Marché du Film. I have been saying for years, after my first Cannes Film Festival, that the only place in which to hold it would be the pig pavilion of Sydney's Royal Easter Show. An Australian reader will know exactly what I mean. Donald Crombie and I had no idea what we were letting ourselves in for.

Somewhere along the way it had been suggested to us to have our print sub-titled, even though we were only screening in the marketplace of the Festival. We had found an enthusiastic French-speaker to do the translations but when they got to France they were deemed unacceptable. We were unaware of the cultural divide between France and French Canada. Our translator was French-Canadian and their French is significantly different to that spoken in metropolitan France. Enter Ann Head, living in Paris, who quickly re-translated *Caddie* to enable Cinetitres to subtitle the print in time for our first screening.

The newly formed Australian Film Commission had established offices in New York and London. New York was headed by Jim Henry and London by the late Ray Atkinson. Both were attending the Festival, offering considerable assistance to the newly-arrived filmmakers from Down Under. Whilst waiting for our first marketplace screening, Donald and I wandered into the local popular watering hole, Le Petit Carlton, for a heart-starter and encountered producer Richard Brennan and director John Duigan. They were there with *The Trespassers* and, like ourselves, were wondering what they were doing there. On reflection, one is more likely to meet one's peers at a film festival than at home, where we were working all the time.

We proudly put our one-sheeter poster up on the board provided outside the humble Cinema Rex, entered and waited for the lights to go down. It is an excruciating experience watching one's film unfold in front of an audience whose sole purpose in being there is to evaluate whether the film is worth buying or not. The buyers watch the opening of the film for about fifteen minutes, then walk out to catch another film, return halfway through and watch for another ten minutes, then disappear again, and if you are lucky they will return to see the last ten minutes. For two hours you have this continual movement of people coming and going. It is soul-destroying.

Donald and I were carefully taking down our poster to store till our next screening a couple of days later, when a voice said 'Why don't you write on your poster your film has French sub-titles? It is very rare for films in the Marché to be subtitled – hello, I'm Jeannine Seawell.' We quickly introduced ourselves. 'Who is looking after your wonderful film?' Jeannine asked. We explained we were there with the help of Jim Henry and Ray Atkinson of the Australian Film Commission. 'You need a sales agent, I would be honoured if you would allow me to represent your film.' We thanked her and said we needed to get permission from the Film Commission.

We scurried round to see Jim and Ray. Atkinson was quick to respond. 'If you have Jeannine Seawell wanting your film, then you are in very good hands. You must accept.' We had a sales agent! We advised Jeannine immediately, who was delighted, and so began a professional and friendly relationship of some thirty years. Before we left Cannes, Jeannine had sold *Caddie* to almost every European country, including the UK and Germany, and the film was invited in competition to the San Sebastian Film Festival, then regarded as one of the top five festivals on the international film calendar.

Jeannine only represented Europe and South America at this time. The film was playing to capacity audiences at home and Greg Coote had introduced it to Marshall Schacker, an American sales agent trading as Premiere Films. Marshall was married to the actress Ursula Theiss who had been the second wife to Robert Taylor. Marshall was a quietly spoken gentleman, in the true sense of the word, whilst Jeannine was a feisty, never-take-no-for-an-answer lady. Between them, on two separate continents, we and our film were in very good hands.

It was on our way home via London that we experienced an interesting encounter with one of the world's most famous film stars. We were booked into the Cumberland Hotel at Marble Arch, a huge pile of a hotel. These were the days of huge switchboards, with as many as twenty or thirty operators. It was about 7.45 when the phone rang. 'Can you take a call from New York?' said the operator. 'Yes, but who is calling?' I enquired. 'A Miss Hepburn, sir – putting you through.' 'Good morning, Miss Hepburn.' 'Oh, call me Kate, Tony – Bobbie gave me your number,' came the husky voice down the line. 'Bobbie' was Robert Helpmann. After *Don Quixote* he had told me of his desire to get a film about *Daisy Bates* up, a project writer Eleanor Witcombe was developing, and to persuade Katherine Hepburn to play Daisy. I suggested that perhaps she might be too old, when Bobbie squinted his eyes determinedly at me and said through gritted teeth, 'They can do wonders with make-up these days'. 'Tony, I'm too old for the role, Bobbie won't listen, will you be a sweetie and tell him for me – but my niece would be absolutely right for the part.' I assured her I would. 'It's been very nice talking with you – goodbye,' and she hung up. I could also hear the switchboard hanging up too.

San Sebastian, September 16, 1976: *Caddie's* gala screening. Helen Morse and Donald Crombie were there to receive a standing ovation at the end of the screening. Better was to come. *Caddie* was the first film announced, Best Actress, all nine members of the jury suddenly shot their hands into the air. Helen had been awarded Best Actress unanimously.

Jeannine Seawell had been told of the jury vote for best actress and got a tip-off about the Jury Prize. Donald remembers the gentlemen of the press rushing down the corridor toward their rooms. Helen had asked the Crombies to hold them at bay whilst she prepared herself, so a very pregnant Judy Crombie stepped out of their room, held her hand up like a traffic policeman and said the immortal line, 'Later boys – later.'

Finally to the Jury Prize: *Caddie* had won this coveted prize. It was a significant moment for Helen and Donald. I was holidaying at The Fijian, Nadi, Fiji, totally oblivious to all this. I was just relieved we had been honoured by the invitation. Mrs Crombie soon had Donald on the phone.[3]

It was a huge boost for the sale of the film to Spain and subsequently every South American country. We had no less than a fourteen-week season in Buenos Aires, which was amazing in itself, but nothing surprised Jeannine Seawell more than the Argentinian distributor lodging returns from the picture, which she claimed was a first for South America. Jeannine sold to Hemdale, an active and vigorous distributor of the day in the UK, but we had to wait nearly a year before they could get screens on Rank's Odeon circuit. It sends a tingle up the spine to open *The Times*, London, October 7, 1977, and read the banner headline across the top of the broadsheet's The Arts page: AUSTRALIA PROVIDES THE BEST FILM OF THE WEEK.

Whilst at San Sebastian, Donald and Helen received a cable from San Francisco. It was an invitation for *Caddie* to open the San Francisco Film Festival. To be invited to an international film festival is always an honour but to *open* an internationally respected film festival is something especially honourable indeed. Our US agent, Marshall Schacker, was elated. As soon as the news broke, Marshall had received an offer from Atlantic Releasing which we (gratefully) accepted.

Caddie opened at the prestigious Plaza Cinema on 58th Street to extraordinarily glowing reviews. Their banner on their poster was WINNER OF 4 AUSTRALIAN ACADEMY AWARDS, INCLUDING BEST ACTRESS. We were to play the Plaza for twelve weeks, exclusively, for four sessions a day.

At home at the beginning of our 52nd week at Pitt 3, Roadshow's team, headed by Greg Coote and Robin Ball, held a celebration at the Orient Hotel in Sydney's historic Rocks precinct for cast and crew. Our season concluded in our 54th week.

---

3 Silent and early talkie star, Dolores Del Rio, was the Chair of the Jury. One day the hotel ran out of milk. It was alleged that Ms Del Rio bathed in milk every day. Donald reckoned she smelt sour when she kissed him, had very white skin and looked considerably younger than her age.

(Top) The Odeon, High Street, Kensington, where the "gang" from 189 Cromwell Road would spend most Sunday evenings of the year in 1960. The projection beam had to pierce a wall of cigarette smoke from the balcony patrons before reaching the screen. Later triplexed to be London's most luxurious film centre, where *Caddie* was to play with success.

(Right) The splendid 'front of house' of the Metropolitan Theatre, Buenos Aires, November 1977. Winning the San Sebastian Jury Prize and Best Actress to Helen Morse, ensured the chance of success in Spain. Dubbed into Spanish and subtitled where the audiences prefer the original version. In Argentina *Caddie* had a fourteen-week season at the Metropolitan. The exhibitor spared no expense, including the neon billing which, if I had known, being a neon lover, I would have had shipped back home. Jeannine Seawell was delighted and was even more surprised when she received overages well above the distributor's minimum guarantee. Jeannine said that in all her experience it was a first time for South America.

A gross of over $2½ million on ten screens, when the ticket price was only $2.50. Today any distributor in Australia celebrates if a film grosses over two million. How times and tastes have changed.

Christmas 1976 was one of the worst Donald and I faced, particularly for him with a wife and two young mouths to feed. *Caddie* had been playing to capacity since April 8 and as the season wore on played to solid business, yet we had seen no returns. I made enquiries to both the AFC and Roadshow to no avail. I finally wrote to Greg Coote in Sydney and he promised to enquire. It was apparent to me that I would have no money for Christmas (credit cards weren't yet a reality) and I would have to sell something, but what? There is nothing worse than the Buckley pride factor. I used to visit Ashwoods secondhand record store in lower Pitt Street on Saturday mornings to browse their incredible selection. I enquired if they bought records, they did, what did I have? I listed various categories and the mention of Broadway shows attracted the man's attention. Off home to cull the collection and back into town on Monday morning with about sixty LPs, now referred to as 'vinyls'. I was paid far more than I expected which meant close family and friends could expect a present for Christmas. About a week before, Greg Coote rang to say he was sending a cheque in the post. $4,000 arrived, but it wasn't from Roadshow, it was from Greg personally, something I have never forgotten.

Caddie was to be the starting point of the careers of so many of us on the picture. Many of our paths still cross in the making of our belief and commitment – Australian stories.

I am going to leave the last words for this chapter to Dymphna Cusack, Caddie's mentor and champion to get her story put before the people.

'In the years since Caddie's book was first published, she has become a legend. Letters come to me from all over the world, asking "How is Caddie? What is she doing now?" … I think of her as she wrote to me in 1954, from the home where she lived out her life at Penrith. "The copy of Caddie you airmailed to me is on the table beside me. I cried when I opened it. I feel my life has been worthwhile." Worthwhile, indeed! Who could ask for more than to have a book of lasting courage and a name that is a symbol of courage and humanity. And so Caddie lives on.'

She most certainly does.

19

My Sons, My Horses
– The Anatomy Of A Motion Picture

Whilst raising the money for *Caddie,* I was editing what was to be my last feature as an editor and Tom Jeffrey's first feature, *The Removalists.* The film was adapted by David Williamson from his own successful play, and he was fast becoming the nation's most successful playwright. Unlike Peter Weir and Donald Crombie who had emerged from the documentary school of filmmaking at Film Australia into drama, Tom came from an equally successful career in television, working for the ABC and BBC. He directed one of my Australian favourites, *Pastures of the Blue Crane* in 1969 for the ABC. Tom was also at the coalface with the rest of us in the late 1960s fighting for the revival of an Australian film industry.

The Removalists was also Margaret Fink's first feature film as a producer. In fact from my perspective as the editor it was really a 'producer's film' as opposed to a producer and director working together. I think overall it wasn't a terribly happy experience for Tom.[1]

Williamson's play was first performed at La Mama, Melbourne, in 1971 and Margaret Fink secured the film rights. Williamson was also a writer of screenplays. He wrote *Stork* for Tim Burstall and *The Family Man* for David Baker, one of the four stories in *Libido,* whilst his plays *Don's Party* and *Jugglers Three* were touring the country to full houses. He was asked by Dave Jones in an interview for *Cinema Papers* (January 1974) if he distinguished much difference between writing for stage or screen and which did he prefer.

Williamson: 'Whether I'm writing a screenplay or a stage play it will be about social or interpersonal relations, because that's what I'm terribly interested in. But when you are doing it for the stage, your dialogue can be much denser. In a

---

1   See David Stratton, *The Last New Wave* p. 117.

sense the thing can be more static. I'm very aware that up on the screen you can have a large close-up of a head, you can convey an awful lot by the twitch of an eyebrow. You can show facial reactions and take away the need for dialogue. In other words, film-writing for a start needs to be sparser. And you tend to feel that there needs to be greater velocity. You tend to think there's a huge big screen and I want something to happen. I don't want people to be just chatting, whereas on stage it can work. And you want to use film's affinity for time flexibility. In fact, the original screenplay I wrote takes a man's life over the course of six months to a year. You can do that so easily with film. You can cut from sequence to sequence to sequence, and you can take a long extended time-sequence from the person's life. Devices like these are terribly phoney on the stage. I think film does it so much better that I can't bear writing any devices in the stage work any more…'

Whilst the film has a fluidity in both camera and direction, not to mention superb performances, I felt it was constrained in the artificiality of Bill Hutchinson's austere set, the flat, where most of the action takes place. The opening scenes are shot on location in the inner Sydney industrial suburb of St Peters and have a raw reality that the remainder of the film lacks, because it has the feel of a television studio set, perhaps not helped by the lighting. Nonetheless the strengths of the play were carried across to the screen by Williamson and strongly realised in the performances by director Tom Jeffrey.

Margaret Fink, however, was not entirely happy with the end result and went off to the Cannes Film Festival's Marché du Film to launch the film into the marketplace. She met up with a renowned British film editor who, Margaret admitted to me, only saw the film once and came up with some notes for improving the editing in the opening reel of the film. On her return I was summoned back to the cutting room and Margaret presented me with the British editor's notes. On first glance they seemed to be logical, involving the intercutting of two scenes near the beginning of the film, which I dutifully began to do. I hadn't gone very far into the new structure when I realised the continuity had gone haywire. The British editor had overlooked the fact that in one of the scenes the coppers wore short-sleeved shirts and, in the other, their blue jackets. The cuts were initially hilarious to look at but of course could never work. I rang Margaret to break the news. Into town she came and, peering down onto the Moviola screen, she suddenly burst out laughing. Even she could see the funny side of it despite her disappointment that the ideas didn't work. 'That'll teach me to spend a film festival with an editor,' she chortled.

The Removalists opened at the prestigious Century Theatre in Sydney's George Street on 16 October 1975 whilst I was in post-production on *Caddie*. Reviews were generally favourable but the film failed to pull the audiences in the way the play had.

It was back to editing once more, but for the last time after *Caddie*, with the challenging filmed drama for television, *Do I Have to Kill my Child?* with superb performances from Jacki Weaver and Brendon Lunney, directed by Donald Crombie. A Film Australia production, the studios at Lindfield had no room for me and I was set up in a vast empty space in an office block in Chatswood, a nearby suburb, to edit the film. It was a blustering wet day when in walked a gaberdine-coated man looking rather windblown and wet. He introduced himself. 'I'm Jim Sharman and I am looking for a producer for my next film.' I quickly explained Donald Crombie and I were about to start *The Irishman* and that the dates would clash. We had a good conversation about his film and I suggested he should go and see Hal and Jim McElroy who lived about ten minutes away in Neridah Street. It was still blowing a gale and pouring with rain when an hour later Jim returned. 'I'm prepared to wait till you finish your film,' he said with his engaging smile. Either a feast or a famine when it comes to working in Australian film, and this was only 1977! I thanked him and now I had two films to produce – back to back – unheard of! Patrick White's novella *The Night The Prowler* and *The Irishman*.

I was standing having morning tea outside the ubiquitous tearoom at Film Australia when Donald Crombie walked up to me and handed me the book. 'I think it would make a good film.' It was *The Irishman* by Elizabeth O'Conner (with an 'e'). I knew of Elizabeth through her very popular bestseller *Steak for Breakfast* first published in 1958. *The Irishman* was Paddy Doolan, a stubborn but proud teamster hauling goods and heavy loads for a living across the blacksoil plains of North Queensland with his team of twenty magnificent Clydesdale horses, at a time of the coming of the motorcar and, worse, the necessary evil of the motor lorry. His young son Michael can see the future is motorised transport, not horses hauling ageing wagons across the spinifex, but his father stubbornly refuses to listen. The future for him and his son is his horses – the team.

Donald had written a first draft of *The Irishman* in Adelaide in 1973 when working for a not very busy South Australian Film Corporation (SAFC) to see if he could adapt a novel into a screenplay. He had never expected it to be taken seriously, let alone made!

I secured the option to the book and discovered Elizabeth's real name was Barbara MacNamara. I enquired about the spelling of her pen name O'Conner with an 'e' and not an 'o'. 'Oh, darling!' she said, 'I mistyped my own name when I wrote *Steak for Breakfast* and it has stuck.' We had the book and Donald had a screenplay.

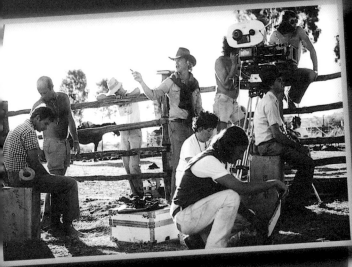

(Top) On location in Charters Towers.

(Right) The dirt-covered main street.

(Bottom) Donald Crombie, left, ponders the next set-up whilst Lyn McEncroe, continuity, talks with composer Charles Marawood, visiting set to get a feel of the picture. Marawood, humming and chants, had the crew very intrigued.

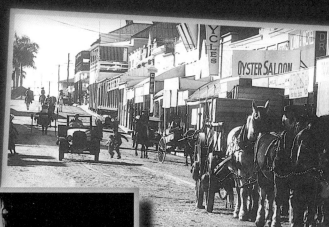

Fred Schepisi knew we were looking for the young Michael Doolan. He rang from Melbourne. 'I've found your boy – be at the Metro[2] Crows Nest Sunday morning – but don't tell anyone. I'm having the first screening of my film *The Devil's Playground*.' Donald and I were there right on the button. Fred had most certainly found our boy. Simon Burke, 'Superjoove,' was to be young Michael.

The financing of any film always finishes up as 'intriguing' and probably the most intriguing aspect of this picture's financing was the substantial investment by the SAFC, even though it was to be filmed in Queensland.

The weeks of preparation prior to shooting are somewhat like a countdown for a rocket launching. Production manager, Ross Matthews, had completed a location survey of the Gulf Country with our director, Donald Crombie, where the early towns of the Gulf had virtually disappeared. Later we returned to Northern Queensland, surveyed Ravenswood and Charters Towers and selected the latter for the film.

On return from the location survey, Donald revised the screenplay and the search for the team of twenty Clydesdales commenced. We didn't have to search far, for in Brisbane we found Don Ross, horsemaster, and twenty Clydesdales, eight of which were already working as a team. Don didn't even blanch when we said we wanted to film at Charters Towers. Then the search for Paddy Doolan commenced. Casting is always paramount and it had been suggested we seek an overseas name, Stephen Boyd had been mentioned and I think a script was sent to him, when he suddenly died on a golf course, and the part of Paddy Doolan was given to Michael Craig. The other leading parts went to Robyn Nevin, Gerard Kennedy, Tony Barry, Marcella Burgoyne, Vincent Ball, Bryan Brown and Roberta Grant (who featured in a small part in *Age of Consent*).

The casting in Queensland had been very successful with twenty-six speaking parts being given to Queenslanders and two discoveries! They were the players for Granny Doolan and Grandfather Doolan. Grandfather was played by Andrew Maguire, the breeder of the mighty Bernborough. Granny Doolan was Tui Bow, stepmother of Clara Bow, the original 'it' girl. It seems that Tui went to Hollywood in the early twenties and fell in love with Clara's father and married him. She had a wealth of stories of Hollywood in the twenties and thirties.

We were taken by surprise with an air traffic controllers' strike so we hired a charter plane which took us eight and a half hours to get there, otherwise we would have lost a week.

---

2   The Metro was formerly the Sesqui, the cinema of my boyhood matinees and, before that, the Queen's, my father's local picture show.

The twenty Clydesdales arrived from Brisbane with horsemaster, Don Ross. When being marshalled into the yards, one of them knocked over a beehive. The bees retaliated by stinging the Clydesdales, who promptly galloped off into the bush. By lunchtime they were rounded up and back in the yards.

The days at Charters Towers are hot and sunny but the nights are freezing. The shorts and T-shirts soon disappeared as jumpers and warm clothing were hastily despatched from Sydney. At one stage our rushes boxes from the lab carried more sweaters than film!

Quietly riding a pushbike at a goat race picnic held for the crew by the local townspeople on our Sunday off, Michael Craig lost his hat in a gust of wind and in trying to stop the bike quickly, fell off. It was obvious he was badly hurt. A tense two hours was spent at Charters Towers Hospital. Verdict, dislocated shoulder, immediate examination recommended by a Townsville specialist. Michael, in fact, had had one too many at the goat races and was greatly embarrassed by this incident.

By 8pm the entire production office had been marshalled and immediate rescheduling of Monday's planned shoot put into effect. There were forty-two extras to be cancelled, most not on the phone, Council to be stopped from starting at 5am placing dirt on the road, all artists to be notified of change.

What to shoot? By the late hours of the night, production manager Ross Matthews and first assistant director Mark Egerton had the day rescheduled. Could the art department cope? The art department of any picture is perhaps the busiest, managing to keep one jump ahead of the schedule. To completely reschedule at less than twenty-four hours notice is taxing that department to the hilt. However, art director Graham 'Grace' Walker and his team were ready for the new scenes next morning and by 7.30am the crew was on the road and the picture back on the rails.

Michael Craig and I flew to Townsville to see the orthopaedic specialist. The dislocated shoulder was going to be painful but he did not recommend pinning it. Michael could return to work provided his workload was eased to give time for the shoulder to heal. If pinning was found to be necessary, then it would be done at the conclusion of shooting. In the doctor's words, 'Michael will just have to "bite the bullet"!'

With Craig back on the set, the picture resumed the planned day, and in the tradition of a true professional, despite the pain, he performed as though nothing was wrong.

The accident caused a major reschedule to vary the workload and by Friday afternoon this had been finalised.

It's the colour of *The Irishman* that's of particular importance and one area where we broke with tradition. After extensive tests it was agreed to film on Gevacolor 680 with prints by Agfacolor. The Agfa-Gevaert company produced these compatible film stocks in Germany and Belgium. Most films are shot on Eastmancolor, however the Agfa-Gevaert colour gave our cameraman that extra dimension we were looking for. In the words of our film editor Tim Wellburn, 'stunning'. The colour in one aspect is rich in greens, browns and beautiful flesh tones, but not as 'bright' as Eastman. In some ways that wonderful Tom Roberts look of the Australian countryside. In fact DOP Peter James issued department heads with a print of Tom Roberts' *Bourke Street, Melbourne* as the standard 'look' and 'colour' for our exterior scenes and a Ray Crooke interior island scene for 'our' interiors.

It was the middle of our second week when the first signs appeared of sickness in our team of Clydesdales and Carl, one of our greys in the shafts, went down quickly. Don Ross and his boys spent a cold, sleepless night in the hope that Carl would survive. Then four other horses became sick and Tiger, our lead horse, particularly so. Although Carl was on his feet early Friday evening, by 11.30pm he was dead. This news reached us at 5.45am on Saturday morning when we had all arrived on set to shoot the early morning scenes at the beginning of the film. Then tragedy struck at 8.10am. In the middle of a 'take', Tiger, our prized lead grey, dropped dead. One of Queensland's leading vets had already left Ayr at 6am to join with our top vet from Charters Towers to do the autopsy on Carl. However, the sudden death of Tiger was a total shock to all cast and crew.

A virus strain that passed through Charters Towers about a year before is thought to be responsible. No expense was spared to ensure the horses received the best treatment. A light plane stood by all Saturday to fly to Townsville to obtain quantities of hard-to-get drugs the vets required. The horses were serviced and treated every four hours. The men once again spent a cold night with them on the Saturday. Sunday morning Donald Crombie and I arrived at the yards to find all horses on their feet and responding well to treatment.

Michael Craig and Simon Burke were particularly affected by the death of Tiger and Carl for they knew all the horses by name and worked with them just as a teamster would. A dreadful feeling of depression fell over the crew but, in that crass showbusiness term, 'the show must go on', and go on it did.

Our composer, Charles Marawood, came to The Towers to witness the filming of the main titles and the crossing of the great Burdekin River by the team. The day couldn't have been better. Sunny and clear and the horses in fine form. Our replacement Clydesdales had settled down well and fitted in well with the team.

Charles had already worked on some guide themes which we actually used on set to put our actors and crew in 'the mood'. This was a common practice in the Silent Days when some directors had small orchestras on set to create atmosphere. Well, we didn't go that far but the playbacks certainly created the right emotional atmosphere. Our composer, though, wanted to get the 'feel' of the horses, walk beside them, watch the team at work in this spectacular country that few Australians ever see.

Tim Wellburn arrived with the first seven reels of rough cut. It's at this stage of production that the director, producer and editor sit down and assess the rough cut to see if everything is working and whether any 'pick-up' shots are required, or re-shoots necessary. Our senior department heads were all delighted by what they saw.

The main titles: To reach the river crossing was by four-wheel-drive or a long walk. Crew call was seven and the day had to match Friday's shooting. The first master shots were completed just on eleven when cloud cover became total. By lunchtime the sky was black! While lunch was served, first assistant director Mark Egerton and Donald Crombie conferred on what to do. Abandon the day and move on to another location to do whatever other scenes could be arranged, or sit on the riverbed and WAIT. To come back and re-shoot would cost us $10,000 (on our operating cost of approximately $11,000 a day) and put us a day behind schedule, but there's not much you can do about the weather, which that year at Charters Towers had been completely unpredictable.

Our decision? To sit it out and hope that the afternoon sky would break. The crew got back to it straight away, the team stood by on the other side of the river, and our visitors joined us to give moral support. It looked pretty grim but at five to three the sun broke through, Mark Egerton yelled 'turn over' and three cameras rolled as the team lunged forward and completed the spectacular crossing of the Burdekin. At 4pm the sky was black, but it was all in the can and Mark's decision had paid off.

Grant Page, our stuntman to do Paddy's death fall, had spent two days preparing special cardboard boxes, four layers of them, covered with mattresses and then a tarpaulin. Grant was very happy about the stunt and was all set to go. He had to grasp for the logs on the jinker to prevent going under its wheels as the Ford truck overtaking forced the team to the side of the bridge, then appear to lose his grasp and fall to his 'death'. No sooner had the film crew arrived at the location than the weather began to close in again. The location was a difficult one, a narrow road and bridge, and sharp drop below the bridge to jagged rocks over which a waterfall was tumbling.

The team instinctively did not like the location or the bridge. Just prior to the weather finally closing down filming for the day, the master scene of the truck coming down the road and overtaking the team on the bridge was shot, only to have the end of the scene interrupted by a prang. The T-Model Ford has very direct steering and hit a displaced board on the bridge and ran into one of the company's parked vehicles on the other side of the bridge, destroying headlamp and mudguard but, worst of all, breaking the Ford's steering rod.

Then the very worst happened. Crew had wrapped and were packing their equipment and the horses were being led back to their stalls by the owner Don Ross. For some inexplicable reason Rose, one of our remaining lead Clydesdales, suddenly shied, lost her footing and fell over the bridge. Under the bridge our electrics were working, packing lighting gear, and narrowly missed being seriously injured. Despite her forty feet drop, the poor horse staggered to her feet and managed to remain standing. However, her collarbone was broken and there was no hope. The location was cleared and the horse destroyed. The effect on the crew was one of extreme shock and sadness, only two days from the end of shooting. Indeed it was Black Thursday for *The Irishman*.

In the early hours of Friday morning our director had a comprehensive storyboard worked out and filming could continue but would need the truck by 11.30am.

The sun shone! Elaborate dolly track set-ups were in place by 8am and filming commenced of all the lead-up scenes to the accident. Everything went well, the team, cast and crew were determined to win this day.

11.30am the sound of an antique truck was heard chugging up the hill. We could not believe it. The T-Model was back on deck. Standby Propsman Ken James had found a retired toolmaker who knew all about T-Model Fords, had parts and tooling equipment. It took the toolmaker only an hour and a half to make the necessary parts and install a new steering rod. The mudguard and light had been straightened out.

By 3pm everything was set for the stunt. Grant Page was dressed and made up as Paddy Doolan. Three cameras were set and we waited for the director's call, 'action'. The team rolled on to the bridge, the jinker swung to the side, 'Paddy Doolan' lost his grip at the right moment and fell to the rocks below. Grant's stunt was superb, but as cameras whirred one always waits to see the stuntman finish his 'act'. 'Cut', and a beaming Grant Page reared his head, 'How's that, okay?'

Just one week after our return from Charters Towers and Cardwell, we sat down at the United Sound Studios in Sydney and viewed the rough cut of *The Irishman*.

This first cut was two hours thirteen minutes which is a good length at this stage of editing. It gives both the director and the editor room to manoeuvre, that is, enough time over to pare down and polish each scene to its final length. The overall result of this first screening was very pleasing and the reassuring aspect was that we knew we had a strong film.

The Irishman locked down at 107 minutes. A few selected visitors experienced in assessing a film at this stage without music and sound effects were invited to this screening, purely to get some 'outside' reactions. All were highly favourable and we noticed some moist eyes when the lights came up.

David Williams, managing director of Greater Union, our principal backer and staunch supporter, was elated with the film and plans were set for its premiere at their flagship, the Pitt Centre, home to *Caddie* for fifty-four weeks. The music, however, wasn't going well. Charles Marawood had the themes sorted but was having extreme difficulty conveying how he wanted the choral voices arranged. On location he would walk with the horses and came up with a beautiful but extremely unusual chanting chorus which he would demonstrate to us as the principal sound, sitting with and above the orchestral arrangement. The 'chant' was evidently not something that could be written down musically. It caused great consternation with Alan Dean, our arranger and conductor. At the music recording sessions in a cramped studio in Sydney's Glebe Point Road, we could see and feel Marawood's desperate frustration, trying to convey how he wanted the choir to interpret his melodic chant. Dean and the choir couldn't interpret it and a musical compromise had to be settled upon. The result was less than satisfactory and caused distress to Charles Marawood for the rest of his career. What one hears on the soundtrack is an adequate but pretty standard choral theme. Kim Williams, David's son, had just returned from India, and had come to our Sunday morning preview before the opening. On coming out of the cinema he commented about the film but added – 'pity about that music'. Sadly, I knew exactly what he meant.

We could not have chosen a worse time in the twentieth century to have a film titled *The Irishman* going into release. The English-speaking world was horrified with the escalating troubles in Northern Ireland, David Williams had not been comfortable with the title from the outset. We racked our brains to come up with another title but this completely eluded us. Jeannine Seawell, our Paris-based agent, had sold *Caddie* to practically every country in the world and had a queue of buyers waiting to see *The Irishman*. One of these was Klaus Hellwig of Janus Films, who was to become the principal acquirer and supporter of Australian films for well

(Top) The team begin to cross the Burdekin River for the main titles of the film.

(Bottom) Watching anxiously with me, costume designer Judith Dorsman and director Donald Crombie.

over a decade until his untimely death. He saw the film, loved it and came up with its German title, which translated as *My Sons, My Horses* – if only he could have seen the film before its release I think we would have adopted his title.

The world premiere at the Odeon, Townsville, February 28 1978, was a huge success, followed by its Sydney opening, as planned, on St Patrick's Day, March 17. Greater Union's team, headed by John Reid, spared no expense on the publicity and scored a coup by bringing Don Ross's team of Clydesdales down from Queensland and had them entering Sydney by walking the team across the Harbour Bridge. It literally brought traffic to a halt and caught every evening news bulletin and the front pages of the newspapers.

The reviews were mixed. Some quite positive, others cool, and it infuriated good old Paddy McGuinness at the *National Times* who, if you remember, had had a gutful of nostalgia at the time of reviewing Tom Jeffrey's *The Removalists*, which is why he found Tom's film like a breath of fresh air. Nonetheless we had a respectable season of ten weeks at the Pitt Centre and around Australia – but if only we had thought of that bloody title!

No reflection on Joan Long's script for *Caddie*, or the superb execution in the making of the film, but I feel quite strongly *The Irishman* is the better film. Script, production and direction. Our only flaw, the music.

It performed extremely well overseas and returned money to our investors and in particular our four very important, independent investors who had put in $25,000 each, a not inconsiderable sum in 1976. One of them, a knight of the realm from Queensland, rang me somewhat agitated that he had just received a cheque for $15,000. 'Hey, Tony, you told me this film wasn't going to make any money!' Whoops, sorry, another tax problem?!

POSTSCRIPT

In Charters Towers, Donald Crombie gave a lift to a young hitchhiker travelling from Melbourne to Darwin. The hiker had been dropped at the motel and wanted to get to the other side of town to pick up the main highway again. Donald said nothing about the main street being closed and covered in dirt for *The Irishman*. The hiker pondered as he looked at our deserted and fully dressed street. Walking a short distance, looking in the shop windows, he turned to our director, quite perturbed. 'Struth!' he said, 'I was told they were a bit backwards up here – but look – they're still using pounds, shillings and pence!' Our director didn't explain and the hiker has moved on to northern climes, no doubt still very mystified.

20

'This Bizarre Work'
– *The Night The Prowler*

The first letter I ever wrote to a newspaper, the afternoon *Sydney Daily Mirror*, was, surprisingly, published at the top of their letters page. I was castigating their correspondent for demonising, denouncing and demolishing Patrick White's *The Season at Sarsaparilla* which I had seen two nights before at the Palace in Pitt Street. Little did I know then that I would later be teamed with Patrick White and Jim Sharman to produce *The Night The Prowler*. Jim had directed *Summer of Secrets* with fellow filmmaker Michael Thornhill as producer. Michael wasn't available for *Prowler*, hence Jim came to see me in Chatswood that wet and windy day I was editing *Do I Have to Kill my Child?* Jim was only sixteen when he saw an early production of *Sarsaparilla* and likewise probably never thought that one day he would be directing a commercial production of Patrick's play. It resulted in a long friendship and Jim later directed two more White plays, *Big Toys* and *A Cheery Soul*. In an interview with David Stratton,[1] then director of the Sydney Film Festival, Jim describes the friendship with the writer as an exhilarating and refreshing experience: 'I was enriched by his viewpoint by being able to see universal issues – life and death struggles – enacted in my own environment. In our naïvete we tend to think the world is happening somewhere else, in New York, or Paris, or in a film, but he brought home to me that it's happening *here*. It was an eye-opener for me.'

Jim relates his discovery of *Prowler* to Robyn Anderson and Sue Adler in *Cinema Papers* (March–April 1979): 'I remember seeing his plays in the early 1960s.

---

1 'The Last New Wave' by David Stratton, pp.167 to 171.

It was the first time I had seen situations that I could relate to in terms of being an Australian. *The Season at Sarsaparilla* was my first association with Patrick; after that I did *Big Toys*. Actually, it was out of our conversations on *Season at Sarsaparilla* that the idea developed to film *The Night The Prowler*. He thought the story would make a good film, so I asked him whether he was interested in writing the screenplay. But since his writing was so visual – I think we share a frustration for painting – I was sure it would be an interesting experiment.'

The first draft was particularly good, overlong as they generally are, but I thought a little heavy-handed in the sequences in Canberra. 'I'm not sure I want to tell Patrick that,' said Jim. I was prepared to – 'No, leave it to me.' The phone rang. I can hear Patrick's clipped voice now. 'I believe you think the scenes with Felicity in Canberra are too long?' There was a pause and I was about to answer when he continued – 'Well, I've rewritten it – you will have it in the morning.'

Jim: 'When I read the screenplay of *The Night The Prowler* I thought it was a remarkable piece of writing for the screen. I never had any doubts about it … Throughout the film I tried to prepare the audience for what was to come. The tone at the beginning is of domestic comedy, but as the other theme emerges, the film becomes serious and mythic. The film then becomes something of an odyssey as Felicity assumes a larger-than-life character in her quest. Felicity goes through all different layers of society and confronts different situations, until she finally achieves, in the most unlikely of situations, some comprehension of compassion. Till then, her life has been devoid of passion. This is largely because of her environment. It is only when Felicity discovers humility that she finds compassion. That is why, contrary to a lot of opinion, I consider the film to be optimistic … I think the humour in the film is heavily laced with irony, yet that irony is not detached from compassion. Ruth Cracknell, for example, gives an extraordinary performance as Doris Bannister, and it is a role in which many actresses would have gone overboard. While Ruth doesn't miss the comic opportunities, she doesn't betray the essence of her character to that comedy …

'… we had a period before filming during which Ruth, Kerry and John (the Bannister family) worked on the script. This was done on the location we used for all interior and exterior scenes. This enabled the actors to get to know the house, and each other, before we started filming. We didn't rehearse in the way you do in the theatre. In theatre you rehearse people so that they can produce, each night, certain emotions, feelings and ideas. In films, however, you only want them to achieve these emotions, ideas and feelings for the single moment when the camera is turning. Consequently, I didn't try to find these moments during rehearsals.'

Three rare snaps of Patrick White on the set. With me on his first visit, and on two other occasions with Jim Sharman. His visits spurred him on to write two more screenplays, regretfully not produced.

The money-raising is a story within itself. My letter either brought no reply or phone calls of incredulity. It was as though I was seeing that Rural Bank manager all over again, only now I was beginning to believe it might be April Fool's Day! I do wince though at my naïvete with some of the approaches I made.

Greater Union, as usual, had a positive response albeit a cautious one. David Williams wrote that he, Warwick Hind and John Reid (of their distribution arm) had re-read the script, respected my whole approach to marketing the film, but still had reservations. David expressed faith in Jim and me as moviemakers and he generously offered an advance if they liked the film on seeing an answer print.[2]

John Daniell, director of projects of the Australian Film Commission, wrote to say that although the Commission was behind the premise of the film, they would only reconsider it if Patrick re-wrote the end of the film which they thought 'could be disastrous at the box office'. I didn't fancy passing this news on to Jim or Patrick.

Finally, maverick head of the NSW Film Corporation, Paul Riomfalvy, came in to fund the entire picture. We got the original budget down from $440,000 to $385,000, deciding to shoot on 16mm for a 35mm 1.185.1 blow-up. The decision to film in 16mm turned out to be an advantage for it gave Jim and director of photography David Sanderson more mobility in the confined interior location of the home we used to film *Prowler*.[3] Jim: 'By the time I came to *The Night The Prowler* I was not concerned with technique. I felt sufficiently confident to pay less attention to it and could concentrate on the relationship between actor and camera – how I would tell the story and how I could achieve the performance level it required. Somebody once said that we used to make films about people and now we make them about real estate. I would like to think that the major landscape in *The Night The Prowler* is the faces of the three central characters.'

David Stratton, director of the Sydney Film Festival and today one of Australia's top film critics, invited the film to launch the 25th festival, which was to be opened by the Premier of New South Wales, Neville Wran. His government's NSW Film Corporation fully funded the film and it was the first film from their investment slate to be publicly screened. The opening night of the film festival is held in the 2,200 seat State Theatre, where the audience comprises the regular subscribers in the stalls and dress circle, and the VIPs, sponsors and the glitterati in the mezzanine. The latter group hated it! When the lights went up there was welcoming applause from the stalls and dress circle, which only created a startled

---

2   The first print of a completed film to be made from the negative.
3   The house was actually in Vaucluse though meant to be facing Centennial Park which was the principal location. The art department provided the wrought-iron fencing to match that at Centennial Park.

Sydney Film Festival 2001 audience response to the restored print of *The Night The Prowler* slightly overwhelmed all of us compared to its original launch. L to R, John Derum, Kerry Walker, Ruth Cracknell, Jim Sharman, Sara Bennett (editor) and me.

reaction from the mezzanine mob. Many people criticised David Stratton for selecting the film as an opening night film, but Jim and I supported the decision and felt it most certainly was not a mistake.

What we were not prepared for was the savagery of the Australian critics. Both Jim and Patrick were shocked by the hostility to them personally and the film. Jim Sharman: 'This was only the second time in my career – the first was the Melbourne stage production of *Don Giovanni* – that I have been devastated by criticism of my work. I had been really looking forward to that evening. I thought it would be the most marvellous evening, because here was a film that I was very pleased with, that tackled a contemporary subject and that I thought everyone would respond to positively. And then when I read the reviews ... I thought I detected undercurrents of the kind of attitudes there were in America in the fifties – you know, "If you don't like living here why don't you go and live in Russia?" I was astonished and quite disturbed.'

There were three exceptions. Bob Ellis in the *Nation Review* : '... for almost the first time in our history we have an Australian film with levels of meaning, wit, irony, plot complexity and something to say.' Elizabeth Riddell in *Theatre Australia*: 'What distinguishes *The Night The Prowler* from the general run of Australian films ... is the intellectual content, the evidence that a mind has been working behind the speeches and action.'

Later in the year, November 28, 1978, the film played in New York at the Lincoln Center in the first Australian Film Festival. *The Night The Prowler* had the New York critics intrigued.

Norma McLain Stoop, *After Dark*: '*The Night The Prowler* is a strange, eerie incursion into the mind of Felicity, the pudgy, rather plain daughter of bourgeois parents who, though they live in Sydney, Australia, would feel equally at home in Claude Chabrol's France. Actually, the film is more a searing indictment of the worldwide middle-class morality and mentality than a story of a desperate, strong misfit of a girl pushed from childhood into the confines of a fluted cookie-mold of gentleness and submission that cannot contain her nature. It is a brutally direct film that flinches at nothing, and in it Patrick White, who wrote the screenplay from his own short story, displays the genius that won him the Nobel Prize. Gutsy, funny, horrifying and tragic.'

Robe in *Variety* Nov 15/78 couldn't cope with it! 'Sharman evidently thinks of himself as the Down Under Alejandro Jodorowsky and, certainly, his films have that touch of the unreal that mark *El Topo*. A hodge-podge of flash-forwards, flashbacks and even some flash-sideways, it tells the story, as one pundit put it, of a female slob's search for self-identification.'

Before New York our film played the Toronto Film Festival in September and, contrary to its competitor *Variety, The Hollywood Reporter* found favour with the film: 'The new film is a fascinating, often rather horrifying black comedy detailing the empty values of modern society and exploring the lack of sensibility that has resulted in the punk attitude of today's youth. It is a harrowingly bleak, but also bizarrely funny work that is ultimately optimistic. The performances expertly underscore the exaggerated black comedy with an attitude of reality and Ruth Cracknell is particularly outstanding as the mother ...'

Sadly, the positive response from overseas and the comment from Derek Malcolm of the *Guardian*, who saw the film at the Sydney Film Festival – 'one of the boldest and most original of the new Australian films' – couldn't persuade Greater Union to release it for a year and then ironically opened it on the opening night of the 1979 Sydney Film Festival. It played two weeks at the Pitt Centre and was not commented on or reviewed by the press.

The filming had gone well, restricted as we were to schedule and budget, but it gave Patrick White a completely new lease of life. My duty was to drive him to set in my humble Morris 1100. Picking him up at Martin Road, Centennial Park, to drive him to our Vaucluse location, terrified the wits out of me. He would sit grandly on set and observe all. One morning he said to me in the car, 'I have written another script, do you think you would have the time to read while you're filming?' I said of course, I would be pleased to. Then and there he presented me with *The Monkey Puzzle* which he informed me he had written for Barry Humphries. I later told him how much I had enjoyed it, when he suddenly presented me with yet another script, *Last Words*, a very dense work. At the time Jim hadn't read either script and couldn't till he had wrapped filming. *The Night The Prowler* had inspired Patrick White to continue writing screenplays, obviously.

Sadly the failure domestically of *The Night The Prowler* put paid to any of Patrick's new works becoming a reality.

POSTSCRIPT

The film was one of fifty Australian films to be included in the restoration programme known as the Kodak/Atlab collection for the National Film and Sound Archive in 2000, and *The Night The Prowler* was presented back at the State Theatre for the 2001 Sydney Film Festival. The place was packed and when Jim and I appeared on stage for Q&A one young man, who must have been a babe in arms when we made the film, stood up, said how much he enjoyed it and what was the audience reaction when it was first shown in 1978. We could hardly control ourselves and assured the young man we only wished this audience had been the one in seventy-eight. A film twenty years ahead of its time?

21

The Very Strange Case Of
The Unknown Industrial Prisoner

During the period between 1975 and 1978, and while I had been producing *Caddie,* *The Irishman* and *The Night The Prowler*, three important events occurred. The first was my appointment to the board of the Australian Film Commission. The government established the Commission as a statutory body to replace the Australian Film Development Corporation in 1975. The task of the Australian Film Commission (AFC) was to fund script development and invest in production. The chair, appointed by the government, was ex-ABC bureaucrat Ken Watts, whose charm and bon vivant manner hid his other side. The board was made up of two permanent commissioners – Peter Martin (television producer and journalist) and John McQuaid (federal secretary of the Australian Theatrical Amusement Employees Association or ATAEA) – plus, initially, three part-time commissioners – Graham Burke (managing director of Village Roadshow), Frank Gardiner (lawyer from Queensland) and me, with Jill Robb being appointed later. Regretfully the government decided to place Film Australia under the charge of the Commission, which was to frustrate and aggravate its producer-in-chief, Denys Brown, for the remainder of his tenure. The Australian Film Commission's board overall did not understand the culture and craft of Film Australia, with perhaps the exception of Jill Robb and me. Chairman Ken Watts made no attempt to encourage and support the venerable organisation.

As described previously in Chapter Seventeen, as the Commonwealth Film Unit and just after the name change, Film Australia worked and existed in a rarefied and somewhat cocooned environment. The early seventies, thanks to the vision of Gil Brealey, Richard Mason and others, began the slow, tortuous turnaround to producing a livelier approach to documentary and to innovative drama. The

Chair of the Australian Film Commission, the late Ken Watts, with Minister Ellicott. The late John Morris, head of production, Film Australia, in the background.

Australian Film Commission wanted Film Australia to be 'more commercial'. God! How many times have I heard that in my long career in this industry?

Thankfully Richard Mason's production of the children's feature *Let the Balloon Go*, directed by Oliver Howes, had been well received, was moderately successful playing children's matinee sessions and obtained an American sale, extremely rare at the time. However, Dick wanted to do something more substantial and something provocative under the 'National Program', a program entrusted to Film Australia by the government to tell Australians about themselves and their country, separate from the staple of propaganda films made to supply the Australian embassies and consular offices around the world. Richard Mason had optioned David Ireland's novel *The Unknown Industrial Prisoner*, a contemporary and controversial allegorical tale about Australian workers' industrial issues, set in an oil refinery. Playwright Alan Seymour (*The One Day of the Year*) was engaged to adapt Ireland's book to the screen, the result being an extremely powerful screenplay. It was to be funded out of the 'National Program' vote at around $500,000 and had to receive AFC board approval and that of the Minister, R.J. Ellicott QC, known to us as Bob.

Film Australia had secured the use of the Total oil refinery at Rydalmere in Sydney, which was being put into 'mothballs' by the oil company as it was leaving Australia, as the principal location for the film. The scale and scope of the film had raised a few eyebrows at the Commission but the majority of us thought it worthwhile, visionary, adventurous, and felt strongly it was worthy of our support. Not so our chair. Ken Watts was determined Film Australia was not going to make the film and went to great lengths to see it stopped. We all knew that Commissioner Burke did not like the project and could not see it being commercially viable, which was his prerogative, and Watts was to use this view to his advantage.

The project was vigorously debated over no fewer than three Commission meetings, none of which Graham Burke could attend because of his overseas commitments. Watts requested outside assessments be obtained. Peter Rose[1] of the South Australian Film Corporation was asked. Rose didn't much like the project though admitted the script was 'well written' but thought the work was far too allegorical for the general public. Phillip Adams thought quite the opposite, though Watts was to use one of Phillip's comments negatively, to Watts' advantage. From Phillip's notes taken at Film Australia: 'Astonishingly interesting script, confronting the system. Amazing political audacity.' (This comment wasn't to go down well in Canberra.) 'A huge tonic for me – actually means something!' However a comment about directors was seized upon by Watts and totally misrepresented by him to Minister Ellicott. Adams had been asked if he knew of any Australian directors who could direct it and had replied not one, meaning there were none available at the time because they were all working. In fact he was delighted when told it was to be a new upcoming director from Film Australia, (the late) Arch Nicholson.

Watts was furious with the majority board decision to support the film and despite our vote the duplicitous Watts went behind our collective backs and wrote to the Minister on April 28, 1978, putting paid to the film by quoting Commissioner Graham Burke's written report expressing his concerns about the film in its entirety. In fairness to Graham, I don't think he was aware that Ken Watts would go to these lengths. But Watts went one better, by asking Burke to see the Minister in Canberra to ensure it was knocked on the head. Burke did, at his own expense too, but claimed to me later in a letter that the discussion that ensued was about the general state of the industry and that *The Unknown Industrial Prisoner* was only 'mentioned' for a minute. Nonetheless, the damage was done; Watts' letter was replied to by Ellicott almost immediately, stating he was not prepared to give his approval to the production of the film.

Richard Mason and his entire team were devastated, Denys Brown demoralised and not entirely aware of Watts' treachery. I had been quite outspoken about the Commissioners' handling of the affair. By now I was en route to the Cannes Film Festival and was unaware of the Minister's letter to me of 25 May thanking me for my 'valuable service rendered during your recently completed term as a part-time member of the Australian Film Commission'. Watts had struck again!

Naïvely, I admit, I wrote to both the Minister and Graham Burke giving them both a piece of my mind, which in hindsight I know was quite a stupid thing

---

1 Peter is now CEO of the Premium Movie Partnership, Showtime and Encore in Australia.

to do, but I was outraged at what had taken place despite our majority vote. It was a rather long tirade but in part I said to the Minister, 'My dear Minister, I returned from Cannes this week to find your kind note re my term on the Australian Film Commission. My term was a most interesting and invigorating, if at times frustrating, experience, but above all for me, a totally encouraging one. There has been one branch of the Australian Film Commission that I have always strongly supported and defended, but which, I regret to say, has not been and is not fully understood by some of the part-time Commissioners. 'Film Australia' has always been the Australian Government's filmmaking division and it has an incredible track record. When the AFC Act was adopted it clearly spelt out that Film Australia's continuing role was the important National Program as well as servicing the various government departments.

'If Film Australia has to become commercial then it will be the beginning of the end of Film Australia. One does not expect the National Gallery, or the National Library, to be commercial just as we all know that opera and ballet cannot support themselves. I urge you to look closely at the nationally important function that Film Australia has to play and give it all your support.'

The second event of this period was the establishment of Forest Home Films by Donald and Judy Crombie and me. Under John Daniell's administration of the Project Development branch of the AFC, he had presented a plan to support producers in developing a package of projects, rather than applying for funding for each individual project to be developed. As Jill Robb said, thumping the Commission's board table, 'Back the producers – not the films.' She was right. I think Bob Weis was the first producer to be granted package support and we were second or third. The plan was to support the producers to be set up as a business and to develop a slate of films over four years, fully funded by the AFC to an approved budget, covering enough for us to live on, cover overheads and be able to option and commission scripts without having to return to the Commission cap in hand all the time.

This was unfortunately misunderstood by Susan Dermody and Elizabeth Jacka in their otherwise excellent book *The Screening of Australia*, as favouritism to the same few.[2] They felt that a 'kind of club' existed that favoured only the 'club' members, naming Donald and me along with Joan Long, Tom Jeffrey, Errol Sullivan, Pat Lovell, the SAFC (!) (my exclamation), Hal and Jim McElroy, Fred Schepisi, Ken Hannam and Phillip Adams. It was a plainly absurd suggestion to have made and could not have been further from the truth. In Donald's and my case we were given one-off funding for the development package and that was

2   *The Screening of Australia*, Currency Press 1987, pp. 93/94.

it. When I look at my desk diary for 1980 I wonder how both of us didn't have a nervous breakdown when one considers the development slate we had embarked on. No doubt the following chapter will reinforce this when I analyse the pitfalls of 10BA financing we were both to suffer.

In development we had *The Killing of Angel Street* with Michael Craig, *The Bagman*[3] with Philip Cornford and John Burney, *Buddies* with John Dingwell, *Morrison of Peking* with Cecil Holmes, *Sugar Train* with Anne Deveson, an untitled comedy with Christine Stanton and *The Reach* with Ian Coughlan. The intention was for Donald and me to be a 'producing team', employing other directors in addition to Donald to enable both of us to generate some form of ongoing production, something Australian producers are still waiting to achieve. Out of all of this we still managed to get two of the films off the ground and John Dingwell to get his project up on his own.

Event number three was my being awarded the Order of Australia, an AM for my services to the industry, in 1977. I had been notified by the office of the Governor-General of their intention and asked if I would accept. I would and did. We were on location in Charters Towers, Far North Queensland, with *The Irishman*. I thought 'good', no one will know. The Sydney papers didn't reach the Towers and the crew working a six-day week wouldn't have time to scan the local paper, and therefore it could be kept a secret. WRONG. 6am a telephone call to the motel. It was Bill Gooley, our doyen of Australian film laboratories, in charge of our daily rushes. 'Congratulations,' Bill chortled down the phone line. Now one must remember that Charters Towers in 1977 was the last manual telephone exchange. Nothing was ever a secret for long in the Towers! I begged Bill not to tell a soul. 'But it's in all the papers.' It was a Saturday if I recall correctly. The day's filming went like clockwork and the production office hummed along as usual. Lunch came and went and afternoon tea. Not a word had been said so Bill hadn't said anything? No one knew? Oh really?! Our company always provides refreshments at rushes, an age-old custom, except on this particular night, after wrap and waiting for the projector to roll, I spied Ross Matthews, our production manager, secreting a large carton of champagne under the stage beneath the screen. Curious, but I thought this might have been props for tomorrow's shoot. I didn't twig. The lights went up at the conclusion of the screening and all hell broke loose. The cat had been let out of the bag at about 7am when Bill Gooley made his customary call to tell the production manager the negative report of the previous day's filming. The entire cast and crew had known all day, a superb achievement in acting by all. It was a great night.

3   Later changed to *Kitty and the Bagman*.

22

Not In The Public Interest
– The Juanita Factor

The negatives and the positives.
Firstly, the negatives.
The Juanita Factor was most certainly 'not in the public interest' or, to be more specific, not in the interest of one of Sydney's leading property developers, the underworld, the police, government, one of our principal investors and mysteriously a future Minister of the Crown. In fact it was going to be, for Donald and me, an investment and production nightmare.

Michael Craig, our star of *The Irishman*, had been intrigued by what had become known as the Juanita Nielsen affair. Nielsen was a member of the Mark Foy family and an heiress to part of the Foy estate. The Foys had come to Australia at the time of the goldrush on the Victorian goldfields. Mark Foy later came to Sydney and established its most prestigious department store in 1909.[1] Nielsen published a lively and controversial local newspaper, *Now*, in which she attacked both the authorities and the developers who wanted to demolish one of Sydney's grandest streets, Victoria Street, in the heart of the city's bohemian and cosmopolitan centre, Kings Cross. Juanita was called to a meeting with a couple of the Cross's 'heavies', to be persuaded to give up her valiant crusade. She has never been seen since, nor has her body been found. We thought Michael's idea for a film about the subject a worthwhile inclusion in our Forest Home Films package for development.

Michael began a first draft of *The Juanita Factor* which was to become *Not in the Public Interest*, then *Hot Property* and, finally, *The Killing of Angel Street*. We were to very quickly realise that we could not adapt the Juanita Nielsen story and would have to fictionalise the facts to protect ourselves. One of the incidents

---

1   This glorious art nouveau/deco building still stands, with its splendid signage in tiles for gloves, hosiery, haberdashery etc. Its storefront windows still grace its splendid piazza and is now the Downing Centre Courts.

which had aroused Michael's interest and curiosity was the horrific story of the old man, living in Victoria Street, who had refused to move and died when his house burnt down. The Coroner's inquiry concluded the fire had been caused by a faulty fuse box and that there were no suspicious circumstances, ignoring the fact that the electricity had been cut off for some time because the old man hadn't paid his electricity bill! Residents were continually being harassed by the police and the thugs. It was clear, after several incidents of this kind, that people 'at the top' were compliant to the big end of town. In fact it would have been more appropriate to call the film *Complicity*, for what was to follow.

Michael had to return to London for film commitments but continued to work endlessly to get a first draft screenplay to us to begin the financing and casting of the picture. David Williams and his Greater Union Organisation, who had championed the release of *Caddie* and the co-financing of *The Irishman*, was to come on board first with enthusiasm, but which to our dismay was later to change to a degree of hostility. Because it had to be fiction based on fact, we would have to build the street. Although the budget was $1.2 million, the head of the Australian Film Commission, Joe Skrzynski, felt it needed the support of an international 'star' to play the lead, based on Juanita Nielsen, to protect the investors in the film. Joe became very supportive through the troubled months ahead. First choice was Julie Christie, David Williams at GU thought we should offer the role to Helen Morse, but it was decided to pursue Skrzynski's suggestion of an international lead.

Michael Craig continued to work on the script and had received a phone call from an investigative journalist, Tony Reeves, who had written extensively about Nielsen's disappearance. Reeves had his ear to the ground and had received threats to his life when reporting the case. He didn't want us to continue. What he heard we don't know, but we were certainly being warned off. Tony Reeves and his co-author Barry Ward, when writing their book about Juanita Nielsen, were all the time expecting a brick through their office window. The pair lived under daily death threats and eventually Barry left the country to return to the UK. His wife, who was pregnant, said it was a choice between the Juanita story or their marriage and the baby back in England. Barry Ward was a pretty tough kind of guy who had been a London cop and a cop in Bermuda. Their literary agent was also receiving odd worrying phone calls at the office during this time.

Because of Michael Craig's British television commitments he couldn't continue past a third draft of the script and we engaged Cecil Holmes to continue. Cecil became more of a script doctor than a new writer of Michael's work, because of his knowledge of and involvement with the union movement and in particular

'Angel Street' specially built for the film on the harbour foreshore, and its spectacular demolition.

the goings on in Victoria Street, which was just around the corner from his Kings Cross flat.

Christie indicated positive interest in working on our film. I subsequently dealt with the Los Angeles office of ICM who were somewhat amazed at our breakthrough. When news of Julie Christie's potential involvement broke, Hilary Linstead, the producer of *Heatwave*, loosely based on a similar theme, objected to the importation of a foreign star to Actors Equity and the Immigration Department. This complaint astounded us but thankfully didn't move Actors Equity. Hilary was also Donald Crombie's agent.

Meanwhile a parallel drama was unfolding with the financing of the film. Although very nearly a chapter in itself, what transpired here is a lesson for any aspiring film producer.

To raise the private finance for the film, Forest Home Films prepared the usual investment brochures and sent them to various potential investors, including some who had invested with us previously. One group – UAA (United American Australasian Cinema) – came forward and indicated they had unlimited funds to invest in our picture. Their principals had checked out our bona fides and had checked with Miss Christie and her agent in London as to the validity of our claim that she was to star in our film.

UAA assured us they were behind us. However, we could not get a written commitment from them. Because we had doubts, a meeting was arranged between UAA and the general manager of the AFC, and it was at this meeting that UAA indicated they had no available funds that would ensure Miss Christie's participation in the film!

Difficulties in communication with Christie, and the failure of UAA to guarantee a bank draft on London to lock in her available dates, forced a situation upon us where we finally had to withdraw our offer. Her London agent did attempt to keep the door open but after careful consideration it was decided to offer the picture to Helen Morse.

Ms Morse indicated interest but requested another draft of the script. Although it was a punt, it was decided to fly noted English writer, Evan Jones, out from the UK to Sydney for a period of three weeks, to meet the actress and to re-write the script. Helen indicated she would submit some script notes to us in a week. Pages of script notes were received which showed that Morse was seeing an entirely different film to ourselves. In an endeavour to clarify the situation, Donald Crombie answered all Morse's points in a very detailed analysis of her notes in relation to the script.

On December 21 a letter was received from Morse withdrawing from the picture. Her agent had not been notified and was as shocked as we were. All potential investors were notified by telephone and letter of Ms Morse's withdrawal.

On December 22 a representative of Jones Grice and Partners – Max Weston – made contact with us with a view to underwriting the film. Ironically they had been introduced to the film verbally by a sales agent of UAA, but when printed matter was requested of UAA none had been forthcoming. Weston made contact with the AFC and in turn met with me for two hours on Christmas Eve and agreed to underwrite the film. Holds were immediately placed on crew. After lengthy meetings New Year weekend with Max Weston, he indicated that Jones Grice would definitely underwrite the film but did not particularly want to deal with UAA. However, if they had raised funds from their clients, Jones Grice would be happy to enter a commission-sharing[2] arrangement with UAA for funds introduced by UAA.

I sought legal advice when UAA called for a meeting with Jones Grice. It was clear that UAA wanted all commission rights to our film, based on the premise that UAA had introduced our film to Jones Grice. They would not hold with the argument that the AFC had, in fact, pointed Jones Grice in our direction and that Forest Home Films had supplied the detailed paperwork.

The meeting was adjourned by mutual agreement until 8am the following day.

I sought counsel with our solicitor, Lloyd Hart, and he accompanied me. It was all over in fifteen minutes and the picture had collapsed. Neither party would shift from its position. I felt more than sick in the stomach when I walked out into the glare of a bright Sydney summer day. Max Weston had been a thorough professional gentleman throughout.

Looking at the gravity of the situation, I sought a meeting with Joe Skrzynski, whose advice that day was welcomed. He urged us to carry on with the aid of the AFC until private funds came forward.

That very same day two offers were received, one of them a total surprise. A representative of Corporate Consultants, Adelaide, rang to enquire if we had heard from their solicitor in Sydney. The reason: they had raised our funds before Christmas and didn't know what to do with them!! The other offer came from Filmco. Although Filmco's representative, John Fitzpatrick, was keen for his company to become involved, we decided, after lengthy meetings with the principals of Corporate Consultants, to go with them as our private backers. A

2   Companies specialising in raising funds for the financing of motion pictures charge a commission or percentage on the funds raised and sometimes take an equity in the film.

On the set at Peacock
Point, Balmain, with stars
John Hargreaves, Elizabeth
Alexander, and director
Donald Crombie.

(Bottom) Clapper loader
Andrew Lesnie, operator
Danny Batterham.

letter of underwriting was tabled to the AFC on January 15. This group were involved in two other productions – one with the SAFC and one with the VFC. They had formed a subsidiary organisation, Endeavour Communications Ltd, as their film production arm and their head office was situated at the SAFC's studios, with producer Jim George as their executive in charge.

Our overseas journey the previous year for Donald to meet Julie Christie and for me to meet with Dick Blodgett, her agent, also involved the two of us continuing on to New York and Los Angeles with our finance-raising for two films in our package, *Angel Street* and *Kitty and the Bagman*. We saw Thom Mount at Universal, at his request, and Mace Neufeld, an enterprising and successful independent American producer. Donald and I saw twenty-two individual companies and/or producers in the UK and the US but Mace Neufeld liked *The Killing of Angel Street* the most. Donald had to return home and I agreed to stay on to await Neufeld's decision, but had to suddenly curtail my stay when an inflamed ulcer condition was suspected. Our mentor, Al Daff,[3] warned me I couldn't afford to go to hospital in America and to get home, quick. He also suspected something was amiss with no news from Neufeld and politely suggested, 'Listen kiddo, I think you are being kissed out the door'. In a mild state of depression and stomach pain, I made my way to LA airport. How could this be? Donald and I had been swanned around Hollywood in Mace's maroon Rolls Royce. We thought we were made! On arrival at the airport I picked up a copy of *Variety*, being somewhat of a masochist, and was astounded to read MACE NEUFELD TO BACK AUSSIE PIX. There in black and white, for all to read, it said Neufeld was going to finance our picture. Well, if nothing else it relieved the stress of the plane trip home, all twenty hours of it via Honolulu and Nadi.

Back at home I had approached Paul Riomfalvy, the chair and CEO of the New South Wales Film Corporation, to invest, who initially was enthusiastic because it was a Sydney-based film. Later he called me in to say they couldn't invest in the film. He confided in me that he had received a telephone call from a knight of the realm to advise him not to take it on.

Nonetheless we seemed to be in business and Donald had tested Elizabeth Alexander for the lead role of Jessica Simmonds, which met with everyone's unanimous approval. What's more, she didn't ask for a rewrite. However, we realised we had to change our lead male actor. Bill Hunter had been cast when the picture was to star Christie. With the change in casting and Elizabeth not being an international name, it was felt the 'chemistry' of casting would be potentially

---

3   See chapter twenty-three.

more commercial if John Hargreaves were teamed with Elizabeth Alexander. Our investors were very happy with the decision. Donald describes the moment of breaking the news to Bill Hunter as positively one of the worst moments of his life. Bill hasn't spoken to Donald to this day.

With the picture entering pre-production the word 'complicity' was to come well and truly to the fore. Filming *Caddie* in Balmain had brought enormous support from the local community and the local police. The senior sergeant at Balmain had provided every facility and assistance, particularly when we were filming on the suburb's very narrow streets. Not so this time. The senior sergeant advised us that he had received instructions from police headquarters not to provide assistance to our production and to have absolutely nothing to do with us. But he did break the order by telling art director David Copping he could photograph the livery of the police vehicles in the backyard of Balmain station so we could make up our own police cars.

Leichhardt Council were only too happy to have us back in the district and provided us our spectacular harbour location. Peacock Point was being extended by the Council into a much larger public precinct, along the waterfront from the Point north to Balmain ferry wharf. Work wasn't to start for about three months which gave us the opportunity of building 'Angel Street', filming, then removing our set in time for the park extensions to commence.

I was also at this time deputy chair of the Australian Film & Television School. The phone rang in the production office. It was Storry Walton, the director of the School. He had received a call from a member of the Opposition (Liberal Party) in the New South Wales Parliament, requesting an inspection of the School and would I be present when he visited. Neither Storry nor I, nor the deputy director, Frank Morgan, could fathom why this senior figure in the state parliament wanted to learn about the School when it was a commonwealth facility. I obliged and attended, also as the acting chair, for the School had been waiting for nearly a year for a new chair to be appointed.

After the tour of the School, we repaired to Storry's office to have morning tea. It was then the member dropped his bombshell. Looking directly at me, he asked, 'And what is this film you're making about Juanita Nielsen?' I carefully explained to him the film was not about Nielsen but a totally fictional story loosely influenced by the events of Victoria Street and the subsequent disappearance of Juanita Nielsen. He was obviously not convinced. He went on to point out the potential dangers we might face as filmmakers if we were to continue. I asked for an example. 'Well, do you have a dog?' (pause) 'You don't want to come downstairs one morning and find the dog dead on the lawn do you? And find your number plates have vanished from your car do you?' Then came this sinister message. 'Doesn't your director have two children?' This startled all three of us to the point that I responded, 'Well, if anything were to happen to us it would be great publicity for the film.' It was the only thing I could think of to say. He was not expecting this response, hearing this, rose, thanked us and departed. Storry, Frank and I sat in stunned silence. All of us were extremely perturbed by this bizarre encounter. Likewise, Donald and his wife Judy were equally troubled by my account of the meeting. Donald, Judy and I decided to continue, despite the intimidation.

Filming proceeded but I felt we were forever looking over our shoulders. On our night shoots, a police paddy wagon could be seen at the end of our street where it joined Darling Street, the suburb's main thoroughfare. This was thought unusual, for Balmain police had always been most friendly and cooperative. On enquiry of the senior sergeant as to why they were doing this, we were informed that the paddy wagon wasn't theirs but came from police headquarters. Complicity with whom?

David Williams, Greater Union's managing director, who had been a champion for the film because it was going to appeal to the under-25 age group, being an 'anti-authority' film, became quite cool towards the time of release. In fact it completely puzzled us why GU were premiering a Sydney-based film in Melbourne, and at a time of year when the under-twenty-fives were sitting for their exams. Matters weren't helped when the senior publicist for GU, on being introduced to Donald Crombie, said, 'I'm afraid I don't like your film.' This caused matters between ourselves and the Greater Union publicity department to grow to a level of hostility which we had not experienced before. In fact there was no publicity for the film until two weeks before its opening.

Though the first week's figures were soft – it had unwisely been put into the largest screen at Sydney's Pitt Centre where the house 'nut'[4] was high – the figures were beginning to grow in the third week when David Williams phoned to tell me he was pulling the film and it would not play the other capital cities. He said he very much regretted the step and added, 'I may explain the circumstances at a later date.' That day has never come. After the film came off, Williams advised the investors that Greater Union had written the film off. It was a shattering blow to all of us.

The positives.

4   The house nut is the term used to describe the rental charge for the cinema in which the film is screened and deducted from the box office gross.

A failure at home doesn't necessarily mean a failure elsewhere. Producers and directors must never throw in the towel when failure occurs. *The Killing of Angel Street* was turned around overseas thanks to the Berlin Film Festival and two young, enterprising, maverick distributors, making their mark in New York.

The film was invited in competition to Berlin. Liz Alexander and Donald were flown to represent the film and to have the honour of receiving a Jury Prize. Our timing could not have been better or more fortuitous. The irony was, similar events to those depicted in *Angel Street* had occurred in the city of Frankfurt, and a German film had been made only to be completely banned by the authorities. Its plotline evidently paralleled *Angel Street*. Klaus Hellwig, Janus Films, who had had success in Germany with *Caddie* and *The Irishman*, seized the opportunity, had *Angel Street* dubbed into German[5] and released it with considerable success and great curiosity from the German audience.

The year before, the two enterprising Americans referred to had visited Australia and expressed keen interest in our film. Ernie Sauer and Gary Conner had formed their own company, Satori Films, and were hungry. We liked them and were to get to know them quite well. Sauer and Conner acquired the film for American distribution and suggested Liz Alexander and I attend the New York opening to help launch the film in the US. We left for New York on tickets generously provided by Qantas through their San Francisco-based representative, Graham Behn. We arrived on the same day at 5.40am and although not compelled to attend the opening that night, both Liz Alexander and I felt it essential to get a New York audience's 'feel' for the film, so we grabbed four hours' sleep and prepared ourselves for the preview.

Wednesday was a particularly invigorating day for Liz and me. I was to address the National Board of Film Review Society who annually hand out the D.W. Griffith Awards, whilst Liz was to be interviewed by the important youth-oriented magazine, *Good Times*.

The afternoon session was even more lively when Liz and I attended a screening at the Department of Film at Brooklyn College. The college has 14,000 students and the Film Department filled the cinema. It was probably the most rewarding and enjoyable session of our visit and, more importantly, we had reached a young audience who liked the film.

Liz enquired whether it was really worthwhile doing the Cable News interview so while she was waiting to go on, I asked the producer how many subscribers they had. Our jaws dropped – CNN had fifteen million subscribers which in real

---

5   The Germans are renowned for dubbing 'foreign' films into their own language, lip-sync perfect and maintaining the tone and nuances of the actor's original tongue.

(Top right) Front of house, New York's D.W.Griffith cinema where distributor Satori launched a successful season for *The Killing of Angel Street*.

(Bottom) Donald Crombie, Liz Alexander and David Stratton at the Berlin Film Festival when *The Killing of Angel Street* won the Jury prize.

terms meant approximately forty million viewers. Liz's interview was on air that morning and was then repeated at the weekend.

Our first reviews had appeared that morning and it was the beginning of a diversity of opinions. New York's biggest seller – the *New York Post* – lauded the film, whilst the *Daily News* was less than enthusiastic. Later one paper was to claim we had overstated our case and another (the same afternoon) stated the film was too subtle for its own good!

Judith Crist, WOR TV: 'Would you believe an Australian thriller about urban development dealing with corrupt developers in league with the powers that be? *The Killing of Angel Street* offers a fascinating topical story, marked by very good performances – with menace and terror coming to horrifying suspense in a breath-bating climax and a disheartening ending. Your remaining consolation is that it can't happen here … Oh yeah?'

However Vincent Canby on *The New York Times* described the film as 'an earnest, self righteous attack on ruthless land developers riding roughshod over the little folks of Sydney … but it so overstates its case that it's likely to give social activism a bad name.'

I leave the last words with Dolores Dwyer in the *Daily World*. 'Overall, though, *The Killing of Angel Street* is an excellent movie. It shows people can fight back, and it shows that through unity and perseverance, they can win. Bravo!'

FOOTNOTE

The Village Voice, having praised Liz Alexander, went on to say: 'We have Liz Alexander to thank for the fact that not since *Cousin Cousine* have we had such a sexy woman on the screen plainly not suffering from anorexia nervosa. Finally with *Heatwave* looming over the horizon, we can welcome a new Australian genre: The Real Estate Western.' Phillip Noyce, director of *Heatwave*, arrived in New York to promote his film the day *The Killing of Angel Street* opened.

23

Flight Ten From Honolulu – A Complete Change Of Direction

Being 'kissed out the door' is possibly my favourite American expression when it comes to the business of motion pictures and, in particular, Hollywood. Al Daff, the Australian-born head of Universal International at the time of Donald and me making *Caddie*, had introduced me to the expression when Al was warning of the pitfalls of hanging around Hollywood waiting for answers. He pointed out the fact that 'the Yanks, kiddo, never like to say no'. He was right. The Hollywood movie bosses at every level of the administration are very curious to know what it is you have that may be potentially of interest to them. They will meet you for breakfast at short notice, whereas to meet their counterparts in London, you can wait three weeks in your hotel for your call to be returned. You'll be advised that casting is critical to the process and 'let's see how we can put this together'. One will always leave their offices feeling optimistic – but, alas, that will be the last one will hear of it. One has been, albeit pleasantly, 'kissed out the door'.

Al Daff had heard about *Caddie* from Ken G. Hall and had asked to see it. I arranged a preview for him at the austere Commonwealth Centre theatrette in Phillip Street, Sydney, thankfully long demolished. Al asked me to stay through the screening. This experience was a long way from the ambience of the Universal Pictures screening rooms, let me tell you. Al was extremely impressed with the picture and thought it would 'have legs' in the US. He wanted to know how I had cast the picture with such superb actors. I told him I hadn't. He looked at me with incredulity. I continued, 'the director cast the picture, I believe it's their prerogative.' Al was somewhat gobsmacked. He said, 'Listen, kiddo, you're going to make one helluva producer.' Al then went on to explain that in Hollywood the producers took credit for everything and most certainly never gave directors the credit for anything. He claimed the majority of producers in Hollywood were a bunch of schmucks! Al himself was an enigma, with curious connections with the intelligence authorities in Washington.

Al Daff was born on August 18, 1902, in Erskine Street, Hotham Hill, Melbourne, the third child of Ernest and Ruth Daff. Like myself starting out in life, Al was fascinated by the movies from a small boy. Every Saturday would be spent at the open-air picture show in Abbotsford Street, North Melbourne. He got his first job at Selznick Studios distribution office at eighteen years of age, film repairing and distributing posters to the Melbourne cinemas contracted to playing Selznick pictures. He was then to move to Universal Pictures as an assistant projectionist, quickly graduating to film booker and selling Universal's films to the independent theatre owners. To learn more about audience reaction to their movies, Al worked at night as the assistant projectionist at the Moonee Ponds Theatre. It was at Universal that Al found his mentor in Herc McIntyre, who became the legendary head of Universal's Australian operation for the rest of his life, and a vigorous supporter of the production of early Australian films, including those of Charles Chauvel. Herc despatched Al off to Universal Studios in 1935 to gain more experience at the coalface of their head office, but before returning to Melbourne, Fox Films, just prior to their merger with 20th Century Productions, offered Al a lucrative position. He tells Fox that he will think about it and confides in Herc McIntyre.[1] Herc tells him to take it for it's the most important job in the country.

On arriving at the Melbourne office of Universal, Herc walks into Al's office and says, 'I told you as a friend to take it. I'm here now representing Universal, how much do you want to stay?' Al says he won't take anything, to which McIntyre replies, 'Well, I'll split my commission with you.' He does – which Al discovers is £60 ($120) a week! Extraordinary money in 1935. Al goes on to represent Universal in Japan, the Far East and finally, in 1946, becomes president of Universal International, a merger between Universal and International Pictures, a small independent studio set up by William Goetz and Leo Spitz in 1943. Al is to create the studio's two most successful series of pictures; *Francis*, the talking mule with Donald O'Connor, and the *Ma & Pa Kettle* series with Marjorie Main and Percy Kildare, who had created their characters in Universal's big hit of the forties, *The Egg and I*, with Claudette Colbert and Fred McMurray.

Al was to get himself embroiled in the 1973 Tariff Board inquiry into the Australian film industry, which didn't make him too popular with the locals here at home. Al had been sent to Australia by the president of the American

---

1   Interview with Roger Climpson, *This is Your Life*, 1979

Producers and Distributors, to give evidence to the inquiry and to 'assist them in their inquiries'.

Al Daff:[2] 'Yes, we had a problem here. All kinds of wild statements were being made about the terrible American distributors, producers, what they were taking out of the country, a figure of $AUD80m was mentioned on one occasion when the whole of the theatres in Australia were not even grossing that amount of money. That will tell you how stupid and ridiculous it was and I spent a year preparing the facts and researching the facts for the benefit of the Tariff Board and I placed those facts before the Tariff Board. I made a personal submittal to the Tariff Board and I must say that when the final verdicts were given that the American companies came out absolutely clean-skinned, even they could see on the facts and figures submitted to them, not hearsay but actual figures submitted to them, that all of the allegations that were made were false. The question is how much damage would they do if they encouraged fast-buck producers or incompetents to go out and make pictures with an assurance that those pictures were going to be distributed by an American company. An American company is no more capable of forcing people into a theatre to look at a lousy picture than any other country.'

(Hhmmm! Not quite so, methinks.)[3]

I always made a point of seeing Al on my infrequent visits to LA. Always dapper, Homburg hat, bespoke tailored suit, and though in his early eighties, a sprightly walk with a sense of purpose and he still had an eye for the girls and would flirt outrageously with waitresses at some of the popular Rodeo Drive eateries to which I would be taken. It was Al who told me that, when he turned eighty to still find his 'best friend' looking up at him when he awoke of a morning, he knew he was still alive and there was yet another day to enjoy.

At home the authorities weren't at all concerned with a film to be made about Kate Leigh and Tilly Devine, the two queens of Sydney's underworld in the 1920s. *Kitty and the Bagman* was the brainchild of John Burney and Philip Cornford, two Sydney journalists who were writing a book about the two crime queens. We liked their script very much. It was overlong and overwritten but nonetheless we could see its potential and included it in the Forest Home Films package. At the same time, raconteur and advertising guru Phillip Adams had persuaded media

---

2   From an interview with Ken G. Hall filmed by Keith Salvat for the Australian Council for the Arts, now Australia Council.

3   It is interesting to note in 1976, when David Williams had three Australian films playing at the triple-screen Pitt Centre (*Caddie, The Fourth Wish* and *Mad Dog Morgan*) the international head of UIP (then CIC) had arrived from London to enquire why.

mogul Kerry Packer to form Adams Packer Films, initially to start with a slate of four feature films with independent producers and then go on from there. The four chosen were Paul Cox's *Lonely Hearts*, Michael Caulfield's *Fighting Back*, Igor Auzins' *We of the Never Never* and our production of *Kitty and the Bagman*. Cornford and Burney worked with Donald Crombie extremely well, both reacting positively to script changes and script editing. Greg Tepper was head of production for Adams Packer, based in Melbourne. It was an unusual experience for us for we never knew what the above-the-line costs of the picture actually were. We were told we had $2 million with which to make the film and any overages would be borne by Adams Packer. The film was to cost $2.4m.

Ours was a lavish production set in Sydney's roaring twenties, based on two extremely tough and jealous (of each other) crime queens, one who owned the brothels and the other the sly grog trade. It was back to Balmain again but this time to build an authentic street set of the time, which merged at the end of the set into the real streetscape of Balmain. It was an ingenious design by Owen Williams and superbly dressed by art director Stuart Burnside. There was only one problem. The street was built in perspective, the view up the street was perfect, but it made reverse angles extremely difficult. It was also our first production in the anamorphic process (Panavision) with director of photography, Dean Semler, at the helm. Donald had worked previously with Dean on the short drama *The Choice* and I had worked with him on *A Steam Train Passes*.

Donald had assembled an extremely strong ensemble cast headed by John Stanton, Liddy Clark and Val Lehman, and with Dean Semler's wife, Annie, leading our raunchy bunch of chorus girls. A caper film in the true sense of the word, enhanced by Brian May's zesty music score. It was no caper, however, when James Vernon, a fellow producer who was lobbying and politicking for tax concessions for investors in film, telephoned to see if he could bring Federal Treasurer in the Fraser government, John Howard, to set. All was arranged, though we were all somewhat sceptical, when Howard arrived and showed a keen interest in the filming. All went extremely smoothly. Mr Howard thought it would be a good idea if the PM could come down to experience being on a film set and to meet some of our cast and crew, to hear their views on the state of the Australian film industry. The Treasurer left and we really thought that was that. Wrong.

The phone rang next day – could the Prime Minister visit the set the day after tomorrow? Struth, I thought, Howard has really bent his ear. Friday, everything was prepared. Despite a few 'rumblings' from the crew, all agreed to be on their best behaviour!! A Commonwealth limousine, number plate C1, pulled onto the exterior street set and out stepped the Prime Minister of Australia, Malcolm

LIDDY CLARK JOHN STANTON VAL

Gerard Maguire   Colette Mann   Danny Adcock
Anthony Hawkins and John Ewart as the Tr

LIDDY CLARK JOHN STANTON VAL LEHMAN
with
Gerard Maguire   Colette Mann   Danny Adcock   David Bradshaw
Anthony Hawkins and John Ewart as the Train Driver
Executive Producer Phillip Adams   Produced by Anthony Buckley   Directed by Donald C

(Top) Lobby cards for *Kitty and the Bagman*.

(Right) Director Donald Crombie welcomes
Treasurer John Howard whom independent
producer, James Vernon, persuaded to visit
the set to convince the Treasurer the tax
incentives under 10BA were working.

(Bottom) Four days later the Prime Minister,
Malcolm Fraser, visited set, here with James
Vernon and me.

Fraser. We found him to be genuinely interested in the proceedings and he also made all of us relaxed and comfortable in his presence. The PM was particularly interested in the Panavision camera and Dean Semler sat him on the operator's seat and explained what the various handles did, to pan and tilt the camera. It was a coup for James Vernon to have persuaded the Federal Treasurer to visit, but for Howard to have got the Prime Minister to come four days later was really some feat.

Kitty and the Bagman finally wrapped and I felt the end result was extremely pleasing, as did David Stratton, director of the Sydney Film Festival, who invited the film to open the 1982 Festival at Sydney's mighty State Theatre. To be selected for opening night is not just an honour, but important for the film to gain its credentials or 'legs' and to be recognised by the cinema-going public when the film goes into general release. These were still the days of single-screen city releases, four sessions a day. A film could play for months in the city before reaching the suburbs. Greater Union were firmly opposed to *Kitty and the Bagman* opening the Festival. I pleaded with them, as did David Stratton who went in to bat for us too. John Politzer at GU explained it could be another year before the film could open as there were no screens. David Willliams advised strongly against it but said that in the end the decision was finally ours – Donald's and mine. My gut reaction was to accept, but it was wise not to antagonise our distributor, who was also our exhibitor. We decided not to accept David Stratton's invitation. It was producer's mistake number one. David was particularly upset and I knew it was the wrong decision for the film. What did it matter if the release was still a year away? In hindsight it was a serious error. The opening of the Festival was given to the Melbourne-based *Squizzy Taylor*, also set in the twenties, but I thought lacking the punch and pace of *Kitty*.

But worse was to come. Not quite a year had gone by when GU announced an opening day for the film at their flagship triplex, the Pitt Centre. An elaborate opening was arranged for the Russell complex in Melbourne, only to be marred by being the tragic night of Ash Wednesday, the bushfires that swept Victoria. In Sydney the media were treated to a steam train trip to Wollongong, south of the city, for the preview, a stunt which was impressive but which I thought didn't quite come off. Producer's mistake number two was to be away for the opening. The previous year I had booked to take a cruise/freighter ship from Manila to Hong Kong via the islands of the Philippines. The opening was to now clash with our departure. Everything was in place, there seemed to be plenty of enthusiasm in the GU team, so I decided we would go. Not a good thing to do, to let your eye drop from the ball. The first weekend's figures were considered soft. Sydney $13,600,[4] Melbourne $6,205, Newcastle $3,157, Wollongong $4,383, Canberra $3,610. By the time we returned three weeks later, 'last days' had been posted and the season closed just after four weeks. In fairness GU made one last desperate attempt to change the 'tone' of the advertising, but it was too late. They themselves blamed an aspect of the campaign for the film's 'non performance.' We also came home to some pretty mixed reviews.

The late Matt White in the *Sydney Daily Mirror* was positive about his feelings for the film: 'There's plenty of action in *Kitty and the Bagman* and at least one principal character comes to a violent bloody end. But there is humour too, and this takes the film out of the routine gangster melodrama, lifting it into the realms of fun entertainment and sending the audience away feeling glad they had spent a couple of hours with *Kitty and the Bagman* ... This is Val Lehman's first feature film ... She's even tougher in this film than in the television series *Prisoner*. Liddy Clark turns in an impressive portrayal of Kitty ... But top acting accolade must go to John Stanton. As the aloof and cold-blooded detective on-the-take, he comes over as a man you hate, but can't help admiring.'

As with *Angel Street*, the film received extraordinarily positive support overseas.

In *The Hollywood Reporter*, Charles Ryweck was honest when he observed: '*Kitty and the Bagman* may not be a critic's picture, but its raw vitality and affectionate salute to the American gangland genre from Australia could very well make it an audience pleaser ... This wild and wooly film from Down Under has some good actors to inhabit the colorful characters. ...'

Variety and *The Hollywood Reporter's* reviews helped influence sales of the film enormously. Greg Tepper, the amiable and personable head of production for Adams Packer, our backers, secured several sales at Cannes, the most significant of which was to Quartet Films of New York, a small distribution company helmed by Arthur Tolchin. Like Lou Edelman and Marshall Schacker, Tolchin came from the old school of American film chiefs, well mannered, quietly spoken, immaculately dressed, and as I was to discover, a perfect gentleman. However, at our first encounter at the venerable Algonquin on West 44th Street, I was to meet a very perplexed Tolchin. He had been waiting to hear from Greg Tepper, who had arrived in New York to deliver the film to Quartet but hadn't appeared. It had been ten days and Tolchin was now concerned for Greg's safety. Play dates right across America had been scheduled. It was to be an ambitious launch. So I took over the arrangements

---

4   I mention our figures for today if a screen grosses $13,600 a week that film is considered a hit. If it is grossing $3,000 plus, the film is kept on. How times have changed, though I do wonder how some exhibitors' screens survive.

of securing the delivery items from the laboratories in Australia for Arthur's team to ready the film for release. We were later to learn that Greg had been totally overwhelmed on arrival by the new wave of 1980s liberation for gay males – the phenomenon of the New York steam rooms. The exclusive all-male establishments not only provided all facilities but full luxurious accommodation as well. Greg didn't emerge till he was due to catch his plane. Arthur and I soldiered on!

What Donald and I weren't aware of was that prior to the release of the film, Arthur Tolchin had added a 'Director's Statement' to the beginning of the film before the main titles, dedicating *Kitty and the Bagman* to 'Bogart, Cagney, Robinson, Muni and everybody at Warner Bros who made the roaring '20s roar.' American critics picked up on this title and in many ways it 'coloured' their view, to the detriment of the film. Others found it cynically amusing. Arthur was certainly brave and obviously had the contacts to roll the film out across the States in an attempt to break a 'foreign' film out of the 'arthouse' mould which John Hawn in *The Indianapolis Star* astutely observed: 'Distributors and exhibitors will be watching the local release of *Kitty and the Bagman* with great interest. That's because the "art" film is being given general release in four theatres in the Indianapolis area instead of being tucked away in a repertory house or in a foreign film series. The distributor, Quartet Films Inc, believes the experiment with *Kitty and the Bagman* will work. The success of *Kitty and the Bagman* would prove to be a great boon to fans of art films, especially those who might miss them because of their sporadic appearances. One has to wonder, though, why *Kitty,* and not any of a dozen other superior films, should be the one to test the tastes of general audiences.'

It was whilst I was with Arthur Tolchin at the Algonquin that a telex came in from Leslie Halliwell to me, who was the spotter and buyer for Britain's ITV network, with an offer of US$40,000 for two plays on the network. Mr Halliwell thought *Kitty* a 'crowd pleaser'.

Right across the board the reviewers and critics, whether liking the film or not, all agreed on one thing, *Kitty* was an 'audience pleaser'. Yet that audience never came. I suppose for the exhibitor, the distributor and the producer, it goes to prove that old Hollywood adage that 'nobody knows nothin'!'

⟨⟩ ————— ⟨⟩

It was Greg Tepper who took the call. It was 7.30am and the woman's voice on the telephone said 'Flight ten from Honolulu', at least that is what Greg thought the woman said, waking one Saturday morning from his slumbers. In fact it was Ayten Kuyululu, a Turkish migrant who sang in the chorus of The Australian Opera. I had first encountered Ayten in 1973 when she was preparing to make *A Handful of Dust*, a powerful short drama about a working class migrant in which Ayten played the lead. Ayten's performance was totally believable. She followed with a feature film in 1975, the first from a woman director in Australia for thirty years, *The Golden Cage*. Her passion, however, was to make *The Battle of Broken Hill*. Greg Tepper had rung me that Saturday morning to check out 'flight ten's' bona fides. Ayten had introduced her script to Donald Crombie inviting him to direct. Donald was intrigued with its potential, even though it was from the Turkish point of view.

The battle of Broken Hill occurred on New Year's Day 1915 when Gool Mahomed, an Afghani ice cream vendor, and Mullah Abdullah, a butcher believed to have been from India, both Muslims and well-known town identities, raised the Turkish flag and fired upon a train crowded with members of the Manchester Unity Order of Oddfellows, travelling to their annual picnic.

Michael Craig had also come up with his own version of the story and Donald attempted to bring his and Ayten's projects together. But it wasn't to work. At about this same time, John Power (*The Picture Show Man*) was developing his own script about the battle, *The Ice Cream Wars*. None of the planned films were ever made.

For me, it was time to move on. The suspected ulcer, which caused Al Daff to suggest I get home quickly whilst I was in Hollywood waiting to hear from Mace Neufeld, was diagnosed finally as a reality. The specialist warned me to 'ease up' as I began a course of Tagamet. Being fully aware that my mother had died twenty-two years earlier at the age of forty-nine from blood poisoning as a result of a burst ulcer, and that I was in my early forties, I felt I was suddenly looking down the barrel of a gun. I resigned from the deputy chairmanship of the Film School, of which I had been acting chair for the past year, quit as president and acting director of the Feature Film Producers Association (FFPA) (now the Screen Production Association of Australia – SPAA) and resigned as a director of Forest Home Films. Drastic actions or dramatic decisions no doubt, but that first weekend I slept peacefully for the first time for a long, long while.

I think the initiative of the Australian Film Commission in supporting packages such as Forest Home Films, rather than developing films piecemeal, was a great one and gave us enormous confidence and zeal to achieve something worthwhile, and experience in handling the bigger picture of the film industry, both at home and abroad. I think it is a scheme worth re-introducing to give producers and directors an anchor for the development of their ideas and to encourage them to bring them to fruition.

Ken Watts had resigned from the Australian Film Commission to move to Melbourne and to take over the reins of Adams Packer Films. But to his horror he was to find the cupboard was bare. The $7 million Kerry Packer had invested in the company had been totally spent on the four films, leaving no money for salaries, overheads and development expenses. It was in the last weeks of the production of *Kitty* that I received a phone call advising me that Kerry Packer wanted to see how his money was being spent. He was invited to visit the set and this was arranged for a Friday afternoon about 3pm. My office was a spartan concrete bunker devoid of any form of decoration, overlooking the art department and the street set outside the window. I had one chair, the one I sat on, and used to steal one from the accounts department when anyone wished to discuss anything.

The 'Big Man' arrived with an entourage of executives from Channel Nine and Packer's headquarters at 54 Park Street, all eager to get home early this Friday afternoon. After a tour of all the departments it was apparent he wanted to talk so I invited him up to my bunker. Strangely I think he enjoyed the austerity of the surroundings. At least he could see his money wasn't being wasted! I also found him easy to talk with. The hour-long visit was entering its second hour and I could detect a sense of unease among his executives pacing outside. It reached 5pm and there was no sign of the Big Man leaving. What we talked about I can no longer remember, but it certainly wasn't small talk. He suddenly asked if his daughter, Gretel, could come and visit the set to watch filming. I suggested she should come at a time when she could perhaps enjoy lunch with the actors. 'Would tomorrow be okay?' he enquired, 'I'll see what she's got on.' He then took his leave, much to the relief of his executives who by now were perpetually looking at their watches. The time was 5.50pm. Saturday morning, 10am, phone rings. 'Could Miss Packer come to watch the filming?' the voice enquired. An hour later the black, chauffeured limousine pulled onto the set and out stepped Gretel Packer. She was a delightful young lady and stayed with the company on set for three hours, enthralled with every minute.

It was some time later when I was invited to the San Francisco Grill at the Hilton Hotel to dine with Lynton Taylor and Len Mauger, two of Kerry Packer's senior executives. I knew Len quite well but hadn't met Taylor before. They put to me a proposal of setting up their own production company to be called PBL. Would I be interested in heading up the enterprise? I explained that I had just quit everything and was going to take some time out. I was asked to think about it; there was no hurry. Well, so they thought.

9.45pm the phone rings in my flat at Lane Cove. Lynton Taylor – 'Mr Packer would like a few words with you.' I recognised the gravelly voice straight away. 'Are you one of these arty farty types, what's this about refusing my offer?' I quickly responded that if I was one of those arty farty types he wouldn't want to employ me. He laughed and then I explained my situation. Lynton came back on the phone and thanked me. Before Packer finished, I took the liberty of suggesting he didn't need a production company and that he should only finance those shows the network needed from the best of the independent production sector. But it was obvious he wanted control, which he hadn't had over Adams Packer Films.

I felt ill when I put the phone down. Had I made an enemy of him and the network? I wrote by hand a personal letter of apology to him. A week later I received the nicest short note from him wishing me all the best and simply signed Kerry. I have the letter to this day.

Adams Packer Films continued to limp along with Ken Watts having raised enough capital to pay salaries from its owner and keep the doors open. Watts was interested in two scripts by advertising writer Peter Carey and his business partner Ray Lawrence, then already Australia's leading creative television commercials director. The first was a highly imaginative work, *Dancing on the Water* which, apart from anything else, required a huge swimming pool and horses that had to be trained to swim and like water. (Horses are instinctively wary of water and avoid getting their ears wet.) The second, *Spanish Pink*, was as different again, very black, somewhat risqué, but could be made on a much smaller budget. I was introduced to Peter and Ray and both projects were put into continuing development, with budgets and schedules being prepared. Regretfully distributors were clearly not interested in these two innovative works and Adams Packer Films weren't in a position to fund them.

I had been asked to head the Australian delegation to the Asian International Film Festival, a hobby-horse of John McQuaid, one of the full-time commissioners of the Australian Film Commission. That year the festival was to be held in Kuala Lumpur. I suggested to Ray and Peter that as soon as I returned, we should all meet to decide a strategy for *Dancing on the Water* and *Spanish Pink*.

September 8, 1982: I was preparing to leave for the airport when Ray knocked on the door. 'Here's something to read on the plane, I think you'll like it.' He handed me a hardcover book and I quickly put it in my carry-on bag for the plane. The MAS flight took off on time and after the plane had levelled out and the inflight service had commenced I opened the book. Eight hours later, as we began our descent into KL, I closed the covers of the novel. It was *Bliss* by Peter Carey. Cleared customs, checked into the hotel, threw my bag onto the bed and picked up the phone. I had read the most remarkable book in all my life. The phone at the studio in Sydney answered and I said, 'Ray Lawrence please, it's Tony Buckley in Kuala Lumpur. Yes, it's important.'

24

A Landmark Australian Film

THROUGHOUT HISTORY MANY GREAT ARTISTS HAVE
DEPICTED THE TORTURES OF HELL.
BUT NEVER BEFORE HAS ANYONE DARED TO SUGGEST
THAT HELL IS A PLACE WHERE AN ELEPHANT
SITS ON YOUR MOTORCAR.

Ray Lawrence came to the phone. I told him what I thought of Peter Carey's wonderful book. 'Why aren't we making this?' I wanted to know. Compared with the two very good but unknown screenplays, *Bliss* was screaming out to be put on celluloid. 'It's the most visual book I have read in years – we have to make it.' It wasn't to be that easy. Ray explained that Peter had optioned the book some time ago to a British producer for Gillian Armstrong to direct. The screenplay had been written by the producer's boyfriend and evidently wasn't considered to be very successful. Peter advised his agent of my reaction and willingness to try and get it made.

The book had just won the 1982 Miles Franklin Award for literature, Australia's most prestigious literary award. Before the year was out it was to win two further awards, the New South Wales Premier's Literary Award and the National Book Council Award.

Why *Bliss*? I think our synopsis for the film best describes both the novel and the film-to-be:

'BLISS Somewhere between HEAVEN and HELL. A highly original and entertaining comedy – a story about a man who so misunderstood the world he almost got it right! The man is Harry Joy. A good fellow, a genial story teller, a successful advertising executive, Harry Joy is all this and more. But Harry's death changes his life. In four minutes of Harry's death, he recognises the worlds of pleasure and pain. Brought abruptly back to life, Harry finds the comfortable images of his former existence have dissolved into uncertainty and with fumbling sincerity sets about discovering the truth. The absurdity of Harry's antics in doing this land him upside down from a tree branch in his garden, swathe him in the luxury of a hotel penthouse, incarcerate him in a mental institution of bizarre dimensions. Into the infernal comedy of human relationships created by this behaviour comes the enchanting Honey Barbara – the beautiful child of nature – who offers Harry the pathway to redemption. Finally, Harry follows this path to bliss ... planting trees ... telling stories ... working with his hands ... and eventually winning Honey. He was happy enough. And many years later a bloody great tree fell on him and that was the end of Harry Joy.'

Home to Sydney and a late night call to London. The agent Stephen Durbridge confirmed there was an option on the novel and its renewal date was fast approaching. It was $10,000 per year. Where on earth could I get $10,000? Funding authorities would accept an application for script development but would not fund options. They see this as the function of the producer. Depending on the property, sometimes an option can be secured for anything from $1 to $500 but $10,000 was absolutely out of my reach. I hit the ground running. September 20, 2.30, an appointment with Jenny Woods, the general manager of the New South Wales Film Corporation, headed by Paul Riomfalvy. Jenny listened attentively and agreed to broach the subject of the option with Riomfalvy. Then across the harbour for a 4.30 appointment with John Daniell at the Australian Film Commission. Yes, they would consider script development of *Bliss*, but not the option money.

I didn't have long to wait. Next morning Jenny Woods rang to advise the NSW Film Corporation would cover the option and I should make the offer to Durbridge immediately. He was impressed that a decision had been made so quickly and advised our offer was firmly on the table. We would have to wait till the option had expired or the British producer renewed. Their producer would be advised there was another offer on the table only when he came to renew.

The wait of three months was agonising. Finally the date of expiration came and the phone rang. It was Durbridge in London. The book was ours. The British producer hadn't renewed and our offer was accepted. The NSW Film Corporation immediately guaranteed script development funding and Peter Carey and Ray Lawrence commenced work breaking down the book in preparation for writing the first draft screenplay. It should be noted at this point that the NSW FC was the most innovative and adventurous of all the funding authorities at this time and had supported me previously with the financing of Jim Sharman's *The Night The Prowler*. They were prepared to take risks and *Bliss* was most certainly a risk – a very big one for all three of us.

It was announced to the media that we had acquired the rights to *Bliss* to make a feature film and Peter, Ray and I formed Window III Productions to produce the film (Window being their television commercials production company). I was at the offices of the Australian Film Commission when I encountered Errol Sullivan, our unit manager on *Caddie*, in the corridor. He was walking toward me and said, with a smile of incredulity, 'Tony, you haven't really optioned Bliss have you?' I nodded. 'I've read it,' Errol said, 'you can't make a film out of it!' I said 'One most certainly can – wait and see.' He walked past, shaking his head. This encounter illustrates graphically how two filmmakers (Errol was to become a very successful television producer) can read the same book and/or screenplay, yet see it so differently. It is one of the wonderful challenges of being a producer, and why NOBODY KNOWS NOTHIN'.

How to raise money for a first-time director? Ray's commercial savvy came into play. He knew whom he wanted for his two leads. Barry Otto and Lynette Curran. Lynette was a seasoned player on stage and screen and had played a significant role in *Caddie*, but Barry was known only to theatregoers, unknown on screen. Ray had a very strong hunch that Barry was Harry Joy. Why not film a scene from the script with our two nominated stars? We had no money, but we scraped together enough to acquire film stock and hire a 35mm Arriflex camera and a marvellous volunteer crew. We hired a heritage private hotel near Double Bay, Sydney, for the weekend, but had the scene shot in a day. Edited and with the widescreen gate letterboxed onto the tape transfer, it looked like any quality feature film. One would never have thought of it as a screen-test.

The NSW Film Corporation had contacted an investment group, Qantum, then operating out of Sydney and Melbourne, but later to operate exclusively out of Melbourne, to raise the private investment moneys. It was a daunting morning when I entered a boardroom to see about ten men seated at a round table looking at a television monitor on which our scene from *Bliss* was playing. It did the trick and reassured the NSW FC's management that they might be onto something.[1]

Whilst our scene did reassure the Corporation and the private investment managers, it gave no comfort to the distributors. Hoyts and Greater Union asked to see the film when it was finished. On December 2, 1983, just over a year from securing the option to the book, with maverick flourish, Paul Riomfalvy, the head of the NSW FC, wrote the following in part: '... We gave thoughtful

---

1   Whenever in doubt about supporting new people, or to reassure one's backers, it is always wise to do as we did and film a test scene. The average investor and even some distributors are unaccustomed to reading scripts but film a test scene and both investor and distributor can see where you are coming from.

consideration to your choice of Ray Lawrence as director. We are very proud to state that producers of New South Wales Film Corporation-backed motion pictures were very successful with their choices of young and new directors such as Gillian Armstrong (*My Brilliant Career*), Phil Noyce (*Newsfront*) and recently Carl Schultz (*Careful*).[2] All three pictures won Best Film and Best Director in the AFI Awards.'

With Riomfalvy's letter and the investment of $500,000, the Qantum group was able to issue a prospectus to raise the remainder of our $3.3 million budget. Though the tax concessions were attractive to prospective investors, one could not take for granted that the required moneys would be in place by June 30, the end of the Australian financial year. Nonetheless, Ray and I began putting a team together – DOP, editor etc – realising the marketplace for our creatives was going to be a very competitive one, along with the marketplace for the available investment funds for the twelve or more pictures competing for those funds. One big one was *Burke and Wills*, an epic saga about the failed explorers, to be directed by expatriate Graeme Clifford returning home for the occasion. Little did Ray and I know how *Burke and Wills* was going to affect us and how we were to learn a lesson as to where loyalties lay.

The months moved slowly by with Peter and Ray working diligently on each draft of the screenplay, and me working with our allies at the NSW Film Corporation, cautiously planning our shoot dates for the second half of the year. The month of June was agony for all of us, including the investment managers at Qantum. In these 'halcyon' days of 10BA, many investors didn't make their minds up until the very last minute. I can remember vividly Monday to Wednesday, June 25, 26 and 27, joining in the fray and driving from suburb to suburb to assist Qantum in picking up cheques from individual investors to enable the cheques to be banked in time to be eligible for their precious tax concession.

Ray and Nonie Lawrence had invited me to dinner for the Friday night. The phone rang. It was Jenny Woods at the NSW Film Corporation. 'Hello Tiger, Paul wants to speak to you.' Riomfalvy came on the line and in his heavily accented Hungarian voice exclaimed, 'You are going to make zee picture Tony. All zee money is in.' Broke as I was at the time, I bought a bottle of Moet Chandon at the Figtree Cellars at Lane Cove. Ray opened the door and peered at me apprehensively. He could see the top of the bottle of French poking out of the brown paper bag. 'We've got the money – we're fully financed.' Ray opened the door a little wider, stared at me and said, 'I won't let you down.' Nor did he.

2   *Careful He Might Hear You.*

What none of us knew, however, at this defining moment in our lives, was that Ray was going to deliver a 'landmark Australian film'. Our great adventure was about to begin.

Burke and Wills had also been financed. This was discovered when I rang those heads of department we had invited to join us on *Bliss*. 'Oh, Tony, sorry, we didn't think you would raise the money, I'm doing Graeme's picture,' was the general answer. So suddenly we had no DOP, no editor, etc. *Burke and Wills*, however, was not to be the dawn of any new prosperity for the Australian feature film industry.

So we began again. Probably, in hindsight, we put together a crew, including our first feature DOP Paul Murphy, who excelled themselves in every department. It also put together Ray Lawrence with long-time associate of mine and unquestionably Australia's best camera operator, David Williamson, who was in turn to become Ray's DOP on *Jindabyne*. Film history buffs please take note.

Bliss is a comedy but it wasn't a comedy on August 6, 1984 when we commenced pre-production and couldn't find office space! For our production manager, Carol Hughes, the week quickly became a nightmare. The end-of-year financing for films caused a 'bunching' effect on production and several features and television films had stolen not only a march on us but had 'stolen' most of the valuable office and studio space available in Sydney. After a week of operating out of three motorcars continuously travelling, and umpteen telephone calls, we finally found a home in Artarmon. The building was formerly Pacific Film Laboratories and bore a close resemblance to a concrete bunker. With the help of some cheap dressings and humanising touches it was transformed into a very liveable and workable bunker!

Finalisation of the cast took until the final two weeks of our pre-production period. It was the right actress for the role of Honey Barbara which confounded us the most. Extensive testing was carried out, sometimes calling the same artist back for second tests. Finally Ray made a discovery in Helen Jones. Helen was a graduate from NIDA (the National Institute for Dramatic Art) and *Bliss* was her first major appearance.

The task of finding an American to play the role of Joel, Harry's partner in his advertising agency, led us to apply to Actors Equity for permission to bring in an American actor to play the role. Equity were considerate and advised us that our request did fall within the parameters of their guidelines pertaining to 'ethnic' parts. However, we said we would look here first, which we did, and soon Ray Lawrence found Jeff Truman to be 'just right' for the character of Joel. Could he perfect an American accent convincingly? Surely if he was right for the part he could perfect the accent. Our casting director, Susie Maizels, arranged with the Juilliard Academy in New York for a month's tutoring for Jeff with Lillian Mansel, one of America's top drama tutors. So Jeff was despatched to the Big Apple. He was firmly warned by our director on departure that if he landed back in a month and said 'g'day' he would be fired! Jeff's term in New York was very successful and to the consternation of all of his friends, he spoke with a fluent and soft Bronx accent. We think this approach was the first time it had been used by Australian producers.

Rehearsals for all the principal cast commenced the last two weeks of September in a nearby motel and video was used to assist the development of the actors' performances. Each rehearsal was carefully recorded and perfected again and again. In the evenings the tapes were carefully studied by the director, producer and co-writer, Peter Carey, to see if any scenes needed deleting or rewriting. This whole experience was of extreme value for the artists and the director/writer team. It saved time on the set too.

Bliss opens with a flooded town in 1920 and a sky full of thundercloud. In a relaxed, deep voice, Harry Joy begins his story of the Vision Splendid (his mother) and the story moves immediately on to 1983. Flooded towns don't come easy you'll agree, so it was decided to build. Budget restrictions had to be a first consideration but after careful thought and planning it was decided to build a church, graveyard with picket fence and submerge a motorcar and a dray. But where to film it? Narrabeen Lakes (used for *Newsfront*) was out of the question as coloured water was to be used and the terrain of the surrounding countryside was unsuitable. A private property with a dam was found near Windsor, an historic town almost two hours drive from Sydney. Although carefully sand-bagged by the crew, the set flooded in a sudden rainstorm.

Reshoots on a picture are generally determined as a result of an accident, or a laboratory malfunction and damage to the negative. It is extremely unusual for a producer to order a reshoot. The 'Vision Splendid' is the opening scene of *Bliss* and clearly establishes the mood, character and genre of the piece. Ray expressed reservations at the end of the day's shoot, which was quite uncharacteristic. We weren't screening rushes on Saturday as an economy measure but I also had sensed from the crew an unease about the day, so I asked for rushes to be called for the Saturday morning. The rushes looked good, they were good, but there was 'that certain something' missing. Discussion led to 'it will be okay when edited'. My editor's eye didn't quite sense this feeling of confidence. If the scene had been somewhere in the middle of the film, then okay, no one may have noticed or have understood what *we* were looking at. However, it *was* the opening of the film.

I looked at Carol Hughes and we adjourned to discuss reshooting the opening. Neither of us knew where we would find the money but we both agreed the opening of the film had to be right. I told Ray we would accommodate reshooting the entire scene and rescheduled it for the following Tuesday. Morale soared and the end result was absolutely perfect. A good example of finding ways to meet an 'end' by being prepared to 'bite the bullet'.

This opening scene called for rain, fog and red water. Safe organic vegetable dyes were used and twenty-two special effects men manned the fires around the lake used to create the fog. Rain machines were hoisted to the top of four scaffold towers floating on pontoons. The Vision Splendid, played by Sarah de Teliga, was required to appear in a rowing boat travelling across the lake towards camera as Harry tells his story in the narration. The boat was rigged to a cable and pulley submerged beneath the water and radio remote-controlled.

For Harry Joy's descent from 'Heaven into Hell', Ray Lawrence wanted rain and lots of it! Through the cooperation of the Council at Hunters Hill, our Sydney location, and the residents in Lloyd Avenue, permission was given to bring in three cherry pickers and a huge 200 ft crane from The Men from Marrs. Cherry pickers are normally used to replace street lamps etc, but in this case they were being used to hold the large rain hoses of our special effects expert, Keron Hansen. The 'rain' was to be pumped from two large water tanks installed nearby. Our master camera was held in a cradle, called a 'hot head', attached to the underside of the crane's bucket, in which were the camera operator and dogman. The camera operator, David Williamson, manipulated the movements of the camera by remote control on a video monitor installed in the bucket. Weeks of planning and rehearsal took place to perfect this highly imaginative operation. The overcast sky was an extra plus, which we had hoped for but hadn't really expected to get. After hours of careful preparation the operation was finally set in motion, the director called 'action', the cameras rolled, the crane began to move, our 'rain' began to cascade down and the heavens opened up!! This was the second time on our shoot that nature had upstaged our special effects man. The result was quite spectacular but the filming operation left the locals completely mystified and possibly wondering about film people.

The residents of Fay Place, Marsfield, our next location, could have been forgiven if they had looked somewhat incredulous as three elephants strolled past their homes in a rainstorm on a sunny day. The elephants were involved in the scene where Harry Joy's Bambino car is sat on by an elephant while Harry is talking with Aldo in Milano's Restaurant. The script also calls for rain but naturally it was a sunny day. This is where our special effects and the fire brigade came to our aid and supplied the required rain for the day. The elephants didn't mind the rain but couldn't see the sense at all in being required to walk backwards to sit on a motorcar!

After the elephants sit on Harry's Fiat the news is broken to him at his table in Milano's Restaurant by Aldo, the head waiter (Jon Ewing), the dwarf from the circus (Marco Colombani) and the elephant trainer, De Vere (Tommy Dysant). The comedy in this scene is only eclipsed by the following scenes of Harry driving his somewhat squashed Bambino through the peak hour traffic of Sydney, much to the incredulity of the arresting officers of the law. To set up these scenes presented our team with two major problems. Where to find a restaurant not open for several days, and how to set up a major scene in peak hour traffic? The Department of Main Roads weren't too impressed with a suggestion to close one of Sydney's bridges and there were no restaurateurs willing to close for a few days. We had completed some hospital scenes in a disused section of the old Rozelle Hospital when our director found a section ideal for the restaurant scenes. Art director Owen Paterson designed a delightful set for Milano's but the traffic scene was more difficult. One has to be extremely careful and conscious of safety when filming with actors in busy streets and therefore locations in continual use were out of the question. Then someone in our team thought of Sydney's old Pyrmont Bridge. It was closed some years ago after the opening of the Darling Harbour fly-overs. Although cut off at one end and permanently open to shipping, the Department of Main Roads agreed to close the bridge for one day. Thirty 44-gallon drums filled with water were placed at the cut-off end of the bridge to stop us driving off into space and the local boat charter operators cooperated in adjusting their timetables to fit in with our filming. We supplied our own vehicles, semi-trailers and police car, all driven by specially trained stunt drivers who understand the requirements of filmmaking. The scene worked very well, Harry driving his crumpled Bambino, menaced by a huge semi, with the city skyline in the background, and without disrupting the city's traffic.

Milano's Restaurant is also used for another major scene in *Bliss,* which can safely be described as 'risqué' but extremely funny. Joel (Jeff Truman) makes advances to Bettina (Lynette Curran), Harry's wife, at the lunch table! Their conversation continues whilst their lovemaking proceeds and fifty businessmen continue eating their lunch, not noticing what is going on, except for Aldo of course who turns to camera – 'See, I told you … They think they're fooling everyone, but not me. Poor Harry, everyone loves him except his wife.' The scene is one of the high points of the film.

Another high point is Harry's open-heart operation. In the middle of the operation Harry wakes, looks at his heart pumping away in the surgeon's hand and says 'Oh! I've died again – hurry up and do something!' This scene was filmed with the help of the surgeons at the Royal Prince Alfred Hospital. Harry's heart was specially made by prosthetics make-up expert Bob McCarron, who was also responsible for making up Harry as an old man at the end of the film.

Apart from rain machines and elephants the art department also had to provide live fish and live cockroaches for some of the film's more bizarrely funny scenes. This last fell to set dresser Alethea Deane to organise. A marine biologist caught our fish at Port Stephens and Taronga Zoo kindly kept them alive for us. The University of Sydney supplied the cockroaches that lived in a specially designed bucket with an 'electric fence' that prevented them from escaping and causing havoc! The careful handling of these creatures, and persuading them to do what we wanted them to do, was entrusted to standby props Colin Gibson, who actually had mastered the art of catching the cockroaches after the completion of the scene. There was only one escapee. An ear-piercing scream from Jenny Miles (standby wardrobe) revealed that one of the cockroaches had nestled comfortably into her note file. It was quickly apprehended and returned to its 'electric' bucket.

The latter part of the film is told by Harry Joy as an old man and is set entirely in the bush. In continuing his story Harry tells us about the character Clive and how he finally dropped a match in the Hare Krishna's lantana patch – 'but he also burnt out five hundred acres of good timber'. The script called for a 'big eucalypt forest the day after an intense fire: huge black leafless verticals rise from an ash blue forest floor. Smoke rises from everything.' In pre-production our location manager, Robin Clifton, had found the perfect site – but it was at Gloucester in New South Wales – a good two days travelling for the heavy equipment. No end of searching could find a closer alternative that would reduce our time, and subsequently our costs. Each week Robin would ring the Gosford Bush Fire Brigade to enquire if any fires had broken out. Always the answer was 'no'.

So the plan was to move to Gloucester at the end of the Gosford shoot. Then the weather closed in and we knew delays were going to be unavoidable, making the Gloucester shoot look more and more difficult and adding considerably to our expense. Till one night Robin's phone rang. It was an excited member of the Gosford Bush Fire Brigade to announce they had had a fire and it was a beauty! What's more, it was an hour's drive from our motel. In the first break available, director Ray Lawrence and director of photography Paul Murphy went out to inspect the fire site. Plans were immediately put in train to relocate our Gloucester scenes to Gosford. The location was only accessible by four-wheel-drive vehicles so a huge ferrying operation was set in place to get the crew and the heavy equipment into the fire area. Not only was this exercise extremely successfully achieved but the filming was completed in the same day, thereby saving us three valuable days. One can imagine how pleased the completion guarantor was!

Ray worked long hours with editor Wayne Le Clos to fine cut the film in time for it to be submitted to the Cannes Film Festival for consideration for competition. Because we didn't have a distributor it was felt essential to gain exposure at Cannes. The long road there had commenced when I approached Giles Jacob, the director of the Festival International du Film, informing him of the production of *Bliss,* which at that time had just commenced pre-production. Our schedule made it impossible to deliver a finished print of our film for the selection committee's viewing. However, they kindly agreed to view a videotape of our cutting copy. The film was in a very raw and unfinished state. To assist the selection committee in evaluating the film, we engaged the help of the Special Broadcasting Service (Channel 0/28) who reversed their usual role and sub-titled *Bliss* into French. The SBS translators achieved this task in the remarkable time of less than three weeks. So off went *Bliss* to await the selection committee. Then an extraordinary series of events occurred. The selection committee first invited *Bliss* into 'Un Certain Regard', a prestigious but 'fringe' part of the Festival, not in competition. After very careful evaluation it was decided to decline the invitation in the best interest of the film's commercial future. At the same time the director of the 'Director's Fortnight' at Cannes, Pierre Henri-Delau, asked to view the tape and immediately invited *Bliss* into that section of the Festival. We naturally accepted and notified the Festival of our wish to accept the Director's Fortnight invitation when suddenly – and I mean suddenly – we were informed *Bliss* was invited into competition. *Bliss* could very well be the first film to have been invited into all three sections of the Cannes Festival! The politics of the situation that had arisen did not escape me.

Our 'in competition' screening was to be held in the Palais de Festivals on the Saturday night. Beforehand there is a screening for the international press contingent. Ours was at 9.30 on the Friday evening. About 1500 attend. Ray and his wife Nonie and I were there with Bob Lewis and his wife from the Australian Film Office of the NSW FC in Los Angeles, and our publicist and his staff. I was standing in the foyer about to go into the cinema to see how our screening was going when I thought I heard applause. No, it was the banging of seats going up as no fewer than 400 people stormed out of the cinema and across the foyer in outrage. What had gone wrong? It was only twenty minutes into the film. Was it the fish scene in the hospital that was too much for them? No, it was the cockroaches bursting forth from Harry's chest. Ray emerged from the cinema ashen-faced and rushed away with Nonie to their hotel. Bob Lewis appeared, threw his hands up into the air as much as to say 'what can I do now' as the film's sales representative. I was left in the foyer alone, perplexed as to what to do. My companion, Gary MacDonald[3] and Susie Maizels our casting consultant, couldn't believe what had happened when I returned to the Carlton Hotel.

It was about 12.45am when the phone rang in our hotel room. I was still sitting on the end of the bed wondering what we were going to do and in fact what had we done? The voice was quietly spoken, a soft American accent. 'Hi! You guys have had a bit of a rough night. My name is David Thomson. I represent the New York Film Festival which is by invitation only. I am inviting *Bliss* officially to the New York Film Festival. You have a very fine film there.' I was speechless. I quickly gathered my wits and asked Mr Thomson would he telephone Ray at the Majestic next door 'before he jumps off the balcony'. I was convinced that if Nonie had not been with Ray, he would have jumped! 1am – Ray rings – 'Do you think this guy is for real?' I said I thought so, for David Thomson had a formidable reputation as one of the world's finest critics of film.

It was the next morning though that caused Ray and me to take fright! Walking along the Croisette, there coming towards us was the familiar, cheery face of Derek Malcolm, film critic for *The Guardian* and co-selector for the London Film Festival. Walking beside him was the gaunt, lanky figure of John Gillet, the film critic for London's *The Daily Telegraph*. 'Tony, Tony! *Bliss*, it's the best Australian film since *The Night The Prowler*.' Before I could shush him, he quickly continued. 'I'm inviting *Bliss* to the London Film Festival.' Gillet looked at him aghast. 'You're not inviting *that* film are you?'

Ray and I were 'dressed' as we had been invited to present our credentials to the director-general of the Festival International du Film,[4] Giles Jacob, that morning. Jacob, a tall, impressive man, impeccably dressed, welcomed us. We were joined by the Minister for Culture, Jack Lang. Jacob had been initially annoyed because we hadn't shortened the film for the Festival as asked for, but being the gentleman he is, didn't mention it. He was quick to observe also that we had had a rough night of it by the walkout. He said something about being in good company because 'you have the distinction of having had the second biggest walkout in the history of the Festival'. Ray and I looked at each other. I gingerly asked who had had the biggest walkout. 'Oh, it was *L'Avventura*,' Jacob said, 'There were only Antonioni

---

3   Not the actor.
4   Now the Cannes Film Festival.

and his producer left in the theatre.' Well, I suppose we were in good company but I didn't think of it as much of a comfort at the time.

It was still about nine hours to our gala black-tie presentation at the Palais de Festivals. Already the first news had broken in Australia. Sydney's *Daily Telegraph* screamed CANING AT CANNES–*BLISS BOMBS*. How were we going to cope with the night? There was no doubt the Australians present in Cannes were fearing the worst.

Bliss was presented to the world for the first time in the official competition of the 18th Festival International du Film on Saturday night, May 18, in the presence of the Australian Ambassador to France, His Excellency Mr Peter Curtin, and 2500 guests in the Grande Salle Lumière, Palais de Festivals, Cannes. Representatives from the Australian film industry included the delegation heads of the New South Wales Film Corporation, Mr Robert Lewis and Mrs Lewis, Mr Danny Collins, Ray and Nonie Lawrence, the chairman of the Australian Film Commission, Mr Phillip Adams, and their chief executive, Kim Williams.

The French tricolour and the Australian flag hung on either side of the proscenium. The lights went down, the curtains opened, *Bliss* began to unspool. Not ten minutes into the film, two people hurriedly left their stall seats and flew up the aisle. Ray Lawrence shot from his seat and chased after them, demanding to know why they were leaving. God, was this going to start yet another exodus? Ray came back to his seat straight away. The couple were Italian, couldn't understand English and didn't read French! Excused.

The international press warmly welcomed the film, except the French! Derek Malcolm in *The Guardian* declared 'powerfully mordant black comedy often very imaginatively handled indeed'. *The Financial Times* referred to 'its wacky vitality and visual wizardry'. David Stratton in *Variety* had reservations but commented it was 'bursting with ideas, originality, inventional daring'. *Time Magazine's*: 'Bliss has such a loopy visual imagination and such sympathy for its half-mad hero that, for a couple of hours, hell seems a nice place to visit'. *Paris Soir:* 'Lamentable in its pretentiousness, idiocy and coarseness'. Ray had T-shirts printed with the above quote and we wore them proudly.

At home the press were to have a field day. It was open slaughter. Under the heading MEDIA SLAUGHTERS GOOD CHANCES FOR BLISS in Arts & Entertainment (*The Sydney Morning Herald*, 10/6/85) Richard Glover bravely and forthrightly came to our and the film's defence. Richard had watched the filming of the Vision Splendid scenes and had written positively about the film's making some months before. Even he was left incredulous by the media's attack on the film and in three cases from writers who hadn't even seen the film. Explaining clearly to his readers what had happened at Cannes, 'You can see it as a story of how Australians cut down tall poppies; as a story about the Australian media and how it works; or as an example of how a myth is being created among us, on little evidence, that the Australian film industry is artistically dead,' said Glover. 'They were besieged with offers from the world's key film festivals keen to have the adventurous, albeit flawed film on their programme – New York, London and Toronto all invited *Bliss*. Late last week the two arrived home to find Lawrence's mother in tears, the cast suicidal and their hopes of an Australian distributor for the film rapidly evaporating. While they were away, *Bliss* had been slaughtered by the Australian press. The chief executioners had not been to Cannes and had not seen the film.'

Richard Glover then drew his readers' attention to Dorian Wild's CANING AT CANNES piece in the *Sydney Telegraph* which was not only damaging but totally untrue. '… Bliss is bombing so badly at this year's Cannes film orgy the tremors are being felt on the Richter scale.'

What Wild and others failed to mention was yes, 400 stormed out of the first screening, but 600 stayed and applauded loudly. Ray Lawrence to Glover, illustrating *Bliss* was not a turkey – 'We have not made a film about a singing dog.[5] Believe me, it is a respectable film. It has been killed by three gossip columnists who have never seen it and I'm stunned by their power. … There were three films in the Festival with a strong Australian influence – *Bliss, Coca Cola Kid* and *Witness*.[6] That's three films out of twenty[7] from a tiny industry with fourteen million people. We should be celebrating that.'

I was even angrier: 'I think a reviewer has every right to rip into a film, but I don't think it is right to be torn to shreds by the general press before we've even had an Australian screening.'

Despite the invitation to three of the world's top festivals, the New South Wales Film Corporation had become extremely nervous, in particular its chief, Paul Riomfalvy, and their marketing director, Danny Collins. GU and Hoyts turned the film down as being uncommercial and film rental estimates they claimed would not cover the costs of prints and advertising. Independent distributor and exhibitor Ronin Films estimated film rental to be $100,000 but this did not convince the NSW FC who were determined not to have the film labelled 'arthouse'. GU and Hoyts offered straight exhibition deals if we were prepared to distribute it ourselves. Hoyts' terms were quite unsatisfactory, yet favoured by the

---

5   A reference to *Molly – The Singing Dog* directed by Ned Lander, produced by Hilary Linstead.
6   *Witness*, the opening night film of the Festival.
7   The number of features in competition was nineteen plus the opening night film.

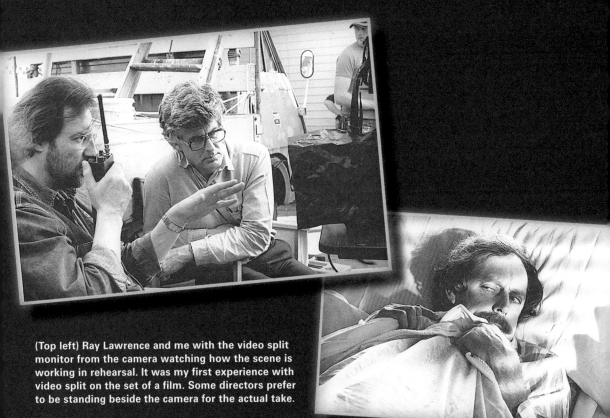

(Top left) Ray Lawrence and me with the video split monitor from the camera watching how the scene is working in rehearsal. It was my first experience with video split on the set of a film. Some directors prefer to be standing beside the camera for the actual take.

(Top right) Harry Joy was superbly played by Barry Otto.

(Bottom left) Harry Joy's spectacular ascent to heaven and descent to hell was shot with the help of a Men From Marrs crane. The camera is suspended from the box in which is operator David Williamson. The box with operator and camera was raised and lowered by the crane with David using a remote control to operate the camera.

(Bottom right) Camera operator David Williamson rigged up for the burnt-out bush scene. David was also operator on Ray's *Lantana* and director of photography on Ray's *Jindabyne*.

Film Corporation because Hoyts weren't 'arthouse'. Ray and I favoured GU and thankfully we won. GU offered us State 2, a retired newsreel theatrette which GU's John Politzer had transformed into an arthouse cinema with *Heat and Dust*, with spectacular success. The cinema had just 173 seats and I figured if we could play six sessions a day, instead of the obligatory four, with feature only, we might have a chance of breaking even. In Melbourne we were offered Russell 4 that seated 250. In the meantime Ray and Wayne Le Clos had re-edited the film to 106 minutes, which had been Ray's intention in the first place before we were suddenly selected to be in competition in Cannes. The running time certainly enhanced our chance of six sessions a day. We were scheduled to open on September 19, 1985. Our first preview was held for the critics at State 2. I stood in fear and dread at the top of the cinema's stairs in Market Street waiting for the audience to ascend the stairs at the conclusion of the screening. The first person I recognised was Paul Byrnes, the respected critic of *The Sydney Morning Herald*. His gleaming eyes stared at me, I cannot remember if he said anything, but he had that 'look' of having seen quite some film. Was the tide beginning to turn?

The nominees for the annual Australian Film Institute Awards (AFIs) were announced in the first week of September. Nominated for best picture was *Bliss* with thirteen nominations. Michael Jenkins' *Rebel* featured prominently in the technical and craft categories. Journalist Walter Sullivan thought the selection was a 'dreary lot' with the exception of *Bliss* which he drolly observed 'has not seen the end of controversy yet, but is a film to see'.

Just when we thought things were improving, the Commonwealth Film Censor slapped an R Certificate on the picture, which was absolutely absurd. We appealed immediately. The morning Ray and I were to appear before the appeals board, to reach the censor's office we had to run the gauntlet of a queue of fifteen-year-olds that extended a quarter of a block, waiting to be admitted to the Ascot to see *Rambo*. The irony didn't escape us. The censors had completely misinterpreted the brother and sister scene of fellatio and the brother's sudden appearance in a Nazi uniform, which was his fantasy, and had objections to the sex scene in Milano's restaurant. A unanimous verdict of the appeals board reduced the severity of the classification to an M. This didn't stop *The Sydney Morning Herald's* editor taking the censors to task in the paper's editorial of Saturday, September 13. This was publicity one could not possibly buy. Under the headline THE CASE OF THE BLUNT, BLUE PENCIL the *Herald* said: 'The controversy over the new Australian film, *Bliss*, should be a lesson to our film censors. Sadly, though, their learning curve does not seem to be particularly steep. Two scenes from the film, one involving incest between a brother and a sister and the other a sex scene on a restaurant table, resulted in the film being given an R rating. The producer of *Bliss*, predictably enough, was incensed at the lack of 'sensitivity to a quality film'. He was supported by the Film Board of Review which unanimously rejected the R rating. The Board of Review, which consists of several former public servants, an academic, a journalist and a film expert, had no difficulty in distinguishing *Bliss* from the normal run of R-rated films.

What provoked the censors, then, to single out *Bliss*? The Film Censorship Board is often attacked for being too permissive, especially regarding scenes where sex is involved: the best it can do is exercise as much commonsense as possible. In the case of *Bliss*, something went badly wrong. Given the fact that only one film currently being shown in Sydney in major cinemas has an R rating, the decision was an extraordinary one. But it was no accident. The film was first rated by a small panel of censors and then checked by the full Censorship Board. Perhaps there is a clue in a similar judgement by the board several years ago relating to the art film, *Pixote*, which had incest as a central theme.

The then Attorney-General, Senator Gareth Evans, was so annoyed at the board's decision to stop the film being shown that he removed its power to approve or censor film festival films. The point that Senator Evans was trying to get home to the board was that the intrinsic merit of a film and the integrity of its makers were relevant considerations. This sensible approach reflects the High Court rule, formulated in 1968, that the standard to be applied to indecency had to take into account the circumstances in which the material was shown. It is a little worrying when an important Australian film, one that is trying to be more than a typical horse opera, is so blatantly misinterpreted by the film censors, not once but twice. If the censors can be so wrong about giving an R rating to *Bliss*, how reliable is their judgement about the hundreds of other films they have to censor?'

The acting chief censor, K.F. Barton, was outraged. 'In summary your editorial's beat up 'controversy' on the 'Bliss' classification is nothing more or less than that.' He must have left some *Herald* readers gasping though, for in his defence of his Board's actions he went on to describe the fellatio scene in minute detail.

The countdown to our opening on September 19 had begun. Saturday, September 14, Her Majesty's Theatre, Sydney and the AFI Awards. The early part of the evening was dominated by *Rebel* winning most of the craft awards, then came the big ones. Best Adapted Screenplay – Peter Carey and Ray Lawrence. Best Direction – Ray Lawrence. Best Picture – *Bliss*.

Monday morning the phone rang. It was John Rochester, then head of GU Theatres division. 'Congratulations on your AFIs. We are going to move you from State 2 to Pitt Centre 3 for two to three weeks, but you'll have to perform!'

Jenny Woods and the team at the NSW FC were ecstatic with the news. Paul Riomfalvy wasn't so sure but wished us well. John Politzer was very supportive of a suggestion from me that on Thursdays, Fridays and Saturdays we have two evening screenings, one at 7.30 and the other at 9.45. We agreed on no previews, we would just open. Pitt 3, 480 seats, where *Caddie* played for fifty-four weeks in 1976/77. Was this a good omen? I encountered the manager outside the cinema on the opening night. 'You are making a great mistake you know, 7.30 is too early for Sydney and 9.45 positively too late.' At 7.30 we turned away over forty people and at 9.45 turned away another thirty. This was repeated over the first, second and third weekends.

The morning had seen publication of Paul Byrnes' review in *The Sydney Morning Herald*. We couldn't believe our eyes as Ray and I took in the headline: 'BLISS – NEW TEAM DELIVERS LANDMARK AUSTRALIAN FILM. It is hard to imagine how this film could have been improved. Perhaps it is still a shade too long, and there are a couple of minor problems to do with the narrative structure, but in all other respects *Bliss* seems to be the movie that we have long been waiting for from the Australian film industry … *Bliss* is that rare thing in Australian cinema, a movie of ideas. It is largely about conservation and apathy and the question of collective and individual responsibility, but it's about a lot more besides – the institutionalised corruption of the modern family, the morality of capital, the transience and importance of love, the role of religion, in short, a large slice of life's rich tapestry. What is so nice is that the film explores these questions in such an accessible way. This is not a self-consciously "difficult" film. There is little of the deliberate obfuscation that makes so many 'serious' films into giant riddles to be deciphered. *Bliss* is a comedy of a very black nature and it's wonderfully funny.'

The weekend papers were uniformly supportive, but would people come? The tide was turning. The first week's figures for Pitt 3 were $40,000+. Distributors said it was a fluke. Week 2, $41,000+ which was unheard of. Normally any screen drops a certain percent in the second week. Ray and I had to depart for New York and the Film Festival, but we felt the film was 'safe' in John Politzer's care at GU. I was in the foyer of the Beverly Wilshire Hotel when I encountered Jonathan Chissick from Hoyts. 'Congratulations on your third week's figures,' he said. I hadn't seen them. 'What were they?' fearing the worst. '$43,000 at the Pitt,' beamed Jonathan. The figures indicated we were playing to capacity and turnaway business and our late-evening sessions on the weekend were a positive indicator to the future of late-evening sessions for the multiplexes on the horizon.

Each Monday I would confer with John Politzer, either in his office or on the phone, to decide on whether we needed to advertise that week or not. His advice was invaluable. Some weeks we would skip having a display advertisement but as soon as the next ad appeared the box office would move up again. Greater Union placed it in every capital city of the nation, then moved it through the circuit after the city seasons had finished. We played the Pitt in Sydney for three months then moved to our original home, State 2, for another three months. We had only nine prints (and still have only nine!) yet those nine prints were to gross over $1.3 million and a film rental of $372,000. The tide most certainly turned.

It is not often that an Australian film makes the *Variety* top fifty films at the box office but *Bliss* did, two weeks in a row. Thanks to the launch at the New York Film Festival, New World Pictures were convinced it had an audience in the States. Bill Shields, New World's president of sales and marketing, changed the advertising campaign which we did not think represented the film well at all, but despite this the critics warmed to it and our opening in New York for a 'foreign' film matched our figures at home. It took US$7,000 in its opening session at the prestigious Plaza Cinema and grossed a total of US$12,000 for the weekend. I have always found it interesting how other countries 'see' our films and with *Bliss* the American take on the picture was extremely reassuring. Kevin Thomas in the *Los Angeles Times*, under the headline '*Bliss* is offbeat but right on target', said: '... What *Bliss* does have is a sensational cast with the runaway dottiness of a vintage Ealing comedy. Although not without precedent, *Bliss* (rightly rated R) represents a bold departure from the genteel traditionalism of mainstream Australian movies. We'll never be able to think of Australia or its cinema in quite the same way again.'

It was to be two years before *Bliss* arrived at the Odeon Haymarket in London's West End. It received a standing ovation at the London Film Festival, an unnerving evening. In New York the audience bubbled and chuckled from the opening scene, causing Ray and me to miss out on the hospitality waiting for us as the film unspooled. So responsive was the audience, we just had to stay and take it all in. A month later, on the South Bank, not a murmur from the audience. Paul Riomfalvy, Ray, me, we were becoming more and more anxious at no audible or physical reaction to the film. Then the surprise of our lives. As the image faded from the screen and Harry Joy's last words were spoken, the audience stood to its feet and tumultuously applauded.

I suppose the following represents the crass side of being a producer, but after all that we had been through, my sentiments are aptly reflected by the late Matt White summing up the local scene for *The Hollywood Reporter*, October 15, 1985:

'*Bliss*, the controversial Aussie movie no local distributor wanted to touch, has become the nation's biggest box office grosser. Last week in only two theatres in Sydney and Melbourne the AUS$3.4 million feature took in AUS$60,000, beating the blockbuster *Rambo* which grossed AUS$37,000 in five cinemas. Even *Desperately Seeking Susan*, despite the Madonna craze here, took only AUS$39,000 in seven Sydney and Melbourne cinemas.'

To this day *Bliss* does not have a theatrical distributor in Australia but thanks to Roslyn Wilson (retired) and Al Thomson at Roadshow Entertainment, both versions of the film can be seen on DVD with our maverick director delivering the director's commentary.

My father had had declining health for some time and it was during the filming of *Bliss* that he was admitted to Gosford Hospital. I used to visit every weekend but I could tell he was in decline. Then the news came that he had gone into a coma and could I come up to the hospital. After returning to Australia I would visit him at his Bateau Bay home where he lived with his de facto, Laura. It took me a very long time before I could accept her, for she was nothing like my mother, who had been a woman full of life and quiet dignity at the same time. I would visit only occasionally, taking my projector with me to show him my latest trip on my favourite mode of transport, freighter ships. These were my halcyon days professionally but difficult years emotionally.

I arrived at the hospital to be confronted with my father in intensive care on a life support system. It was explained to me that he would not be coming out of the coma but it was the medical profession's duty to keep him alive. I sat beside the bed for an hour and reflected on the futility of the situation. My cousin, Tedi, daughter of Dad's sister Ruth, joined me. She explained the whole situation for she was a trained nursing sister. I asked to see the doctors and advised them that if it was their considered opinion there was no chance of him coming out of the coma, and not knowing what brain damage may have occurred, then I thought his life support system should be turned off. Kethel Timothy Buckley died peacefully on the very day we were filming Harry Joy's ascent to heaven.

The long voyage home from Britain on Chandris Lines' *Bretagne* had whetted my appetite for sea travel and my next voyage was on a freighter to the New Hebrides. I had finished editing Gregory Ropert's remarkable and intriguing short film *Willy Willy*. Gregory had been my assistant editor at Ajax Films and I became his mentor. We were very good friends, though at times I found him exasperating, to the point one day I remember physically throwing him out of the cutting room, much to looks of incredulity down the corridor from fellow editors Tim Wellburn, Nicholas Beauman and our old sage, Hughie McGuinness. 'Having a bit of a clean out, Tone?' came Hughie's droll enquiry. Gregory's film was an ambitious exercise involving moving a merry-go-round to the top of a small mountain in the Snowy Mountains. He had selected a promising young talent, Pamela Stephenson, to play the female lead, and cast Chips Rafferty in his last role on the big screen. None other than Peter James was the DOP. 35mm, widescreen, the film was a brave achievement but Gregory chose not to continue as a filmmaker, specialising in opening post-production services. I consider him to be in many ways like my long-time friend Des Freeman, two valuable talents lost to Australian film.

With the film delivered I booked on the thirty-passenger ship *Polynesie* and Peter James, who had friends travelling on her, delivered me to No. 21 Pyrmont. All we could see was a huge freighter at the dock, till we walked to the wharf's upper deck railing and looked down. There was this tiny vessel, not much bigger it seemed than a Manly ferry. It was on the *Polynesie* I discovered the difference between 'tourists' and 'travellers' and to start my addiction to this wonderful form of travel.

After my next assignment I wandered down to Bridge Street in Sydney's business district and home to the shipping companies. Wilhelmsen Line had the *Delos* sailing on Friday to New Guinea, a three-week round voyage to Rabaul, Madang and Lae. *Delos* was a handsome Swedish freighter, carrying just twelve passengers, many of whom got off in Lae where another contingent joined the vessel. On arriving there were a dozen other vessels waiting to berth at the only wharf in the port. The three weeks became five, so I went to Goroka and Mt Hagen, returning on the native bus, an eight-hour journey back to Lae with the trusty 16mm camera whirring away.

But the journey of journeys was yet to come. I had booked on the Blue Funnel Line's *Centaur* from Fremantle to Singapore and Penang some months before the due sailing. New Year's Eve on the Indian Pacific from Sydney's Central Station to Perth seemed not a bad idea at all. I was more than impressed with my first-class cabin from which I waved goodbye to make-up artist Peggy Carter and Grahame Jennings, who had come to see me off. The three and a half day journey across Australia is a must. Travelling across the Nullabor Plain I overheard an American in the club car say, 'Now I really know the meaning of the word "space".' Our last night on board was New Year's Eve and after dinner, returning to the club car I discovered all the first class passengers had retired for the night. A steward came along and invited me to join them with some tourist-class passengers at the front of the train. It turned out to be a brilliant suggestion. The train staff had decorated the tourist class club car and though few stayed up to celebrate, the stewards and I had a wonderful time.

The *Centaur* was a superb freighter/passenger vessel carrying 120 guests at the back of the ship and 5,000 sheep up front. By the time we got to Singapore one knew there were 5,000 sheep aboard! The smell was akin to a floating farm. Being a single traveller one is always invited to someone's table but on this splendid voyage I was allowed a seat at the captain's table, very much in keeping with the Buckley style, I thought.

PART TWO

25

... And Now For Something Completely Different – Television!

Be warned, for we are about to enter a completely different world altogether – the world of television, which bears absolutely no resemblance to the world of motion pictures whatsoever. It's a world where a dolly-bird pop singer will be the preferred star of a drama rather than an actress. A world where directors and producers are basically regarded and treated as a commodity, as opposed to a practising artisan where even Hollywood recognises their talents and abilities. I am not referring to the heads of drama or the programmers at the networks, with many of whom I have had great pleasure working. I refer to 'upstairs', the television executives, and in particular those executives who have become television producers in the independent production sector.

After leaving Forest Home Films and my various industry posts in 1982/83, I had time to reflect while *Bliss* was being adapted by Ray Lawrence and Peter Carey. I could sense the feature film industry beginning to languish in a trough once more. I had learned as a film editor, from the very beginning of my career, that one couldn't put oneself on a pedestal and say one was only going to edit a particular genre of film. More so as a producer. If one was to declare oneself as only a producer of feature films, then one would find oneself quickly falling from that pedestal. The format of the miniseries had attracted my attention with Henry Crawford's two early minis, *Against the Wind* (1978) and *A Town Like Alice* (1981), for which Henry won Australia's first Emmy. Igor Auzins' *Water Under the Bridge* was probably my favourite at the time, and Kennedy Miller's contemporary political drama, *The Dismissal* (1982) certainly impressed me.

How did one get a miniseries off the ground, I wondered, and was it any different to producing a feature film? I supposed one should first find a television network. I thought of Ruth Park's classic Australian novel, *The Harp in the South*.

Ruth was born in New Zealand and came to Sydney in 1942, originally to be a journalist, but she met and married D'Arcy Niland instead and set off touring Australia before settling down in the Sydney suburbs of Surry Hills and Petersham. Ruth was persuaded to enter *The Sydney Morning Herald's* first competition for a short story and a novel, the prize for the novel being £2,000 ($4,000). Though she was known for her children's stories on ABC Radio and felt she had no chance in a serious novel competition, Ruth decided to give it a go and set her novel in the area she knew best, the place where D'Arcy and she had lived, Surry Hills. At the time they were living in a small flat in the inner Sydney suburb of Petersham and had saved enough money to take the family to New Zealand for a holiday. It was here Ruth sat down and wrote *The Harp in the South*. The year – 1946. The winner of *The Sydney Morning Herald's* prestigious prize of £2,000, Ruth Park's *The Harp in the South* was announced on December 28 and all hell broke loose. The *Herald* published a synopsis of the novel, which caused a furore. Ruth Park tells the story best in her autobiography *Fishing in the Styx*:[1]

'Almost at once a hideous clamour burst out, not only in the literary world, but in Australia at large, and this on the basis of the synopsis only of *The Harp in the South*.

'Normally I would not enlarge on this extraordinary row, for after all it happened long ago and far away, and very nearly in another galaxy. But it is, in its way, a unique psychological study of the popular mores of the late 1940s and early 1950s of this century. Old Preposterous, hard-nosed journalist attuned to that peculiar thing, the reading public's common denominator, was right. There was trouble.

'The first nick of the knife at my throat came in a church, where D'Arcy and I attended Mass. It was a thanksgiving Mass for us. D'Arcy, as I have said, was extremely devout. We were stricken when the celebrant devoted his sermon to the *Herald*; its scandalous judgements; wicked books; immorality in print and to what it would lead; young women and their conscienceless slandering of that great race, the Irish. Nay, it was his sincere belief that I had taken the axe to the foundations of Ireland itself, island of saints and scholars.

'"Can you believe this?" hissed my husband.

'The priest was now well away on Our Lady and her chaste example to all. He implied strongly that in her lifetime she would never have stooped to writing a book of any kind, let alone that to be published in the *Herald*.

'"Ah, that a great newspaper should ..."

---

1   *Fishing in the Styx*, Viking Penguin Books 1993, pp. 147/148.

Production design/art direction has always fascinated me, probably since the time my parents were horrified I might become a window dresser. Here Murray Street, Pyrmont, has become Plymouth Street, Surry Hills, designed and dressed by Bernard Hides and Virginia Bieneman, and director of photography Paul Murphy did the rest.

'"It's not fair!" I muttered, "He hasn't even read it!"'

'"Bugger needs a good poke in his godly snoot."'

'Ten years later I would have risen and marched out down the centre aisle, but then I was so shocked, so humiliated I felt faint. My husband was all for going around to the vestry and pulling the priest's biretta down over his lugs, but I needed him to lean on on the homeward journey, for my knees intermittently gave way.

'"Why? Why?"'

'"Don't ask me. Gone mad with all that celibacy."'

Ruth Park was distressed and perplexed, *The Sydney Morning Herald* were also perplexed and absolutely delighted with the response. Publication of the novel occurred in 1948 and to this day *The Harp in the South* has never been out of print.

Donald Crombie and I had wanted to make the book into a feature film after *Caddie* and *The Irishman*. We screened the two films to Ruth Park in 1978 but she was not convinced and felt 'not quite ready'. In 1983 I reapproached her literary agent, Tim Curnow at Curtis Brown, with the idea of a miniseries. This caught her imagination but not so Channel Nine's (who had backed *Caddie*), to whom I took the idea of a mini, who thought it depressing and bleak. This initial reaction was much the same as the one we had to *Caddie* in 1974! Not so Matt Carroll at Network Ten at Ryde, where I had edited their opening night show *TV Spells Magic* for ex-pat director Robert Flemyng. Matt was prepared to find the initial funding for a script but left to be part of the establishment of Roadshow, Coote & Carroll. Thankfully Valerie Hardy became head of drama and champion for the series. However, there was nervousness at the top of Ten. Tom Warne, their programmer, was right behind the series with Valerie, but the network's interstate representatives wanted a meeting. I received a phone call from Valerie asking if I could meet with management and those from the other capitals. Brisbane and Adelaide were the most concerned. I needed to 'pitch' and convince them the series would work. 'I would be delighted. When?' I enquired. 'Could you be here in about half an hour?' asked Valerie. 'Half an hour!' Fortunately, Lane Cove (where I lived) was only a few minutes drive along Epping Road from the studios.

I was ushered into the anteroom with its faux fireplace, adjacent to the boardroom, to be confronted by a platoon of besuited men. I was relieved I had worn a tie. Surrounded by this group, who were all standing, only Tom Warne was in shirtsleeves and he beckoned me to sit down in the only space left in the room. Valerie was the only woman present and revealed later that she was mortified when I was asked to sit. Brisbane and Adelaide immediately wanted to know why the series would work when it was 'so depressing, sorrowful and awful'. I asked them if they had seen *Caddie*. One's wife had. She had liked it. I enquired had she found it depressing. 'Well no,' he said. 'Well,' I said, 'nor will *The Harp in the South* be.' I added, somewhat grandly, 'There will be one tear at one commercial break and a chuckle at the next.' It was a daunting experience and the platoon of standing executives were expressionless to say the least. Later that afternoon Valerie rang with the good news. Evidently I had completely won over the two from Brisbane and Adelaide and it was a unanimous decision to go ahead. They then all congratulated themselves, they were going to make a 'great women's series'.

Who was to direct?

It was in the second half of 1979 that Storry Walton, director of the Australian Film and Television School (later the Australian Film, Television and Radio School), rang to enquire if I was available to take over an important course in what was then called the Open Program, a marvellous initiative of short-term courses for the industry and for those wanting to join the film and television world. The course was Gil Brealey's visionary 'Stage to Screen' course, devised by this master of our craft to give directors in theatre the opportunity to direct filmed drama. 'When?' I enquired of Storry. 'Tomorrow, Tony?'

As mentioned in Part One, Gil Brealey is a visionary practitioner, but he is equally frustrating because he often doesn't finish what he starts. Once he establishes whatever it is, Gil then quietly moves on to the next challenge. I think this time it may have been the setting up of the Tasmanian Film Corporation after his success in founding the South Australian Film Corporation and his revitalisation of Film Australia. I think he is one of the neglected heroes of Australian film.

I thankfully was given the enormous support of a very young and talented production manager/line producer, Julia Overton, with whose help I steered first nine, later seven, well-known Australian stage directors through an ambitious course of writing and directing for film. Regretfully nothing like it has been attempted since. They were all extremely talented. However, it wasn't Richard Wherrett's *Simone de Beauvoir* or Rex Cramphorn's striking *By Night* that caught my eye at their first cut screenings on March 17, 1980, but *Dancing*, a short, visually enticing film about Greek dancing directed by George Whaley. George is the true thespian – actor, writer, director. Would George be the right choice for *The Harp in the South*?

Valerie Hardy reacted positively to the suggestion, as did Tom Warne. George's theatre work was well known to both. Ruth Park also reacted with enthusiasm and thought the step to take a director from the stage to film was a bold initiative.

(Top left) Attention to detail included a Holden yellow cab of the period.

(Top right) Darcy family of Plymouth Street, Surry Hills – Anne Phelan (Mum Darcy), Martyn Sanderson (Dad Darcy), Kaarin Fairfax (Dolour), Gwen Plumb (Grandma Kilker), Anna Hruby (Roie).

(Left) George Whaley with Shane Connor and Martyn Sanderson.

(Bottom) I am the bane of all publicists for they can never find stills of me on set, which somewhat pleases me. Here is one rare exception on *The Harp in the South*.

However, Ruth was adamant that her book be adapted by Eleanor Witcombe, whom I had briefly encountered some years before with Bobbie Helpmann when both were attempting to get *Daisy Bates* off the ground. From the outset Eleanor and George Whaley working together was not a good idea. Eleanor's adaptation was faithful enough to the book, but it would have been twenty, not six, hours of television if she had continued. Something had to give and I consulted Ruth. I was the one who had to break the news to Eleanor, never a pleasant thing to do to any writer but especially one as talented as Eleanor Witcombe. I have never been sure but I felt that she was somewhat relieved not to be continuing with the task. I felt a load had probably been lifted and she could get back to her beloved *Daisy Bates*.

The writing recommenced with George at the helm, ably supported by Ruth's suggestions and observations. It was to be a long road for both of them, but finally all six hours were ready to submit to Ten. It was 'greenlit' immediately. Robert Mercieca's (pronounced Mer-checka) company, Qantum, which had been one of the principal raisers of investment for *Bliss*, had relocated to Melbourne to become involved in 10BA tax investment-raising for feature films, miniseries and documentaries. The prospectus was filled by June 30 and plans for production were already underway.

The art and prerogative of the director is the casting of the actors, and the prerogative of the producer is the casting of the crew, though I have to admit I like to know who our leads are, to ensure the 'chemistry of casting'. George had his heart set on an actor to play the lead male role of Hughie Darcy, the father in *The Harp in the South*. The actor was definitely a good actor but I strongly felt he did not have charisma, or what I call 'celluloid magic', a phrase I continually use, much to the annoyance of most directors. In screen-testing for the female leads, George engaged this actor till one day I said no. Susie Maizels, our casting director, suggested we look in New Zealand and there we found Martyn Sanderson. The 'chemistry of casting' clicked into place with Anne Phelan as Mama Darcy. Susie had also come up with the idea of Gwen Plumb for the role of Grandma Kilker. Her tests were marvellous. Gwen came from the great days of radio, where she had been a star. Before this she was well known on the stage and in fact was the star of the venerable Tivoli circuit's last revue, *One Dam' Thing After Another* in March 1966. She appeared in her first movie in 1960, Fred Zinnemann's *The Sundowners*, and though radio was her forte, she moved into television with ease as the host of *Woman's World* in 1958, which aired till 1963. Her ribald and risqué comments often got her into trouble with the censors. I was interviewed by Gwen on radio 2GB after my return from London working on Nureyev's *Don Quixote*.

There were a couple of asides from Gwen that brought frowns from her producer through the glass panel of the control room. The listeners were lapping it up.

George Whaley and Susie Maizel's casting for *The Harp in the South* was classic casting from our leads to the one-liner parts. Anne Phelan and Martyn Sanderson as Ma and Hughie Darcy, Anna Hruby as the elder daughter Roie, Kaarin Fairfax as the young Dolour, and of course Gwen as Grandma. The ensemble was strengthened by Shane Connor, Syd Conabere and the wonderful veteran Lois Ramsay. We had the good fortune too of being able to bring the principal crew from *Bliss* to the production, my long-time and trusted line producer Carol Hughes, director of photography Paul Murphy, and camera operator David Williamson, along with film editor Wayne Le Clos and composer Peter Best. Production designer Bernard Hides joined our team with art director Virginia Bieneman. Thanks to the cooperation of the Colonial Sugar Refinery (CSR) and the City Council, Bernard and Virginia transformed a mainly disused and derelict Mount Street in Pyrmont, Sydney, to Plymouth Street, Surry Hills.

It was a very happy shoot with a very satisfying result. Ruth's classic work had been brought to the screen with integrity, warmth and humour and, above all, heart. Would the 'suits' find it depressing?

Valerie Hardy and Tom Warne were delighted with the first cut presentation of the six hours. The network had secured sponsorship from Johnson & Johnson and General Motors Holden, and CBS-Fox/Hoyts had secured the video rights, only the fifth miniseries to have done so, for release through the ever-growing video libraries. Ten's Sydney and Melbourne operations were completely independent of each other pertaining to publicity. Each knew their own city better, it was obviously felt. Whereas Sydney held its media launch in the intimacy of an inner-city restaurant, Melbourne went all out with the full three-course luncheon at a five-star hotel, screening the first two hours before lunch and the final two hours after lunch. I would not have expected anyone to have lasted the distance, particularly the media scribes, but last they did, with overwhelming approval. Then Ten dropped a bombshell. We were being programmed in prime time on Monday and Tuesday nights, but skipping Wednesday night for the finals football coverage, and *Harp* returning Thursday night for the final two hours. I thought this was courting a ratings disaster. On the contrary, Tom Warne's programming strategies were exemplary. Monday in Sydney we rated a top of twenty-six, Tuesday a twenty-seven and Thursday a twenty-eight. The football night had seen us increase our ratings in both cities. In Melbourne it was even more surprising. Here was a Sydney story rating even higher in the southern capital with twenty-nine and thirty, peaking at thirty-one. The press coverage in all capital cities had been saturation. For reasons not known or analysed, *Harp*, the making of and its transmission, had caught the attention of the press. Double-pages of photo spreads and column inches of copy and reviews. Here is a sample:

Popular TV columnist Peter Luck in his '5th Column' in *The Sydney Morning Herald*'s Pink Guide: 'Harp has had so many favourable comments, I can't add much. It is melodrama, of course, but so is half the world's literature, three quarters of the world's television and all of Joan Collins's wardrobe. The miniseries is beautifully made – "Aren't they all?" says my wife – but isn't it marvellous that we can be so blasé about the technical standards of Australian products?'

The dour raconteur and sometimes curmudgeon of the media, Phillip Adams, however, had a wonderfully astute and perceptive summing up of the series. He regarded it as 'a quite significant event'. In *The Australian*, under the heading 'Hosanna to the fine players of Harp,' Phillip wrote: 'For yonks Australia has been dominated by the myth of mateship. By and large, the Australian woman cops the rough end of the pineapple in both our popular culture and our high art. All of which makes the miniseries *The Harp in the South* a quite significant event. Just in time for Mothers Day, this is a celebration of the working-class female, as mother, daughter, sister, lover, while it paints a devastating picture of the Australian husband as a weak, beer-sodden apology for a human being. Yet while Ruth Park's novel (and to a lesser extent Eleanor Witcombe's adaptation) show the miserable, mean-spirited side of mateship, it is done with neither cruelty nor bitterness. Both the book and its television counterpart tell their stories with love, humour and compassion. And at the end you wish there were five hours more … I'm faintly ashamed to admit that I haven't enjoyed anything as much in years.'

Needless to say many critics carped about 'yet another period piece', however Jane Heath in an interview she conducted with me for *The Australian* quoted me correctly when I said, 'In actual fact in the last fifteen years there's been more contemporary Australian films made than period … it just so happens that the period films have been successful. And I feel the reason for that is the story. If the story doesn't stand up it doesn't matter when the film is set, nobody will go and see it.' Thirty years later I still stand by those words. Period miniseries have rarely, if ever, failed. Whether it be then or now. For example, two I produced for Screentime, *The Potato Factory* (1999) and *Jessica* (2003), rated their socks off – because they were based on good stories.

With the ratings success behind us, Ten were wanting to commission the sequel to *Harp*, *Poor Man's Orange*. Unbeknown to me, our executive producer Robert Mercieca had received an offer from Channel Nine for the sequel and had begun negotiations with that network. I thought this was all rather odd. Why change networks, particularly in light of the fact that Ten had been a champion for the first series? It would have been very unwise to have turned our backs on those who had been so supportive, and the major risk-takers in the first place. Ten generously offered a higher licence fee for the second series which was agreed to by Mercieca, who was quick to get the prospectus into the marketplace before the end of the financial year.

The adaptation this time was done by George Whaley on his own, though Ruth Park was given the drafts of the four episodes, with which she was greatly pleased.

Our *Harp* team was reassembled and *Poor Man's Orange* began shooting less than a year after the completion of *Harp*. The only setback we suffered was the loss of Mount Street in Pyrmont to the developers and as a result we had to recreate part of our street and the backyards of Plymouth Street in the studio, a big ask for our director of photography Paul Murphy, who achieved amazing results and the right 'feel' for daylight exteriors which in fact were interiors.

The second series was as successful as the first with our audience, the ratings showing they had all come back for more. Of the two series, I think *Poor Man's Orange* is the better. George Whaley's scripts were tauter and tighter, and his direction a little more fluid. To tackle ten hours of superior filmed drama after a ten-minute short was an extraordinary achievement.

Both Donald Crombie and George Whaley have many similarities in their approach to their craft and in particular their skill or 'knack' with their actors, winning their confidence and obtaining a quality of performance that set the benchmark for film and television drama.

26

The Tree Of Humankind – Man On A Limb!

I suppose there is a good side and a bad side to everything we encounter. Certainly in my career there has been a lot more of the good than the bad. However, even after the appalling experience of the skulduggery associated with the abandonment of Film Australia's *The Unknown Industrial Prisoner* by the Australian Film Commission, I was still not prepared for the bad side of 10BA[1] which we were to experience with our ground-breaking documentary series *Man on the Rim – the Peopling of the Pacific*, to be revealed in this chapter, probably to our series' investors for the first time.

Firstly, the good side, the series itself.

The Tree of Humankind was conceived by Dr Alan Thorne, originally as a five-part series, about the development of society from an anthropological viewpoint. Alan was already Australia's best-known anthropologist and archaeologist who had uncovered the earliest Australian human remains at Lake Mungo. Alan had taken his idea for the series to Film Australia's producer-in-chief, John Mabey, in 1982. Mabey recognised a unique opportunity to involve international partners and took Alan with him on a visit to Paris to meet and 'pitch' the project to the principals of the French national film and television production company, SPF. On their return to the Lindfield headquarters of Film Australia, Mabey contacted me, inviting me to be the producer for the series. Alan and I got on well from the outset and I liked his entire concept for the series. I also felt he would have

---

1 10BA was a division of the taxation act that allowed investors in provisionally certified 'Australian' productions to claim 150% tax exemption on their investment, later reducing to 133% then 120% and finally 100%, which virtually made the scheme impotent.

considerable 'on camera' appeal and that we needed a good director who would relate to the subject matter and how best to bring it to the screen. Alan suggested Robert Raymond. At the time I hadn't met Bob, but his reputation was second to none. Alan had encountered Bob at Kow Swamp where Bob was filming Alan's excavation of the burial ground dating back to the late Pleistocene.

Alan: 'What I liked about Bob was that he had a good relationship with Vincent Serventy, one of the best naturalists this country has produced, and his first morning at Kow Swamp I asked him what he wanted to film and he said, "You just go about your work and we will see what it is we want to film." I was used to quick visits by cameramen from the ABC who just pressed the button and filmed everything so that it could be sorted out later. Bob did not film that first day and the next day we talked and he shot exactly what he said he needed. No wastage at all.'

Alan organised a dinner at my flat in Lane Cove for the three of us to get together. The meal was helped along by copious quantities of good red wine, though I was somewhat horrified to hear later that Bob was a renowned chef! That night set the seal on what was to be a most enjoyable and rewarding association. Bob had suggested the series be a little more expansive and centred on the Pacific Rim, the countries bordering the Pacific Ocean and those in the Ocean. We opted for the title *Half a World Away*, hence the decision to call the production company Demimonde, because we were dealing with half the circumference of the globe and, as Alan remembers, 'it had a cheeky other meaning that seemed appropriate'. Alan and Bob immediately set out to construct the content for the series and ten days later had a thirteen-hour outline. This was subsequently reduced to eleven hours, owing to permits and permissions not being granted by two countries.

Alan had signed a letter of agreement with Film Australia committing him to the project for two years. To devote himself full time to the research and development of the series he took leave from his post as a fellow in prehistory at the Australian National University (ANU). I was in the early stages of develop-ment of Ruth Park's *The Harp in the South* when I sensed trouble brewing at Film Australia. The organisation was still under the control of the Australian Film Commission. Then we learned Mabey had resigned as producer-in-chief. Alan and I were summoned to meet CEO Kim Williams and the secretary of the Commission, Brian Gittings. Alan and I thought our meeting with Kim and Brian was very positive and we were asked to prepare a report and submission to the AFC's next board meeting. However, we were to learn from the ANU that the series had already been abandoned. Alan received a phone call from a staffer at the ANU saying the university had received a letter marked 'strictly confidential' from the AFC asking whether Alan could be reinstated in his position as a fellow in prehistory. I sought confirmation from Williams who wrote confirming the decision. Kim Williams got one of my better letters, with a bill for $5,000 for all our work to date. It was paid with no comment whatsoever.

Where to now?

In the development process, *Half a World Away* became *Man on the Rim – the Peopling of the Pacific*. Alan and Bob had prepared a superb synopsis of each of the planned episodes and I took the presentation to the head of television at the ABC, Richard Thomas. Richard liked the whole concept and was to become a champion for the series. He suggested the now legendary Jonathan Holmes be our executive producer. The pre-sale we obtained was the highest ever paid for a documentary series, which brought a barrage of complaints to Thomas and the ABC from the independent documentary sector, of which we were part! Thomas, much to his and the ABC's credit, didn't budge. What our complainants hadn't realised was that I had raised the benchmark pre-sale for all documentaries to what became the new standard fee of $65,000 per hour.

In the meantime Robert Mercieca had secured an international sales agent, Joe McCann in London of McCann International Distributors, later to become known as Vision Ventures. Alas, as it was to turn out, there was very little vision and not very much venture. In the States, Cal Thomas was appointed to represent the series in North America. Qantum Securities issued a prospectus that was filled by over 300 private investors by the end of the Australian financial year, June 1986. Robert Mercieca arrived in Sydney on July 28, the day after my birthday, for a series of meetings with the team related to planning the series and its delivery dates to comply with the regulations pertaining to 10BA investment in filmed subjects. It was at a celebratory luncheon on July 29 at the Camperdown Travelodge, that mention was made of Alan and Bob's planned book of the series. Bob stressed that it had previously been made quite clear that the series only was the copyright of the investors, and that copyright in the book was Bob and Alan's, which was to be written after the delivery of the series.

But for the moment let me stay focused on the 'good' side of the story – the planning and filming of this pioneering, ambitious venture. As Robert Raymond recalled later, 'It is amazing, in television, to find something that hasn't been done before … but the history of half the planet, which is two-thirds of the world's population, the eastern hemisphere, the Pacific, basically has been totally ignored.'

Alan and I were intrigued with Bob's work methodology, of planning and researching before turning over a foot of film in the camera. Working as a team, Alan and Bob prepared the script outlines for the series. Alan prepared the content and ideas for each episode and then Bob worked them into a shooting script, passing them back to Alan for correction and refinement. The series was to be dependent upon rare archival historical and ethnographic footage and to this end we engaged a British producer/researcher, Sue Haycock, to start ferreting out rare film sources. After only a few weeks on the job Sue came up with an extraordinary list of film material hidden away in archives in such places as the north of Scotland and small country centres in Germany.

To arrange filming sites and to view the rare film, Alan and Bob left on an exhaustive tour of archives, museums and institutions in Honolulu, Canada, the US, London, Europe, Tokyo and South America.

Meanwhile, back at the home base our Australian researcher, Venetia McMahon, had been working on making valuable embassy contacts and other arrangements for Bob and Alan's meetings in the United States and Europe. Over fifty countries either border the Pacific Rim or are to be found in the Pacific Ocean. Over forty-three countries had already been approached to try and facilitate the series at this early stage, and to minimise red tape wherever possible.

Sometimes months would go by before we would hear anything from those contacted or written to. One country was Palau in the Pacific Ocean. The phone was already ringing as I opened the door of our production office one morning at eight. On answering I heard a quietly spoken voice apologising for not having replied to a letter I had sent some four months before. They had only received it that morning as the letter had travelled via Los Angeles, sea mail! Then the gentleman enquired, 'You wouldn't happen to have a fax machine?' It so happened we had just acquired this new wonder of the twentieth century, which Palau had installed as soon as it had become available. I imagine that if the internet had been invented we could have shaved a year off our planning schedule.

Bob had worked for many years with editor and production manager John Oakley and suggested to me he be appointed as co-director. This was an excellent move and I'm sure John didn't expect the enormous task ahead of him, not only as co-director but chief of scheduling and production management too! John started with us at the beginning of January '87 and within a few days was en route to South America with Bob and Alan for the next phase of planning and research.

The following is a little indulgence for the armchair traveller I'm sure is in all of us. I quote from Bob's diary notes back to me in the production office, which made me want to pack my bags too at the time: 'The 17th saw us in Lima, Peru, where we arrived at midnight. Next day we inspected the main museum of archaeology and anthropology, and also a separate museum featuring clay figures, depicting people in all kinds of everyday activities, which enables us to bring the past to life in ways that are impossible with just ruined buildings and temples.

'Next day John Oakley asked the head concierge at the Sheraton to find us a good car and a driver for our lengthy trip through southern Mexico. After negotiating all the details, including price, John asked who the driver was to be. "Me!" said the concierge, named Gilberto. It must have been an offer he couldn't refuse. Set off with Gilberto in white pants and shoes to the Gulf of Mexico. Stayed first night at Tuxtla. We then drove out to Tres Capotes, one of the best Olmec sites (the Olmecs were the founders of the Middle American civilisations, flourished from 1200 BC to 300 AD, and are best known for the huge heads they carved from very hard rock).

'We then drove to Palenque, which research suggested was the most spectacular Mayan ruin – not in area or numbers of buildings, but in its setting. Where all other accessible Mayan sites are on the flat lowland plain of Yucatan, and therefore difficult to shoot, Palenque is set part way up the edge of the escarpment, looking out across the plain, and backed by a stunning wall of dense rainforest. Its temples and palaces are few but striking, and make a superb set for our piece on the Mayans.

'We then drove through the mountains of the Chiapas region (where the descendants of the Mayans still live, following their traditional ways) to San Cristobal de las Casas. We needed to find a traditional Mayan village, where the people still weave Mayan patterns and cultivate their corn and grind it with flat stones, etc. We picked the most remote village, at the end of what looked on the map like a very bad, dead-end road. Triple jackpot!!! Wonderful women weavers, only too happy to be filmed, men in traditional costume (most of them, including the president, flaked out in the street after a three day cactus-cocktail party) corn everywhere, grinding stones, strangely dressed street musicians playing bizarre instruments, etc. In short, the works.

'We then drove to the airport through spectacular mountain scenery and flew to Mexico City where Gilberto set off on the 1200km drive back. On the 25th we drove out of Mexico City to the 'floating gardens' – the surviving section of the extraordinary system of canals and gardens which surround the Aztec capital of Tenochtitlan, and which so astonished Cortez when he came over the mountains and saw this "Venice of the New World". Took a boat trip along the canals, past the gardens, which still provide most of Mexico City's vegetables. Opportunity for a most evocative sequence.

All in all, a highly successful survey, as the result of which TWO COMPLETE EPISODES can be regarded as all wrapped up.'

Whet the appetite to travel? Bob makes it all seem so effortless, but there was a monumental task ahead. Only two countries proved to be difficult – Malaysia

(Top) Our intrepid *Man on the Rim* team on location. Writer/director Robert Raymond, writer/presenter Alan Thorne, camera assistant Andrew Birbara, DOP Pieter De Vries, stoic production manager John Oakley and sound recordist Grant Roberts.

(Left) Meditating for a quiet moment whilst the crew were setting up, Bob Raymond had devised a meticulous shooting schedule where there was never a day or moment wasted.

(Bottom) Alan Thorne, palaeontologist, archaeologist and presenter, was able to expand and develop his ideas on the peopling of the Pacific in an entertaining way that pleased the viewers. Many of his speculations have since become fact.

and Indonesia – and it was quite clear early in the piece that permissions to film would be most unlikely.

We did, however, have an unexpected windfall when our team obtained accommodation on the *M.V. Illiria*, visiting some remote islands of the Indonesian archipelago. The journey had been arranged by the American Museum of Natural History and places were found for Bob, Alan and our second unit cameraman, Mike Dillon. This preliminary filming enabled us to visit some remarkably remote sites and peoples not normally encountered on regular air routes or scheduled shipping services. Our team disembarked at Port Moresby where Bob and Alan stopped over to plan our filming requirements with the Papua New Guinea authorities.

A similar incident actually occurred during production. Crucial to one of our episodes was filming in Siberia. We had waited eighteen months to hear from the Soviet authorities, but as with all good bureaucracies, letters became mislaid and overlooked and embassy staff in Canberra would return home for leave, and as time wore on our requests faded into the top drawer. I had been to Antarctica with Lindblad Expeditions in the summer of '83 and was now firmly on their mailing list. When we were about to give up and try and find another country in the same region in which to film, a large envelope was received through the mail from America. Out dropped a glossy brochure announcing Lindblad Travel's *Siberia*! Not only were Lindblad announcing their first-ever journey to Siberia but they were going to all the archaeological sites Bob and Alan wanted to go. So Alan, co-director John Oakley, cameraman Michael Dillon and sound recordist Grant Roberts boarded the *MV Demjan Bedny* on the Lena River heading for Lensk, Derin Yourjakh and Shkalik Islands on which are the excavated sites of humankind's earliest settlements.

I must stop here for I am getting ahead of myself. After just over a year of pretty much continuous travelling, research and scripting, Alan and Bob had eleven episodes prepared for filming. The ABC had readily agreed to the reduction from thirteen to eleven hours owing to permissions not being given for filming in certain countries. On returning from this mammoth task Bob Raymond cheekily commented 'all we have to do now is go out and do it!'

The eleven episodes[2] commenced filming with episode one, *The First Footsteps* on Melville Island, May 1987. Heading the team was renowned documentary cinematographer Pieter De Vries. Winner of several Australian Cinematographers

---

2   *Man on the Rim* Ep. 1 'The First Footsteps', Ep. 2 'Hunters and Gatherers', Ep. 3 'Into the Deep Freeze', Ep. 4 'Flaming Arrows', Ep. 5 'Changing the Menu', Ep. 6 'The Cutting Edge', Ep. 7 'The Powerhouse', Ep. 8 'Pure and Simple', Ep. 9 'Roads Without Wheels', Ep. 10 'The Feathered Serpent', Ep. 11 'The Last Horizon'.

Society awards, Pieter had left many years of service with the ABC to join us in filming his first independently produced series. He was probably best known at the time for the superb photography of the ABC series *Sweat of the Sun, Tears of the Moon*, which won the Logie Award for Best Documentary of 1985. In pondering our thirty-two week shooting schedule in forty-nine countries he said it was impossible. What Pieter wasn't used to at the ABC was Bob's extraordinary strengths in organisation and research. The year's planning probably saved us thousands of feet of unused footage. Pieter was amazed and impressed that on arrival in each location, Alan and Bob knew what they were going to film and whom they were to interview, and artefacts researched months previously were ready on display at the various museums to film. Joining the team as sound recordist was Grant Roberts who, like Pieter, had a considerable number of years in the documentary field, most recently with *Beyond 2000* and *Extra Dimensions*. Grant had worked with Alan Thorne previously on Alan's successful documentary *Entombed Warriors*. We had two Andrews joining the team – Andrew Birbara, assistant cameraman, and Andrew Cunningham, assistant editor. Andrew Cunningham had the onerous task of collating, assembling and filing all the footage being filmed for the series, and the archival film coming in from countries all over the world. Last but not least was Venetia McMahon, our researcher, who had been with us for some months researching stills material and historical footage, and liaising with the various embassies and libraries.

I won't detail all the episodes, you may be relieved to read, but I do wish to mention my two favourites – episode seven, *The Powerhouse*, and the following episode, *Pure and Simple*. *The Powerhouse*, on China, is remarkable for its content. We look at the incredible dynamism of the Chinese and their extraordinary record of innovation and invention. One of China's most famous inventions is also one of the oldest. We follow the entire process of silk-making from cocoon to cloth in, I think, one of the most detailed and fascinating sequences I have ever seen. Then the episode continues, to reveal the secrets of the Grand Canal, the amazing achievements of Li Bing's Dujiangyan water control project built 2,000 years ago and still operating today; the pioneering in China of iron and bronze casting; the development of the horizontal bellows, never used in the west; the invention of printing. Without question the highlight is the sequence on Chinese bell design. All over China there are bells of all sizes, in iron, bronze and brass, very like those in other countries. But in 1978 archaeologists in Hubei Province unearthed a set of bronze bells like no others anywhere else in the world. They were found in the tomb of Emperor Zenghou Yi, who died two and a half thousand years ago. What makes them different is that each bell can play two distinct notes, separated by a major or minor third – equal to about four or five notes on a piano. Staff of the museum in Wuhan play the bells, bringing to a climax this extraordinary episode.

If one finds *The Powerhouse* absorbing but a little exhausting, then *Pure and Simple* absorbs and relaxes. Here is an episode on the arts and crafts of the people of Japan – an illuminating look at the skills and patience of the artisans of this Pacific country. We study in beautiful detail the ritual of the Japanese tea-making ceremony; the development and crafting of bamboo; Japanese calligraphy; the craft of brush making; the exquisite process of fan making, a wholly Japanese invention; the hair comb; the Tatami mat; and last, the most revered of all Japanese bamboo products, the Shakuhachi flute.

Thursday, June 1, 1989, *The First Footsteps*, the first episode of *Man on the Rim*, premiered at 8.30pm on the ABC. The advance publicity and reviews were universally praiseworthy but it was Phillip Adams on the Saturday after, in the *Weekend Australian*, who made me laugh and also feel very proud for Bob and Alan, and an unsung hero of the piece too. Under the heading A HUGE OCEAN OF HISTORY, Phillip wrote of Thorne: 'It was Dr Alan Thorne, one of Australia's best known anthropologists and archaeologists, whose investigations at Lake Mungo revealed Australia's earliest human remains dating back 30,000 years.' And, of Bob: 'Then, by digging a little deeper, he unearthed the perfectly preserved Robert Raymond who, in the olden days of 1961, launched *Four Corners*, destined to become the ABC's most enduring and admired programmes.' (Nothing has changed! My emphasis.) 'Now, Alan knows his old bones. He is to the skeleton what Professor Higgins was to the flower girl. None of your "Alas, poor Yorrick". Nothing makes him happier than a shovel shaped tooth, a bit of jawbone or a fragment of forehead. Equally, Robert knows his filmmaking and together they're pretty formidable.' Phillip then goes on to explain the detail of the series to his readers, later observing: '… Thus, *Man on the Rim* is immediately significant because of the extensive anthropological material it contains – footage that Raymond insists on editing at a measured pace. Indeed, that's one of the things I like most about the series – it doesn't rush you through the complicated ideas hidden within apparently simple cultures. It takes its time so that you can watch and think and appreciate.'

The culmination of three years work had paid off, not only in the quality of the series, its critical acceptance and viewer response, but the realisation of one man's dream, Alan's, to be able to tell a story that had not been told before. I used to become exhausted at lunches with Alan and Bob, listening to endless anecdotes of their encounters away. There is one that stands out for me but I'm going to let Alan tell it: 'The single most memorable was when we were on Easter Island, where I thought to myself that if there was a single visit that for me was a reason to be glad to have done the series, it was Easter Island. And then a couple of days later we were out filming on the southern coast shooting a piece to camera by my good self, talking about Thor Heyerdahl and how brave he was and yet quite wrong about humans going from west to east. I was halfway through my second take when I noticed Bob looking over my shoulder and heard the camera click off as everyone looked off into the distance behind me. I said something like "I thought I got that right" but Bob just pointed over my shoulder and as I turned around I could see a Concorde with its nose down coming in to land. Sort of summed up our series with an ultramodern human discovery linking up with Easter Island that was part of our ancient way of life.' They should not have turned the camera off! A missed metaphor of the series.

Secondly, the bad side:

At our luncheon at the Camperdown Travelodge three years before production began, with our executive producer Robert Mercieca, Bob Raymond, Alan Thorne and me, the deal we agreed upon was for Demimonde Productions Pty Ltd to deliver a series entitled *Man on the Rim*, and the book rights were to belong exclusively to Bob and Alan. The book was not referred to again, nor is it referred to in any of the legal documentation pertaining to the series.

As the ABC began to issue the publicity about the forthcoming series, they also announced the joint publication of the book with Angus & Robertson. Mercieca telephoned me one evening from Melbourne in a fury, claiming Bob and Alan had received a quarter of a million dollars for their book. I said, quickly, that it didn't sound quite right to me. Mercieca warned me he was suing the company and its directors on behalf of the investors. I protested that the book had nothing to do with the investors. I rang Bob, who at first laughed uproariously at the thought of a quarter of a million dollars. I also rang Alan to enquire further. He was completely perplexed. It took the weekend to sort out the facts. Yes, Alan and Bob were to receive $259,740 from Angus & Robertson – from which they had to fund the total production, including the enormous cost of printing the book. At the end of the day they would have been lucky to see $20,000 each for their trouble.

However, the horse had bolted. I had no option but to resign from our own company because Mercieca had completely misunderstood the facts of the case.

I suggested to Bob that perhaps a newsletter from him and Alan explaining the situation in relation to their publication of the book would be a fair and reasonable thing to do for our investors. However, the list of investors' names (over 300) and their addresses was private and confidential information that we did not have access to. I decided to ring the investors' rep. I had spoken with him on previous occasions and found him affable enough. But my suggestion that he should circulate Bob and Alan's letter to the investors drew a blank.

The case laboured on with an acrimonious exchange of faxes between Mercieca and me in 1993 and we were never to meet again. The situation worsened in 1994 with the failure of the sales agent, Vision Ventures in the UK.

In 1995 I wrote to the Australian Securities and Investments Commission (ASIC) setting out my request for Bob and Alan's newsletter to be sent to the investors. A officer rang to explain ASIC was overwhelmed by the enormity of cases requiring investigation and it would be some months before they could respond. About a year later a letter arrived from ASIC advising they were unable to assist.

In early 1998 Demimonde's lawyers advised the investors' rep that all rights in the series, including international marketing rights, had reverted to Demimonde, and that they sought his cooperation and assistance, under the deed with Qantum and the investors' representative of 7 June 1986, in facilitating the information required to continue to be able to service the sales of the series.

The sad and unfortunate side of 10BA, which could have been totally avoided by considered and rational examination of the truth of the matter. The ones I feel sorry for are our valued investors who were denied the truth.

27

The Heroes Of The Miniseries

'I really take exception to derogatory statements such as "it's only a miniseries", which fail to reflect the fact that the miniseries may be saving all our bloody necks and we should be appropriately grateful. They're very demanding to produce but Australian miniseries – not just ours but those of Kennedy Miller, David Elphick and a few others – have a feature film quality about them, so there's no compromise of standards. They have a reputation of being among the best.' So I ranted to Mary Colbert in *Cinema Papers*, March 1989. The decision to move into minis whilst making *Bliss* had proven to be the right one. George Whaley, Carol Hughes and I moved from Camperdown to St Johns Road, Glebe, which was to be our development and production base for a few years before the rents were doubled. George was developing scripts for Pat Lovell and Mel Gibson, who had formed their production company Lovell-Gibson, for a miniseries, *My Brother Jack*, based on the novel by George Johnston. George was also working with me on a couple of features. One, *The Trouble With Mr Trethaway*, for a yet-to-be discovered Geoffrey Rush, whilst Ray Lawrence and Robert Drewe were adapting Robert's *Sweetlip*, and Ray was adapting Robyn Davidson's *Tracks*. Meanwhile *Man on the Rim* was halfway through production. It was a busy and rewarding time, even though none of the aforementioned was ever to come to fruition, sadly. I was attending the SPAA[1] conference on the Gold Coast, November '87, the first one to be held there and long before it was to become permanently on the Gold Coast, when Valerie Hardy, head of drama for Network Ten, sighted me – 'Ah, you're the very man I want to see! – I want you to read a script for me.' I said I would be delighted and that I would be back in my Glebe office on Tuesday morning. 'No!'

---

1 Screen Producers (later Screen Production) Association of Australia

she exclaimed, 'I need you to read it while you're here – tonight?' I was attending the conference with fellow producer, Damien Parer, and I announced I would have to leave dinner early. 'To read a script!!?? NOW?' He was incredulous. I was perplexed. I couldn't see what the urgency was till next morning when I met Valerie. The script was *The Heroes*, adapted by Peter Yeldham from Ronald McKie's novel about the heroic exercise Operation Jaywick to blow up the shipping in Singapore harbour in World War II.

'Well, what's your verdict?' enquired Valerie. 'Well it's been a pretty quick read; it's pretty good, but that phoney love story has to go,' I answered. 'Oh no, don't you start too,' said Valerie. She then went on to explain the fictional love story had been included at the insistence of the English. 'Who are the English?' I asked. 'James Gatward,' said Valerie. Ah! Here was a name I recognised. I was to have edited a television series a decade or more beforehand entitled *Elephant Boy* for James Gatward, being filmed in Ceylon (Sri Lanka). My ulcer condition, discovered in LA, put paid to that and I engaged film editor Tim Wellburn as my replacement. Gatward was forever grateful and I became de facto Australian production supervisor which entailed me going to Atlab at Epping in Sydney on Sundays to view rushes, which at that time came in from Ceylon only once a week. Gatward had approached Pat Lovell to be the Australian co-producer of *The Heroes* but when his British production man, Dickie Bamber arrived, Pat sensed the job was not for her. Because *The Heroes* was based on fact and involved mainly Australian servicemen, the 'phoney' love story would have to go, as it would be insulting the memory of these men and their surviving families. 'You'll have to tell them that,' said Valerie. I indicated I would consult Peter Yeldham first. 'You do that – do you think George would be right for it?' She was referring to George Whaley. I said I thought so. 'What about the Poms?' I enquired.

I rang Peter Yeldham and said what I had to say about the love story. 'Thank God,' came his immediate response. It had come about because of Gatward's concern re the 'women's interest' for a war story. But there was no need to worry. Gatward had left the production side of TVS[2] and had been replaced by head of drama Graham Benson, and Bamber was no longer in the picture. I presented the script to George on my return to Sydney, telling him the love strand was going. In the meantime Peter Yeldham sent the first draft for me to read – minus love story – and the later drafts were firmly based on his first draft.

2   TVS, Television South, based in Southampton, part of the ITV network. They were later to lose their licence under the Thatcher regime which was re-allocated to Meridian, who acquired the Southampton studios.

Benson had seen *The Harp in the South* and *Poor Man's Orange* and indicated George was okay by him. Graham Benson eventually arrived from the UK to discuss with Carol Hughes and me the setting up of the production, which was being totally financed by TVS. This was the beginning of a very rewarding and long professional relationship between Graham and me, and a personal friendship with him, his wife Christine and their daughter Fay.

My Brother Jack was also by now looming on the horizon and George became concerned he may not be able to do *The Heroes*. I figured he could do both if they were scheduled back to back. From my perspective it was possible. Carol agreed. She had scheduled and budgeted the entire four hours impeccably (as is her wont!) and we were in a position to commission casting. Sadly, Carol was committed to another project and her task was very ably taken over by another long-term colleague, Rosanne Andrews-Baxter. Benson and TVS were delighted that progress was finally being achieved. I thought the best thing to do was to put my plan to Pat Lovell. We lunched at The Wharf on Thursday, 26 May 1988. Pat is full of life and enthusiasm for whatever she is doing and in particular the development of a script. On this day she was in fine form and in full flight. *My Brother Jack* was going to be the breakthrough miniseries for the Lovell-Gibson company. I could sense my idea of doing our respective series back-to-back was going to be a futile suggestion. I was right. Pat was somewhat taken aback at first that I would dare suggest such a proposal, but after a little further discussion she reached the conclusion that George working on both series could compromise her working relationship with Mel and Bruce (Bruce Davey, Mel's business partner). I said I thought it was a pity. I broke the news to George and rang Graham Benson that evening.

I sat at my desk looking out the window into St Johns Road, pondering what to do. Instincts were telling me *My Brother Jack* wasn't about to happen. It would have been extremely inappropriate of me to ring Bruce Davey or Mel. George suggested I ring Bill Shanahan, who happened to be Mel and George's agent. Bill was the most highly regarded of all agents and none has equalled him since (and no offence to all those agents I have worked with and still do). Bill was a listener, a confidant to his stable of actors and actresses, an advisor and polite and skilled negotiator with the producers and casting directors. Bill was also the epitome of discretion.

I rang Bill. He listened, pondered, and said that he was going to be very frank with me. 'Tony, it's not going to happen. Don't ask me why or how but I know, I just know.' I was completely taken aback and assured him I wouldn't say a word to anyone. George couldn't be asked to make the decision for fear of completely jeopardising his relationship with Mel and Bruce. It would have been treason. George had been placed in an invidious position.

I rang Benson and advised Valerie Hardy. Benson asked for three names overnight. The only one I could think of and recommend was Donald Crombie. Valerie also suggested her then husband, Rod, so I put only two names to Graham Benson. He chortled down the line, 'We're not having nepotism on this production, thank you – I know Crombie's work, see if you can get him.' I had asked Donald's permission to nominate him, and I think he thought I was completely mad and that it wouldn't happen. Valerie was most gracious and said, 'He's absolutely the right man for *The Heroes*.' So Donald Crombie was appointed director, and practically in the same breath was whisked away to London with Susie Maizels to cast the British leads.

Z Force headquarters was in Cairns, the capital of Far North Queensland. It was from here in 1943 that Operation Jaywick was planned, and became one of the great naval accomplishments of World War II. Sailing in a stable but leaky fishing boat called the *Krait*, fourteen men left Cairns via the inside reef to 'Potshot' in Western Australia, then north to Singapore to blow up the enemy shipping. Heroic? Many in high places thought it suicidal. This Z Force contingent was led by Captain Ivan Lyon, a Britisher who was described as a nervous, tense and obsessively driven man. He was also shy and introspective. Susie Maizels and Donald Crombie, armed with photos of Lyon, began the task of finding the 'right' actor for the role. There were several contenders offered by the leading London agents, but one stood out from the rest, who could also be described as shy and perhaps introspective. Paul Rhys, 25, born in Neath, Glamorgan, Wales, was our man. As a boy Paul used to spend his summer holidays at the pictures, often going three times a day. In 1984 he had won a George Bernard Shaw scholarship which was offered only every three years. He had been spotted by the principal of RADA and was selected from nearly 5,000 applicants. Two years later he graduated with the Bancroft Gold Medal as their most outstanding student.

Timothy Lyn won the role of Welshman 'Taffy' Morris, by sending a performance tape to Crombie in Welsh! The real Taffy Morris was still alive and Tim had the good fortune of being able to spend time with him before leaving for Australia to commence filming. He told Tim that right from the beginning of Operation Jaywick he knew he would survive. 'He told me in Singapore he offered his place on a boat home to England to a man whose wife had been injured. The boat was bombed and all on board were killed. Another time, people on either side of him were struck by bullets. It was because of this belief in his resilience that he was able to keep morale high aboard the *Krait* during the long and difficult voyage.'

(Top) Our executive producer, Graham Benson from TVS UK (right) came to Queensland for our location filming. To Graham's right: director Donald Crombie, Mark Lewis Jones (Ingleton), me, and last but not least, Craig McLachlan.

(Middle) The crew of the *Krait* line up for inspection.

(Bottom) Christopher Morsely as Bob Page and Miranda Otto as his wife, Roma Page.

To cap off the Australian casting, Susie urged Donald to cast Jason Donovan as the young Harry Houston. Jason was the popular star of the forever-running series, *Neighbours*. Would it throw the rest of the casting out of kilter? From New Zealand came John Bach to play the second lead, Donald Davidson. John Hargreaves, our unsung hero of Australian stars, cast as Ted Carse, Bill Kerr as engineer Paddy McDowell, Cameron Daddo as 'Joe' Jones, Christopher Morsley as Bob Page, Wayne Scott Kermond as 'Boof' Marsh, Jeff Truman from *Bliss* as 'Cobber' Cain, Don Talbert as 'Moss' Berryman, Mark McAskill as 'Poppa' Falls, Gerry Skilton as Andy Crilley, David Wenham as 'Horrie' Young, Tim Robertson as Col. Mott, John Ewart as Bill Reynolds, John Bonney as the rear admiral, with Lorna Lesley as Pat Carse and Briony Behets as Alice. If ever there was a pattern for the chemistry of casting, this ensemble certainly took the candle. Unquestionably the charismatic John Hargreaves' finest role, and Jason fitted like a glove.

Crombie[1] about the series: '*Heroes* does not follow the usual traditional war story format ... unlike the usual perceptions of war, it's not an action piece, but a character-based drama with no shoot out to resolve the mounting tension through battle. Rather it's maintained in the pervasive though rarely sighted presence of the enemy. There are close calls but no conflict. In fact there is only one shot fired in the entire four hours and that's when a gun goes off when they're cleaning it. The bullet hits the tomato sauce bottle which shatters and severs an artery in a man's leg, so what starts out farcical becomes serious – unexpectedly. It's the type of reversal which makes *Heroes* different from all the usual action pieces, which are gung-ho about the fighting.'

Although the actual *Krait*[2] still existed, it was considered unseaworthy and impractical to use for filming. It was also awaiting heritage listing. Enter Bernard Hides, production designer, and his art director Virginia Bieneman. Bernard had an exact replica of the *Krait* made, without a keel, built onto a flat-bottomed barge with a cleverly concealed outboard motor for propulsion. The design was a life-size replica to hold the fourteen cast and at the same time provided for the thirty-strong crew a platform on which to work. An additional pontoon was provided as a camera platform. On looking at the series today one would never know it was not the real *Krait*. A scale model was also made for the very few special effects shots in the film. There were no computer-generated images (CGI) used. Filming was done in and around Cairns and our 'at sea' locations off Mission

---

1   To Mary Colbert, *Cinema Papers*, March 1989
2   *Krait* is fully restored and afloat at the Australian National Maritime Museum at Darling Harbour, Sydney.

Beach, opposite Dunk Island, the island on which I had spent six weeks editing Michael Powell's *Age of Consent*.

The location at Mission Beach was one of the most pleasant and happiest of my experiences. Our motel faced the beach and Dunk Island, and all our actors were very comfortable. Jason was looking forward to Kylie's arrival for a week's holiday while he was filming. I took the precaution of reminding him that his room was next to mine. He beamed!

Queensland is an ideal location for recreating the watery straits leading to Singapore. Bernard's biggest challenge came with the design and construction of the studio tank to hold the *Krait*, film crew and 800 tons of water. This was constructed in the old Ralph Symonds warehouses at Homebush, Sydney, built for the manufacture of the plywood mullions for the Sydney Opera House. The tank was a temporary fixture whereby the crew could work in the water at waist height, allowing an incredible degree of manoeuvrability of the craft and the camera pontoon.

The Heroes was a challenging production but working for our UK executive producer, Graham Benson was, for me and Donald, a revelation and a pleasure. We had total creative control and support from both Graham and Valerie Hardy at Network Ten. It was the best example of a co-venture to cite as an example of an international co-venture working satisfactorily without the clutter of a platoon of executive producers and their respective egos. In 1989, though the series was originated on film, the finished program was delivered on two-inch master tape, one of the last to be completed this way before the arrival of one inch tape. The delivery components were completed about fourteen days before the UK's scheduled April transmission dates. The only way to guarantee delivery was to take the tapes with me as hand luggage on QF1 to London, first class. Special arrangements were made with customs at Heathrow, and Qantas made the closet at the front of the first class cabin available to hold the two heavy tapes, which I guarded all the way to London. It was only the second time I had flown first class and it was to be the trip from hell. I was seated in row one, aisle, starboard side. The window seat was occupied by a mother and her six-month-old baby. On the aisle seat, port side, a mother with her recently arrived baby! Sleep to London was a figment of my imagination!

I arrived somewhat of a wreck at Heathrow, to be met by a liveried chauffeur and whisked away, with tapes, to the Southampton headquarters of TVS. I was greeted on arrival by the cheerful, forever-beaming face of Graham Benson, then straight into master control to check that the tapes met with all the stringent British technical standards of the day. Previews had already been arranged later that week in London for the media, only days before the world premiere. TVS was part of the ITV network serving the south of England, but *The Heroes* was being transmitted by the entire ITV network, north to south, east to west, over three nights. This meant the greatest percentage of the advertising revenue went to TVS, thereby covering the production cost domestically, leaving the rest of the world as profit wherever it sold.

The first night's two-hour episode gained fifteen million viewers and the second and third nights' one-hour episode fifteen and a half million on each night. Figures not achievable today. It was the highest rating for a miniseries from anywhere in the world ever for the ITV network. Though TVS were ecstatic with the results, they paled into insignificance by one phone call. I was in my London hotel room the Wednesday morning after the previous night's final episode, when the phone rang. It was Peter Hider, our ever-supportive production manager/liaison at TVS. He was somewhat breathless. 'I've got news for you – the palace has just rung.' 'The palace?' I queried. 'What palace?' Hider could hardly contain himself. 'BUCKINGHAM PALACE!' came the shout. 'Ma'm' had evidently called on her staff to enquire if they could have a copy of *The Heroes* for viewing by Her Majesty and the family for the weekend. The ultimate accolade.

The casting of Jason Donovan also became a godsend. Though he wasn't the lead, from the media's perspective he was most certainly the star of *The Heroes*, for he could be found on the cover of every television magazine and guide in the country. The same was to be repeated in Australia a few months later when Ten successfully launched the series, but not before their rival, Channel Seven, rained on our parade. Seven had owned for many years a film made by Lee Robinson in 1982 entitled *The Highest Honour* about the same subject. In an act of absolute commercial bastardry, the Channel changed the title to *Heroes of the Krait* and programmed it a week ahead of Ten's *The Heroes*. Mike Harris, columnist in *The Bulletin*, August 29, 1989, was scathing about Seven's actions: '… and to say that it languished on the network's inventory would be too euphemistic. As I noted recently, television is the only aspect of showbiz that deliberately sets out to act to the detriment of any success by the competition.'

Little did I know at the time, Channel Seven was to rear its head once more, much sooner than anyone could have expected. *The Heroes* was an extremely worthwhile series for all of us. 'A sequel, Graham?' I asked Benson. 'Hardly – they all lost their bloody heads!' Operation Rimau was a disaster, it was true, but an heroic sacrifice no less. As a series I felt it would be extremely charged with high drama. Ten were not interested in a sequel. TVS Southampton authorised the sale and disposal of all props, chattels and wardrobe, all of which had been especially tailored for the production. The *Krait* replica was scrapped and the scale model went to a gallery in Mosman, Sydney. Graham and I had grave misgivings about this taking place. That was that.

Some months elapsed, then a phone call came. I was by now familiar with the pause and the quiet sound of air preceding an international call. It was Graham Benson. 'I've got news for you.' He didn't. I knew exactly what he was going to say. I said, 'We're doing *Heroes II*?' Graham laughed. 'Yes, how did you guess?' He continued to explain that TVS and the ITV network wanted it but Channel Ten didn't, and he hoped to persuade them on his coming visit. Graham's visits to Sydney became great social events and I think it must have been at one of these that he impressed the Seven hierarchy to take on the series for Australian transmission. It seemed strange to me not to have such a potentially strong sequel with the same channel and audience. Channel Seven it was to be. Enter into my life Des Monaghan, head of production at Channel Seven. (More – much more – later!)

For Peter Yeldham it was quite a different assignment from the first – there was no book to adapt. Shortly after commissioning the second series it was discovered we did not own the rights to Ronald McKie's book – on which the first series was based. A brief part two in the book told of the second raid and its failure. Only the rights to the first voyage, Operation Jaywick, had been bought – not the return, Operation Rimau. This was fortunate for Peter Yeldham was able to obtain, via Lee Robinson, a large volume of formerly classified army documents. McKie and many others had been badly misled about the treatment of the captured men, and perpetuated the legend that they had been beheaded as heroes in the Bushido tradition, and had gone to their deaths with equanimity and bravado! A study of the army documents seemed to indicate this was quite incorrect. There were various interviews with prison camp guards who told the true story. The presentation of the men's trial in which they had no defence counsel was clearly an elaborate attempt to whitewash those responsible, and avoid them being prosecuted for war crimes.

Graham asked if I could put the same team together again, particularly our director, Donald Crombie. Bernard Hides and Virginia Bieneman were quick to hit their drawing boards, only this time we needed a submarine and, yes, another tank to be built. It was decided to scout for locations closer to home this time and the Gold Coast and the Moreton Bay area south of Brisbane were chosen. Susie Maizels went off to London once more to look for the actors to play Ingleton and Ross. She and the rest of us were not expecting the news that Paul Rhys was not going to play Ivan Lyon. By the time Donald Crombie arrived, Susie had met with 170 actors and had selected thirty for Donald to meet, with no inkling of the Rhys situation. His agent wouldn't give any indication, one way or the other, or that in fact there may have been a problem. In hindsight I suspect they were holding us at bay because the agent may have been sniffing a bigger offer in the wind. On the day prior to Susie and Donald leaving for Japan, Graham Benson advised us, in the light of no firm commitment from Rhys, to immediately recast. Having seen so many actors it didn't take Susie and Donald long to focus on Nathaniel Parker to replace Rhys as Ivan Lyons. Nathaniel played Laertes to Mel Gibson's Hamlet in Zeffirelli's version. Mark Lewis-Jones won the role of Ingleton and Ian Bolt, who Susie had spotted in the West End, was selected to play the young Ross.

Our wet stage was to be rebuilt at Homebush, only this time with beach, jungle, and the tank for our night rowing scenes and model work. However, we were to be completely spoilt, for all our interior shooting, including the interior of a submarine that had to be built, was to be in a studio. For decades Australian filmmakers have had to make do with inferior, non-sound-proofed warehouses and/or inadequate interior facilities. All this was about to change. Ironically, Hoyts Television were now managing the old Channel Ten studios for the Westfield Corporation. Carol Hughes, my line producer, began negotiations after a visit to the facility impressed us all. We had wonderful space for our production office and art and wardrobe departments, not to mention Studio B, thoroughly suitable for our sets and sound-proofed – in fact it was to be the first sound-proofed studio I had worked in for twenty-five years!

After the selection of our English lead cast, Donald and Susie travelled on to Tokyo to audition Japanese actors for some of our principal Japanese leads. Going straight from Narita Airport to the casting agency, thirty-seven were auditioned on the first day and another forty on the second day. Fortunately for our tireless travellers the third day was a public holiday. One of Japan's leading television stars, Ken Teraizumi, was chosen to play the lead role of Furuta, Go Awazu to play Mikizawa and Taro Ishida, Otsuka. Whilst we knew we would be able to cast other Japanese supports from Australia we were pleasantly surprised to find our second Japanese lead here in Sydney, Kazuhiro Muroyama, who played Kamiya, and Ken Senga played Yoshida.

Our strong Australian cast was headed by Christopher Morsley (Bob Page) and John Bach (Donald Davidson) who were joined by Simon Burke (Captain Ellis), Craig McLachlan (Lieutenant Carey), Miranda Otto (Roma Page) and Anne Louise Lambert (Nancy Davidson). Simon Burke came to stardom in Fred Schepisi's *The Devil's Playground* and played the lead in our company's film *The Irishman* opposite Michael Craig. Craig McLachlan needed no introduction but *Heroes II* was to be his first role outside the hugely successful *Home and Away*.

Anne Lambert, remembered for her role in Peter Weir's *Picnic at Hanging Rock*, had been working mainly in England. Wayne Scott Kermond rejoined us to recreate his role of Marsh and an exciting newcomer, Troy Willets, was selected to play 'Happy' Houston.

Our art department had great success with the acquisition of a number of boats in the Surfers Paradise area on Queensland's Gold Coast for the various vessels featured. Existing craft converted into a Malay police launch, Japanese and British patrol boats and even a Japanese landing barge had been found. A superb lugger, the *Cornelius*, had been generously offered to us by the owners for conversion into the *Moestika*. The art department's research team had discovered the spellings of various words were different prior to 1948, hence used the above for the *Mustika*. We had also researched for our actors the correct pronunciations of various island names used at the time by the Indonesian, Malay and British colonial authorities.

The *Moestika* was a brilliant conversion of the *Cornelius*. Her owner visited us and couldn't recognise his own vessel. He even suggested leaving it that way! Production designer Bernard Hides cleverly cladded the vessel in such a way that it could be reinstated immediately filming finished. However, her disguise nearly got the ship arrested. Returning to base after shooting was completed, the *Moestika* was making her slow way up the channel when two customs launches intercepted her, wanting to know her origin and the skipper's name. When Captain Bruce 'Tibby' Manson and deckie Adam Lowe waved and said, 'Hi, it's us, it's the *Cornelius*,' the customs officers wouldn't believe them. 'We know the *Cornelius*, come off it Tibby, where did you get that junk?' The customs officers were left incredulous when they inspected the craft and needless to say the *Moestika* was no junk either!

The one thing they always tell you about filmmaking is not to do films with children, animals or boats. Well, you would think we would have learnt our lesson on the first series, but alas we hadn't. Our flotilla, which sometimes resembled the departure for Dunkirk every morning, set sail on schedule for our first day's filming on Saturday, 27 April 1991. On the *Krait* we had had a cast of fourteen. On the *Moestika* we had twenty-three and it was quite a feat getting them on the boat, together with crew, considering the vessel was ten feet shorter than the *Krait*. When rolling for a take, director Donald Crombie called 'action', only to have Ivan Lyon (Nathaniel Parker) lean forward and say, 'Don't you think he should be awake?', pointing to one of our 'raiders' fast asleep on the deck. With twenty-three actors to check on, no one had noticed our sleeping beauty.

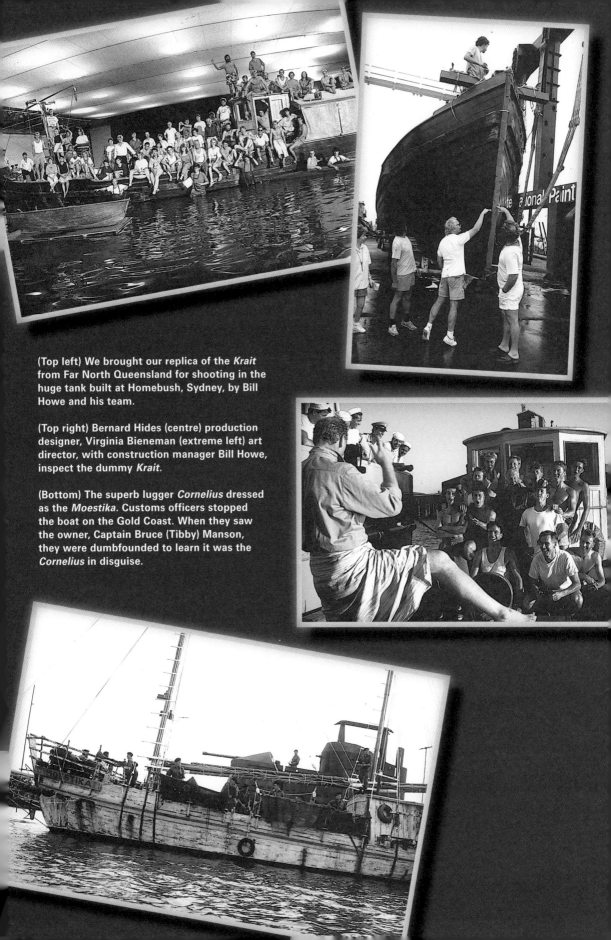

(Top left) We brought our replica of the *Krait* from Far North Queensland for shooting in the huge tank built at Homebush, Sydney, by Bill Howe and his team.

(Top right) Bernard Hides (centre) production designer, Virginia Bieneman (extreme left) art director, with construction manager Bill Howe, inspect the dummy *Krait*.

(Bottom) The superb lugger *Cornelius* dressed as the *Moestika*. Customs officers stopped the boat on the Gold Coast. When they saw the owner, Captain Bruce (Tibby) Manson, they were dumbfounded to learn it was the *Cornelius* in disguise.

On the first series, *The Heroes*, there was a minimum of interference from TVS in England, but for some reason this was to change with the second series. There was far more effort to influence the show. Peter Yeldham and Donald Crombie were continually sent copious notes – often after scenes had been shot. Many of these 'notes' were vague, difficult to fathom and in the end just angered and irritated us. It became a 'them and us' situation with, thankfully, Peter and Donald in accord on almost all points. I finished up becoming the referee and diplomat between the opposing camps. The main problem was the English script executive or, as Peter aptly described her one day, '… a real pain in the arse!'

Then the rains came. And they weren't the rains of Ranchipur either. The rains in Queensland normally fall between December and March, with some in April but generally very little. The rains in May were certainly not expected. Poured, it did. And all one could hear were the locals continuously exclaiming, 'Funny, but it never rains this time of the year.'

Director of photography Roger Dowling was always worried about our jungle locations losing light from the sun very early in the afternoon. Well, Roger didn't have to worry for there was no sun. In fact the jungle canopy turned out to be an advantage. Although a wet and muddy location to work in, the canopy kept the light rain out for the best part of the time. The generators were moved closer to the set to provide light and I would defy anyone to know it wasn't sunlight.

As I have mentioned earlier, the public at times must think we are completely mad. One of our jungle war scenes called for rain. Naturally our special effects people arranged for rainmaking machines to be installed ready for the appropriate time. Needless to say, it poured that day. So much so, in the middle of one take Toby Pease, our first assistant director, called 'cut'. The rain continued. Toby called 'cut' again, only to hear the distant voice of the special effects person plead, 'But it *is* raining'. Life imitating art? *Bliss* all over again!

As a result, a reschedule had to occur with many of our incomplete jungle scenes being moved to Sydney. We had found a 'jungle' on a private property at Otford, about an hour and a half's drive south towards Wollongong. Wednesday, 12 June 1991, will be long remembered by this producer as Black Wednesday. Otford was chosen for our jungle scenes because it was private property, the jungle canopy for Singapore was just right, and gunfire and explosions were permitted. The site had been used previously for *The Damien Parer Story*, *Emma, Queen of the South Seas* and *Emerald City*. To gain access we had to reconstruct a road approximately two kilometres in length. On the Thursday beforehand, Sydney began to be deluged. The rain was never-ending! Locations manager Henry Osborne, production manager Elizabeth Symes, unit manager Will Matthews and I visited the location to inspect the road. All was okay. Associate producer Carol Hughes revisited on the Monday and found the road was holding well. To allow the water to run off we decided to go to studio interiors on the Tuesday and definitely film at Otford the following day.

The advance unit were preparing base on Tuesday afternoon when the rains came heavier than before. In attempting to get back to the farmhouse rented for the unit and catering, the unit driver stopped to inspect a small bridge ahead of the vehicle, to discover what he estimated to be a ten-foot high wall of water rushing past. The only way the unit could get back was to drive along the railway line. At ten that night, the railway line was washed away. When I arrived on set at six on the Wednesday morning I was greeted by an ashen-faced location manager who said he feared we had a major problem. It was still dark and we had to wait till first light at about 6.45 before we could take a four-wheel drive vehicle into the location to see the result of the rainfall the previous night. The morning headline in the *Herald* had declared SYDNEY – HIGHEST RAINFALL SINCE 1884! The sight that now greeted us was devastating. The entire road had been washed away and our four-wheel drive could only travel half the distance. We walked, or should I say waded, the rest of the way. Even if we had been able to get the crew in, it was totally unsafe for electrics and the ground was completely awash with rushing streams of water. It was a sight to see, but worse was to come.

For the first time in my career, we had to send the entire cast and crew home for the day.

It was clearly evident it would be many days before we could get the road rebuilt, if in fact there was anyone available to do it. Every man and piece of equipment in the district had been commandeered to start rebuilding the railway embankments, which of course were far more important.

So on our unofficial day 'off' Donald Crombie, with Peter Yeldham, devised a rewrite of our jungle scenes, to be filmed without explosions and gunshots. Donald went off that afternoon with Bernard Hides and found a location at Narrabeen, very close to our home base. Application to the local Council was made. We held our breath. Yes, we could use the location, provided there were no gunshots.

I have related this story as an example of what a producer does and must do. Remain calm no matter what the circumstances and, most importantly, make decisions and make them quickly. In production one can't postpone decisions till tomorrow. Department heads need decisions, then and there. Strangely it is better to be mistaken than not to make a decision at all.

Post-production flowed as it always does, though for Donald and me we found the 'culture' at Channel Seven quite different to that of Ten. At Seven everyone seemed to be intimidated by Des Monaghan and I sensed Des would have liked to have been more hands-on in post than he was allowed to be by Graham Benson.

The second series was successful, even with the change of channel, though ratings were not as high and it had been programmed in late April after Anzac Day when I think viewers had had enough of the 'war' coverage. Young Craig McLachlan became the 'star' this time. It was to be another six years before I would encounter Des again and under quite different circumstances. For me, I think the second series is the better of the two, though thankfully both were a huge success for Graham Benson and TVS.

For George Whaley it was a regretful experience as *My Brother Jack* didn't happen and the Lovell-Gibson partnership folded.

28

Prostitution – Adapting Bryce Courtenay – And The Mysterious Case Of The Stolen Logie

There are two executives of our industry who deserve closer scrutiny – Dame Patricia (as she is known in the industry) Edgar, and Des Monaghan.

'I would regard Patricia Edgar as a sort of human tank. Patricia is a sort of centurion in her abilities to kick down doors and push walls over. She is annoying, irritating, relentless, drives people mad, but she gets things done … There is also the difficulty that Patricia Edgar does not conduct herself like an Avon lady. I don't think she's read *How to Win Friends and Influence People*. She is relentless, she is a missionary, she's a zealot, she's also trodden on toes that belong to people at television stations and toes that belong to people on self-appointed committees. So clearly it is going to be drama.' So wrote Phillip Adams, in his impeccable, understated way.

Drama indeed. Make no mistake, Patricia Edgar can be credited and highly praised for making the Australian Children's Television Foundation (ACTF) become a reality against all odds, and ensured its survival and continuing existence in a climate of considerable industry indifference.

My first encounter with Patricia was when I was invited to produce one of the 'More Winners' series, *Mr Edmund*, a delightful television hour written by Steve J. Spears and directed by George Whaley. We had a strong cast, headed by Robert Grubb, and I was fortunate in obtaining director of photography Andrew Lesnie. My production manager, Elizabeth Symes, and I had noticed, in the early stages of production, Patricia's preoccupation with publicity and the publicity machine. I hadn't encountered the ACTF's Melbourne-based publicists before. Our shoot for *Mr Edmund* was short and well-managed and the publicists were controllable, but most certainly had a completely different approach to the Sydney-based publicists I had used previously.

It was during the final week of shoot that Patricia enquired of my availability to produce a telemovie for the Foundation. I should explain at this point that independent producers like myself should never look a gift horse in the mouth, for the times between gigs can sometimes be lengthy. At the same time, I cannot do anything just for the money. If the script is not 'me', then I pass. I have to be able to go to rushes (dailies in the US) at the end of the day and believe in what we are setting out to do. If one's heart is not in it, one mustn't produce the film. The script of *Skytrackers* was by one of our better writers, Tony Morphett, so I opened the pages with optimism but my enthusiasm and optimism soon faded. I couldn't understand where Tony was coming from. It was a hybrid story involving Americans and Australians at a tracking station at Tidbinbilla, in the Australian Capital Territory. It was a complete cop-out to American movies, and therefore a 'B' script. I rang Patricia and asked why on earth the ACTF wanted to make it. It soon became clear. She was hellbent on having Disney involved in the financing and production of program material which was suitable for the Australian children's audience and American viewers of Disney programs. Well, the two couldn't be more poles apart if you tried.

Elizabeth Symes had a thorough look at the budget and quickly concluded it was $100,000 under-budget. Whew! Thank goodness. I could safely decline. I telephoned the 'Dame' and told her the bad news about the budget. She listened attentively and said 'I'll get back to you later today. Oh, and by the way, John Power has agreed to direct.' John Power? Well that was a step in the right direction. I rang John. 'I've told her I don't want to do it,' he exclaimed. He thought much the same as I did, that the script was a complete cop-out to the Yanks. I told him about the budget and said not to worry as it wouldn't be happening. Well, that was foolish of me.

Elizabeth Symes put her head through the door – 'The Dame is on the phone.' I asked Elizabeth to sit down and took the call. In her characteristic raspy voice, Patricia proudly said, 'I've raised the money you need, we can go ahead.' I was dumbfounded. The centurion tank had gone to work and knocked down the doors of the bank. Elizabeth leant across the desk and whispered, 'Think of the mortgage.' Bugger! She was right, and so for the first time in my career I was doing something for the money. I would live to regret it. I rang John Power. Patricia, contrary to her own memory,[1] had been begging John to agree to direct.

---

1   In her 'memoir' *Bloodbath*, Patricia Edgar suggests the US producer had over-ruled her on cast and the choice of director.

Now there was no way out for either John or me, the money was there. God knows how much blood had been left on the bank manager's carpet. John and I were beginning what was, for both of us, one of the unhappiest experiences of our careers. It was, for the ACTF, a serious lapse of judgement. The star was Pamela Sue Martin of *Dynasty* fame, a pleasant and extremely competent actress who gave it her best.

Little did I or my colleagues know that *Skytrackers* was to start World War III with the Dame. The publicists arrived in force from Melbourne and set up camp, to the consternation of us all, demanding access to, and on, the set every day of the shoot. Media and publicists are allowed access generally on the easier days of the shoot, and preferably when on location. The publicists demanded access every day, which I quickly pointed out was a demand that was neither feasible nor permissible. Patricia Edgar rang to demand I accede to the publicists' demands. I refused.

All hell broke loose when our first assistant director telephoned the production office seeking my immediate presence on the set. Chris Webb is one of the very top ten of first assistant directors in Australia, and the calmest, most quietly-spoken professional a director and crew could wish to have on set. Something had really blown up. I arrived to meet a tense, angrily-frowning first AD who made it politely but perfectly clear to me that if the publicists did not leave the set immediately, the filming would not continue. I ordered the publicists off the set and to my office. I was not in a position to fire them but was able to ban them from the set. I telephoned Patricia to advise her of the morning's events and that from now on the publicists were banned from the set. Needless to say, she went ballistic. Despite Patricia Edgar's protestations, that was the end of the matter. The centurion tank had been disabled.

Ironically *Skytrackers* much later became a successful series but not connected with the telemovie, which regretfully was probably Patricia Edgar's biggest mistake in her twenty-three years guiding and building the Australian Children's Television Foundation.

If Patricia Edgar was the centurion tank, then Des Monaghan has to be the bullyboy of television. I wasn't aware of Monaghan's moniker, until a colleague of mine in New Zealand asked me on the phone what I was doing. I told her I was going to work for Screentime, a relatively new production set-up established by Bob Campbell, the former CEO of Network Seven, and Des Monaghan, head of drama for the network. 'Not old Mogadon?' she exclaimed, and then laughed uproariously. It seems Des was given the moniker when he worked for Television New Zealand. The reason why was never made clear to me, but it had certainly stuck on his move to Australia. Producing *The Heroes* for Network Ten and *Heroes II – The Return* for the Seven Network were quite different experiences. The cultures of the two networks could not have been less alike. At Ten, working for Valerie Hardy and Tom Warne was a collaborative relationship. At Seven I found a culture of intimidation caused, I think, by the authoritarian manner of those at the top. Fortunately, being primarily a production for TVS and Graham Benson, my team and I were somewhat shielded and protected from this.

Coming to work at Screentime was somewhat of a coincidence. I was holidaying on the island of Lombok (across the way from Bali) at the Sheraton, reading. The book I had picked up was Bryce Courtenay's *The Potato Factory*, a real page-turner. I thought to myself, it would make a bloody good miniseries. Little did I know Screentime were optioning the book for a miniseries for the Seven Network. Rob Marchand (*Kangaroo Palace, Come in Spinner*) had been engaged to direct, and Alan Seymour, one of our top playwrights (*The One Day of the Year*) and television writer for the BBC, was commissioned to adapt Bryce's bestseller. A good team.

I was given an office at Screentime from where the production was planned and organised. *The Potato Factory* is set in England and Australia in the mid-1800s, and for economies of scale it was decided very early in the piece not to dramatise the lengthy voyage out to Australia by Mary, Ikey Solomon's mistress, played by Lisa McCune, but focus the story in London and Hobart Town in Tasmania on Mary, Ikey and Hannah, his wife. Overseas funding to match the Australian investment was coming from Golden Square Productions, a subsidiary of Columbia Television headed by Victor Glynn. International, and top Australian casting was a requirement of Golden Square, but Des Monaghan and I were to spend many nights at Screentime on the phone to London trying to pin Victor Glynn down on the money, and to approve our casting recommendations, and to lock down the cash flow requirements Screentime needed. Dealing with Victor Glynn was a nightmare for Des and me. Meantime both of us went down to Tasmania for a reconnoitre of possible locales to ascertain whether we could find London locations as well as those set in Australia. While we found possibilities in Tasmania, it became apparent that the cost involved in taking cast and crew there was going to be prohibitive. So back to the drawing board we went.

It was decided to take the bold step of building 'old' London and searching for locations for old Hobart Town nearer Sydney. Old Sydney Town, a run-down and defunct theme park north of the city, was suitable for part of our requirements, but for the main part of our location, the city of Goulburn, south of Sydney, proved to be a significant find, so we moved south while our city of London was being built in an old warehouse at Leichhardt, an inner suburb of Sydney. Whilst

(Top right) Early 19th century London, a labyrinth of lanes, alleyways and streets, built in a vast warehouse in the inner Sydney suburb of Leichhardt! Production designer Nicholas McCallum had his team build this vast set in six weeks whilst we were in pre-production, and our first four weeks of location shooting.

(Right) Lisa McCune's stunning costumes were designed by Jennie Tate.

(Bottom) Fog and rain machines were installed to get the right atmosphere for this 'interior' shoot.

'THE POTATO FACTORY'
ROLL   SLATE   TAKE
A153A   583   1   FPS
DIR: R. MARCHAND
DOP: K. BATTERHAM
DATE: 17.2.99

production designer Nicholas McCallum was designing his ingenious set of streets and alleyways of old London, director Rob Marchand was despatched to the real London to lock down our English lead actor for the role of Ikey Solomon. On arriving at Golden Square's offices, the elusive Victor Glynn was nowhere to be found. Ben Cross of *Chariots of Fire* fame was available and suitable for the role of Ikey and Rob recommended we offer him the role, but when Glynn finally appeared he was not convinced our 'name' casting was strong enough to sell the series.

Meanwhile, back in Sydney Des and I would stay back at Screentime till the late hours waiting on Glynn's phone calls or attempting to find him to secure our casting approvals and, more importantly, our cash flow requirements. Also, there were contracts to be signed in conjunction with the Film Finance Corporation, which had heavily invested in this co-venture and were waiting to sign off on the Production and Investment Agreement. The contracts were eventually signed mid-way through pre-production, despite the fact that Victor Glynn was nowhere to be found. Nor has he been heard of to this day.

Enter Columbia's representative from the US, Fran McConnell, and their Asia representative from Hong Kong, a gentleman who I'm sure arrived to close the production down until he and Fran saw the enormity of the sets built at our primitive warehouse in Leichhardt. The mystery man from Hong Kong returned and Fran McConnell realised that her pre-production had gone too far to sensibly put a stop to it. An acreage of sets had been built, wardrobe was virtually complete, and our scheduling indicated we were to start shooting in about three weeks. I'm convinced Fran had been sent to curtail the production, about which it was obvious Victor Glynn had told Columbia very little. We adjourned for the Christmas/New Year break and commenced the shoot in January 1998 in Goulburn, New South Wales. Fran McConnell returned to LA, no doubt to advise her employer that Columbia were getting a miniseries whether they liked it or not.

Alan Seymour's scripts went through several drafts, mainly for length, but with suggested rewrites coming from Rob Marchand, at times to Alan's disquiet. Contractually the scripts had to be signed off by Bryce Courtenay, but I was never convinced Bryce actually read them. He was satisfied that one of the country's best writers and playwrights was adapting his work, and he was very happy I was producing. Professionally, Bryce and I go back a long way, to the days of Ajax Films where I was one of their television commercials editors and Bryce was a senior creative writer at George Pattersons, the leading advertising agency, for whom Ajax produced most of their work.

Our shoot was relatively uneventful until we got back to the 'studio', our huge corrugated-iron barn of a place under the flight path leading to Sydney airport. I remember the first sound recordist invited to record the series walking into the place, taking one look, listening to the aircraft overhead, looking at me, saying 'it's impossible' and walking out, never to be seen again. It wasn't going to be easy, but sound recordist Rob Schreiber coped as best he could with a remarkable degree of enthusiasm considering the circumstances.

The only irritation for director Rob Marchand was Ben Cross's concern about his own dialogue, which had become a major discussion point prior to every take. It all became too much for Rob one morning when Ben began questioning yet another line of his dialogue. Rob blew his stack and told Ben what he thought of him. I was sitting at the end of our open plan production office and looked up to see Rob walking towards my desk. This was unusual, for one only sees the director in the breaks during the day and/or at rushes. Rob came to tell me Ben Cross had walked off the set and was in his caravan. I urged Rob to stay calm and have the first AD call Ben back to the set. Ben delivered his lines and at least we stayed on schedule.

Network Seven were delighted with the 'director's cut' and locked off on the series without any significant alterations to the work. I was pleasantly surprised, as was Des Monaghan, when John Holmes, head of drama for Seven, and one of the real gentlemen of the television industry, got up from his viewing seat to exclaim that it was a lock-off as far as he was concerned and asked when we could deliver. Chris O'Mara, head of programming for the network, was equally delighted and was to pull out all stops to make it Seven's premier program for the following year.

The Australian extras in *The Potato Factory* were fine, but their accents weren't of the period. We were booked in to a recording studio in London to post-sync some of Ben Cross's dialogue, not necessarily for performance but because of the noise level on the original track caused by the over-flying aircraft. We decided to take advantage of the time in London to re-voice our extras with genuine cockney and other English accents. This brought an authenticity to the dialogue which we could not otherwise have had.

Composer Carl Vine claimed that he had retired from film composing when I went to see him at his Balmain terrace. On viewing a cassette of the series he thankfully relented and came out of retirement. I think it a very satisfying miniseries and it rated its socks off for the network, which in itself was an achievement, for one would have expected to have seen *The Potato Factory* on the ABC, not a commercial television network. More importantly, it began making significant overseas sales for its backers.

By this time, Columbia had set up an Australian production base and commissioned Screentime to make a telemovie, *My Husband My Killer*.

Screentime offered me a retainer when we were developing Sara Henderson's *From Strength to Strength* for Kris Noble of the Nine Network. The retainer was to be recouped from the first production to get up. In reality, my being paid a retainer was not going to cost Screentime a cent but *From Strength to Strength* was proving to be problematic and promising a long, difficult road ahead. Michael Laurence was the adaptor, a writer of considerable television experience, but it was not coming together. The first draft was faithful to the book but trying to achieve too much storywise, and from then on each successive draft, though improving, was just missing the mark and the development of the project became extraordinarily protracted. Screentime were developing several strands of television entertainment and had their new soap, *Breakers*, in production.

Dave Gould, a young experienced television producer, had been hired to produce the all-film telemovie *My Husband My Killer* for the Ten Network, about the Kalajzic murder case. Kalajzic was the hotelier of the Pacific International Hotel, Manly, a Sydney seaside suburb which the Manly ferries used to advertise as being 'seven miles from Sydney and a thousand miles from care'. Kalajzic was sentenced to life imprisonment for organising the murder of his wife whilst he was at home in bed with her at their Fairlight residence. It had become a cause célèbre and he still proclaims his innocence. Director Peter Andrikidis, who had an established reputation in series drama television, both tape and film, was engaged to direct. A wise choice. I had first encountered Peter and his regular DOP, Joe Pickering, at the Film School, and had followed his career with interest. He has the knack of getting the most out of a location with a miniscule budget and in fact an episode of the popular series *GP*, shot in Greece, still impresses me after some twenty years. Greg Haddrick, son of noted Australian actor Ron Haddrick, a relative newcomer on the block to film, had written a superb script.

It became apparent that all was not going well from Des Monaghan's point of view and I was called in as supervising producer, a role I had not encountered before. Through no fault of Dave Gould's, he was obviously feeling out of his depth, to a point, in the very able and professional production office. I also detected a personality problem from the 'Des' perspective. It was further exacerbated by the arrival of the newly-appointed head of Australian production for Columbia, Fran McConnell, who had been brought out to replace Jackie O'Sullivan. Screentime had two telemovies in production simultaneously for Columbia which was stretching

Fran, who was totally unfamiliar with the way we produce film. The second telemovie, *Ihaka – Blunt Instrument*, designed to be an ongoing series, was having production problems. I think this was also contributing to Des's state of anxiety.

I was called to his office at 6pm. On arrival he informed me he had summoned Dave Gould with the intention of firing him. I protested that this was not the way to go about things and that it would be extremely disruptive at this late stage of pre-production. I said I would move into the production office and be on hand for the entire shoot and Dave and I would share our responsibilities. Des was clearly unhappy but agreed not to dismiss the producer and accepted my proposal. It was winter and a miserably cold night as I walked the short distance from Screentime to the corner of Alexander and Albany Streets with Dave, trying to restore his confidence and urging him to stay with it. It wasn't an ideal situation for anybody but I wasn't going to accept the television mantra that people like ourselves are just another commodity.

It was a shoot lasting a few weeks, with a change of location and suburb nearly every two days. It was a demanding schedule in one of the coldest Sydney winters on record. The casting of Colin Friels as Detective Sergeant Bob Inkster, and David Field as the assassin, was to give us some of the most powerful performances seen in Australian television and for which David would win an AFI. Colin had the reputation of sometimes being difficult on set, though Peter Andrikidis and I were not to experience this. Nonetheless it was decided I would be on set all day every day. This action also had a calming effect on Fran McConnell and after the first three days' rushes we didn't see her again till the end of the shoot. I had to leave set for two days in the last week of the shoot and issued a note on the call sheet accordingly. Colin, on reading this, evidently said cheekily to his driver, 'Mmmmm, this means I could play up doesn't it?' She looked at him sternly and said, 'I don't think Mr Buckley would appreciate that.' Colin replied, 'No, I don't think he would.' The shoot concluded smoothly.

It is strange how people earn reputations, particularly actors. I had been warned not to cast John Hargreaves in anything, nor John Stanton, and that Colin was 'difficult'. Yet I had no problems with any of them and if Hargreaves were alive today I would find the right vehicle for him to star. What many producers don't realise is that actors are like high-quality porcelain, fragile and needing care. Treat actors as human beings and masters of their craft from day one of the production, and not just another commodity, and they serve you, your director and the production with all they have to give – and more.

Fran McConnell phoned. Could I come into town to meet John Misto, writer, to talk about *Survivor – the Thredbo Story*, an account of the rescue of Stuart Diver in the landslide at the Thredbo ski resort some years before. 'I would like to do it,' said Fran. I accepted the invitation and thought I should advise Des Monaghan that Screentime would no longer have to keep me on a retainer. I bounced into Des's office and broke the news I had been asked to do *The Thredbo Story*. 'Aren't you relieved you won't have to keep me any more?' I joked. This was no joke. Des looked at me aghast. 'But we're doing that for Ten, David Mott confirmed this to us at New Orleans in January.' He reached for the phone and I thought it prudent to leave immediately. I raced home to Lane Cove and rang Fran. She was not in the building. I urged her capable assistant, Elizabeth, to try and find her, as it was imperative that we talk. I thought it better if I stepped aside straight away, to avoid any ructions between the network, Screentime and Columbia. It was very late in the afternoon when Fran returned my call. I told her of my encounter with Des and that to avoid any embarrassment I would step aside. 'You are doing no such thing,' she retorted, 'I have asked you and your company to do this and I will ring Des and tell him – oh, I've just noticed he has called four times so I will do it now.' Fran hung up and I thought, oh dear, this will be the end of it now. Some minutes later she called. 'Well, that's all done – we will see you in here in the morning.' And that was that.

The Thredbo Story very quickly developed into *Heroes' Mountain*. John Misto, the screenwriter, is a master of his craft. Fran and I would concur on our script notes and how best to deliver our view to John. He would arrive and arrange himself at her production table. One of us would mention our first note only to have John reply, 'Oh, I have done that already.' We got through the script in no time at all because John had anticipated all our reactions and had already either deleted a particular scene or had completely rewritten it. He has a remarkable sense of what his producer is going to say. The final draft met with Stuart Diver's approval, but who to play Diver?

Susie Maizels is a remarkable casting director and consultant. She has the ability to come from left field with her suggestions and is generally spot on. Trying to convince a television executive, though, is an entirely different matter, as you are about to learn in two specific cases. Peter Andrikidis screen-tested the best of the best available for the lead role of Stuart Diver and he and I agreed that Susie's recommendation of Craig McLachlan was definitely the one. Fran McConnell agreed but the network would not have a bar of it. Sue Masters, Network Ten's head of drama, wasn't the problem, but upper management was, and they would give no reasons. So screen-testing continued. Craig's role in *Heroes II – The Return* had been stunning and propelled the series on to international sales as well as being a ratings winner for Seven that year. A supporting role in *My Husband My*

Killer was highly praised and admired by the Ten Network, but this time they were really digging in their heels. None of us could fathom why. Crunch time came when the final screen-tests were rejected. Peter Andrikidis and I sat in my office. I rang Sue Masters and said it had to be Craig. It was one week and three days from principal photography. It was 3.10pm when she agreed to go back to management with our ultimatum – that Craig was our choice and by far and away the best actor for the role. At 4.15pm Sue rang to give the go ahead, albeit reluctantly. Not a good start but I knew we were making the right decision.

To avoid opening old wounds at Thredbo, where the residents and relatives of those who had lost their lives were still trying to put the trauma behind them, as a mark of respect we decided to do one week's shooting at Falls Creek over the border in Victoria and recreate the disaster in a massive quarry at Moorebank on the outskirts of Sydney. The collapse would be recreated in the studio. I was to work with Jon Rohde, production designer, for the first time (and certainly not the last). He designed the tunnels dug by Diver's rescuers to where he was trapped underground in modular form in the basement of our production office and then erected them to form the three-storey set in the studio, allowing the camera enormous flexibility. Diver's wife drowned before she could be rescued, a harrowing scene of the two of them together as the swirling waters engulfed them. A special tank was built with pumped warm water to make the scene as comfortable as possible for Craig and Jodie Dry. It was scheduled for the morning of 12 September, 2001.

Australia is fifteen hours ahead of New York. I had gone to bed at about 10.45 having watched the first half of *Lateline*, the ABC's late evening current affairs show. Just after I retired, *Lateline* was carrying the news and the first pictures of the September 11 holocaust. I normally listened to the 5am ABC radio news, which I did this morning when I awoke, only to think I was on the wrong station. What was this science fiction nonsense? Nothing made sense to me initially, then I realised what I was hearing. I dived downstairs and watched with awe and horror what was unfolding on the television. Craig had gone to bed earlier than me at his home because the next morning was his biggest scene in the picture. He got up about 2am to have a hot drink and kept the sound off on the portable television in the kitchen. He noticed the picture on the set and thought it was a B science fiction movie. He arose about 4.30 to get ready for his early call when he noticed the same footage was still playing and thought it was an awfully long movie, when he turned the sound up and became transfixed.

I reached the studio just before 7am to find our crew, like everyone else in the world, numbed by what they had seen. A little cluster huddled around the small TV in the make-up van. It was an incredibly hard morning for any of us to concentrate fully on what we had to do. Craig McLachlan's sense of humour kept our morale up by singing jingles dedicated to Rheem hot water services. Craig got us and himself through the morning and at the same time gave the best performance of his career. The true professional.

Whatever management thought originally about our choice of Craig to play the lead of Stuart Diver, they must have had a change of heart after seeing the show, because David Mott, head of programming, could not have been happier with the end result, getting right behind the promotion of *Heroes' Mountain* by dismissing their advertising agency's submission and creating the excellent publicity themselves, coming up with the line 'The rescue that made us believe in miracles.' *Heroes' Mountain* won the ratings outright on the night of its world premiere, Sunday, 10 March 2002, went on to be nominated best telemovie in the AFIs and won the Gold Hugo at the Chicago International Television Awards for best feature length telefilm, 2003, and Peter Andrikidis the Silver Hugo for direction. This was up against the very best from the BBC, HBO, PBS and many other countries' product.

Regretfully for our industry, Sony Pictures (owners of Columbia Pictures) decided to curtail production in Australia and Fran was recalled to LA and later Rome to supervise European production. Fran McConnell to me was the true Columbia lady, though no longer carrying the torch.

Early in 2001 I could see that a gap in production was looming again so I decided the time had finally come to up-anchor and move north to my home in Port Douglas that I had bought two years previously. I had a good tenant and gave her plenty of notice I would be leaving Sydney in 2002 once and for all. Mind you, my close friends and associates thought it was some sort of fantasy I was having, and speculated that I would be back in eighteen months. Eight years later and I'm still here. I had been visiting the Far North for over twenty years, alternating with Bali for nearly thirty years. Long before the troubles in Bali I had reached the conclusion one couldn't live there but one could certainly live in Far North Queensland. For about twelve years I had been visiting Port Douglas, Yorkey's Knob and Palm Cove. The latter is very beautiful, but it's all resorts and at the time no one actually lived there. I felt that Port Douglas and nearby Mossman had a sense of community that was still very much alive after all the tourists had left at the end of the season. *Jessica* had been in development since the completion of *The Potato Factory*, but the money was taking some time to come together, so up-anchor I did. Packed and catalogued forty-eight boxes of my life in film and shipped them off to the National Film & Sound Archive in Canberra, and kept ten boxes to enable me to check my memory from time to time while writing this tome.

Of course, as you can imagine, I was happily ensconced in Port Douglas for six months, setting up house etc. Gary, my long-time friend from before *Kitty* and *Bliss* days, had taken six months long-service leave to help drive the loaded Forester the 2,300 kilometres from Sydney, help set up the house and establish the garden. The time had regretfully come for him to return to work in Sydney, which he didn't want to do, but we both survived that trauma and continue forward. I had just finished sorting out my superannuation when a call from Screentime came. *Jessica* had found its overseas finance and it would be going to the December meeting of the Film Finance Corporation (FFC) and we could start pre-production in January. So back to Sydney it was to be, but also a very strange coincidence in finding a sitter for my house in Port Douglas.

Jessica regretfully is also somewhat of a horror story for being taken for granted as a commodity and a classic example of how not to produce. The schedule and budget had been carefully prepared by Carol Hughes, who I think is the best in the business, and we have worked together for a very long time. Our original budget was $10 million which we knew was too high but Screentime's overseas partner wanted some 'name' casting, which is called 'above the line' on the budget. Carol whittled away till we finally had an acceptable and workable budget at $8.2 million, which could go to the board of the FFC. By this time Carol had accepted another picture because of the delays we had incurred and I lost my line producer – and, as I was to discover, in more ways than one.

When I reached Sydney, Screentime presented me with a different budget from the one we had prepared and it was now $7.4 million. A mere $800,000 had been stripped out! I exploded. I studied it with amazement. First thing I noticed was my and Peter Andrikidis' fees had been reduced by $35,000 each. No 'ifs', 'buts' or 'I beg your pardons' about it. No phone calls asking did we mind. No, it was take it or leave it. The company accountant, David Turnidge, had been instructed to slash and burn. I'm quite sure David is a good company accountant but there is a very big difference between company accounting and production accounting, which is the very reason production accountants exist. Items deleted from the budget left me incredulous. A typical example was the wranglers had been deleted, but the horses remained. Hello? And to top it all off, the important post of line producer was deleted. I rang the completion guarantor seeking help. All they would say was they thought it was tight. Tight!! It was strangulation time. I had been backed into a corner.

Before cash flow can begin from all investors, the completion bond must be signed. This can't be signed until the director and the producer sign off on the budget. No sign off, no bond, no picture. This, from my point of view, was plain blackmail. I signed off, but for the first time in my career I put a rider on the document to Film Finances, the completion guarantor, that I was signing under protest and that it would be difficult to contain. They had to accept it. Our first meeting in the production office to discuss the budget with the guarantor's representative, Annie Browning, was with Bob Campbell, Des Monaghan and the accountant David Turnidge, and my able production manager, Sam Thompson. The line producer had been cut from the budget. When I protested at what had occurred Des said, 'Well, you signed off on the budget.' I knew then this was going to be my last production ever for Screentime.

Worse irritations were to come. Screentime's overseas partner demanded at least one 'name' cast but the above the line budget had been savaged. I suggested Sam Neill for the role of the drunken barrister, Runche. I felt that with a bit of juggling we might be able to afford him. For the role of Jessica we needed a consummate actress. For this Susie Maizels had drawn up a list of the very top contenders for Peter Andrikidis to screen-test, including one that Susie had a hunch, or we say 'gut reaction' about, whom she had seen recently on the stage. I was also instructed by Des to enquire about the availability of a dolly-bird pop singer. I did what I was told and emailed her manager in London. Her manager was quick to respond with a phone call next morning. He was very courteous and had taken my enquiry seriously. 'Mr Buckley, she has concert and recording engagements for the next eighteen months.' I invited him to call me by my first name and he did likewise. He paused and quietly said – 'but Tony, she can't act!' He was in no way putting his client down, just stating a matter of fact. I rang Des to break the news.

In the meantime Sam Thompson had been re-jigging and rearranging the budget where possible to enable me to make an offer to Sam Neill. I told his agent, Ann Churchill-Brown, with whom I get on very well, what we could afford, but there were to be no extras! She thought the offer was respectable. I informed Des who thought I was wasting my time. Sam Neill loved the script and the part 'made for him', would do it if we could fit him into a window he had during our schedule. First AD Russell Whiteoak scheduled all of his scenes into a contained three-week period of our eight-week location shoot. Sam Neill was signed. Sue Masters, head of drama for Network Ten, was thrilled with the news, but Des remained impassive, although he did say 'well done'.

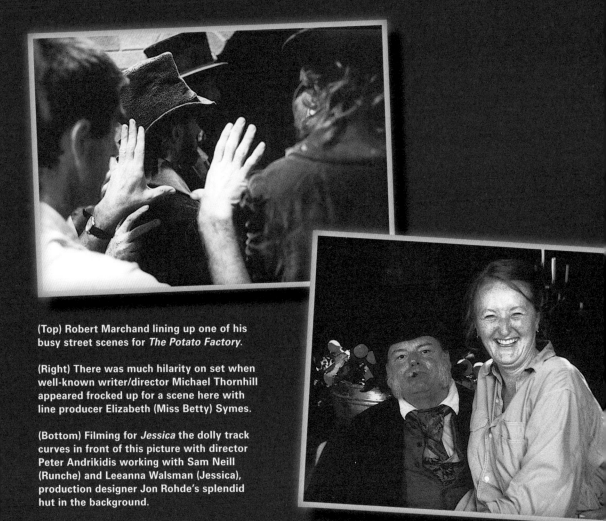

(Top) Robert Marchand lining up one of his busy street scenes for *The Potato Factory*.

(Right) There was much hilarity on set when well-known writer/director Michael Thornhill appeared frocked up for a scene here with line producer Elizabeth (Miss Betty) Symes.

(Bottom) Filming for *Jessica* the dolly track curves in front of this picture with director Peter Andrikidis working with Sam Neill (Runche) and Leeanna Walsman (Jessica), production designer Jon Rohde's splendid hut in the background.

There was going to be a clash over our choice for Jessica which Peter and I could see coming. We narrowed the thirty-something tests down to five. There was not a dolly-bird among them. All five on our reel were good, but one shone. Des was not convinced and told us to keep looking, only there was nowhere else to look and as far as Peter, Susie and I were concerned, we had found her. Sue Masters had seen some tests during the process but had not seen our final five. Des reluctantly said he would present them to Sue. I said fine, but Peter and I must be present to discuss the actors and to enforce our preferred choice. Des was not at all happy with this proposition and made it clear he would do the talking at the meeting at Ten. We rendezvoused at the coffee shop next door to the network's headquarters ten minutes beforehand. Sue Masters and her deputy head of drama, Rick Maier, ushered us into a narrow boardroom which had a plasma wall-mounted screen at the far end of the room. Peter and I had designed the screen-test reel to have our choice in the middle of the reel in number three position. Sue looked at Peter and then to me and said, 'I presume you are both in agreement on who you want to play Jessica?' We nodded our heads in unison. Des wasn't asked and said nothing. The tests rolled. Halfway through the test, in position three, Sue suddenly said, 'It has to be her – surely?' We didn't comment and I couldn't see Peter's reaction in the dark, nor Des's. The lights went up and Sue was quick to query if number three was our choice. We assured her it was. Sue and Rick were sincerely enthusiastic and excited at what they had seen. Des still had nothing to say. Sue automatically assumed Des must have agreed with Peter's and my choice and we weren't about to tell her. 'Well then, go ahead – congratulations, I think she's going to be terrific,' said Sue. Peter and I beamed. Leeanna Walsman was to be our star. Susie Maizels would be elated. The three of us left the building, Des bade us farewell and went to his car, not having commented on our victory.

Adapting Bryce Courtenay to the screen is no easy task. His books are wonderfully detailed in description and incident. Peter Yeldham was my choice to be the adaptor, with which everyone agreed. Peter and I go back to *Age of Consent* in 1968 and I consider him to be one of the very best screen adaptors in the country. His first draft is always faithful to the book, then you ask him to put the Yeldham touch in, and you get a freer-flowing interpretation of the original, more filmic, with a fresh eye now translating the original to the screen.

The city of Orange in central western New South Wales was chosen as our base for the film. With a daily train service, actors could be brought from Sydney in four hours, a trip which they enjoyed, and the marvellous, unspoilt heritage towns and villages in the surrounding districts were easily accessible by road. The book is set in Narrandera, further south and economically just too far away to take a full film crew. So it was decided to combine the three towns of Milthorpe, Carcoar and Lucknow as the centre Narrandera of our story. Milthorpe is a quiet backwater on the main railway line but where the trains no longer stop. It was ideal for our town, for the main street becomes a dead end at the railway station. Carcoar, a branch line, had a superb courthouse and the rural hills of Lucknow were ideal for locating Jessica's hut. Filming took place over a period of seven weeks before returning to Sydney.

Casts and crews like country towns, for houses can generally be found to rent instead of hotels and motels, though many are quite happy with a motel. Cast need privacy, especially known or recognisable actors like Sam. A superb house was found for him out of town. The owners were moving to Cairns in tropical north Queensland and though the owner was staying elsewhere in Orange, his wife was in the north looking for the place where they were to settle. Could she house-sit my home whilst she was looking? A weird coincidence and very convenient.

Jon Rohde rejoined us as production designer, Lorraine Verheyen costume designer and Colleen Woulfe as costume supervisor. It was a big period production with a large cast to design for and dress. Our cast was top drawer, right down to the minor roles. Leeanna Walsman as Jessica, Lisa Harrow, formerly married to Sam, as Hester, Tony Martin as Joe and Sam Neill as Runche.

With no line producer to assist us, the load on Sam Thompson, my production manager, forced her to stay back in the production office many nights well beyond the call of duty. Nonetheless we kept to schedule, even though the budget was stretched to breaking point. Fortunately Sydney left us alone and rushes were satisfying everyone at Screentime and the network. A VIP visit was scheduled for Des and Bob and the day of their visit we were filming Sam and Leeanna at Jessica's hut out at Lucknow. Des arrived in his very classy dark green Jaguar, too good, I thought, to travel on the dirt and gravel road to Lucknow, so I offered to drive out in my humble rental car. There was no need, he informed me. He had traded the Jag in that week on his new BMW. So the Jaguar was driven to location, without harm I was relieved to see, though the risk didn't seem to bother Des. Now, motorcars don't mean a thing to me one way or the other, so the fact Des was getting a new BMW didn't register. Little was I to know its arrival would cause the crew to come close to striking on the picture.

We had one week of interiors to complete in the barns out at Homebush next to the former Olympic site, where we had shot *The Heroes* and *Heroes II – The Return*. Used by many other companies too, they are non-sound-proofed but adequate. What we hadn't realised was that Sydney's famous Royal Easter Show and its noisy, vibrant sideshow alley had been moved from their city site to make way for the Fox Studios and had set up next door to our Homebush facility and, you guessed it, it was Easter and the noise unrelenting. Actors were forced to deliver their lines robotically just to get the take in the can, and give their performance later in post-sync.

The phone rang at our Leichhardt office. It was director Peter Andrikidis. I had never heard him so angry. 'Could you come to set straight away in case the crew go on strike.' What on earth was the matter? It's a 45-minute drive to Homebush and I was on my way. Peter was white with rage when I arrived. Des Monaghan had arrived earlier – in his new BMW – and parked at the open doors of the set showing it off for all to see. Peter observed the crew's reaction to the arrival of the car because, according to them, it was only one of nine BMWs of that marque in the country and worth something like $300,000. When I saw the car I fully understood their anger. Here we were, exhausted and stretched to the limit on a strait-jacket budget, and there was Des flaunting it for all to see.

The launch of the series by Ten was exemplary. On Sunday, 18 July 2004, its initial rating was 1.8 million and on the second night, Monday, 19 July, when we ran nearly fifteen minutes over, the audience peaked at 1.85 million and stayed with us to the end. It had already won the Silver Hugo for miniseries and the Gold Hugo for direction earlier in the year at Chicago, where *Heroes' Mountain* had won Gold and Silver the year previously. I ordered copies of the Hugo's for Des, Bob and Peter Andrikidis, and the series was destined for AFI and Logie nominations. Despite all our upsets and angst and lack of support from our executive producers, I think *Jessica* is the best miniseries I have ever produced and consider it in the top ten of all minis made in Australia.

I had to have unexpected major surgery early in 2004 and Des rang during my recuperation. He asked how I was progressing then said, 'Now it's time for you to get back to work – we are ready to start…' I interrupted. 'No, Des, even before this happened I had decided to have a year off.' And that was that. I wasn't going back to Screentime again. He was stunned, I could tell, but he listened to me politely and he knew this time I was serious.

I wasn't privy to the entering of *Jessica* to the Logies but if winning the Logie or any award was important to Screentime, then they only had to ask this producer to give the award to Screentime or, better still, share the producer credits, where both would be recipients.

The phone rang. A softly spoken young lady at Ten wanted to know if I was accepting my invitation to the Logies. What invitation, I enquired. This somewhat confused her. I said I would enquire but I doubted if anyone would be prepared to fly me down from Port Douglas to Melbourne. She reiterated that an invitation

The cast and crew shot is a tradition in motion pictures and television. Here our cast and crew shot has been designed as a vintage lobby card, as Columbia were backing *Heroes' Mountain*.

had been sent. I suspected it had gone to Screentime so I emailed Des Monaghan asking what was happening and why Ten were enquiring. He emailed back that he would look into it. About two days later, Screentime rang to tell me they didn't know what was going on but were attempting to find out. By the end of the week Screentime came up with the odd explanation of what was intended to occur at the Logies, which on the surface I thought plausible at the time – the Logie organisers had decided not to have producers accepting the awards, in favour of 'personalities' receiving them on their behalf. Okay, producers are not 'personalities' and if we were to win, no doubt Sam Neill would accept on our behalf. I thought no more about it.

I happened to be in Sydney that weekend for it was a board meeting week for the FFC, on which I sat. I had drinks with Brian Rosen, our CEO, who was off to the Logies and couldn't understand why I wasn't going to be there. I am not a late-night viewer and I was staying at my friend Gary's flat at Redfern. I was thinking of going to bed when he asked if I was going to look at the Logies.

I said I would look at the opening and then retire. After the first opening round of dolly-birds strutting their stuff, the serious awards began to filter through the gloss. The first was for children's television, extremely important from my perspective. The award was announced and the producer went up to accept. I thought this strange, considering what I had been told about not being required to be present at the event. I think the next recipient was one of my peers, Curtis Levy, for documentary television. And so the evening went on and I sat transfixed as one producer after another went up to receive their Logie. Sam Neill won best actor and thanked me and Peter. *Jessica* was announced winner of the Logie for best miniseries (rightly so, I thought) 'and to accept the award, Greg Haddrick for Screentime.' I cannot remember his opening words but he finally got round to 'and I must thank the creative team...' We turned the television off. I kept relatively calm, opened the laptop and composed an email using an expletive I never use, and using it twice! It was addressed to Greg Haddrick (the fall guy), copied to Des, Bob, Sue Masters and my lawyer. Weren't moral rights involved somewhere here? I felt a lot better having exploded and went to bed and slept soundly.

At the AFI awards later that year Greg Haddrick came up to me to apologise. We had a long talk and later walked back to our respective hotels together. He had been greatly embarrassed by the whole affair. Earlier I saw Des walking towards me with that cheery hail-fellow-well-met look on his face. I did something I have never done in my life before. I looked at him and said, 'Des, I haven't anything to say to you, sorry,' and turned away from him. Well at least I said 'sorry'. I was told later in the evening he was very upset. So be it. He obviously didn't care how I felt, or have any conscience about what he had put me and my cast and crew through to get *Jessica* to the screen.

PART THREE

29

Back To The *Reel* World

'I ain't workin' for no black sheila, mate!'
Well, that's what the voice on the other end of the phone kept saying to me with many expletives thrown in for good measure. 'A black f...ing, work for some f...in' black f...in' sheila? No way mate!'

Welcome to 'beDevil'.

I had been gardening all day at 27A, my Lane Cove home, and had just come in to hear the phone ringing. A pleasant voice introduced herself. 'Oh, hi, I'm Tracey Moffatt and I have a script I am hoping you will read for me, I need a good producer and I like what you have done.' I knew Tracey's work through her wonderful short film *Night Cries*, in which she also appears. She was wondering if it would be okay to drop the script in and I said she was welcome to do so. 'I'm home all weekend.' My home had French doors which led to the garden and which, like the front door, were open all the time I was home. It seemed as though only ten minutes or so had passed when I heard a knock on the door. 'Come in,' I called, thinking it was probably a neighbour. It was Tracey, looking charming and very smartly dressed, and me looking like nothing on earth in my gardening clobber. I apologised for my appearance, which didn't seem to faze Tracey at all. I had the disturbing feeling she may have been ringing from the nearby Lane Cove shops in the hope I would be at home. There were no mobile phones in 1992. We sat in the lounge room as I listened to her tell me about the script she had just finished and the film she wanted to make. There had been films made here featuring or about Aborigines, like Charles Chauvel's *Jedda* in 1955, but none by Aborigines. Here was one ready to be made and by an Aboriginal woman. This was a breakthrough, but not destined to be an easy one.

beDevil is a compendium of three unrelated ghost stories written by Tracey, as 'fantasy' and 'factual' (or documentary) with the 'fantasy' elements in each story

The second story in Tracey Moffatt's trilogy *beDevil* is my favourite, *Choo Choo, Choo Choo*. Based on her mother's stories, who had lived at Charleville, outback Queensland, we went in search of her home beside the railway line, but no remains could be found. Here with co-producer Carol Hughes, Tracey and production designer Stephen Curtis. Despite the distance to travel, Carol made the budget work to enable Tracey to film in the actual location of her story.

being filmed entirely in the studio, and the 'factual' on location. 'Mr Chuck', the first story, is set on Bribie Island, 'Choo Choo, Choo Choo' (my favourite) in Charleville, outback Queensland, and 'Lovin' the Spin I'm In' set in the city and completely studio-bound.

After a very pleasant hour Tracey excused herself and went into the night. I'm not a Saturday night going-out person, so after an overdue shower and dinner I settled down and began to read Tracey's script – and couldn't put it down. Next morning I accepted her invitation.

The Australian Film Finance Corporation, as it was called at the time, had initiated an innovative $2.5 million film fund for one or two feature films, at this budget, per year, that were not likely to attract distributor interest but would attract first-time film directors who had established themselves with a repertoire of short drama films. *beDevil* fitted the AFFC's criteria perfectly and would also be the first Indigenous feature film. The fund was inundated each year with applications, too many by far, and regretfully gained the derogatory moniker of 'the chook raffle'.

Carol Hughes also liked the script but, along with all the other applicants, we had to come up with a budget that wouldn't exceed $2.5 million. The studio side wasn't the greatest problem to tackle, though a significant cost factor nonetheless. It was the locations required in the second story, 'Choo Choo, Choo Choo', which posed our greatest challenge. It is the story closest to Tracey's heart, based on stories told to her by her mother who lived a little way out of Charleville, a day's drive west of Brisbane. How could we possibly afford to go out there to film? Wisely our sage Carol Hughes marshalled locations manager Robin Clifton, to drive with Tracey and me from Brisbane to Charleville and to stop at various towns on the way in the hope of finding a suitable substitute for Charleville closer to Brisbane, to minimise our travel costs.

It is not until the bitumen runs out and you hit the vibrant red dirt of the unsealed roads in Australia that you realise how different that 'outback' environment is. We were about half an hour out of Charleville when we spotted the derelict white-ant-infested house to our left on the other side of the railway line that was to become the 'ghost house' of the story and the basis of Stephen Curtis's amazing production design.

To stand in the main street of Charleville makes you realise the wonder of the outback. The town has sealed roads and historic buildings dominated by the huge hotel straddling the main corner with its adjacent Victorian ballroom. Turn your head 180° and there is nothing to see except the dusty scrub plain of the channel country and the railway line disappearing into the vast distance to Quilpie.[1] The four of us stood on the corner looking at the bulk of the hotel one way and the enormity of the outback behind us. Tracey spoke first: 'We can't film here can we? – it's just going to be too expensive.' Carol quietly said, 'Let's see, I'll look at the budget when we get back.' Carol and I could see the emotional importance and significance for Tracey of being able to film in the home of her mother's stories. I knew that somehow or other Carol would find a way to enable us to come back to Charleville to film. That afternoon we drove out of town beside the railway line to try and find the stumps of the railway fettlers' homes and Tracey's mother's house. We searched in vain.

We repaired to the cool vastness of the nearly empty public bar of Charleville Hotel. We were just settling down to enjoy our long-awaited cold beers when a voice said, 'You must be the fillum people?' Word travels fast in the outback. Standing behind us with his female companion was a short, stocky man with the biggest ten-gallon black hat on I had ever seen. I assured him we were 'the filllum

---

1   At the time the train still ran to Quilpie but now terminates at Charleville.

people'. 'Ah! youse wouldn't know about the fillum made about me father out here,' said the stockman. For once in my life my brain clicked in immediately. 'You must be Tom Kruse's son. Hi, I'm Tony.' He was dumbfounded. 'Yeah, how do youse know?' 'Your father is the hero who drives the mail truck from Birdsville to Maree in *The Back of Beyond*.'[2] Well, we had friends for life. I can't remember his name but he had driven in from Birdsville that day to take his wife to hospital. The film crew were most definitely okayed by the good folk of Charleville.

Back in Sydney our application for funding had been shortlisted and Tracey, Carol and I had to face the assessment panel. John Morris, the CEO of the AFFC, and Catriona Hughes were extremely sympathetic to the project and handled their questioning very well, though I knew they were extremely sceptical about the film's commercial prospects. I argued for the chance for the first feature to be made in Australia by an Indigenous person and, important I felt, an Indigenous woman telling the stories of her people. Certainly *Night Cries* and *Nice Coloured Girls* would guarantee *beDevil* would be something different and very special. Funding was approved and we were on our way.

The Mentmore studio, a single stage with production office facilities upstairs, was found in Alexandria, an inner Sydney industrial suburb, which was affordable. The only problem was that the set of the ghost house for 'Choo Choo, Choo Choo' was somewhat bigger than expected and at one point jutted out of the studio doors. There wasn't a lot of room for lighting or the camera trucks. We were very fortunate in obtaining one of our legends of cinematography – Geoff Burton ACS liked the whole concept of the project and gave enormous support to Tracey. Unfortunately not so his crew who at first displayed those stereotyped sexist attitudes towards Tracey and these had to be nipped in the bud. I had not been confronted with such a situation before and called Geoff up to my office one morning between set-ups. He wasn't pleased to hear of our observations for he himself had not been aware. This was fair enough as Geoff was lighting cameraman and operator, a full-on task on such a set. He listened and reassured me he would talk to his boys. Things improved almost straight away. It doesn't matter whether you are black or white, it is still a tough world for women out there in any of the professions, no matter how progressive we think we have become in our attitudes.

What we weren't prepared for was the attitude of most of the Indigenous males to black women when the woman is in charge. To these men no woman can be boss. This we learnt very quickly was anathema to those black males who answered

2   *The Back of Beyond* was produced and directed by John Heyer for the Shell Film Unit and won the Grand Prix at Venice in 1954. It is an Australian classic.

our call for attachments to the production. When told the writer/director was a woman, and Indigenous, they became very hostile. The telephone conversation at the beginning of this chapter was typical of those few males who applied. Tracey was hoping for a broad range of attachments across the production to give Indigenous people an opportunity to gain experience in their respective fields. The result I think was eight women and one man engaged as attachments. We aren't allowed to substitute professional crew with attachments so those lucky to have been given placements learnt from the professionals in whichever department they had either requested or had been seconded to. Our learning curve never stops.

The 'look' Geoff Burton was to give to the film quickly became apparent and evening rushes were eagerly anticipated by everybody on the picture. Then came the challenge of the 'factual' look when we went on location, and this contrast worked extremely well.

Charleville became a reality through the will of everyone concerned wanting it to happen. Geoff said he could film on his own with some small lights; P.J. Voeten, our first assistant director, took on the roles of 1st, 2nd and 3rd! Carol and Robin provided and ran the catering shuttle each day, and so on. With a small cast and crew of just fifteen people the location filming for 'Choo Choo, Choo Choo' was achieved with enormous success. It was an achievement of which everyone deserved to be proud. Likewise in the editing department where film editor Wayne Le Clos and his capable assistant Wayne Hayes were preparing the first cut of the picture for Tracey's return. As with Geoff Burton's astute and sympathetic eye to the 'look' of the film, Wayne Le Clos was bringing that other 'eye' to the rhythms and pace of the picture. The editing was an extremely happy experience for all of us. Then there was the added dimension composer Carl Vine brought to the film, which would have been a challenge for any composer. Carl sensed from the very beginning where Tracey was coming from with her three individual stories and yet managed to bring a cohesion to the whole film with his contemporary and classic film score.

With our film *Bliss* having been invited into the official competition at the Cannes Film Festival in 1985, the selection panel were curious to see *beDevil*. This is the world's most highly competitive film festival and to be chosen to participate in 'official selection' is no mean feat. We kept our fingers crossed nonetheless. We were in the middle of the final mix of the film with Peter Fenton and Ron Purvis at Atlab when we received the news that *beDevil* had been invited into 'Un Certain Regard'. The invitation was gratefully accepted!

Though Cannes is important to any film, whether it be in the official competition as we were, or Directors Fortnight, the highly regarded and respected 'side bar'

One of our finds beside the railway line coming into Charleville was the white-ant-riddled home which became the basis for Stephen Curtis' stunning studio design. The ant hills were a feature of his landscape.

event, or the plain cutthroat good old-fashioned marketplace (Marché du Film), it is imperative to be in attendance to back up your film and your sales agent, if hopefully you have one. None of this fazed Tracey at all as she told journalist Sandie Don: 'Cannes is a crazy circus. It's very trashy. It pretends it's not, but it is a big market, disguised as something arty. I actually preferred the Toronto Film Festival. I got a great reception and a good Q&A after the screenings.' Tracey's observations are spot on. The film's debut in 'Un Certain Regard' gained it serious attention, with invitations to the Toronto, London, Vancouver and San Francisco film festivals.

The London press is particularly important to any film being presented at Cannes, for any positive press can assist the launch of the film at home and the task ahead for the sales agent. And *The Guardian* is no exception. With critics of the calibre of Derek Malcolm and Jonathan Romney, one sits up and takes notice. On the paper's arts page under the heading CINEMA OF THE ABSURD – FESTIVAL FAVOURITES; THE GUARDIAN'S JURY DELIVER THEIR VERDICT, Jonathan Romney observed thus: 'The award for provocative strangeness goes to *beDevil* by the Australian director Tracey Moffatt. Ostensibly a set of three ghost stories, *beDevil* threw narrative caution to the wind, and gave us a discordant, elliptical series of lurid dream images, luscious, stylised decors and Aboriginal myth. Everything in it was strangely evocative, but nothing quite made sense or took you where it promised. *beDevil* was much derided, but Moffatt has a vision of her own – however loopy and hermetic – and will definitely be a name to watch. Messy perhaps, but truly Martian cinema.'

Before Cannes, maverick local distributor Andrew Pike, head of his company Ronin Films, had viewed an answer print and had fallen in love with the film. He felt exposure at the Sydney Film Festival in June, a month after Cannes, would be helpful.

Now the Sydney Film Festival is the bane of this producer's life. In 1993 the Festival was held exclusively in the 2,200 seat State Picture Palace, so if the audience liked the film it was certain to get good 'word of mouth', but if they hated it then the film was certain death at the box office on its release. In recent years the Festival has wisely diversified and spread out to several smaller venues, as well as the vast State, giving 'difficult' films more of a chance. Tracey refused to do the customary walk onto the stage to discuss her work, as she later explained to Anabel Dean of *The Sydney Morning Herald:* 'You usually get really weird questions and I just wasn't in the mood for it. I found North American audiences far more open … the Europeans [at the Cannes Film Festival] are sort of closed off to art films in a way – they've done it – and now other people are doing it – but the Americans are so swamped with Hollywood they're hungry for alternatives.'

Ronin Films prepared for an October opening for the film, four months after its launch at the Sydney Film Festival, five months after Cannes but two weeks before its London opening. Ronin created a strong and effective campaign for the launch of the film at their Academy Twin at the top of Sydney's Oxford Street, at their Walker Cinema, a tiny arthouse survivor in the business heart of North Sydney across the harbour, and Melbourne's prestigious Nova. That 'truly Martian cinema' line from *The Guardian* appeared strongly at the top of the display advertising, along with 'One of the most visually striking films from Australia or anywhere else in recent years ... Brazenly original'. *Sydney Morning Herald*, 'One of the boldest, most visually intriguing films. *Who Weekly*, 'Bright, original and bizarre.' And 'A dazzling tapestry ... distinctly different from any other Australian feature to date.' David Stratton, *Variety*.

But a strangely prophetic observation was made by Sean Slavin at the conclusion of his brief but positive review giving the film four stars. After praising Carl Vine's expressive score, Slavin continues, 'Forget about everything you would normally expect from this genre and you will start to see some of the possibilities of this extraordinary film. It opens up questions about landscape and time as well as slyly subverting the cinema itself. This is a very significant Australian film unlike any local product we've seen before. *For this difference I wouldn't be surprised if it's politely ignored initially.*' [my emphasis]

With positive reviews, strong display advertising, an impressive 'front of house', we still decided against a gala premiere and went for a 'soft' opening. You certainly knew the film was on. But nobody came. Oh, about a dozen on opening night, which included loyal cast members and crew. A stoic Andrew Pike put a brave spin on it, saying it was as a result of Thursday late-night shopping. We both stood there alone in the foyer knowing the night was not a good omen. Worse was to come. The Australian Film Institute Awards (AFI) nominations were announced and absolutely no mention in any category of *beDevil*. Lynden Barber in *The Sydney Morning Herald*, lamenting many other omissions in the AFI nominations, noting the omission of Bob Ellis's *Nostradamus Kid* which Geoff Burton also photographed, observed, 'Yet to punish one of this country's leading cinematographers, Geoff Burton, for his stylish work on the film seems not just unfair but perverse. Burton has drawn a double blank this year. Tracey Moffatt's experimental *beDevil* may be annoyingly flawed but it would be ridiculous to deny the power of Burton's camera work or Stephen Curtis's production design (it was filmed mostly on stylised indoor sets). Yet both, incredibly, were left out of the final poll.' If Lynden was left incredulous, David Stratton, God bless him, was totally outraged! In a full length of the page in the broadsheet *The Australian* arts page under the heading AFI JURIES OFF KEY IN THE PIANO'S YEAR, David questioned every aspect of that year's nominations in a year he described as '... a year of fine Australian films, one of the best years ever, but I would have thought the AFI preselection juries (which consist of professional film practitioners making decisions in their own area of expertise) would have noted the astonishing production design, the splendid music and the glowing cinematography, if not Moffatt's striking vision.'

Ronin kept the film on for a few weeks but finally had to announce 'Last Days'. The accolades from Cannes, London, Toronto, Vancouver, Lynden Barber and David Stratton and others had very little effect. The audiences stayed away.

If *The Night The Prowler* and *beDevil* were ten years ahead of their time, wait till you discover the film that came ten years too late!

30

On Their Selection
– The $24,000 Lunch!

The night of Friday, January 4, 1980, should be indelibly stored in my memory bank, for it was to become a fateful night indeed. It was the night I attended the Nimrod Theatre in Sydney's Belvoir Street to see George Whaley's highly praised and commercially successful production of Steele Rudd's *On Our Selection*. George had created the production at NIDA[1] in 1979 with his young protégé Mel Gibson playing the role of Sandy in this classic play, which in its original form first appeared at Sydney's Palace Theatre in 1912.

It wasn't the sparkling freshness of the new production that caught my attention as much as the incredibly positive audience reaction to it. There were the regular Nimrod subscribers of course, but the place was packed with young people who were obviously not your regular theatregoer and were enjoying every bit of this genuine period Australian comedy, so much so seasons were being extended wherever the play was performed. George Whaley had gone one better though than just putting on a revival. He had gone back to Steele Rudd's original stories and characters for this adaptation. The thought of a new film version for the 1980s had me intrigued and subsequently was to become probably the longest gestation period for any Australian film in history!

Steele Rudd was born Arthur Hoey Davis at Drayton, near Toowoomba, Queensland, on November 14, 1868. He was the eighth child of thirteen. His father was Thomas Davis, a Welsh blacksmith, and his mother was Irish. Brought up on his father's 'selection,'[2] he left school at the age of twelve to work on a pastoral

---

1   National Institute of Dramatic Art
2   The squattocracy of Australia, mainly upper middle class English, established themselves in the early 1800s by taking up vast tracts of crown land. By the 1860s, with an increasing number of unemployed gold diggers, the colony of New South Wales implemented radical land reforms, encouraging people to

station. He joined the public service in Brisbane when he was eighteen, at which time he took up rowing as a recreational activity. Davis began writing a weekly column for the local paper about rowing, using the pseudonym Steele Rudd, 'Steele' after the famous essayist and 'Rudd' an abbreviation of the word 'rudder'. As Steele Rudd, Davis sent a short story, or sketch, to the Sydney *Bulletin,* which was published on April 6, 1895, and subsequently became the first chapter of his collection of 'sketches', *On Our Selection*, published in 1899. Initially selling over 20,000 copies, it eventually went on to sell over a quarter of a million copies in the next thirty years. Between 1899 and 1916 Rudd was to write five 'Selection' books, all of which were enormously successful. In 1907, playwright and later successful filmmaker, Beaumont Smith, bought the rights to *On Our Selection* to dramatise into a theatrical production. Entitled *In Australia*, it was a disaster and Steele Rudd withdrew his support for the play. Smith was to later plagiarise Rudd's *Selection* stories in a series of silent films and one talkie, under the moniker *The Hayseeds*.

New Zealand actor Bert Bailey, with his fellow actor Edmund Duggan, had had success with their play *The Squatter's Daughter*, and bought Beaumont's script and revised it, caricaturing all of Rudd's characters. A copyright dispute erupted between Bailey and Rudd, and Bailey and Duggan went ahead forming the Bert Bailey Dramatic Company to launch their own version of *On Our Selection*. Though the play bore very little resemblance to the originality of Rudd's characters and stories, it became a huge success, touring the country continuously from 1912 to 1929.

In 1919 theatrical entrepreneur and film producer E.J. Carroll bought the film rights to *On Our Selection* from Steele Rudd for the princely sum of £500 for his imported American director, Wilfred Lucas, to direct. Lucas felt uncomfortable with such an intrinsically Australian story and wisely declined Carroll's invitation. Carroll turned to Raymond Longford, who by now had established himself as Australia's premier film director with his early films for Cozens Spencer and his recent success, *The Sentimental Bloke*, and its sequel *Ginger Mick*. Longford rejected out of hand using Bailey and Duggan's play and went back to Steele Rudd's original work, retaining the episodic structure of Rudd's stories. Thus Longford's version preserved the authenticity of Rudd's characters and the Australian bush in which they toiled. Writing in *The Picture Show*, April 1, 1921, Longford said: 'I'm making an Australian picture and I want the people in it to be real Australians. Now, your average Australian is about the most casual person under the sun; so if I put the players through their parts over and over again, worrying them, striving to perfect

'select' a small land holding, a 'selection', on crown land, sometimes land already allocated to the squatters. This was in turn to cause disputes between the 'Selectors' and the 'Squatters', the latter calling the former 'cockatoo farmers' or 'cow cockies' because the 'Selectors' scratched the earth for a living.

them, they might do good work but they wouldn't look like Australians. They'd be actors, perfectly conscious that they were acting. My way is to let them know the action I want and allow them to go right ahead with it. For a picture like *On Our Selection* in which it is absolutely necessary that the characters look natural, I think that's the best course.'[3] Thankfully much of Longford's 1920 version survives and one can 'feel' the Rudd characters when watching it.

Bailey, however, was not to be deterred and paid Steele Rudd £620 in 1925 for the exclusive rights to make films of all of Rudd's stories, and buying out Beaumont Smith's share of copyright in the stage version in 1930. Despite having done this, Bailey and Duggan's play was the basis of Ken G. Hall's 1932 talkie. *On Our Selection* opened at Sydney's Capitol in August 1932, where it ran for six weeks! The *Capitol* was a massive 3,000 seater, 'atmospheric' picture palace, operating on a weekly change of program. The film became a massive success wherever it played. Hall made a total of four *Dad & Dave* comedies, all champions at the box office.

How would this perennial Australian classic transfer to the screen in 1980? Judging by the audience reaction to the stage production, and the number of young people finding something in it to relate to, I felt it had a chance. George Whaley was intrigued with the idea but we had other things to do. Looking back, the 1980s were a very busy time for both of us, with much of the time being taken up with the development and making of *The Harp in the South* and *Poor Man's Orange*. However, the thought of a new version of Rudd's classic was never far from my mind. During this time George and I commissioned a writer to do a first draft screenplay and another writer submitted an unsolicited script. Neither were anywhere near capturing the spirit of the original stories so George sat down to prepare a screenplay. Like Longford, George chose to work from Steele Rudd's original stories.

We submitted an application to the Australian Film Commission to develop the script and were successful.

George and I thought it might be a good idea to consult with Ken G. Hall about the film, for his version in 1932 had been hugely successful. We met with him at his Mosman home and the meeting was to prove a grave mistake. Hall was totally possessive about his version and was adamant that we had to use the Bailey-Duggan play that he adapted for his version. The meeting became very heated when George pointed out that the play bore very little resemblance to

---

3 Strangely, after all these years, reading Longford's piece in *The Picture Show* I can actually *hear* his voice, for it was exactly how he spoke to me at our afternoon teas at Gilles Street, Wollstonecraft, in 1956 (chapter two).

the original Steele Rudd characters and stories and in fact had become, in Hall's version and likewise in George Edwards' radio serial, caricatures. Hall exploded, confessing he had never read Steele Rudd. We were horrified at his admission and sought our leave. It was an extremely sad encounter with the ageing pioneer.

George and I were excited by the suggestion of Leo McKern to play Dad Rudd. I had first met Leo in 1970 when he recorded the narration for my film on the life of Frank Hurley, *Snow, Sand & Savages*. Leo wouldn't fly, always travelling the world on freighter/passenger ships (the latter a hobby I had also taken up many years before). I flew to Cairns where I met local radio personality Ian Coughlan[4] who recorded Leo's dulcet tones. Later in the eighties I was to fly to London to record Leo again, narrating the commentary for Part 3 of Film Australia's series about Australian cinema, *Now You're Talking*. So access to Leo was easy. We had stayed in touch through the years. He was delighted with the prospect of playing Dad if we could get the show off the ground.

Who to play Mum? Enter supremo of casting, Susie Maizels. She came up with many names of note in the film and stage world who would have adequately played the role but were no match for Leo's commanding screen presence. Susie rang. 'Darling, Leo is the ubiquitous Australian – larger than life – so is Joan Sutherland.' Susie describes the silence from my end of the phone as deafening. 'Dame Joan Sutherland?' I stupidly enquired. I thought about it. George Whaley's reaction when I rang him was one of incredulity. More so when he realised I was seriously contemplating making an approach to Dame Joan. 'Do you think she could do it?' I asked George. He rang back later. 'I think Susie is on to something here. Why don't we give it a go?' I made contact with Richard Bonynge and he agreed to see George and me at their apartment at Potts Point. It was a very agreeable meeting. Richard was quite taken with the proposal but cautioned that Joan would take a bit of convincing. However, he would do his best on our behalf. Richard was on his way back to Switzerland shortly and would present the idea to her when he arrived. It was August 31, 1989. It would not be till November 18, 1993, that we would get a decision from Joan.

George worked continually on the script and it finally went off to Richard Hatton, Leo's agent, on May 7, 1990[5] and Dame Joan a little later. By this time,

---

4   Ian Coughlan was to become a lifelong friend until his untimely death at the age of fifty-three from cancer whilst I was filming *Heroes' Mountain*. I took a weekend off from the shoot and with Damien Parer flew to see Ian in Calvary Hospital, Cairns. I was very glad we did, for a week later Ian was dead, the week of his birthday. Ian had become a successful screen writer and director, notably *Alison's Birthday* and his unproduced thriller *Bloodstream* (*The Reach*).

5   I mention dates specifically in case a prospective producer may be reading this tome, to indicate how long the process can be in getting a picture off the ground.

though, Joan had already indicated through Richard that she thought it not a very good idea – not the film, her good self playing Mum Rudd. Would she agree to meet with us to discuss further? Richard rang and George and I were summoned to an afternoon tea with them both. A more relaxed couple one couldn't wish to meet and it was clear Richard was backing us all the way. Joan served the afternoon tea with grace and style, telling us at the same time she thought the whole idea a bit of a joke. Here George Whaley came into his element as only a good director of theatre could. Talk about the gift of the gab! I could sense Her Ladyship wavering, but only slightly, mind you. Joan assured us she would give it further consideration but not to expect a quick decision. We assured her we weren't in a hurry.

I went to see John Morris, CEO of the Australian Film Finance Corporation, to discuss what the organisation expected us to deliver to the table. Our budget was about $5 million, which was a big ask for the time. John advised we would have to bring nothing less than $2 million to the table, which for us was also a big ask. He further said that we would have to have a local distributor attached.

It was the evening of August 22, 1991, at Seaworld on the Gold Coast where Ronin Films staged a spectacular show to launch to Australian exhibitors their newly acquired film for 1992, *Strictly Ballroom*. The Australian Movie Convention is held every August on the Gold Coast by the Motion Picture Exhibitors of Queensland. I am one of the few producers who have attended the convention for nearly twenty years. I figure that if I am making movies for an audience, then it's wise to eavesdrop on the exhibitors to ascertain their moods and reactions to the films previewed at the convention, for if anyone knows their audience, it's the independent exhibitor. I had met Andrew Pike, the founder of Ronin Films previously, but on this occasion he asked me what I was planning, knowing that I had segued into miniseries to survive the slump in feature production. Ronin's *Strictly Ballroom* was instrumental in bringing the feature production industry out of its slump in 1992, followed by *The Adventures of Priscilla, Queen of the Desert* and *Muriel's Wedding*. I told Andrew of my desire to make *On Our Selection*. He warmed to the idea immediately and committed to be the film's distributor. Andrew's strategy was to play Queensland first, then move into the other states, only playing selected cinemas in the capital cities. Suddenly we had a distributor with not only a strategy but enthusiasm for the project as well. All we needed now was the money!

I had been appointed to the committee to organise the celebrations for the Centenary of Cinema in 1995/96. What better subject than *On Our Selection* to launch the centenary.

(Top) Joan Sutherland (Mum Rudd) and Leo McKern (Dad Rudd).

(Middle) One of the few bright and sunny days on our location.

(Bottom) As with *The Irishman*, nearly twenty years before in Charters Towers, the main street of Braidwood NSW was dirt covered for period authenticity. Director George Whaley with David Field, whilst camera operator David Williamson lines up the shot.

Ideally George Whaley saw Mel Gibson playing Dave in the film but Mel's career had taken off and he and his business partner, Bruce Davey, had established their own production and distribution company, Icon. Would, perchance, Icon be interested in *On Our Selection*? Bruce Davey was also George's accountant! So we saw no harm in approaching Bruce re the possibility of Icon's involvement. Bruce was receptive to the idea and suggested we meet with Mel and himself when we had a budget together, script and casting preferences to discuss, and further suggested George and I should meet with them in London.

The development of the screenplay had moved quickly. Enter composer Peter Best. Though a comedy and definitely not a musical, the script had been written to include songs, bringing a unique approach to the dramatisation of Rudd's stories. There could not have been a better choice than Peter Best. I had first encountered Best's work in a film I had nothing to do with[6] when I had been invited to the answer print screening of Igor Auzins' *We of the Never Never* (1982). I walked out of the theatre in Double Bay, Sydney, to run into the film's mixer, Phil Judd. 'Who did the music?' I asked Phil. 'Peter Best – isn't it terrific!' It certainly was. The film was very impressive on every level but Best's score lifted the entire work to a much higher plane. It was to be three years before I was to meet Peter when Ray Lawrence said he would like him to score *Bliss*. 'Ah, the man who scored *We of the Never Never*,' I said. I had not been aware that Peter was also Australia's top TV commercials composer. I think the best score for motion pictures is *Bliss* and thereafter he wrote the scores for our miniseries *The Harp in the South, Poor Man's Orange, The Heroes, Heroes II – The Return*, and gave very special attention to the series *Man on the Rim*. So I felt very confident of his involvement with *On Our Selection*.

Crunch time had come. Leo McKern thought casting Dame Joan ingenious, maybe he could convince her? We submitted the script to the Australian Film Commission (who had funded the initial development) for funds to go to London to put the deal in place with Bruce Davey, and to take Leo and Joan to lunch to see if he could convince the Dame to say 'yes'. With our application, we submitted an

---

6   Not quite true. Hoyts had picked up *We of the Never Never* for distribution and then CEO Terry Jackman organised a world premiere in Canberra with Prime Minister Malcolm Fraser in attendance, and to which I had been invited. At one point in the film the audience became restless. The film was too long. When the lights went up, Jackman spotted me. 'Buckley, I need to take twenty minutes out of this film before we open on Friday – you're our man.' I protested and pointed out that I had nothing to do with the film and that it was Wednesday! I am not aware of what transpired with the film's producers, but I was available and I was hired. There were two places where a sub-plot could be deleted from the prints. So with a bottle of Indian ink to bloop out the sound on the splices, I physically cut all six prints, deleting approximately twenty-two minutes. However, there were actors only in the sub-plot who went to see the film and never saw themselves.

American view of the script from noted film writer and historian, Arthur Knight, who was visiting Australia at the time: 'Both Rudd and Whaley view their rustics not merely with an eye to their humour (and some of their doings are genuinely funny), but with a warm sympathy and admiration for their efforts to wrest a living from the unyielding soil. In any case, what emerges is considerably more than a cornball comedy. It's like an affectionate look back to the Australia of a century ago – or, what is more important, an affectionate look back to Australia as most Australians would like to imagine it was a century ago ...'

We need not have worried, for the AFC's own assessor sent the following to our project officer at the AFC, Richard Brennan. In part: '... Give Tony Buckley the money – I want to see this film with Leo and Dame Joan – it has the potential of becoming an Australian classic.' The assessor was none other than Brian Rosen, later to become CEO of the Film Finance Corporation.

George and I left for London on Saturday, November 13, having spent the previous week locking down appointments to see Bruce and Mel, Leo and Joan. We awoke the morning after arrival to find it had been snowing during the night. We were staying at the Grosvenor House Hotel on Park Lane, though the grand entrance is actually around the back. It's a great old pile, centrally convenient, and has (or had) wonderfully big baths with their original plumbing. My phone rang. It was George. 'I'm just checking to see if you're still with us,' he chortled, 'I've just read Anthony Buckley's obituary in *The Daily Telegraph*. I'll see you at breakfast then,' the hilarity in his voice barely disguisable.

I went to my door and retrieved my copy of London's most conservative of newspapers. Sure enough, there was Anthony Buckley's obit. Thankfully it was the sometimes Royal photographer, whose studio it turned out was a short walk from the hotel. So through the snow we trudged after breakfast to photograph the 'scene of the crime'.

Our first appointment was 2pm Monday with Bruce and Mel at their hotel. We were both made very welcome and George, who hadn't seen Mel for a very long time, adjourned with him to catch up and talk about the creative side of the picture. Meanwhile Bruce and I sat down to talk through the business and financing side of structuring a deal. He didn't seem to be fazed at all that I was seeking $2 million investment, as I could assure him of a $3.2 million commitment from the FFC. It was a very agreeable meeting and the upshot of it obviously was dependent on our lead casting. They both farewelled us, wishing George and me luck for our luncheon the following Thursday with Joan and Leo.

On the Tuesday George and I met with Leo's long-time agent and confidant, Richard Hatton. The money we were offering was acceptable and Richard was enthusiastic about the script, which he found 'delightful'. Wednesday we caught up with my old friend Graham Benson for a splendid luncheon at BAFTA in Piccadilly. That night George and I saw the National Theatre Company's superb production of *Carousel* at the Shaftesbury. The previous evening we had had a 'royal' box to ourselves, practically on the stage of Her Majesty's in the Haymarket, to see our own 'star', Simon Burke, in *The Phantom of the Opera*. We both felt very proud for Simon and repaired to Joe Allens in Covent Garden for supper, a venerable late night oasis, where Simon was obviously known and got a welcoming ovation as he descended the stairs ahead of us. Around the time, just up the road from where Simon was playing in *Phantom*, Jason Donovan was at the Palladium playing the lead in *Joseph and the Amazing Technicolor Dreamcoat*, and further along in Tottenham Court Road at the *Dominion*, Craig McLachlan was wowing them in *Grease*. At home, though, I doubt if anyone was aware of this trio's stunning success. It's moments like these that relieve the tensions of travelling on business. I describe the days as very often being long and dark, and the nights short and light.

By late Wednesday we were becoming decidedly nervous and apprehensive about our Thursday rendezvous. I had sought advice as to the best restaurant to book, for not only the food but for privacy, and for Joan and Leo to meet us at the hotel beforehand. Now Leo had a resonant, booming voice at the best of times, made even more so by his deafness. They both arrived early and the concierge rang to alert me. All George and I could hear as we exited the lift was Leo's booming voice and Dame Joan echoing across the hotel foyer. We found them both in the lounge off the foyer, getting on like a house on fire. The restaurant, as it turned out, was just around the corner from the hotel in Mayfair, though I didn't know this when I called for the cab. Judging by the look on the cab driver's face, recognising our 'royal' guests, he figured we weren't going to walk, and cheerfully drove us around the block for a fiver!

We were greeted grandly by the maître d' and shown to a spacious table in the centre of the restaurant. Beautifully set and sensibly separated from the other tables, fully booked with diners, who all came to a halt eating their meals or looking at their menus upon our arrival. So much for privacy! I don't remember George or I getting much of a word in for quite some time, as Leo boisterously entertained Dame Joan – and the rest of the restaurant – with the occasional ribald story. The meal was superb and the attention of the waiters exemplary. Coffees were ordered. Joan looked at Leo and said, 'So you think I should do it?' Leo lowered his voice and assured her, 'Yes!' She looked at George. 'And you, George, think I can do it?' and before George could reply she continued, 'Well then, I'll do it!'

I called their cabs, we bade them farewell and George and I walked back to the hotel and repaired to its lounge for a stiff drink. Graham Benson hosted a celebratory lunch for us on the Sunday, with special guest Verity Lambert, at Graham and Christine's splendid home in Larkhall Rise at Clapham, before we departed for the airport. Two twenty-six hour plane trips, and a week in London, for lunch! Or as long-time friend and colleague Damien Parer was to exclaim, 'Cripes, $24,000 for lunch!' That journey to secure Dame Joan and Leo has been known as the $24,000 lunch ever since.

Back at home everything wasn't all that rosy. Although there were only two investors – Icon and the FFC – negotiations over contractual procedures between my solicitor, Paula Paizes, Icon's solicitors and Catriona Hughes at the FFC, were to continue from March to September and were becoming uglier. Enter Jonathan Shteinman, my executive producer and later my co-producer till now, one of the wiser and better decisions of my career. Shteinman took on Catriona Hughes at 'howitzer' level, who retorted with her own 'rocket launcher' attacks, but Shteinman was thankfully to win the protracted battle that ensued. But another missile had been fired from across the Pacific and when it landed was to devastate me and subsequently, though not realised at the time, the future of the film's success. It was afternoon in LA when it was fired, next morning here. Bruce Davey on his mobile from his car: 'We are changing distributors, I have just spoken with Greg Coote and Roadshow will be taking the film on as distributor.' I was dumbfounded. Long before Ronin Films and Andrew Pike came on board, Alan Finney, head of Roadshow's distribution arm, had rejected the script as not one for Roadshow, and Alan had expressed the strong opinion there was no market for *On Our Selection*. I protested to Bruce and pointed this out as a recipe for disaster. Now Bruce Davey, with whom I do get on quite well and have got to know him over the years, has a forthright way of saying things and a manner of using expletives I had not quite heard the like of before. 'It's either Roadshow or no Icon.' Click went the phone. I sat devastated. I had a distributor with an excellent strategy for the release of the picture and now I was being told to take a distributor who didn't want the film and whom I didn't need and – didn't want! I regard Greg Coote as a friend, and along with Graham Burke, father of *Caddie*. I rang Greg in LA. Mistake number one. Greg assured me Roadshow would do the right thing by the film and Alan Finney 'would have to take it'. I knew Greg and Bruce to be good friends. Phone call number three. Bruce back on the phone to blast me off the face of the earth for having interfered with his company's affairs by ringing Greg. I was not to make contact with Greg again. Click went the phone. Though my day was already ruined, I had two immediate tasks at hand. The first to break the devastating news to Andrew Pike, the second to contact Finney in Melbourne.

Ringing Andrew Pike is still one of the worst phone calls I have ever had to make. Andrew was taken aback and extremely disappointed with the news. He took it on the chin and magnanimously wished me well. I later wrote to him to confirm my distress and disappointment too. We have remained friends all these years.

There was no point in beating around the bush. I wrote to Alan Finney that afternoon advising him he was getting a film he didn't want and likewise I was getting a distributor I didn't want. We had better talk about it. He telephoned telling me not to worry. He didn't seem at all fazed and I suggested I fly to Melbourne to sort the whole ugly mess out and whether we both liked it or not, we had to work together for the next two years to make the film a success. He agreed and assured me of his support.

Meanwhile Catriona Hughes and Jonathan Shteinman continued to scream at each other, with Icon's solicitor Craig Emmanuel apologising to all parties continuously, and my own solicitor, Paula Paizes, retreating in defeat.

A loan of $300,000 had to be obtained from the Australian Film Commission to guarantee commencement of pre-production whilst we waited for the Production Investment Agreement (PIA) to be signed, and to pay for Leo McKern's and Dame Joan's air fares to Sydney.[7] I offered my house at Lane Cove as security but the AFC's head of development and long-time colleague, Tim Read, refused to allow this and offered the loan guarantee against the picture. These were very tense weeks and Tim was doing everything to ease that stress and the load being placed on me and the picture.

The PIA was finally signed. Everyone had stopped screaming at each other, though I knew the FFC, and in particular their chair Chris Lovell, were uncomfortable about their investment. Chris made it clear to me on more than one occasion that 'the film doesn't stand a chance'. Makes one feel good when one is about to start production.

I had wanted to surround George Whaley with the very best people, as we had done with *The Harp in the South* and *Poor Man's Orange*, but even here I was thwarted by other events. We had both wanted Peter James, ACS, ASC, to be director of photography, primarily because of the 'look' he gave to Donald Crombie's *The Irishman*. Peter accepted the invitation and asked for David Williamson as

7   Passenger-carrying tankers and freighter ships were becoming harder to find and Leo had had to become accustomed to flying to Australia. He could fly, provided he was comotosed with a prescription drug. Even then he and his wife Jane would only go as far as Darwin, and drive the rest of the way.

operator. This presented no problem for us as he had been on *Caddie* and *The Irishman* and was operator for Paul Murphy and George on *Harp* and *Poor Man's Orange*. It was only weeks before pre-production when Peter rang me from LA to say he was sorry but he and director Bruce Beresford were on a hold to film *The Bridges of Madison County* and as a result, our dates would clash. Peter had shot most of Bruce's pictures to date, including *Driving Miss Daisy* and *Black Robe*, so I understood the dilemma our respective pictures' dates caused him. I queried whether *Bridges* was actually confirmed. It wasn't but it was 'very likely'. I had to let Peter go.[8] We were now in a difficult situation with most DOPs contracted for the rest of the year. Fortunately Martin McGrath, a very capable DOP, was available and willing to take our film on at short notice.

In the meantime, while I was coping with the dramas associated with financing, distribution and finding a DOP, George Whaley was diligently working away honing his script and working in liaison with composer Peter Best on the music and songs. I sensed an unease at the time between composer and director and couldn't put my finger on it. I was preoccupied elsewhere and Peter assured me everything was fine. I know I had to remind them at one stage that the film wasn't a 'musical', which I knew hadn't gone down very well with either of them. Peter was also working to an unrealistically low budget, which didn't help matters.

Steele Rudd's stories are set on the Darling Downs of South Queensland, centred around the town of Nobby. We surveyed the entire area hoping for authenticity's sake to find our locations there. None suitable were to be found and it also became clear that such a move from Sydney to the Downs was going to be too expensive for our budget. An area near Braidwood in New South Wales, not far from Canberra, was found to build the Rudd family's 'selection' and the town lent itself beautifully to the period of the late 1890s and had the added plus of ample accommodation for our cast and crew. In fact the politics of this area in the 1890s was no different from where Steele Rudd had set his stories. Though Braidwood had a Station Street and a stationmaster's cottage and Railway Street, the railway never came, going instead to the town of Bungendore a few miles further down the track.

George and casting director Susie Maizels had put together a marvellous ensemble cast, a wonderful balance of our known thespians and two refreshing newcomers – Essie Davis and Murray Bartlett. Geoffrey Rush, as George had earlier predicted, was absolutely right as Dave Rudd; David Field as Dan; Celia Ireland, Sarah; Noah Taylor, Joe; Nicholas Eadie as Cyril Riley; and last but

---

8   Regretfully neither Peter nor Bruce were to be engaged to do *The Bridges of Madison County*, the picture being taken over by Clint Eastwood.

certainly not least Robert Menzies as 'Cranky Jack' – 'It's me father, it's me father', a hilarious scene where every time Cranky Jack looks in a mirror he only sees his father. It is a classic piece in both our film and the 1932 version by Ken G. Hall.

In Braidwood production designer Herbert Pinter designed and built the entire 'selection', bark hut, the farmhouse, the dam, the paddocks with their post and rail authentic fencing, and the cemetery! Roger Kirk was wardrobe designer, having a field day with the period. Though Peter James was unable to shoot our picture we stayed with the Agfa stock we had ordered to contribute to the 'look' of the picture. We had first used Agfa/Geva stock in 1977 for *The Irishman* with superb results.

If you want to break a drought, bring a film crew to town. We did our first location survey in the January, a second in July and our final in August. No rain all year. We opened for business on September 19 to prepare for our forty-two day shoot. In the weeks between then and December we had three hail storms, two snow flurries (we are approaching the Australian summer), a few gale force winds and, to top it off, a day of complete fog. We had two weeks rehearsal but George Whaley, accustomed to his background in live theatre, would have preferred four weeks. Such luxuries are not allowed for in Australian budgets. Despite the hazards of unpredictable weather, the shoot got underway, even though the grass in the paddocks had to be sprayed brown to simulate our Queensland drought conditions.

Rushes were good, though we had to look at them on video, which is not good with a big widescreen motion picture. Despite always being together in the evening to view rushes, I felt communication between the director and myself wasn't all it should be. I had the impression the George Whaley directing *On Our Selection* wasn't the same George Whaley I had worked with on *The Harp in the South, Poor Man's Orange* and *Mr Edmund*. Whether the pressure of knowing his former student at NIDA was backing the picture, with the FFC, through his company Icon, was causing some strain or not, I attempted to find out. Sunday, normally the day one can sit down with the director to talk through any problems we may be having on the set or with the schedule. I wandered around to his house to see him. On answering the door, he seemed surprised to see me and quickly said he was too busy working on his script preparation for the week, and not to worry, everything was fine.

Carol Hughes, my co-producer, advised me David Williamson, our camera operator, wished to see me after work if I was available. Yes, of course. Now David and I go back a long way to *Caddie* and there are no secrets between us about the business. However, I sensed, being mid-week, it wasn't a 'social' he was seeking.

(Top) *Dad & Dave – On Our Selection* was given its world premiere
at Sydney's *State Theatre* to celebrate the centenary of the cinema.

(Bottom) Dress style for the premiere was bushman's attire.
Composer Peter Best, director George Whaley, Mel Gibson,
co-producer Bruce Davey and me. The night was a huge success and
the party continued to 2am.

We repaired after rushes across the road to a veranda overlooking the street. He lit his usual trademark cigarette and then dropped his bombshell. He wanted to leave the picture as soon as possible. He could find an operator to replace him, although he knew Martin McGrath, our DOP, would probably prefer to operate as well as light. I always believe the 'chemistry of casting' is basically the prerogative of the director and the casting of the crew and his heads of department that of the producer. Here I had a crisis on my hands, for the chemistry of casting the crew had failed. We talked through frankly about everything that was troubling him but basically he could not relate to his DOP. I knew George relied heavily on David. He was doing a marvellous job in setting up the master shots, liaising with George how many set-ups would be needed for the comedy scenes, and in particular had a sense for the lenses to obtain the big country look the film required. I implored him to reconsider and that both of us couldn't afford to let George down.

It was a long night.

I went to location for breakfast next morning. David quietly indicated to me he was staying. I knew the remaining weeks for him would not be the enjoyable ones he and I had experienced on other pictures and minis, but he became determined to get the picture in the can.

Movies are all about shadows and light. It's the lighter moments on a long shoot that make the memories of the moment even more significant than perhaps they really should be. It was just before the end of the first week's shoot when Leo McKern called me from the doorway of his caravan. 'Hey, Tone!' his rasping voice echoed around the set. 'Where's the crew list?' I told him it was in his portfolio, given to him on arrival. 'No, no, Tone, the "screw" list?' he bellowed. He had observed two junior members of the crew already getting very well acquainted. I retreated to the production office. I asked Carol Hughes, who can take umbrage in her Austro-Hungarian manner if you inform her of something she already knows but is confident no one else knows. It's extremely important when making an enquiry of Carol not to reveal your sources. 'I see so-and-so is already an item with so-and-so.' 'How do you know that?' came her retort. 'Ah! So it's true.' I said. (Nothing gives me greater pleasure than to telephone Carol and inform her of one piece of information or other that you know she already knows. All hell is likely to break loose if she hasn't already heard!) I reported back to Leo that his observations were entirely correct and that we would duly confer on this important social activity of the crew every Monday morning.

Leo, Dame Joan and I were accommodated at lovely B&B lodgings a few kilometres from town. The hosts also generously provided Leo and Joan with late evening meals when necessary. After the first few weeks, I moved when accommodation became available in the town, which made it a lot easier to communicate with the production office and our department heads after wrap every day. In the meantime many enjoyable evenings were had at our somewhat luxurious and comfortable B&B. Leo used to send Joan up unmercifully at times and Joan would cleverly meet his match on many an occasion. His partial deafness didn't help matters because of the volume of his voice. One evening Joan was bending over the traymobile serving some food when Leo could be heard around the entire district: 'She's rather large isn't she?' To which Joan retorted, 'Yes, I am, so be careful.'

I was driving Leo and his wife Jane back after rushes in my humble Alfa 33 when I saw a woman in white on the edge of the road. I slowed and thought it better to say nothing when Jane, sitting behind me, said 'Who was that, did you see her?' and Leo, in practically the same breath, said he saw her, 'and Tone, I've only got one bloody eye.'[9] Had we seen a ghost? The fact that we three had seen her so clearly, and that it was a ghostly figure, came up in conversation on more than one occasion. The only poltergeist I had ever experienced was at my home in 27A in Lane Cove. Wearing spectacles one has to be careful one hasn't seen a reflection. This was a bright sunny morning and I looked down the corridor to see a woman in a cream nightdress walk from the spare bedroom into the bathroom. I called out 'Can I help you?' and walked towards the bathroom. I looked in and of course there was no one there. I had often felt a 'presence' in the house and now I had seen it. Many months later I was sitting in my upstairs television lounge talking with a fellow producer when he suddenly interrupted, 'Who's that?' From where he was sitting he could see that same bathroom door. 'She' had walked into the bathroom again from the spare bedroom. 'Oh, you have seen her too,' was all I could say. Leo, Jane and I had seen someone on the road that night, but she wasn't there.

It was approaching Christmas and Joan indicated she would like to go shopping on one of her scheduled days off. I suggested nearby Canberra but she insisted she wanted to shop in Braidwood. The town is small, with some smart gift shops and a splendid old general store. Braidwood it was to be and the general store the first stop. I picked Joan up at the appointed time, drove back into town, parked, and we began our walk. She wanted to go to the town's only bank to get some shopping money. We were halfway across the road when Joan stopped in her tracks. 'F...! I've forgotten to bring any identification.' Having quickly composed myself on hearing her splendid expletive, I assured her that I didn't

---

9   Leo's favourite joke about his glass eye was, 'Tone, I paid ninety bloody quid for it and I can't see a bloody thing with it.'

think it would be necessary. We entered the Braidwood Westpac where three or four locals were being served, when a young lady beckoned Joan over. How could she be of help? Joan told her she had forgotten to bring any identification, to which the girl quickly replied that it wouldn't be necessary. How much would she like to withdraw? Followed by, 'Now, Dame Joan, would that be in the name of Bonynge or Sutherland?'

We had a wonderful afternoon shopping, though I couldn't fathom exactly what she was buying other than lots of wrapping paper. All was to be revealed in the last week of the shoot. The Dame had bought a gift for every member of our cast and crew. All were summoned to the steps of her caravan in a lunch break to receive their presents. Those at the top are always the nicest of the stars.

Bruce Davey and Mel were pleased with the rushes they were seeing back in LA and Bruce managed to find time in his busy schedule to visit us in Braidwood for a couple of days. He is an interesting producer. The contracting negotiations had been protracted and at times not without a degree of angst among the parties, but when it came to the making of the film, we were left completely to ourselves to get on with the job. There was absolutely no creative interference at all.

It was a wrap – back to Sydney where we were to see a first cut of the picture within a few days.

Wayne Le Clos not only knows and understands the craft and style of editing but also how to carefully guide a director if he is ever unsure of himself and his material. Here the 'chemistry of casting' the crew was working extremely well, and soon the director's cut was on its way to Bruce and Mel. Then George and I were off to Hollywood and to my favourite 'lot' of all, Warner Brothers at Burbank, where at this time Icon was headquartered. A few comments from Mel and Bruce, some good, positive and astute suggestions but nothing of serious concern. As George and I were preparing ourselves to go to a screening room to go through the film with them both Bruce said, 'Righto, get back and finish the film, let's go to lunch.' So off we went to the Warners commissary, Mel and George going off to talk about old times and Bruce and I repairing to discuss the finalisation of the film and its release.

Alan Finney had originally suggested having the world premiere in Brisbane, more or less following the line of Andrew Pike's original strategy for the release of the film, but the Centenary of Cinema put paid to this plan. We had arrived at the time to screen the answer print for Alan Finney. It was at Atlab, our laboratory, on Sydney's north shore. Screening a film to only three people can be a lonely experience. Screening a comedy even worse. Remember this is the man who very firmly had rejected the idea of the film in the first place, and now we were completely in his hands for the future of the film. Even at this point I saw the film as a limited release, giving time for word of mouth to have its effect on the box office. Alan quietly chortled through the film and had a couple of good guffaws. The lights went up and nothing could contain his enthusiasm.

He was extremely complimentary, staggering me with, 'It's a 150 print picture, Tony, definitely 150 screens.' I was too taken aback to comment immediately. After a pause I queried the wisdom of his recommendation. Could this film sustain a wide release? Leaving to catch his plane back to Melbourne, Alan congratulated us again and stressed it was going to be a big hit and Roadshow was going to be right behind it. George and I looked at each other and he asked, 'Well, what do you think of all that?' I was greatly troubled. Was it all hyperbole? I expressed my unease to George but knew there was very little we could do. I couldn't confer or seek Greg Coote's advice but I quickly conveyed to Bruce Davey Alan's spontaneous response to the film. By the end of the afternoon I had made up my mind to phone Alan at home to suss out what his true feelings really were. His wife answered the phone. His plane had been delayed and she would get him to return my call as soon as he got in and, 'Oh, by the way, congratulations, I haven't heard Alan so enthusiastic about a film for such a long while. I'm really looking forward to seeing it.' So it wasn't hyperbole, he really did like it!

There are various dates between 1894 and 1896 that one could choose to celebrate the centenary of cinema. June 5, 1995, was the date chosen in Australia for the official launch of the centenary and *On Our Selection* was chosen for the opening night celebratory gala at Sydney's magnificent State Theatre. Mel and Bruce would definitely attend and the theme for the evening was to be country, and country attire the dress code for the event. Thankfully the night was a rip-roaring success. The State is a 2,200-seater and premieres are generally reserved for the 'A' list of Sydney society, not the sort one would expect to enjoy Dad & Dave. If the after-show party is emptied very quickly, you know your film is in trouble, but our party filled the upper and lower foyers of the Picture Palace till 2am.

Just before the world centenary premiere, Bruce Davey had arrived at the Hotel Intercontinental in Sydney and telephoned me. 'Have you seen the poster?'[10] 'I have, it arrived about an hour ago,' I replied. 'It's bloody dreadful and I've summoned Finney here in the morning. Can you be here?' 'Yes.' It was a Saturday and a meeting I try hard to forget. We hadn't been consulted on the poster, which I thought a strange collage not particularly aimed at anybody. If anything, by putting our young newcomers – Murray Bartlett and Essie Davis – at the top of

---

10 Known in the trade as a 'one-sheeter', a billboard is a 'twenty-four sheeter'

the poster, we were ignoring the audience we were actually aiming for, the over forties, an audience I still firmly believe filmmakers are ignoring to our cost. Bruce went into full attack. All one could do was listen, and generally agree with what he was saying, albeit somewhat forthrightly. Berating your distributor can be very risky. Though Alan Finney was taking it on the chin and assuring Bruce that the poster would be changed, I knew underneath he was fuming.

I rang him in Melbourne later that day when he had returned, to try and placate him and keep him on side, for I had to be the one to work directly with him, but I knew the damage had been done. The poster was never changed. As far as I was concerned, Alan treated me very well, took all my calls and introduced me to his film booker Paul McKenzie, with whom I was to liaise over the coming weeks working out strategies, in particular the release of the film in the regional cities and country towns.

We opened wide and our first week was okay. Didn't set the world on fire, but was an acceptable take of $276,382 on seventy-eight screens, whilst *Batman Forever* was taking $1,545,136 in its third week! The publicity prior to our opening was positive and very generous, with Dame Joan and Leo rightly being the focus of attention. The reviews in the main were extremely positive – AUSSIE BOTTLER headlined Rob Lowig's review in Sydney's *Sun Herald*. 'The joys of the film are in the superb idiosyncratic casting … co-star and opera diva Sutherland has a rather surprisingly flattened voice on screen, but her radiant, upside down smile more than compensates … George Whaley's ability here to capture on the big screen that very essence of Australian humour – direct, boisterous, whole-hearted, communal – makes *On Our Selection* enormous fun.'

Despite the failure to produce a good one-sheeter, the press display advertising was excellent, here Roadshow excelled. Where the film was not clicking in the capital cities, it certainly was in rural Australia. I suggested to our film booker, Paul McKenzie, that we order some 16mm prints for the country circuit. At first he was hesitant, 16mm was generally only for the 'big' pictures, but concluded it may be worth the risk. We ordered six 16mm prints and Paul hoped for a film rental[11] of between $20,000 and $30,000. The final tally was over $60,000 film rental on 16mm. As always expected, both our 35mm release and the 16mm excelled in Queensland. On Mondays the managers in country towns, where they screen only on Fridays, Saturdays and Sundays, would ring Paul and ask if they could keep the print till the following weekend to save freight costs, to which Paul readily agreed. Toowoomba and Cairns, thirteen weeks; Townsville twelve weeks; holdovers for

---

11 Film rental is what the distributor collects after the exhibitor has taken their expenses and returns from the box office.

four weeks, Roma, Bowen, Windsor; two weeks in normally one-week locations, Bundaberg, Charters Towers; and the same in all the other states. In all there were holdovers in sixty-eight country locations. From the schools perspective, its seasons in rural and regional Australia was helped enormously by an excellent study guide to the film prepared by Atom, the Australian Teachers of Media.

Time to reflect? I think it is a good and greatly underrated film. The timing? I would concede the film arrived about five to eight years too late. In a lengthy lament about the distribution of the film, long-time colleague and raconteur Bob Ellis had this to say (in part) in *Encore*, the local trade paper, on August 14, 1995: 'When I saw *On Our Selection* at its flash centenary premiere (rejoice O Australia in your hundredth year of grovel) I sensed while loving it without reservation that it could go one of two ways. One was the *Crocodile Dundee* way of eerie surprising international success and lavish praise and container-loads of money for Buckley and Whaley, two of my favourite human beings (though Whaley's oft-cited credentials as a Martian, bug-eyed, snickering and wholly in control of his humanoid carapace are considerable and in need, I think, of ASIO[12] investigation), because it is a film of strength, individuality, high-darting wit, clarity of purpose, great writing, great acting, great design, great populist music and anthropological exactitude that is only incidentally as funny as a crutch. The other is the traditional Australian way of projection at 9AM to three surly bitches with hangovers and Evan Williams and immediate extinction.

'True to its traditions, Village Roadshow has opted for the latter course, forgetting that comedy needs an audience, not a jury, and it should never be test-shown to an audience of less than fifty. And so a great film may disappear.

'And it is a great film – as great as *If* which it partly resembles, a film about a whole society satirically observed, and a moment in history, with chapter headings, no structure, no close-ups and the accumulated wit of the *tribe*.

'No one should miss this film. And most now will. Had it quietly toured through country towns and played a few Sunday sessions in the city before it opened it might have prevailed. But no: for distributors it's more important to maintain old habits than pursue success with anything like commonsense. Success is for the Americans. We are only colonials, and we know our place.'

Thanks to his persistence, perseverance and belief in the film, Paul McKenzie at Roadshow got the film to those country towns and the stoic exhibitors out there in the bush, and the film finally found its audience.

---

12 ASIO (Australian Security Intelligence Organisation).

Ken G. Hall was never to see *Dad & Dave – On Our Selection*. Despite his hostility to George Whaley and me that we didn't use 'his' version of the script, which in fact was Bailey's and Duggan's play, he still used to ring on Sunday mornings for his usual chat. His ninetieth birthday celebration was held at the Royal Sydney Yacht Squadron, Kirribilli, on Monday, February 18, 1991. He had had a mild stroke but on this particular day he was in good form. Sighting me sitting to his left in the crowded dining room, he singled me out to say to his audience that there would be nothing to celebrate of his career if it were not for me and Ray Edmondson organising the 'great heist' of all his features and other material from Cinesound all those years ago. He was to suffer another stroke a little later, but the two strokes didn't affect his sense of humour, nor his ability to enjoy a good argument with anyone. He died in February 1994, his funeral being held on February 14 at St Thomas's Church, North Sydney, where in 1933 he had filmed John Longden, 'I am that man' for *The Silence of Dean Maitland*. I felt saddened in more ways than one on that February Monday, for I felt his funeral eulogies were hijacked by those who never really knew him, and had only recently made his acquaintance. I sat in silence thinking how fortunate I had been in having him as mentor and friend for the best part of my career.

31

A Celebration – Then Shadows Fall

An impressive envelope arrived at 27A Lane Cove postmarked Prague. Inside, an invitation to the 32nd Mezlnárodní Filmmovy Festival, Karlovy Vary, July 1997.

I'm told only three Australian films have ever won the Karlovy Vary Prize for Best Film and/or Best Direction. Our own film *The Irishman* won the prize in 1978 for director Donald Crombie. The Czech Ambassador presented the elegant cut crystal map of Czechoslovakia (as it was then known) at an impressive ceremony at the Czech consul's residence in Sydney. Karlovy Vary was always held the alternate year to Moscow and has always been regarded by the northern hemisphere film community as preferable to the Moscow Film Festival because it was more adventurous in program selection.

Since the beginning of the Velvet Revolution, as seven years of freedom at this time were known in the Czech Republic, Karlovy Vary had been held annually. Little did I know that nineteen years after *The Irishman* I would be invited to present our first film, *Caddie*, at a celebration of Australian film at this Karlovy Vary International Film Festival.

The invitation was a result of David Handley's recommendation to the Festival's organising committee. David had had a long association with the Czech Republic and lived for many years in Prague. The Australian Retrospective was his brainchild and most certainly deserved the support of the Australian Film Commission, which it got. The program committee's final selection was refreshingly eclectic, including, among others, *The Cars That Ate Paris, Angel Baby, The Sum of Us, Last Days of Chez Nous, Caddie, Romper Stomper, Young Einstein, Devil's Playground, Breaker Morant, Lonely Hearts, The Chant of Jimmy Blacksmith, The Last Wave* and *Picnic at Hanging Rock*.

(Left) Jeannine Seawell, Karlovy Vary, 1997.

(Bottom) Karlovy Vary 1997: I'm standing behind Yahoo Serious, to his left Stephanie Devine, Peter Duncan and Jeannine Seawell.

The organising committee were totally oblivious of the fact that Donald had received the prize for direction in 1978 and were at first greatly embarrassed.

Karlovy Vary is the largest and best known of the spa towns in the Czech Republic. (It was also known as Karlsbad/Carlsbad.) Two hours drive from Prague, it nestles in a mountain valley in West Bohemia with the river quietly running through the town. Its baroque buildings are a feast for the eye, not to mention spectacular examples of art nouveau. Regretfully another prominent building of the town was built by the Russians in the seventies and is best described as ghastly Russian modern sixties! This is the centre of the Festival and the dire Thermal Hotel. Fortunately none of us were accommodated here. Although out of place in this elegantly beautiful town, it is an ideal venue for the Festival. Screening facilities were excellent – and all the screenings were overcrowded. The Australian Retrospective was held in a pleasant 200-seater, in which 300 people crammed to see *Picnic at Hanging Rock*! The screening of all our films drew crowds in excess of 220 to 250 every day. When one considers the number of films in the main program, and the whopping great Retrospective dedicated to Milos Forman, returning home for the first time, the audiences for our films were all the more remarkable.

However, the big night was Peter Duncan's, and deservedly so. The Australian contingent entered the Grand Hall to be confronted by 1,300 enthusiastic and noisy young cinemagoers waiting in anticipation for *Children of the Revolution*. Peter stood before the huge screen and told the crowd he was 'scared'. 'It's a scary moment, for I know Communism touched you differently to our experience with it.' Peter gave a terrific introduction to his film and had the audience in his hands as the main titles hit the screen. At the end it was an overwhelming response as Peter escaped in the darkness through the exit doors.

The Australian party that evening at the 200-year-old Grand Pupp Hotel was a triumph. Once again, thanks to David Handley's initiative, a business friend of his, Tony Denny, had arranged, with the assistance of the Australian Film Commission, a shipment from Prague of Australian wines. This has particular significance. Whilst not wanting to cause a diplomatic incident, and acknowledging without hesitation that Czech Pilsener has to be the best in the world, the same cannot be said of their wines! Our party was in La Belle Epoque Salon next door to the ornately grand La Belle Epoque Ballroom where the major sponsor of the Festival was holding a party for 1,000 guests (to which we had also been invited), commencing one hour after the Australian party. The word had obviously spread that there was Australian wine being served next door! David Handley looked suitably fazed when we saw elegantly dressed people beginning to infiltrate our party. I told David not to worry if they drank all the wine, it could mean another export order! On the stroke of eleven the party concluded and we repaired to the Grand Ballroom and *two* Czech dance bands – sounding like and playing the music of the thirties and forties – to drink their pilsener!

Also in attendance at the Festival and our grand evening was Jeannine Seawell, still flying the flag for Australian films twenty-three years later. We arranged to meet for drinks the next day, knowing it was to be the last time we would see each other. During our conversation, saying to her how well I thought she looked, Jeannine revealed she was fighting a battle with cancer but was determined to keep fighting as long as she could. Her determination was shining through. It was only a few months later that her sister Bernadette telephoned to tell me Jeannine had been admitted to hospital and was sinking fast. Two days later the sad news came that Jeannine Seawell was dead. *The Australian* newspaper headlined my obituary to Jeannine as MIDWIFE OF AUSTRALIAN FILM. 'Jeannine Seawell was a Paris-based agent who took on the overseas selling of Australian films in the 1970s when the rest of the world hardly knew there was such a thing as an Australian film. *Caddie, Picnic at Hanging Rock, The Picture Show Man, Tim* and *The Irishman* were some of the early titles she marketed successfully in Europe and South America. Seawell was still selling those early films at the time of her death, twenty-four years later. As new video and pay-TV markets opened up, and as the terms of the original sales expired, she sold them over and over again. The result is that the investors in these films, including the Australian Film Commission, are still receiving income from Seawell's efforts.'

Our relationship with Jeannine Seawell began on May 17, 1976, outside Le Rex cinema in one of the back streets of Cannes. Donald Crombie and I had just finished counting the numbers attending the first screening of *Caddie*.

Crombie and I hadn't the faintest idea what we were doing at Cannes – only that we were supposed to be there. In my diary each day Crombie would write, 'Fly home, give up, buy a farm, be admitted to an asylum.'

Seawell offered to represent the film and ourselves and saved our lives. Within a week she had sold to twelve countries and we were in competition at the then prestigious San Sebastian Festival where Helen Morse went on to win Best Actress and the film the Jury Prize. Remember, this was in the days when no one overseas had heard of an Australian film.

Seawell pioneered the way for many of us – Pat Lovell, Jim and Hal McElroy, Joan Long, Paul Cox. The list goes on and on, and for this past twenty-four years she had been a beacon for Australian cinema. She also became an advisor and friend to all of us, guiding us on how to get our films into festivals, the market, which distributors were the best and so on. She took us under her wing and put us all firmly on the learning curve. Although a highly successful sales agent, she also gave her own time to the establishment of the many successful Australian film cultural events in France, Italy and Czechoslovakia. It was at Karlovy Vary that we met again and she revealed she had been having some health problems. She went into hospital in January and battled on regardless. She went to Cannes this year as she had always determined not to let her filmmakers and buyers down.

Her advice to Australian filmmakers lives on. About our films she always said, 'Be yourselves – always be yourselves.'

A year later, Donald and I were to face the death of our friend and colleague, Joan Long. After writing *Caddie*, she wrote another script especially for Helen Morse which was never produced. She became a producer in her own right with her delightful homage to cinema, *The Picture Show Man*, directed by John Power, and, with co-producer Margaret Kelly, the enormously successful *Puberty Blues*, directed by Bruce Beresford. Her next film was *Silver City* directed by Sophia Turkiewicz. Her last feature was David Williamson's *Emerald City*, directed by Michael Jenkins.

I saw Joan hours before she died in the sterile unit of intensive care at Royal North Shore Hospital where one is required to don protective wear and keep a certain distance from the patient's bed. As a result I couldn't hear the last words she was attempting to gasp to me. It was very distressing and a totally unfair way for anyone's life to end.

I'm not afraid of death, nor do I get maudlin about it, for having turned seventy I still have too much to do to even contemplate the thought. However, it's a reminder when one turns over the pages of one's filofax to still see the telephone numbers of those one used to ring who have since long gone. Between 2000 and 2006 I counted that I had been to seventeen funerals and have lost thirty-five of my peers, associates I had worked with or for, and very close friends and relatives. I hope to live to eighty for, as I have said, I have too much still to do, and anyway, I want to be around a while longer just to annoy the buggers in our film bureaucracies!

32

'That Resilient Little Beast'
– But Not Quite A Heart Stopper!

Saturday, 1 December 2001, 11am, Anna Reeves arrived for morning tea at 27A, Lane Cove. It was a bright, sunny Sydney morning and, unlike Tracey Moffatt's arrival, I had had time to dress. Anna had migrated from New Zealand some years beforehand and had become an Australian citizen. I knew her from her Film School days through her short film *La Vie en Rose*, which strangely that morning I discovered still sitting on the bookcase. Anna was looking for an Australian co-producer for a script she had written for her first feature film as a director. She had thought of seeing me much earlier but had been advised by one of her peers that he considered me 'too old' for her and her film, something she confided to me on the telephone when making her appointment. I mused because I knew who had made the remark.

Anna was a lady in a hurry. I was last on her visiting list as she was back off to London that afternoon, where she is based with her husband Frederic and now their son Sebastien. I gave Anna my usual spiel about having to like the script and being able to go to rushes believing in the film we do. Mind you, getting a word in edgeways with her ladyship is no mean feat. Her script was *The Oyster Farmer* ('The' later being dropped) based on her observations while spending every available weekend, when in Australia, with the oyster farmers of the Hawkesbury River. I would read the script and let her know Monday night my time, morning in London. I liked this woman, feisty and full of life – and not suffering fools gladly, that I could tell.

I enjoyed the script immensely. It had a freshness about it, with *Bliss*-like qualities, but nothing like that film of course. The whole premise of *Oyster Farmer* was its originality. The only film I could remember having been set on the river was Ken Cameron's charming *Sailing to Brooklyn*. Anna's script had been financed by Piers Tempest and his partners in Little Wing Films, a London-based company. I didn't get the opportunity to phone Anna to accept her invitation. Piers rang me to introduce himself and to congratulate me on being Anna's and his Australian producer! I thanked him, put the phone down and thought 'well, that was quick'.

We then jointly, Piers and I, set out on the road of money raising. He had good connections in London and I knew how the funding agencies worked, but it was to become a road well travelled for the next two years. I wisely invited Jonathan Shteinman to be our principal executive producer.

It was now early 2003 and I had come back to Sydney to produce *Jessica* for Screentime, not realising I would be away for the rest of the year with the successful financing of *Oyster Farmer*. *Jessica* was no sooner delivered when our team was ensconced at Film Australia's studio for pre-production in October, with a November start date for principal photography.

Our wardrobe buyer was crossing the street when she was stopped by a woman coming in the opposite direction. 'Are you with the fillum people?' she asked. 'Yes,' was the reply. 'Oh, I see, well, my sister-in-law's dog is in your picture.' Welcome to Brooklyn on the Hawkesbury River! I'm sure the dog was an important addition to the cast of our film but not as important as our 'stars' who made up our ensemble cast. I first met Kerry Armstrong (Trish) in the sandhills of Botany when Ray Lawrence and I were screen-testing for Robyn Davidson's *Tracks*. That film, like many, didn't get off the ground, but Kerry went on to become a star in her own right with four years in *Sea Change* and then in Ray Lawrence's *Lantana*, for which she won the AFI Award for Best Actress. It was at the same AFI Awards that David Field (Brownie) won Best Actor for his superb role in *My Husband, My Killer*. Jack Thompson joined us to play the role of 'Skippy', along with Alan Cinis playing 'Slug' and two newcomers we felt were destined to become stars, Alex O'Lachlan as Jack Flange and Diana Glenn as Pearl.

The role of 'Mumbles' was originally written by Anna Reeves for David Kelly from *Waking Ned Devine* but only two weeks before pre-production was due to commence we learned he was not in good health and it was not wise for him to make the journey out to Australia. This was sad news indeed and at this late hour we had no time to waste. Our two casting directors, Susie Maizels (Australia) and Sarah Beardsall in London, drew up a list of possibles for Anna and there was one who stood out from the rest, Irish actor Jim Norton. Jim has had a wide-ranging career on the stage, in film and television. As the Bishop in *Father Ted* he is familiar to both British and Australian audiences. He has also played in *Ballykissangel* and in *Harry Potter and the Chamber of Secrets*. Strangely Jim was already familiar with the script of *Oyster Farmer* and had read it nearly a year earlier when Kelly had been offered the role. Kelly, a good friend of Norton's, lived not far away and had given the script to Jim to read. He was very envious of Kelly. So, in turning full circle, the script came back to him. We were now three weeks into pre-production and all of us were becoming somewhat anxious. Jim had already left for New York when our offer had been made. His UK agent couriered the script to his hotel where he read it three times in the one day. Anna spent a half hour on the phone with him and raced into my office to tell me 'Mumbles' had been found! Jim, familiar to Broadway audiences, had gone to New York to renew his green card with just enough clothes for a couple of days. There was no time to return to London as wardrobe fittings and make-up tests were due that week, followed immediately by rehearsals. His arrival was a day 'late' because the travel agent had forgotten a day is lost travelling west to east from Los Angeles. Like the real trouper he is, he arrived at the airport and came straight to his first read-through with the cast. The cast read-through is the first time one 'hears' the film and it was no doubt a relief to Anna Reeves to know not only did her dialogue 'click', it was also very funny. Since Anna had introduced me to *Oyster Farmer* twenty-three months ago, she had not stopped working on refining her script and the development of her characters. If only all screenplays were this well developed!

Over the four years visiting the oyster farmers on the Hawkesbury Anna had got to know the people and had won their trust. This made it so much easier for our location managers to secure spectacular river sites for the picture. Of the nineteen river locations selected, only four were accessible by road, the others only reachable by boat. This was the first problem to be solved by our scheduler and first assistant director Mark Turnbull. It was apparent that cast and crew would have to be moved by boat. How to do it?

One of the most experienced boat people in the Australian film industry is Pat Nash and thankfully he was available. Pat set forth to muster all the boat owners and sailors of the Hawkesbury to interview them to select the boat people whose services we would need for our five weeks on the river. Of our six-week pre-production period, four of them were spent scouring the river for the locations and preparing the flotilla of boats of all shapes and sizes we would need to ferry our cast and crew each day back and forth from our unit base at Brooklyn. What to do about catering? Oh, and the unmentionable comfort stops during the day?

Then there were the tides! The tide on the Hawkesbury moves rapidly between high and low, so an extensive study of the tide chart was done, to the extent that it showed in many of our locations there would be no room for our equipment on shore and it would have to be confined to watercraft. Working out a shooting schedule at any time is a feat in itself, but we had not been prepared for having to consider the added factor of the tide. So the day's shooting schedule and crew start times were dictated by the tide. The day's tide chart was printed at the top of the call sheet to remind everyone. In some locations, on high tide some crew were knee-deep in water and we had to complete a sequence before the tide began to go out, otherwise the entire flotilla was stranded on the mud flats. At our last pre-production meeting of the department heads and crew, Mark Turnbull took us through every day of the shooting schedule and its relation to the tides of each day.

When asked if everyone was clear about the schedule, one of the boat people assigned to Pat Nash's team, sitting at the side of the hall, gingerly spoke up and said, 'What about the fogs?' Twenty-nine pairs of eyes turned and focused on the boatman – 'the fog' everyone chorused. I will never forget this scene. Mark quietly asked when the fog lifted. 'Aw gees, mate,' said the boatman, 'could be eleven, more likely twelve o'clock.' 'Radar?' Mark asked. 'Nope,' came the reply, 'not even the water taxis will venture out in our fogs – and they've got radar.' Now fogs can be expected in winter but not to any extent in late spring/early summer. Well, this was our collective reckoning.

First morning crew call, 0545. Sunny and clear. Brooklyn was buzzing and the sun glinting on the Hawkesbury was every cameraman's dream come true. The first barges set out carrying grips and electrics, followed by a flotilla of craft of every size and type imaginable. Now the Hawkesbury is not the Amazon but it has many tributaries. Following the barges was the funniest and strangest sight of all. There in splendid isolation, on a flat-bottomed raft, were the two porta-loos, serviced by a speedboat to get cast and crew to them! The main flotilla turned into the tributary they were meant to take only to be enveloped in – FOG! However, the barges and the porta-loos had taken the wrong arm of the river so had to scuttle back, by which time the fog had lifted.

The Hawkesbury River is probably one of Australia's best-kept tourist secrets. It begins in the lower Blue Mountains west of Sydney as the Nepean and becomes the Hawkesbury at Yarramundi, crossing near Castlereagh. It is one of the scenically spectacular rivers of the world. Though only twenty-five kilometres north of Sydney, the town of Brooklyn is not yet on the sewer and this has limited the establishment of five-star accommodation on the river. The suburban train trip from Sydney to Woy Woy skirts one of the principal tributaries of the river and is well worth the trip.

We were very privileged to have cinematographer Alun Bollinger on board. He and Anna had been working closely for weeks planning every shot of the film, a collaboration which paid off handsomely when watching rushes. The super 35mm aspect ratio, which gives us an anamorphic widescreen print for the cinema, was ideal for both actor and river. The images are spectacular. Also on board was Stephen Jones-Evans as production designer, his most recent accomplishment being *Ned Kelly*, for which he won the AFI Award for Best Production Design. Deborah Lanser, a familiar face, was in charge of make-up. Deborah won an Oscar nomination for her team's work on *Mary Shelley's Frankenstein*. The film was in the careful hands of film editor Peter Beston who had arrived from the UK and set up his editing department at Film Australia. Peter, one of the UK's most experienced editors, had just finished editing *Shackleton* with Kenneth Branagh.

Alun Bollinger's camera was discovering nooks and crannies of the river few people ever see. The weather had been topsy-turvy but was showing the river in its many moods, which Anna and Alun were successfully capturing. We had been shooting a five-day week but Alun and Anna had been filming the river and its life every Saturday in what had become known as the 'Albol Nature Unit', quietly capturing the dramatic escarpment, the wildlife of the river, the extraordinary mangroves and the battalions of crabs that emerge from the mudflats as the tide rapidly recedes.

Having mastered the demands of the river, we thought we had conquered all our problems. Not so. Problems always turn up when you least expect them. Our opening scenes depicted Jack Flange, Alex O'Lachlan, committing his heist at the Sydney Fish Markets and posting the proceeds to himself via Australia Post. The Fish Markets refused to let us film a robbery on their premises. It seems there had been several ATM scams at the Markets throughout the year and the management was decidedly nervous at letting a film crew stage a robbery. Fortunately Poulos Brothers, one of Sydney's oldest families of fishmongers, had their premises just outside the boundaries of the Markets under the Anzac Bridge, but we could only film on Sundays. Would the union agree? The crew were happy to cooperate and the union said yes. There was somewhat of a nice reward in this, because it gave us all a three-day weekend off that week.

Australia Post were adamant we could not film in *their* post offices or in any way use their logo. We could not get a direct answer as to why. I wrote to the Minister. He declined to intervene. When pressed, the somewhat officious woman, the head of Australia Post's Public Relations, curtly told us, 'Australia Post cannot be seen to lose mail.' Really? So we had to invent our own mail service, Allied Post, prepare our own truck and find a building to serve as a post office and a mail-sorting centre. DHL came to the rescue with the latter, and luck was on our side at Brooklyn, for the old post office, still with its sign, Brooklyn, in place, was now privately owned, so Allied Post took it over. I'm sure there were red faces at Australia Post when the film was released.

State Rail was quite another matter. They could not have been more helpful and cooperative with a bit of a hard ask on our part. Some scenes were set on the train with Nikki, Claudia Harrison, and Jack, Alex O'Lachlan. In scene 162 Jack tells his sister that he has to go back to Brooklyn and leaves the train at Wondabyne, a little further up the river. State Rail gave us permission to film on their actual trains proceeding north, but not on their trains travelling south, as this was peak hour for trains to Sydney in the morning. To overcome this we scheduled to film the scene on five runs of the train north, disembarking Alex and crew at Wondabyne Station where our speedboat sped them back to Brooklyn to catch the next train. With State Rail's own representative with us, and our security company Who Dares boarding each train at Central Station, Sydney, to keep the top deck of the last carriage clear of passengers, the entire exercise was an enormous success. Perhaps the funniest sight of all was when each train arrived at Brooklyn (actually Hawkesbury River Station) our props department would quickly erect a stepladder to squeegie the windows of the carriage clean, much to the looks of incredulity from the paying passengers on the lower deck. I caught a glimpse of the stationmaster, about to blow his whistle, also looking at the scene with great bemusement.

The anatomy of an oyster is the last thing I expected to learn about on this production. However, learn I did. The success in the organisation of this picture is due in the main to Anna Reeves' continuing contact with the community of oyster farmers over four years. The leaders of this band of farmers were Ian (Egg) Johnson, Peter Johnson and Lloyd Spencer, to name but three. One of our very few days filming onshore was at the depuration tanks at Brooklyn. The oyster farmer's working day is not unlike our filming day, except the farmers can very often start much earlier even than we do. I was down at the set when our line producer, Sue Mackay, introduced me to Peter Johnson who in turn said I had to meet Egg. I immediately said that I didn't think it appropriate that I should call him Egg. 'Why not?' Peter retorted. 'Everyone else does.' 'Good day … Egg,' I awkwardly greeted him. 'Good day – here, have an oyster.' Now if the reader is not a devotee of the oyster, then the following may not be of interest. Having consumed two or three freshly opened oysters, a taste you will never experience in a restaurant, Egg thought it was time for my anatomy lesson.

I have always liked oysters, especially the Sydney rock oyster, but I have more respect for these creatures now than ever before. One doesn't imagine an oyster having a heart – well, it most certainly does. The oyster doesn't die till just after

(Top left) The spectacular Hawkesbury River.

(Top right) Scouting for locations, DOP Alun (Albol) Bollinger with writer/director Anna Reeves.

(Below) Alex O'Lachlan (Jack) with Jack Thompson ('Skippy')

(Bottom) Our ubiquitous porta-loos caused our oyster farmers much amusement.

it is opened. Watching closely as Egg opened an oyster, he pointed out the tiny heart in the top right-hand corner, gently beating. It looks and is about the size of the tiny circular battery in a 35mm still camera. Then, gently lifting the knife under the flesh, Egg drew apart the gills of this extraordinary creature, pointing out its breathing and how it draws the water in and expels it on the other side of its shell. An oyster is sterile – absolutely pure – when the shell is opened. And there's another thing I didn't know. They are known as 'oyster openers' not 'shuckers'. The word 'shuck' does not exist in the oyster farmer's vocabulary, so I presume it must be American. Anyway, the word is taboo on the Hawkesbury. Watching the precision with which Egg opened an oyster with his small but very efficient knife was really something. The flavour of oyster is a rare experience. Slightly salty, but at 'room' temperature all the subtlety of the flesh can be discerned.

It was the end of the day for the farmers and they were enjoying their beers. We still had about an hour and a half's filming to complete. 'Here, have a beer, Tone.' Now it's not the done thing to turn down a 'shout' in Australia as we all know, but I said quickly 'Oh, we haven't finished work yet Egg – later.' Egg looked at me quite perplexed, looked over at the crew filming, then back at me and said quizzically, 'Aren't you the boss?'

Strangely, the very last scene in the film was shot on our last night. In the early hours of the morning of December 20, *Oyster Farmer* wrapped. Our diligent film editor, Peter Beston, must have stayed up all night, for that very same afternoon, just hours before the wrap party, Peter had ready a complete assembly of the entire picture – minus the last scene – for a select few of us to view on the big screen, before he and Anna departed for the UK to commence editing. For Anna I'm sure directing the film must have been a baptism of fire in the very sense of the words, but what was on the screen that day gave all of us, particularly me, great confidence Anna had delivered a very special picture.

Film interruptus

The usual Christmas/New Year break was more than welcome that year. Editing was to commence on January 5 in London and I was booked on Cathay Pacific out of Cairns to London on February 25 for the 'lock off' of the picture and the post-production leading to the final mix. During January I sensed there were problems in the editing suite and felt that the sooner I got there, the better. Anna would be happy with the editor and the editing one day, but not the next. She had the bad habit of taking a video home on Friday night containing the cut, up to the point Peter had reached that week, and showing it to several of her friends. Now the intention may have been to gain confidence in her work by seeking the opinion of others. I know as an ex-editor this is always a fatal mistake and can only lead to confusion for both the director and the poor editor. People who are not experienced cannot evaluate a film in the editing stage without its music and effects and dialogue replacement. This procedure regretfully was to continue each weekend. I was booked for a two-day board meeting of the Film Finance Corporation in Canberra the second week of February, then off to London on the 25th. An edit of the film was coming to me before departure so that I could prepare notes for any last-minute recommended trims and cuts.

Sunday, February 8, 2004. Booked on QF923 at 11.25 to Sydney from Cairns, a three-hour flight, and a one-hour drive from Port Douglas to the airport. My bag, heavier than usual because my Sydney/Canberra visit was for two weeks and not the usual one, was packed and ready to go. 7.59am I enter the shower. 8am on the dot, the most fearsome pain struck in the upper chest, causing me to drop soap and grab the shower taps. I turned the shower off and started taking deep breaths, still clutching my chest. I walked around my rather large bathroom wondering what had happened. All my limbs were working and I was able to speak so I figured I hadn't had a stroke. My pulse was normal and my heart was beating but the area around it felt as though a brick had hit me. It was when I went to pick up my suitcase that I knew something was very wrong. The pain abated but the soreness was extreme. I decided to continue to Cairns at least, where there are two fine hospitals. I asked the coach driver, who knew me as a regular, whether he would mind taking the suitcase. He was very obliging and lifted it off when we got to the airport. My plane had been cancelled and I had to wait until 1pm. I sat in the Qantas Club lounge and began to relax. Eventually my flight was called. Seated in the plane I felt another twinge. I pondered getting off the plane but then this would cause considerable disruption, for they would have to find my suitcase in the hold. I had a glass of red wine with my lunch and the soreness began to wear off. It reappeared sharply when I lifted the suitcase off the carousel.

On arriving at my friend Gary's flat in Redfern in the inner city, although I had a key and was expected, I rang the bell and asked if he would come down to take my suitcase up to the third floor. He didn't think anything of it until I told him of my 'turn' that morning in the shower. He thought it might be muscular or a referred pain from my back. The following morning I drove to Canberra in my hire car and checked into the Hyatt for our two-day board meeting, one day of which was held in Parliament House. I sat through the two days in relative discomfort but not in pain. Wednesday and on returning to Sydney I rang my

GP for an appointment, only to discover that Dr Sue Ridley was on leave and would be back on Monday. Did I wish to see someone else? No, I would wait till Monday.

11am Monday and Dr Ridley arranged three tests for me to have immediately and to return 5pm Tuesday evening. 5pm Tuesday and the three investigative tests were all clear. Fine. Sue Ridley looked at me and said, 'Tony, I don't like this, would you mind waiting outside for a moment?' About 5.30 I was called back in. She gave me a piece of paper with a name and address. 'I want you to be there at 7.15 in the morning. Dr Caspari, a cardiologist, will come in early especially. When are you going home?' It was the next day but it wasn't a problem to cancel and re-book for the end of the week. 7.15am at Chatswood, I was sitting in the darkened foyer of an office block; a besuited man emerged from the car park. Dr Caspari ushered me in, switching on all the lights approaching his rooms. He too thought, like Gary, that it might be muscular. He had ascertained I had had a stress test only four years earlier, which was clear, but he wanted to do another that morning and asked if I could wait until the operator arrived. He had asked me what medication I took but I had forgotten something. 'Oh, by the way, I also take Astrix (a low dose aspirin) every two days.'

An hour later I was on the treadmill, doing quite well, till I suddenly felt that twinge again. I was just about to put my hand up and ask if they could slow the treadmill down just a little, when all hell broke loose. Alarms were ringing, the machine had come to an abrupt halt, a nurse thrust a stool for me to sit on immediately and handed me a glass of water. I could see the operating technician was taken with the graph paper he was looking at. I dressed and had just sat down in the waiting room when an assistant called me to Dr Caspari's room. I think it is the first time I have ever looked at anybody and seen shock on their face. 'Tony, these are not the results I was expecting; I want to do an angiogram. I want you at North Shore Private tomorrow morning at eight. Take four of these tablets now and the fifth in the morning. I suspect we may have to put a stent in one of your arteries – nothing to worry about, you'll be able to go home at lunchtime.' Off I went. Once again I cancelled my flight, leaving it open. Next morning I parked my hire car in the car park at Royal North Shore Hospital and dutifully presented myself.

An angiogram is a fascinating procedure. It involves only a local anaesthetic to pump purple dye through you, which creates a sensational feeling when it's applied, followed by the sensation one is urinating, whereas obviously one is not. Above my head was a television monitor where I could see my rapidly-moving bloodstream pushing its way under what looked like the white cliffs of Dover.

I could sense a flurry of activity in the control room when Dr Caspari appeared, looking over my screen. 'Tony, you won't be going home.' 'That's okay,' I said, 'I cancelled the flight.' 'No, no, you are not leaving the hospital – I will see you in your room in an hour.' 'But I don't have a room,' I protested. 'You do now,' said an obviously concerned cardiologist. He duly appeared to break the news that I was to have a triple bypass in five days and the hospital staff were not going to let me out of their sight. I was evidently a walking time-bomb. The good news was that I had a perfectly healthy heart that would be able to pump throughout the operation which in turn would minimise any risk of infection. The heart had been screaming out for more blood, that was all. It was later confided to me that my taking low-dose aspirin all those years had prevented a heart attack, but I had a week to wait for the blood to re-thicken after the angiogram. I also had a rental car parked in the hospital grounds!

I spent the rest of the day on the telephone creating shock waves to those dearest and closest to me and that evening notifying Piers Tempest and Anna that I wouldn't be coming to London. Dr Caspari reappeared to tell me the good news that he had been able to secure Dr Peter Brady to perform the operation. I could tell he was more than pleased. I would be 'done' at 6am the following Thursday.

Anna's latest cut had arrived and a monitor and VCR were organised to be installed in my room. If I was going to be a prisoner of the hospital for a week I had better, at least, contribute something towards the finishing of the picture. Dr Caspari was very intrigued with my set-up and with what I was doing. He remarked that if ever they were short of patients, they could convert the rooms into editing suites. I assured him the rooms were perfect for such use, and with en suites should command an impressive rental! The staff found any excuse to visit the room to see what I was doing. 'Oh, Kerry Armstrong is in the picture – oh, it must be good,' observed one sister. 'Who's the good lookin' guy?' asked another, transfixed by Alex O'Lachlan. I rang Anna to tell her my notes were on their way and I thought the film was looking good. Some pick-up shots had been recommended and there was money in the budget for Anna to do those in about five weeks time.

Monday morning and Sue Mackay, our line producer, arrived to break the news Anna had sacked the editor. My heart sank, for I knew if I had been there this could have been averted, but what was done was done. The film had to move forward.

The first days of recovery can be uncomfortable but not painful, except I was violently ill on the Sunday morning. Dr Brady was called, which I felt embarrassed about, it being a Sunday and probably a surgeon's only day off. It was discovered I was allergic to high doses of Panadol. I am also allergic to penicillin. The medication was changed and I felt fine in about two hours. Once the external plumbing had been removed (and that is an experience, let me tell you!) one is encouraged to be up and about walking, and on the second day one is walking up and down a flight of stairs. I looked a sight in my surgical stockings with my toes poking out the open end. I could hear loud voices at the end of the corridor and great hilarity. Jack Thompson and Bruce Beresford had arrived, with Jack assuring the sisters on duty they were there to take me down the road to the St Leonard's pub for 'afternoon tea'. The senior sister had obviously made it clear I wasn't going anywhere, as she led the pair into my room with a stern look on her face to Jack and Bruce, and a wink to me. I was sitting in my chair and Bruce roared at the sight of me in my surgical stockings. 'Tony – you look so Japanese – I want a pair.'

Convalescence is about a ten- to twelve-week period and in the first six weeks one is required to have a carer. My long-time friend, Judy Gimbert, offered to care for me at her home in Chatswood. The hospital had made arrangements to put me in a convalescent home but Jude was not having a bar of that. I got to know Judy and her mother when they lived at Penrith after my return from overseas in 1962. All the friends I had made at 189 Cromwell Road and elsewhere in Earls Court stayed in contact on my return and still do to this very day. To help raise money for Jude's church at Penrith, film nights were organised of my overseas trips, all of which had been photographed on 16mm. They were pretty amateur affairs with my 16mm Siemens projector and my appalling, unscripted commentaries, with music played from my reel-to-reel tape recorder. Fortunately my projector had a rheostat and I could slow it down or speed it up when the film went out of sync. Gosh, to think people paid to come to these evenings…

On the day of my discharge Dr Brady noted I lived in Port Douglas and said he, his wife and daughter were coming up in April, so he would do his final checks there.

Convalescence at Judy's was a careful four weeks learning what one can and can't do. Standing in the kitchen I would offer to make the coffee, but when it came to pushing down on the plunger a pain would shoot across my chest. The big shock came some six or seven weeks later when I was allowed to drive the car. Try releasing the handbrake and you will know straight away you have had a bypass. It is amazing, on reflection, what we take for granted as being normal.

Anna arrived from England to do two days of pick-ups on the Hawkesbury, which Sue Mackay organised. Anna came over to see me but it wasn't the time or place to discuss the editing. From hospital I had despatched Tim Wellburn to assist but this was to no avail – no fault of his, I should add.

I was given the all-clear to go home, booked Judy and me on the plane, only to be thwarted by a massive rock fall taking the Captain Cook Highway out, preventing travel from Cairns to Port Douglas.

The patient was improving and it was time for Jude to return to Sydney, her duties to be taken over for two weeks by Carol Hughes. My house is an open one, ceiling-to-floor louvres, French doors to the wide verandas, letting the breezes circulate continuously. Carol noticed a gentleman coming up the driveway. 'Hi! Peter Brady.' My surgeon! After introductions Peter suggested we adjourn to the Combined Club for fish and chips – but no chips for me. 'Tony, bring your medication chart with you and I'll check you over before dinner.' Before dinner? Carol and I looked at each other. Off we went. Sure enough, Dr Brady looked at my hand – but surely not my chest – at the table. 'Let me see your left wrist please,' he asked. He turned my hand over and exclaimed quietly, 'Oh, this is terrific – you are absolutely fine.' Querying him, he explained that what he looked for was the colour of the skin and the blood veins one can see in the wrist. He slashed my medication to what it is now. 'Keep the Astrix up, but make it daily now,' and we ordered fish and chips for four and fish for one. Carol later observed, 'Well, that's the most expensive house call I have ever seen.'

Oyster Farmer was finally locked off. We had missed the deadline for Cannes but were selected in the Discovery section of the Toronto International Film Festival in September, which was to be its world premiere. Our budget didn't stretch to paying for me to go. Anna was the 'official' guest and the Festival provided her fare and accommodation. I thought it wise to be there so decided to raid my bank and booked my friend Gary and me to Toronto via New York (I hadn't stayed at the Algonquin since 1996!) and home via LA. It was strange being back in Toronto where I had stepped off *The Canadian* in 1958 to seek work. Though it has, in many ways I felt the city hadn't changed. Hard to explain.

Our premiere screening at the charmingly quaint Isabel Bader Theatre was packed. Anna introduced the film and we all sat in the back row to observe the audience reaction. The session was very late in getting underway, a good way to get an audience offside, and one disgruntled subscriber made it known he had another session to attend and would have to leave before the film ended. Canadians have a soft accent compared to those across their border, and hearing the Aussie accent coming from the screen in such an environment you did feel it was a 'foreign' film. The audience bubbled and chortled in the right places and it got a standing ovation. The disgruntled patron who had another film to go to

(Top) At our Sydney Film Festival premiere, line producer Sue Mackay, writer/director Anna Reeves and casting director Susie Maizels.

(Right) Associate producer and first assistant director Mark Turnbull with Anna Reeves (Mark was second assistant director on *Caddie*). Note the 'sold out' sign. This also happened at Toronto the year before.

was still there when Anna's Q&A finished. The audience gave another round of rousing applause. The woman in front of me, not knowing who I was, stood up and turned to me and said 'That was a very good film, wasn't it?' I was not about to disagree. Another woman of mature years enquired as to whether Alex's tattoos were real. When assured they were, she blushed, 'Really?!'

The Australian release of our film was still eight months away. Dendy's strategy was for a winter release, June/July. What about the Sydney Film Festival? Dendy asked. I would only agree if it was either opening night or closing night film, but wouldn't accept it being plonked at a matinee in the vast State Theatre. Matt Soulos at Dendy agreed but did want it in the Festival. He felt strongly it would be the right launching pad for the film with Dendy opening *Oyster Farmer* on limited screens the day after the Sydney Film Festival closed. At our preview of the finished print it would be Matt's view of the film that would be the most important. I sat two rows behind and watched his body language throughout the screening. His face, reflected by the light pouring from the screen, told all. He was enjoying the film. If your film booker likes your film then there is hope.

Lynden Barber, the newly-appointed director of the Film Festival, dropped a bombshell when he announced that, of those available, there wasn't a strong enough Australian film to open the Festival. Instead he was programming a British film about two lesbians. I demanded our film be withdrawn from the Festival and I'm sure the Dendy team nearly had a stroke. Lynden, in one fell swoop, had insulted every Australian film, long and short, programmed for the Festival. We had found out from one of the inner sanctum at the Festival that the head of the film selection panel didn't like the film at all and didn't want it in the Festival.

Dendy won out and we played to capacity at their prestigious Dendy Opera Quays, a classy arthouse complex adjacent to the Sydney Opera House, in the last week of the Festival. We were the first film of the Festival to be completely sold out days before the Festival opened. As the crowd began to disperse after a thunderous round of applause, an irate subscriber stormed up to me demanding to know why it hadn't been the opening night film. I politely told her she should ask the Festival. 'I most certainly intend to'. The irony was, the head of the film selection panel was standing next to me and I'm sure she thought I had put the woman up to her protest.

Our audience of course were regular Festival subscribers plus the oyster farmers in the film. We had already given a special preview of the film the previous Sunday for all the oyster farmers of the Hawkesbury and their families. Despite having received their invitations for their special gala, they had also purchased tickets to the first public screening. It was a triumph. Standing in the foyer of the Dendy Opera

Quays listening to the various comments, I spotted a very tall, lanky, well-dressed country style bloke looming towards me. 'G'day.' He introduced himself, I doing likewise. 'I come from one of the other tributaries of the river, so I'm not in your film, but I know all them blokes.' I was getting ready for the blast. 'You've done us proud, mate, you've done us proud.' Writing this now I still get a lump in the throat and a tear, as I did at that moment.

We opened cautiously June 30, 2005 on twenty-three screens, averaging $17,000 per screen in the first week. To say these figures surprised the industry would be an understatement. Exhibitors who had been unsure began booking the film, including Paul Dravet, friend and manager and programmer of the Cremorne Orpheum Picture Palace, the most prestigious cinema complex in Australia. Working closely with Dendy in the weeks prior to the film's release I had queried why Paul hadn't booked the film, yet it was made for his audience. The Orpheum's main auditorium seats over 800 and Neil Jensen is the flamboyant and charismatic Wurlitzer organist. I wrote a jolly and threatening note to Paul Dravet that if he didn't book our film, I would have him put across the organist's knees and given a good spanking. Monday and back came the reply: *Oyster Farmer* starts Thursday! It wasn't anything to do with my jolly note, Paul had seen the figures. Yet this stunning opening success never rated a mention anywhere in the media.

A commentator had observed that the thing with oysters generally is people either love 'em or hate 'em. Well, the same was to apply to the film. The audiences were loving it and the entertainment writers showed an exceptional bias against it. Across the country we had uniformly good and positive reviews but the attempted undermining of the film's success by non-film reviewers became too much for me.

At the end of our third month, and just hitting two million at the box office, *Sydney Morning Herald*'s political commentator/journalist, Michael Duffy, made an unprecedented attack on the industry and in particular the film. Under the headline YEARS OF SUBSIDY AND FILM IS STILL REELING, Mr Duffy opined and lamented the fact that Australian films are subsidised and went on to rant: 'Last week my wife and I did a very brave thing and went to see an Australian film. I know what you're going to say – more fool them, poor survival skills there – but we happen to believe the film industry needs our support for the good of the broader culture. We make the effort every few years, once the last experience (in this case *Ned Kelly*) has had time to fade. We go to see Australian films for the same reason we support African orphans: we are good people … But film, puzzlingly, has been an almost complete commercial and artistic failure. Australia has been far keener to subsidise its films than to watch them. [Well, this was wrong for a start – author.] Anyway, last week we decided to do the right thing again. My heart sank the moment the opening credits rolled. The long, lingering shots of nothing much, the laboriously quirky music ... Nothing of exuberance or passion. Just a drawing-on of the cultural trackies and an aesthetic slouch into the armchair. I knew, after years away watching good foreign films, that I had come home... I don't wish to be too hard on *The* [sic] *Oyster Farmer*. I was once a film reviewer and saw a lot of Australian films, and it's no worse than most of them. But even so it's bad, and surely unacceptable that after 35 years of subsidy and worrying about scripts, so little has changed. Maybe the time has come to stop making films here and put the audience out of its agony. After all, there are so many other good causes to support these days.'

One should never argue with film critics but Mr Duffy in my book had gone too far. I wrote, in part: 'After fifty-two years in the Australian film industry I have resigned myself to ignoring the cretins and critics who continually bag our industry, but I'm afraid I'm not letting you off the hook with your unprecedented and unwarranted attack on our film *Oyster Farmer* (*SMH*, 27/8/05) which I have just read on return from overseas. Don't get me wrong, Mr Duffy, it's the prerogative of any critic or writer to express their opinion, but when you have got it so wrong then it's time to speak. While I don't know where you've been these past few years, it just so happens you might have set out to bag the wrong film. Your po-faced view of our film matches that of your colleague, Gary Maddox, who can't bring himself to mention the name of the film at all. In April this year, after an admittedly bad period of navel-gazing, Film School generic product, *Three Dollars* brought a glimmer of light and hope to the scene. Then on June 30 *Oyster Farmer* brought a gust of fresh air, bringing back our audiences. As I said at the opening the previous week of the Sydney Film Festival, "There is nothing wrong with the Australian film industry that a good film can't cure." *Oyster Farmer* has been that film, I'm relieved to say. Ten weeks at Dendy/Palace cinemas, ten and eleven weeks at Castle Hill GU Megaplex and Macquarie GU Megaplex. The big chains don't leave a film on for eleven weeks as a favour – the film must be doing something right – and what is that, Michael? – entertaining our audience that has been waiting and wanting to be entertained by an Australian film for some time – a film they obviously relate to... Having digested your article, from now on I'm going to call you Huffy Puffy Duffy. You have huffed and puffed and have failed to blow our house down. There are discerning critics but thankfully more discerning audiences.'

It was in our eighteenth week that Andrew Mackie coined the phrase 'that resilient little beast'. From here on, the film was never mentioned by name, only as 'that resilient little beast'. Dendy's carefully planned display advertising, freshened up every three weeks with a variation to the image and quotes, spurred the box office along or, as Mark Sarfaty, head of Dendy Cinemas observed, - '... and (the) current hit *The* [sic] *Oyster Farmer* have been the most successful this year once earnings are weighed against film hire.' Our seven-month season put us fourth in the top Australian films for 2005 and topped the box office for the Cremorne Orpheum in its third week.

The bias and prejudice wasn't confined to the media. It was noticeable within the management of the Film Finance Corporation. The FFC had introduced a two-door policy of film investment – the marketplace door and the new door, evaluation. A lot rested on the success of the evaluation strand. *Oyster Farmer* was marketplace and had come along stealing some thunder from the evaluation door projects. The FFC had prepared a very impressive brochure of the Australian films in the marketplace at Cannes for 2005, except *Oyster Farmer*. When asked why, CEO Brian Rosen brushed it aside by saying they couldn't put every film in, and anyway we had been in the marketplace for a while. This was news to me, we hadn't opened and we were at our first Marché du Film. Our sales agent, Hilary Davis, was furious at the slight. I was totally perplexed, particularly as the FFC had $4 million invested in the film. In the FFC's annual report 05/06 you'll be struggling to find mention of it and no mention of the box office performance, and not listed because we opened on June 30. It's as though, in the eyes of the FFC, the film doesn't exist.

Our opening week's figures may have surprised the industry but nothing surprised them more when *Oyster Farmer* was nominated Best Picture at the AFI Awards, and only one other, cinematography. I observed that the film must have made itself!

Our performance in America was erratic, to say the least, not helped by insufficient P&A[1] allocated to it by our distributor, The Cinema Guild, New York. Reviews in the main were positive. *The Village Voice* in New York hated it, which was fine because they had also hated *Bliss*! *The New York Times* was warm, 'Even though the setting, full of abundant green forests and winding waterways, often takes precedence over story and character, which are both sorely underdeveloped, this uneven but ultimately endearing film manages to portray ordinary life in a refreshingly authentic way, full of grit, pain and joy in the little things.'

Even I would have to admit the venerable New York film critic, Rex Reed, may have gone a little overboard in the *New York Observer*: 'For something refreshingly

---

1   P&A means prints and advertising. The distributor will increase the number of prints available to the theatres based on a film's performance in the opening weeks.

different, check out *Oyster Farmer*, a pleasing slice of Australian life written and helmed by Anna Reeves, a stunning new director making a warm and insightful feature debut. The character development, as natural and satisfying as oxygen, combines with the relationships of an unusual band of total originals – especially the sleepy-eyed charisma of young Mr O'Lachlan, captured in loving close-ups – and the spectacular natural vistas of the Hawkesbury River, filmed with relish in graceful travelling shots, to imbue this film with a winning spirit and a broth of eccentricity that warms the cockles. As an uplifting, enriching series of tableaux of village life in a remote part of the world that few of us will ever experience firsthand, it is never overplayed, but rather beautifully executed by director and cast alike – a quirky, mesmerizing entertainment.'

Our fifteen-week season in New Zealand pushed our Australasian box office to just over $2.6 million and it became the most popular Australian film released in New Zealand in 2006.

Like *Caddie* and *Bliss*, I sense this 'resilient little beast' is going to be part of the Australian film scene for a very long time.

33

An Apple For The Teacher – Food For Thought

If ever there was a resilient little beast it would have to be what is euphemistically called the Australian film industry. From the first flickering images shown at the Kinetoscope parlour in Sydney's Pitt Street in 1894, Australian motion pictures have been through more ups and downs than a rollercoaster, and the ride at times has been more than daunting. Through the boom and bust and boom again of the 1900s and 1920s, the extraordinary output of Ken Hall's *Cinesound* of the 1930s (sixteen films in nine years), the troubled war years, the struggle of the independent producers including Charles Chauvel post-war, to the effective closing down of production by the Rank Organisation in the early 1950s, if this wasn't enough to deter anyone from making pictures, the Australian film 'industry' seemed always hellbent on resurrecting itself.

The so-called renaissance has been discussed elsewhere in these pages. Suffice to say that the three changes made to the valuable but often abused tax concessions in the 1980s and 1990s did not deter those practitioners, including me, from working in the field. The major change to affect all of us was no longer being employed practitioners but freelance contractors. Nonetheless we have soldiered on and I think with a pretty impressive output of quality Australian cinema and filmed drama for television. However, all is not well. The 2000s have introduced an enormous shift in approach and attitudes to production and especially teaching and, of more concern to me, an extraordinary shift in audience responses, not just to Australian films but <u>all</u> films. Forget the 'Tentpole' and blockbuster films and the distributors' hyperbole, the facts are, when one equates the number of screens on which a film is played over a fifty-two week period, the average gross takings for each multiplex is about $3,600 per screen! It is no wonder the queues for the popcorn are so welcomed by the theatre owner. Yet Gold Class, to use a term generically, is packing them in. A clue to this perhaps is venue, then product. In the late 1920s the nickelodeon approach to the pictures was replaced by mighty picture palaces, whilst in the suburbs the worn-out silent barns, badly converted to talkies, were being replaced by art deco gems – the pictures were the places to go and get dressed up for.

The government has replaced the Australian Film Commission, Film Finance Corporation and Film Australia in 2008 with one great bureaucracy, Screen Australia, and I wish it well. The product, though, needs close scrutiny. The FFC's attempt to encourage more creative filmmaking with the introduction of an evaluation door alongside the regular marketplace door was crippled by an archly bureaucratic approach to assessments and the rejection of established directors with considerable credits to their name, resulting in a basically poor performance by both doors.

I don't expect many to necessarily agree with my view but I believe our present malaise is caused by what I refer to as 'film school generic syndrome', which has spread like a disease. In discussion with one of Victoria's most highly regarded and respected professionals, this person expressed dismay at the lack of knowledge displayed by the graduating students of the Victorian College of the Arts (VCA) film school (formerly Swinburne). 'It is as though they have spent three years learning exactly nothing.'

However, if my commenter was disturbed by this observation then one should look at the Australian Film, Television and Radio School (AFTRS) which has completely lost its way, yet is the recipient of extraordinary government largesse. One industry leader described to me 'creative energy at the School is only as good as its leaders.' Its leaders, senior management, most certainly require scrutiny.

My association with the 'Film School', as it is generally known, goes back to the interim School in 1973, where I was employed to teach editing. The School still advertises that year's intake (!) who were Gillian Armstrong, Ross Hamilton, John Papadopoulos, Ron Saunders, Phillip Noyce, Graham Shirley, Wolfgang Kress, James Ricketson, Alan Lowrey, Robynne Murphy, David Stocker and Chris Noonan. My first task was to edit Phillip Noyce's *Caravan Park*, an observant film that nearly became a television series. After Phillip completed his shoot he arrived and wanted to know why I hadn't edited his film. I told him he was here to learn, and therefore I was waiting for his instructions. Phillip dutifully sat down beside me at the moviola and we began. It was a very satisfactory collaboration.

Storry Walton was appointed interim director whilst we awaited the arrival of Jerzy Toeplitz from Poland to head the School. Storry's strength for the School was invaluable and he eventually became director in 1980 after Jerzy retired. I was appointed to Council in 1978, became deputy chair and was acting chair for some months awaiting the appointment of David Ferguson. In 1979 I took over from Gil Brealey to run the Stage Screen Course, and became guest lecturer on Damien Parer's Producing and Packaging Course for about eleven years.

The 'Open Program' was one of Storry Walton's greatest initiatives and achievements at the School. Frank Morgan became deputy director though Storry and Frank did not always see eye to eye, but from my view of the School, Frank's appointment was another good initiative of Storry's.

Even in those early days I used to question the selection process for the School intake each year, which was becoming more and more middle class. I wanted to know where the 'working class' filmmakers were, where were the modern generation of radical filmmakers giving us films that the Waterside Workers Union Film Unit gave us in the fifties? The selection panel, on which I sat, was to come to odds with Storry one year when I suggested an 18-year-old be included in the intake. Storry was totally opposed, claiming the applicant was too young. We argued and the panel won but it was to be the only occasion this would happen. I was dropped from the selection panel. Already an unholy culture was developing in the School, which worsened after the opening of their $18 million purpose-built premises in 1986. On council I fought for a Film School to be in the city. The New South Wales Government's Printing Office in Ultimo had closed and could have been an ideal site. Some staff members strongly supported the idea but the bureaucrats won the day and the concrete mausoleum was built at Ryde. When Dr George Miller walked into the main stage he exclaimed, 'Cripes, they don't even have it this good at Warner Bros.'

My angst was further fuelled in 2003. I was producing Screentime's miniseries of Bryce Courtenay's *Jessica* (Chapter Twenty-seven). In pre-production, our production designer Jon Rohde asked me if it would be appropriate to appoint an attachment from the Film School.[1] I have had attachments at various times over the years and told Jon it was a good idea and I would also ask our other department heads. The response was overwhelming. At the end of the day we had eight attachment opportunities available.

I rang Pat Lovell, head of producing, to offer the opportunity of eight attachments from a week to eight weeks on location in central-western NSW. Pat rang back a few hours later to break the news that the director of the School declined the offer as it would 'interfere with that year's curriculum'. I couldn't believe my

---

1   Attachments are not a replacement for a member of crew but a position offered for the student to obtain 'coalface' experience with the professionals. They are not paid a salary by the production but are housed and fed when on location.

ears. I knew there was no point in protesting. The 'culture' of the Film School hierarchy was shining like a lighthouse. Later that year I went into production with *Oyster Farmer*. My line producer, Sue Mackay, enquired if we were offering any attachments to the School. I said firmly, 'no'. However, during the course of production, the School rang to ask if three cinematography students could come to location. I relented and invited the students. Because of the School's policy the three students could only come for a day each whilst we were filming. A day? Alun Bollinger, our director of photography, would have been only too delighted to have had them for longer. I'm sure the three budding cinematographers enjoyed their day on set but you can't learn much in a day.

Donald Crombie became head of directing at AFTRS in early 2005. There could not have been a better choice. A top professional in his craft, a listener, intelligently caring in the direction of his actors, and the right temperament to be a teacher. Yet on 14 September 2006, Donald Crombie walked into Graham Thorburn's (head of film, television and digital media) office at 4.30 and tendered his resignation, left the building and drove away to a new life.

For any film school anywhere in the world to lose the very best head of directing one could possibly have would be cause for enquiry and concern. Not so at AFTRS. No concern expressed, no inquiry asked for or conducted by the chair or council (board). Worse, no curiosity expressed in the media, no mention whatsoever in the trades.

I was so concerned I rang Donald. He was his usual laconic, cheery self. 'Yes, I've resigned, thank goodness, I should have done it months ago. I thought I was there to support the students but increasingly management's view was I was there to support them.'

It was six months before the head of directing's position was advertised and eight months before an appointment was made. At the time of writing this chapter, Sandra Levy's appointment as Head of the School has been announced. New management initiatives have been introduced to streamline the operation of the School but these initiatives are, in the eyes of some, detrimental to the standards set for the School's various courses. One has to say that graduates were always industry ready, but by cutting some courses by half, a student can't possibly be in such a position on graduation day. Setting the bar was always high, but lowering the bar can be courting disaster. A new one-year course for seventeen to twenty-five year olds, straight out of school, for a general introduction to filmmaking, has to be questioned when these same school leavers can learn the subject from most TAFE colleges in Australia. Recruitment is now done by written application only, no interviews! This is plain foolhardy.

Do we need film schools? Yes, I'm afraid we do. The studio system of employment died in the very early 1970s. Film schools per se can only work if at least six months of a course is spent in apprenticeship to a picture or miniseries in production, and/or attached to an individual proficient in the craft related to the student and that individual is financially subsidised by the School.

I would scrap AFTRS altogether in favour of placing their core strands – producing, direction, cinematography, editing, sound and writing – at NIDA (National Institute of Dramatic Art) where there would be a synergy between stage and screen. In Australia, none of us can afford to put ourselves on a pedestal and claim to work in only one field. Actors, directors, writers, production designers, art directors and costume designers must work across the three fields of theatre, television and film to survive.

I believe we have lost our way. It is the 'thirty-somethings' that worry me and my peers. They seem to have no sense of the audience they are hoping to reach. For example, one of our top writers had to go through the grinding ordeal of assessing over sixty of our thirty-somethings' first feature scripts. The males wrote drugs/slash movies, the females destructive sex/abusive parents, and that was it! They only have two stories to tell until they're forty-five and, oh, they have invented an entirely new genre called 'I don't read or watch television.' I read the weekend papers, and when I read the book reviews I wonder why more of our modern literature isn't being adapted to the screen. Our authors know how to tell stories; our current generation of filmmakers are failing to tell the stories our audiences would like to see. Here, television has stolen a march on our cinema in the adaptation of Australian novels to miniseries and, in a few cases, the telemovie. I am not afraid to claim that the standard of writing and adaptation to the small screen has been far superior to anything we have produced for the screen in the past decade. Network television is to be loudly applauded for the money they invest in the development of the script.

If an Australian film attracts over 100,000 admissions it is considered a success, but how can one possibly compare this with the fact that the average Australian telemovie will attract a million viewers and our top quality miniseries peak with an audience of two million? Here the government is getting value for their bucks. If our audience is preferring to stay at home, then what is wrong with making MOTION PICTURES (not telemovies) for television, and next morning being available on DVD?

We live in a world of change and movies are included. Our audience is changing its preferences. 3D is not going to 'save' the cinema, it will in the long run send them broke, but there's nothing wrong that a good movie can't fix. STORIES please, not techniques.

34

Shattered Dreams
– Broken Promises

Joseph Losey's production of Patrick White's *Voss*, Ray Lawrence's *Tracks* – Robyn Davidson's epic journey of discovery, James Ferguson and Stephen Dunn's cutting edge *'Bidgee Boys*, Robert Drewe's *Sweetlip* – also with Lawrence, Brian Trenchard Smith's *Harper's Gold* – a rollicking adventure in modern Kalgoorlie, Philip Cornford's chilling and timely *The Taipan Negative* set around the Tyndall air base in the Northern Territory, and Rob Dupear's very commercial *The Turtle Run*. That's only for starters, the years of work in development, in film and series in which you and your creative partners believe, only to end in disappointment when no one else shares the vision. John Heyer's production of Xavier Herbert's *Capricornia*, Cecil Holmes' and Bob Raymond's *Call Me By My Proper Name* and Cecil's *Morrison of Peking*, George Whaley's *The Trouble With Mr Trethaway* and Justin Fleming's brilliant *Lord Devil – the Emperor as Artist*, the colourful life of Australian artist Donald Friend. The list goes on. All tightly packed away in their archive boxes for someone to investigate one day whether they may have been worth making or not. There is no point in lamenting their loss; it is a fact of life about producing. You must have more than five 'balls' in the air at any one time for you don't know which of the five may fall back into your hand and be the one to be financed. A producer can only survive by having a slate of projects and diversifying into all three areas of production – features, television drama and documentaries. I feel though, quite deeply, for those whom I have failed, left behind because others didn't see what we could see in the project. If it is not moving after five years, you must stop and take stock of the situation. After ten years then you must give it away. There are a couple of projects I have spent probably twenty years on that haven't as yet been archived in their boxes, but time is running out.

Let's take a look at three of the above. One I was, and am still probably, passionate about, another I was 'attached' to but it wasn't my project and its history is interesting.

Voss: I was sitting in the back garden of Graham and Christine Benson's at Larkhall Rise, enjoying the late sunny evening, the sort that London can be blessed with in summer, once again waiting to go to Heathrow for the long journey home, when Graham suddenly asked, 'What could be the great Australian film?' I didn't hesitate. '*Voss* of course, Patrick White's *Voss*, but it will never be made, it will never happen.' 'Why?' asked Graham. 'It's all to do with a man called Stuart Cooper who owns the rights in perpetuity.' Graham was astounded. 'But I know him, we stay in his apartment when we are in LA. You two should get together.'

All I knew of Stuart Cooper was that Patrick White despised him. Tightening his jaw and gritting his teeth when I asked Patrick what had happened to *Voss*, he said, 'Tonee, Mr Cooper made a film called *Disappearance*, which is exactly what it did.'

My association with *Voss* started in 1977. Before my involvement, Harry M. Miller, at the time one of Australia's top theatrical entrepreneurs and agents, and still one of the country's leading agents representing a diversity of professionals in the entertainment industry, had acquired the rights of Patrick's novel. He had acquired them in perpetuity, for a flat fee with no percentages to follow from any profits the film might make. Many in the industry, including me, are still mystified how this happened. Patrick was later to become very bitter over the deal and his association with Harry. In 1975 Harry Miller's company signed a contract with British screen writer David Mercer to adapt *Voss* and for a first draft screenplay to be delivered in January 1976. Miller succeeded in attracting Joseph Losey to the project, signing him up in 1976 to direct the picture. Both Mercer and Losey met with Patrick's approval. Coincidentally Losey had been wanting to make *Voss* from the very first time he had read the novel. Losey prepared a summary, his vision for the picture: 'I read *Voss* when it was first published in 1957 and made tentative notes for a film then.

'The story is rich and elaborate but at the same time simple in the manner of all greatness. Its images are multifold and startling. This would be Australia's first international film in the true sense. It also would be Australia's first real filmic presentation to the world. Additionally it will provide a significant opportunity for Australian actors and technicians, as well as some international stars.'[1]

---

1   Losey prepared his 'statement' to assist in the raising of finance for the film, however I can find no evidence that it was ever used.

As the reader will discover, it was this last sentence that was going to be the undoing of the film getting off the ground.

Klaus Hellwig of Janus Films, Germany, was attracted to the idea of *Voss*. He was to become probably the biggest buyer of Australian films of the late seventies, early eighties. Klaus invited me to be the Australian producer representing Janus Films. David Mercer's script met with Patrick White's approval. My job for Klaus and Janus Films was to raise some of the Australian capital through the film funding agencies, whilst Harry Miller was handling the private sector.

From 1973 to 1979 Australian feature films were costing between $250,000 and $950,000 with a couple breaking the one million dollar mark. *Voss* was budgeted at $2.8 million, with $1.2 million being sought locally. The budget, however, wasn't the main factor influencing our government film funding agencies or the unions, it was Losey's demands: The following personnel were to be from overseas: his producer, production designer, director of photography, film editor, make-up and continuity. So much for Losey's assurance in his vision statement of 'significant opportunities for Australian actors and technicians'. None of the government funding agencies was supportive of Losey as director, and the unions, rightly in my view, rejected Losey's wish list.

This news depressed Klaus Hellwig who had got wind that Harry Miller had involved Phillip Adams in putting the money together for the picture and had proposed either Weir, Beresford or Schepisi to be director. Did I know anything about this, Klaus asked down the telephone from Frankfurt. No, I didn't.

Then a bizarre twist to this tale occurred. Patrick White rang. 'Tonee – who is this pompous prick Jack Lee? He says he knows you.' I knew Jack well, having cut TV commercials for him in the 1960s at Ajax Films. Jack's association with Australia had begun with his directing Nevil Shute's *A Town Like Alice*[2] in 1956. What on earth was Jack enquiring about *Voss* for? He met with Patrick at his Martin Road home, suggesting that Peter Weir should direct the film. Jack was quickly despatched by Patrick who immediately telephoned me.[3]

Patrick rang to tell me he had received a letter from Phillip Adams that morning, enquiring after *Voss*, with his recommendations for directors. There is no need to relate here what Patrick had to say.

Klaus Hellwig was becoming increasingly frustrated with the Australian situation and dealing with Miller. In a telex of March '77, Harry told Klaus of his own frustrations with the government funding organisations which he was

---

2   The US title of *A Town Like Alice* is *The Rape of Malaya*.
3   It is not known whether Jack was representing himself, or as a board member of the SAFC. He didn't tell Patrick.

convinced were controlled by the unions and Losey would have to be released from his contract to pursue other work offers. In February '78 Klaus dined in Sydney with Patrick and Rupert Chetwynd and Luciana Arrighi. Patrick reaffirmed his support for Klaus's involvement with the project and Losey as director with Mercer's script. In March and April a promising exchange of telexes occurred between Klaus and Harry, indicating Harry's willingness to accept a buy-out from Janus Films for Harry's rights, David Mercer's script and Losey's contract. The offer included a producer credit for Harry and a percentage of producer's net profits. But by August '78 the negotiations were in the hands of Harry's London representatives, Richards Butler and Co. Klaus wrote to Richard Fletcher at the company expressing his dismay at Harry Miller's involvement with Phillip Adams. Fletcher replied to Klaus saying that he, Klaus, should not be surprised if Harry was exploring alternative purchasers of the rights, since they had not been able to reach an acceptable agreement with Janus Films.

Klaus wrote to me, October 18, 1978: 'Considering the very dubious situation of Australian financing we have therefore decided that *Voss* should be abandoned for next year, which probably means that Joseph Losey is not going to make the film at all.'

The truth of the matter is the film had no chance whilst Losey held to his demands about crewing. The funding authorities, principally the NSW Film Corporation, gave a very reserved 'yes' to the project and a reserved 'yes' to Losey, though privately they had expressed to me he was 'too old', but an absolute 'no' to his crew requests. They argued, I think convincingly, that times had changed and that it would not look good politically if taxpayers' funds were invested in an overseas crew. The equity of the proposed parties was also at a disadvantage with their proposed European partners.

1979 and Klaus Hellwig notified all parties concerned that because of Janus Films' ever-increasing production schedule, they would not be pursuing any further interest in *Voss*. Unbeknown to Klaus or myself, Sawbuck Productions Ltd of London (Stuart Cooper) purchased the full film and TV rights from Harry Miller on 30 September 1979. There the matter was to lapse as far as my involvement was concerned till 1997.

15 July 1997, sitting in the Benson's garden, having returned from Karlovy Vary in the Czech Republic as a guest of honour at the Australian retrospective with *Caddie* at their annual film festival, Graham Benson was quite taken with the thought of being involved in what could be the 'great Australian film'. He wrote immediately to Stuart Cooper to enquire where he was at with his plans for *Voss*. Some time elapsed before Tim Abel Smith from Sawbuck Productions

furnished Graham with all the details of their ownership of the rights in the property. Graham was all for applying for script development funding to kick-start the project. Cooper had previously commissioned a new script from noted playwright Louis Nowra, which Cooper noted to Graham was 'an interesting contrast to the Losey version'. Cooper had forwarded Nowra's notes, the script and a proposed development plan to the Australian Film Commission which was never proceeded with. The NSW Film Corporation rejected supporting Louis Nowra's script proposals.

I had suggested to Graham Benson recommending to Cooper the writer and playwright Justin Fleming, who had completed a lively screenplay for me on the life of Australian artist Donald Friend. Some examples of Fleming's work were subsequently sent to Cooper for consideration. He had also sent out an impressive locations portfolio based on the David Mercer script. Cooper had also indicated he would be interested in novelist David Malouf. I sent a fax to David but I was uncertain as to whether he had written a screenplay. For Graham in London and me in Sydney there were months of silence from Cooper, to the point that on June 15, '98, Graham sent a short fax to him: 'I presume, having heard no further from you of late, that we have made no more progress. I think we missed a trick with Justin Flemying [sic]. After so long, an imaginative and limited risk is needed. A leap of faith to relight a great bonfire. I'd urge you to think again. Track record and success rate are not what's needed now but an instinctive move with a new voice and face.' What Graham wasn't expecting was my return fax of June 16! 'Received your fax this morning regarding Mr Cooper. Now comes the big shock – I had lunch with Mr Cooper last Saturday!' It was the coincidence of all coincidences. Stuart Cooper had arrived in Australia about a month before to direct a movie of the week for Paramount Pictures at the Gold Coast Studios. He had rung the week before to say he would be in Sydney at the weekend, could we meet? So I organised a Saturday luncheon which was to go for the rest of the day. Keeping in mind Patrick White's terse comments, I really didn't know who to expect. He was in town casting with Maura Fay. He sounded okay to me on the telephone.

I found Stuart Cooper to be a very nice man, quite astute and very intelligent. I challenged him on why he hadn't made a decision re the writer and he said the work I had sent to him was quality writing, but it didn't lead him in the direction of *Voss*. Cooper said he had toyed with an English writer but I pointed out that the writer should be Australian, and suggested he try and obtain new funding for further development of the picture. With this Cooper agreed. He had had positive meetings on the Gold Coast with Mike Lake, head of the studios, and with Robin

James, the CEO of the Pacific Film & Television Commission (PFTC), who were wanting to secure *Voss* for Queensland and were ready to back it. I urged Cooper to reconsider Justin Fleming who was about to return from Paris and said I could arrange a meeting before Cooper returned to LA to finish his movie. It was an interesting day and the man must have returned to his hotel exhausted, for I had quizzed him about every aspect of his career and ambitions. Cooper's departure date from Australia meant he was going to miss meeting Justin but with some lateral thinking the two agreed to meet at Sydney international airport as one was coming in and the other was going out.

Justin reported in quickly that his meeting with Cooper had been a success. All of the above and more was discussed and Cooper liked what he heard. Cooper emphasised to Justin he wanted me as co-producer and that he would fax a proposition to Justin and me on his return to LA.

I wrote immediately to Graham, my birthday in fact, July 27, to advise him that the meeting between Cooper and Fleming had gone well and that Justin felt very positive we would be able to proceed with further script development. Months went by and neither of us heard anything until I received a phone call from Cooper asking me to enquire about Nick Enright as a potential writer. I knew Nick's agent quite well and rang Kate Richter. 'But Tony, my computer shows Nick passed on *Voss* on August 26, 1998, the producer Jim McElroy was notified.' Jim McElroy the producer? I remembered that Jim had phoned me in 1997 asking who owned the rights to *Voss* and I told him, and that was that. I rang Jim McElroy, telling him nothing of the above, except that Kate Richter had said he was the producer. Jim revealed that the PFTC had recommended him to Stuart Cooper and that he had met with Cooper in LA the previous year. He said he was looking for a writer, mentioned a few names, all of them hopeless. I thanked him for the information and wished him luck with it.

I let fly with a forthright fax to Cooper, 10 February 1999, concluding with: 'Now it's strictly your prerogative to work with whomever you wish. However, this is most definitely not the way I do business. To ask me to follow up one writer and another producer to follow up another writer or two is plainly unprofessional. There is no need for any reply to this correspondence either by fax or phone. Suffice to say I am no longer interested in being involved. I am paying Graham Benson the courtesy of notifying him of the above for he may wish to continue to be involved in the development of the project with you.'

Cooper's actions troubled me for some time. If he was doing this to a friend of his, namely Graham Benson, and me, was he also behaving in the same way with Jim McElroy? The McElroy brothers I have known and admired since the beginnings of the recovery of the Australian film industry in the early 1970s. I decided to write to Jim: 'I have been procrastinating for some time about the subject of *Voss* in relation to a fax I sent to Stuart Cooper in February. At the time I didn't think it important to send on to you but having had second thoughts, I believe it is only fair that you should know as a friend what has elapsed over the past twelve months between me and Mr Cooper. I just copy you to alert you to keep your ears and eyes open whilst you develop the work with him. I would hate the same thing to happen to you as happened to me, hence this short communication.'

Patrick White's terse words were ringing in my ears: 'Tonee – He made a film called *Disappearance* – which is exactly what it did.' Now Mr Cooper had disappeared from our lives. The irony would have pleased Patrick. The film Cooper was making at the Gold Coast was called *Chameleon*!

In 2006 the *Weekend Australian*'s colour magazine published a profile on Cooper and yes, *Voss* was going to be made. There he stood in the double-page spread on Sunset Boulevard.

───────

Mention of Louis Nowra reminds me of his excellent breakdown and first draft miniseries adaptation of Xavier Herbert's *Capricornia* for veteran Australian filmmaker John Heyer. John's dream of a major motion picture of *Capricornia* had been nurtured for over twenty-five years, from the time he first optioned the book. He was still paying the annual option fee at the time of his death in London at the age of eighty-four in 2001, his dream unrealised. I was introduced to his project by Tim Read, a fellow producer who was having to stand aside when he was appointed head of development for the Australian Film Commission. John, Tim and I were led on a wild goose chase, along with a few of our peers, by two 'producers', Ann and Rob Chapman, who had produced a miniseries *Emma – Queen of the South Seas*. They had set up a company in Paddington, Sydney, with the promise of raising private finance for a slate of motion pictures, including John Heyer's *Capricornia* and our own *On Our Selection*. Months were spent going to meetings with the Chapmans where each time we were told they were nearly ready to go. Well, go they did. I arrived at their offices to have a showdown with them only to discover the doors were all padlocked.

John, however, was devastated with this news. His own adaptation of *Capricornia* I felt 'old-fashioned', if not 'wooden'. I tentatively suggested considering it as a miniseries, citing changing audience patterns, and how the format would suit the large canvas of Herbert's book. He was far from being convinced but agreed to meet with Louis Nowra, whom I had already approached. Heyer was unsure but felt, after due consideration, it may be worth a go. I took the idea to Penny Chapman, then head of drama of the ABC, who was immediately inspired by both the idea and that Louis was going to adapt. Progress was being made and John was beginning to see this was the best way for the project to go, to the small and not the big screen. It was going to be expensive, and would have necessitated co-financing from the UK, but there were reservations being expressed about the ability of Heyer to handle the gruelling schedule of a miniseries and of course his age. Then Penny left the ABC and the project languished.

Twenty-five years is a long time to stay with a project and I am equally guilty of doing the same. In this tale I have mentioned my penchant for travelling on passenger/freighter ships. It was on one of these journeys that I made a major discovery. One of my very early trips was on the veteran Messageries Maritimes vessel *Polynesie*, a thirty-passenger freighter sailing every three weeks to the New Hebrides (Vanuatu) and New Caledonia, to Vila and Santos. My policy, as far back then as it is now, is to leave film scripts behind and only take books that have been waiting a year for me to read. On this fateful journey I discovered Cyril Pearl's *Morrison of Peking*, also known as 'Chinese Morrison'. He was the famous Australian journalist for London's *The Times* based in Peking at the time of the Boxer rebellion. I found Pearl's account of this man's life riveting. Here was an Australian to make a big picture about, who few would have heard of, our 'Lawrence of Australia'.

In 1979 I took an option on Pearl's book. Although the material was in the public domain, having access to his book made the adaptation a more straightforward task. The Australian Film Commission provided first draft funding and Cecil Holmes began the long journey, which was to continue for the next eight years. The AFC initially supported the concept. 'This type of blockbuster film is rare these days mainly because of the high cost involved … However, this could prove to be a commercially viable property.' Dr Stephen FitzGerald, our first Australian ambassador to China, came on board as our advisor and interpreter. Despite FitzGerald's appointment, the chair of the AFC, Joe Skrzynski, thought the whole project too ambitious and subsequently the AFC withdrew their support.

The NSW Film Corporation took on the project for further development and financed an exploratory journey for FitzGerald, Cecil and me to China to meet with the China Co-Film officials. The door to China in 1983 was only ajar, not as it is today. Beijing was a city of several million bicycles, hardly a car to be seen, and a watchful guide and interpreter who was assigned to the three of us constantly. He was a friendly young man, used to being a guide to the tourist.

(Top left) In search of Morrison; Cecil Holmes, writer *Morrison of Peking*, walks with our guides down one of the hundreds of streets of Old Beijing in 1983.

(Top right) Dr Stephen FitzGerald, Cecil Holmes and me with head and principals of the Beijing Studios.

(Middle) Dr Stephen FitzGerald ponders what was believed to be the roof of Morrison's library and rear courtyard.

(Bottom) Cecil Holmes stands on the permanent set of Peking 1900 on the backlot of the Beijing Studios.

When we made it clear we did not want to go out to see the Great Wall of China, he was not only relieved but immediately curious as to what we wanted to see. We wanted to see Old Peking, the top, right-hand quarter of the map of Beijing, a place few tourists ever ventured and probably didn't know was there.

Our guide received an all-clear from the authorities, and for him too it was an adventure of a kind, for he was about to discover old Peking with us for the first time. The narrow streets, barely a car-width wide, and alleyways comprised of endless walled buildings, windowless, with an open doorway every fifty yards or so, for mile after mile. What was at the end of these open doorways was what we had come to see. Ageing but beautifully maintained courtyards, in most cases, surrounded by Chinese homes, some of which were hundreds of years old. This was the Peking we had come looking for, a film production designer's dream come true. Our guide's eyes were a joy to see as he led the way through more open doorways to yet another group of courtyard homes. I think for many of the occupants we were the first foreigners to venture here since Morrison's time. They didn't seem to mind, welcoming us with smiles and looks of curiosity. It was probably the most important day of our visit.

China Co-Film had indicated no objection to the film, or filming in China, but politely warned us permission would take time. Between 1983 and 1987 Cecil continued with one draft after another, but even he was to admit finding Morrison the man was proving elusive. The background was there in strength, but not the man. Causing stress to Cecil, I commissioned the material be redrafted by writer/director Ian Coughlan into an extensive treatment for a four-part miniseries. His treatment for *Morrison*, whilst attempting to do too much, put the spotlight on the project with potential overseas participants. Our miniseries concept was submitted to the BBC, Meridian, Central – all thought it exciting and fascinating, including the BBC who claimed they were developing two of their own. Zenith thought the production 'admirably ambitious and clearly has a tremendous sweep'. However, not one was prepared to proceed and the BBC's series didn't happen. By 1989 there was no further funding available and I had run out of money. I advised Stephen FitzGerald, Ian Coughlan and of course Cecil Holmes that the project had to be shelved indefinitely. Cecil became extremely bitter and wrote to me the most abusive and offensive letter I have ever received. It was beyond replying to, though I did eventually, because it was so irrational and full of hurt. No one deliberately sets out to fail but Cecil couldn't see this side at all.

1990: Stephen FitzGerald phones from his office. 'I've just received our permission from China Co-Film and they would like to know when we would like to start.' He laughed with incredulity. I couldn't see the funny side of it at all. Then he explained that one of his clients, BHP, had had to wait a similar period of time for permission to build a steel mill. Seven years?!

In 1999 Errol Sullivan, CEO of Southern Star Television, telephoned to enquire about the status of *Morrison*. I prepared a full report for him but obviously it just became too hard.

I have given you three examples only of the many projects that have taken time and money, perseverance and belief in them, to no end. If you are a young aspiring filmmaker I hope these accounts don't discourage you. I have detailed them deliberately in the hope that it gives encouragement never to give up on the subjects you believe in and want to see made, until you reach a stage where circumstances prevent you and, through no fault of your own, you have to let go of that particular dream. This is what producing is all about, belief in yourself, and the projects, and the aspiration to achieve and succeed.

The Final Reel – The Full Circle

'**M**y father said he could remember the Picture Show behind the back fence. As a boy he would stand on the upstairs veranda balustrade of our family home and watch the flickering images and the pianist playing under the screen.' This I wrote at the beginning of our journey together on page two. I had failed to find any evidence of this picture show in 1995 when researching for the centenary of cinema. So for this book I thought I would make one more attempt. My first discovery was at the Lane Cove Library where a volunteer woman of mature years said she had something that might interest me. She produced a brochure issued by the Department of Main Roads in the twenties pertaining to the proposed widening of Lane Cove Road (Pacific Highway) for the approaches to the Sydney Harbour Bridge, then only a plan on the architects' and engineers' drawing boards. There was a panoramic shot of Crows Nest featuring the Queen's Theatre with its retractable roof. Further along to the left one can see the site on which the picture show 'behind the fence' once would have stood.

Back to the Stanton Library at North Sydney. The librarian revealed that she had been on furlough overseas at the time of my enquiries in 1995. 'I know exactly what you are looking for,' she assured me. The photo she produced would be about 1912 to 1914. There, as large as life, to the left of a panorama of Crows Nest, is a large tent facing Lane Cove Road which is obviously the picture show behind the fence. However, it was not the first site chosen. On 13 May 1910, Sherard Becher, architect, wrote to the town clerk advising there were difficulties with the owners of the site and applying for permission to move the proposed picture show to Lots 8 and 7, Section 2 of No. 1 of the Crows Nest subdivision of the Berry Estate – the blocks facing the intersection of Lane Cove Road and Alexander Street. It was also opposite the tram stop for the trams from Chatswood and Lane Cove to North

Sydney. Department of Main Roads archives reveal a photo, not of the picture show but the tram stop opposite, showing a row of one-sheeter billboards for the picture show opposite.

So my father's memory had been proven true. Fifty-nine Sinclair Street, Wollstonecraft, our family home, built behind a picture show, where my journey in film began, a journey I will be ever thankful for and a journey not yet over, strange as this may seem to Bert Cross.

Perhaps the most relevant picture
of all – the picture show over the
backyard fence. A double tram heads
through Crows Nest Junction (left) for
North Sydney. At left centre of photo
is the large tented Rialto picture show.
Right centre above the vacant block
of land are my grandfather's homes of
61 and 59 Sinclair Street. The librarian
at the Stanton Library, North Sydney,
found this rare photo. I date it about
1912 as 'Glen Garrig' was built in 1909
and 'Glendalough' in 1910.

Sources and References

The following books were referred to for quotes and reference checks, and to people, dates and places mentioned.

Australian Film 1900–1977, Andrew Pike and Ross Cooper, Oxford University Press, Melbourne, 1980

Australian Cinema, Graham Shirley and Brian Adams, Angus & Robertson/Currency Press, 1983

The Avocado Plantation, David Stratton, Pan Macmillan, 1990

Cinema in Australia, edited by Ina Bertrand, University of NSW Press, 1989

Entertaining Australia, edited by Katherine Brisbane, Currency Press, 1991

The Last New Wave, David Stratton, Angus & Robertson, 1980

Photo Play Artiste, Marilyn Dooley, National Film & Sound Archive/Alani Publishing, 2000

Screening Australia, Susan Dermody and Elizabeth Jacka, Currency Press, 1987

Plus the journals *The Picture Show, Stage and Screen, Theatre World, Footlighters*, to be found in the Mitchell Library of the State Library of NSW. The Library also holds the bound volumes of *Everyone's* (later *The Film Weekly*) from 1923.

Index

Italicised text refers to names of films and/or documentaries, miniseries or television programs
Page numbers underlined refer to photographs, illustrations etc.